Wallenstein

Also by Geoff Mortimer:

EARLY MODERN MILITARY HISTORY, 1450–1815

EYEWITNESS ACCOUNTS OF THE THIRTY YEARS WAR 1618–48

Wallenstein
The Enigma of the Thirty Years War

Geoff Mortimer

© Geoff Mortimer 2010

All rights reserved. No reproduction, copy or transmission of this publication may be made without written permission.

No portion of this publication may be reproduced, copied or transmitted save with written permission or in accordance with the provisions of the Copyright, Designs and Patents Act 1988, or under the terms of any licence permitting limited copying issued by the Copyright Licensing Agency, Saffron House, 6–10 Kirby Street, London EC1N 8TS.

Any person who does any unauthorized act in relation to this publication may be liable to criminal prosecution and civil claims for damages.

The author has asserted his right to be identified as the author of this work in accordance with the Copyright, Designs and Patents Act 1988.

First published 2010 by
PALGRAVE MACMILLAN

Palgrave Macmillan in the UK is an imprint of Macmillan Publishers Limited, registered in England, company number 785998, of Houndmills, Basingstoke, Hampshire RG21 6XS.

Palgrave Macmillan in the US is a division of St Martin's Press LLC, 175 Fifth Avenue, New York, NY 10010.

Palgrave Macmillan is the global academic imprint of the above companies and has companies and representatives throughout the world.

Palgrave® and Macmillan® are registered trademarks in the United States, the United Kingdom, Europe and other countries.

ISBN 978–0–230–27212–5   hardback
ISBN 978–0–230–27213–2   paperback

This book is printed on paper suitable for recycling and made from fully managed and sustained forest sources. Logging, pulping and manufacturing processes are expected to conform to the environmental regulations of the country of origin.

A catalogue record for this book is available from the British Library.

Library of Congress Cataloging-in-Publication Data

Mortimer, Geoff, 1944–
   Wallenstein : the enigma of the Thirty Years War / Geoff Mortimer.
     p. cm.
   Includes bibliographical references and index.
   ISBN 978–0–230–27212–5 (hbk.) — ISBN 978–0–230–27213–2 (pbk.)
    1. Wallenstein, Albrecht Wenzel Eusebius von, Herzog von Friedland, 1583–1634. 2. Thirty Years War, 1618–1648. 3. Generals—Holy Roman Empire—Biography. 4. Holy Roman Empire—History—1517–1648. 5. Nobility—Czech Republic—Bohemia—Biography. 6. Bohemia (Czech Republic)—History—1526–1618. 7. Bohemia (Czech Republic)—History—1618–1848. I. Title.

D270.W19M67 2010
940.2'4092—dc22
[B]   2010012501

10 9 8 7 6 5 4 3 2 1
19 18 17 16 15 14 13 12 11 10

Printed and bound in Great Britain by
CPI Antony Rowe, Chippenham and Eastbourne

Contents

List of Illustrations	vii
Conventions, References, Author	viii
1. A Riddle Wrapped in a Mystery inside an Enigma	1
2. No Great Expectations	6
Early manhood	9
Maturity	15
Gradisca	18
3. A Scandal in Bohemia	22
4. Richer Than All His Tribe	35
Minting money	38
A man of property	41
5. The Fault Is Not in Our Stars	52
6. Some Achieve Greatness	68
War without end	70
A general and a duke	75
7. Go, Captain, Greet the Danish King	82
The Dessau bridge	82
1626: A campaign and a conference	88
1627–28: Denmark and Stralsund	95
8. At the Parting of the Ways	106
The Edict of Restitution	111
An Italian entanglement	114
The limits of power	117
9. The Wheel Is Come Full Circle	123
Dismissal	123
Intermezzo	132
Resumption	138

10. Once More unto the Breach	139
Wallenstein's second army	142
Towards confrontation	147
11. From the Fury of the Norsemen Deliver Us	153
The Alte Veste	153
Lützen	164
12. Of Peace and Other Demons	177
Exile intrigues	182
Fruitless endeavours	186
13. Decline and Fall	199
The gathering storm	201
Hope springs eternal	209
Condemned unheard	213
14. Assassination Is the Quickest Way	221
Death, a necessary end	227
Aftermath	232
Requiem	238
15. But Brutus Says He Was Ambitious	240
References	254
Bibliography	264
Index	269

List of Illustrations

Maps and plans

1. The Holy Roman Empire, c.1630 — x
2. The battle at the Alte Veste — 159
3. The battle of Lützen — 172

Plates

(Between pages 152 and 153)

1. The old image: 'Seni predicts Wallenstein's death'
2. Wallenstein, aged about 30, c.1614
3. Wallenstein, aged about 46, c.1630
4. Emperor Ferdinand II, aged about 55, c.1633
5. Elector Maximilian I of Bavaria, aged about 60, c.1633
6. The battle for the Dessau bridge
7. The defences at the Alte Veste camp
8. The murder of Trčka, Ilow, Kinsky and Niemann

Conventions, References, Author

Conventions

Dates given in this book are 'new style' according to the Gregorian calendar. Recognised anglicisations of the names of people and places are used where they exist, but otherwise the Germanic form is normally employed in preference to Czech or equivalent versions, although the ubiquitous 'von' is omitted from aristocratic German names. All translations are the author's own.

References

There are no notes, but source references are given throughout the text. These are limited to author names and page numbers, with details given in the bibliography. Works by the same author are distinguished by the abbreviations shown.

Author

Dr Geoff Mortimer studied history and German at Oxford University, where he also taught at St Edmund Hall.

x

1. The Holy Roman Empire c.1630, showing territories relevant to Wallenstein's biography (Switzerland and part of northern Italy were also theoretically still within the Empire.)

xi

1
A Riddle Wrapped in a Mystery inside an Enigma
(Churchill)

An enigma, according to the *Oxford English Dictionary*, is 'a puzzling thing or person; a riddle or paradox'. Whether viewed through the eyes of seventeenth-century contemporaries or modern historians, Wallenstein fits this definition. A minor Bohemian nobleman who within the space of a few years became a prince and one of the greatest landowners of his age; a military entrepreneur who twice saved the Holy Roman Emperor from disaster with armies he raised, financed and led, but was then twice dismissed; an able general who rescued the Empire from Swedish invaders, but was accused of planning to defect to the self-same Swedes; the emperor's commander-in-chief, but assassinated on the emperor's orders; a successful soldier who fell because he tried too hard to make peace; Wallenstein was all these things.

Widely believed to have been insatiably ambitious, Wallenstein was nevertheless content to languish in obscurity on his country estates until the age of 35, when the rebellion of 1618 which started the Thirty Years War turned Bohemia upside down, and with it his own life. As a Catholic he remained loyal to Emperor Ferdinand II rather than siding with the mainly Protestant Bohemian rebels, losing his lands as a result and enlisting as a colonel in the Imperial army. Three years later he was the military commander of Bohemia, and within five one of the richest men in the Empire. Despite the defeat of the rebellion the war widened and turned against the emperor, and in 1625 Ferdinand had neither the men nor the money to match the armies of the Protestant king of Denmark and his allies. Wallenstein came to the rescue, volunteering to raise and finance an army, with which he led the Imperialist side to victory in the campaigns of the following three years. By 1629 he was a prince, possessor of three duchies, and commander-in-chief of the largest army seen in Europe since Roman times, and he was reputed to be so powerful that even the emperor hesitated to cross him. This power was an illusion, as Ferdinand exploited the military and political advantage which Wallenstein had won for him to pursue policies of which the latter strongly disapproved, notably militant counter-Reformation and entanglement in the wars of the Spanish branch of his Habsburg family. With no immediate external threat facing the Empire Wallenstein came under pressure, and in 1630 his enemies among the Catholic princes coerced the emperor into dismissing him and dismembering his army.

Their timing was spectacularly bad, dropping their defences and dispensing with their champion just as a new and more formidable enemy appeared, in the person of Gustavus Adolphus, the warlike king of Sweden, who invaded north Germany in the same year. Within fifteen months Gustavus had gathered Saxony and Brandenburg as allies, routed the remaining Catholic army, and advanced to Frankfurt, Mainz and the Rhine, from where he was threatening to over-run Bavaria and the emperor's own Austrian territories. Desperately Ferdinand appealed to Wallenstein to resume the command and to raise a new army, which the general, already ill and old before his time, reluctantly agreed to do, accomplishing this seemingly impossible task in less than six months. Even so Gustavus had taken Munich and ravaged Bavaria before his preparations were complete. In mid-1632 Wallenstein moved south, trapping Gustavus in Nuremberg, where he kept him besieged for two months while the king waited for reinforcements. In the engagement which followed the Swedes suffered a tactical rather than a decisive defeat, but Gustavus's wider plans were left in tatters, and when Wallenstein moved against the king's Saxon ally he had to hasten northwards to the rescue. The armies met at Lützen, near Leipzig, where the resulting battle, the longest and hardest fought of the Thirty Years War, was effectively a draw, although Gustavus himself was killed.

With the Swedish threat neutralised for a time, Wallenstein devoted most of 1633 to a series of attempts to make peace with Saxony and Brandenburg, negotiations which were mainly conducted during prolonged truces. His efforts were unsuccessful, and when hostilities were resumed in the late autumn Wallenstein first recaptured the Habsburg territory of Silesia from the Swedes, but then failed to react in time to prevent them from advancing once more into Bavaria and taking the fortress city of Regensburg. Although of no great military significance this setback enabled Wallenstein's enemies to mount a new political campaign against him. Rumours were spread that he had ulterior motives for his peace initiatives, and that they concealed other potentially treasonable contacts with the Swedes and their French allies.

Early in 1634 a secret report claimed that Wallenstein was preparing a *coup d'état* against the emperor, and that he had already planned the division of the Imperial lands among his allies and supporters. He himself, so it was said, was to become king of Bohemia. The men around the increasingly ill Wallenstein persuaded almost all of the army's generals and colonels to swear an oath of loyalty to him in an inept attempt to shore up his position, a move which was interpreted at the court as a further sign of imminent rebellion. A secret tribunal was convened and hastily condemned Wallenstein, without charge or trial and in his absence, whereupon the emperor authorised four senior officers to arrest him, dead or alive. Realising the danger only at the very last moment, Wallenstein and his closest associates sought to escape towards Saxony, their flight taking them to the Bohemian border town of Eger (Cheb). There the garrison commanders received them with a pretence of loyalty, but over dinner armed men set upon and murdered Wallenstein's officers, following which the invalid general was assassinated in his bedroom.

Subsequent Imperialist propaganda and the undoubtedly dubious contacts of some of Wallenstein's circle combined to turn unsubstantiated suspicions into received wisdom. More paradoxes appeared. The man who had twice been the saviour of the Catholic cause became the object of Catholic vilification. A pamphlet written anonymously by the emperor's Jesuit court preacher described him as 'repudiated by the church, arrogant, wild, mad and vindictive', and claimed that he dealt with the issues of war and peace according to the position of the stars.[1] A body of sober-sided Imperial lawyers pronounced that he had been 'manifestly and permanently engaged in *lèse-majesté*, rebellion and treason', arguing that because of his 'incontestable notoriety' there had been no need for any kind of trial to establish his guilt. The officers who in January 1634 had sworn to 'stand by him honourably and faithfully, and to offer their all with and for him, down to the last drop of blood' deserted him in February, and by March many were eager to testify against him, even though they had nothing of substance to report.[2] One of the main stumbling blocks in the peace attempts of 1633 was Wallenstein's insistence that the armies of Saxony and Brandenburg should join with his to drive the Swedes out of the Empire. Now it was taken as proven that he had been planning to combine with those same Swedes to drive out the emperor. The Saxon army commander, who had played a central part in the negotiations, was appalled at Ferdinand's authorisation of the murder of his own general. 'I know', he wrote, 'of no instance where such a thing has happened in the realm of a Christian emperor.'[3] In another paradox Wallenstein, the leading Catholic general, became something of a posthumous hero on the Protestant side.

The picture of Wallenstein presented by the propagandists and the contemporary popular press had acquired the status of a 'well-known fact' by the time that nineteenth-century historians began to search out primary sources from the archives, and consequently they often failed to draw the logical conclusions from their own researches. Modern historians have sometimes still struggled to put the established image out of their minds in interpreting the evidence, which although voluminous overall can be scarce at critical points. Paradoxes remain. One distinguished British historian of the Thirty Years War noted that Wallenstein showed great judgement and discretion in his financial affairs, but claimed that in military matters he trusted to the horoscopes of his officers rather than to their talents. Another stated that where religion was concerned he was as calculating and pragmatic as any modern business executive, but nevertheless this writer considered that Wallenstein might well have entertained dreams of becoming king of his native Bohemia. Both suggested that his efforts to negotiate a peace settlement were only a cover, beneath which he was pursuing his own interests, although without advancing any evidence to support this view. Terms such as 'measureless ambition', 'egomania' and 'unscrupulousness' have often been employed as though these qualities were self-evident and well-established facts rather than requiring proof. The concept of Wallenstein as obsessed with astrology is still a 'well-known fact' in biographies and German popular opinion, although the evidence for this has rarely been subjected to critical analysis. Historians seem to have been content to identify what one called a 'contradiction between the hard-headed man of the world and the superstitious idealist', without enquiring whether such a paradox is psychologically or practically credible. Can a star-struck fantast really have been the 'organising genius' or the 'logistical genius' the same historians describe? Can he really have outmanoeuvred Gustavus Adolphus, the leading general of the age, on the strength of horoscopes? Can he really have been as loyal as his actions indicate, but as disloyal as the dreams and schemes imputed to him imply?[4]

This book sets out to resolve the enigma, and to do so upon the basis of the evidence and without being unduly influenced – one way or the other – by tradition. This is of course not the first attempt to do so, and some recent German historiography provides a more balanced view of Wallenstein and his career. However this book is also intended to provide a modern interpretation for the English-speaking reader. In Germany the Thirty Years War is still regarded as one of the most important events in the nation's history, and Wallenstein is well known as one of its leading figures. There have been literally dozens of serious biographies and major studies from the late 1700s onwards, as well as large numbers of articles, pamphlets, plays and novels about Wallenstein. This is not the case in the English-speaking world, in which the Thirty Years War is seen as one major European war among many, and one in which England, though a participant, played a supporting rather than a central role, notwithstanding which many English and even more Scottish and Irish soldiers served in the armies of the principal combatants.

There have only been three biographies of Wallenstein published in English, one in 1837, one in 1938, and one in 1976, the last a translation of Golo Mann's truly *magnum opus*, some 900 pages of main text. The first two were reprinted as military historical studies in the 1960s, but none are now available. There is thus a need for an up-to-date academic study, but this book is also directed towards readers who are not necessarily familiar with seventeenth-century European history, the Thirty Years War or Wallenstein himself. Mann's level of detail would be inappropriate, and a more selective approach has necessarily been adopted. Hence some topics have had to be largely omitted, such as Wallenstein's striking success as a progressive and economically effective landowner, while it has been possible to do no more than touch upon his innovative and widely copied methods of military organisation and financing (although the latter subject is more fully discussed in Mortimer, Contributions, listed in the bibliography.)

The modern German biographies of Wallenstein noted in the bibliography have been valuable reference works in locating the sources and compiling the core information upon which this account is based. Those apart, the author's principal debt is to the dedicated nineteenth-century and early twentieth-century historians, mainly German and Czech, who painstakingly located, transcribed and published volume after volume of relevant letters and documents from archives spread across half of Europe. Without such essential groundwork broader historical analysis would be very much more difficult, and often impossible.

2
No Great Expectations
(After Dickens)

Monarchs apart, the early lives of the great of the medieval and early modern periods are illuminated only in flashes, if at all, by the sketchy records available to the historian. Wallenstein is no exception. We know that Albrecht Wenzel Eusebius, as he was christened, was born on 24 September 1583, and that the happy event took place at the village of Hermanitz (Heřmanice), on the Elbe in north-east Bohemia, near the border with Silesia. For his childhood only the barest facts are recorded, and apart from a couple of striking incidents his adolescence is little better documented.

The background can be quickly sketched. Bohemia was a Habsburg province, albeit one with a nominally elective monarchy, and while most of the people were of Czech stock there were many German influences. There were both Czech and German forms of the family name, and indeed several variants in an age when spelling tended to be phonetic rather than consistent, but it originates from the German words *Wald*, a wood or forest, and *Stein*, a stone. Its source was the name of a thirteenth-century ancestral castle which indeed stood on a rock outcrop in the forest, and it will have worried no-one at the time that a culturally Czech family from the Bohemian aristocracy had a Germanic name. Albrecht signed himself 'Waldstein' in his earlier years, confining himself to initials in his later correspondence, by which time his title had effectively replaced his family name in the wider world. Illustrating the variability of contemporary spelling, one of his closest associates and officials wrote 'Waldtstein', 'Waldtsteyn' and 'Waldstein' in various extant letters, while in a document of 1632 Albrecht himself referred several times to 'the family of Waldtstein' but nevertheless to his cousin and heir as 'Wallenstein'. Clearly there is no right spelling, but 'Wallenstein' is the variant which has passed into history, appearing in historical works as early as 1640, and as such is adopted here.[1]

Bohemian aristocracy the Waldsteins definitely were, distantly descended through female lines from a medieval king of Bohemia and related through a long history of inter-marriage to virtually all the other families in this small but tightly knit elite.[2] Nevertheless they were not rich, and indeed Albrecht's father, one of nineteen children, owed his modest estate of Hermanitz to a fortunate bequest from a childless uncle. Some of his own smaller family died early, so that Albrecht was the only surviving son by the time of his parents' death, leaving him heir to the property and the title of *Freiherr* (baron) at the age of twelve. That he looked back with affection on his childhood may be surmised from two later acts. On taking up his inheritance at the age of nineteen he had fine memorial tombstones for both parents erected in the local church, and when he later reached a position of power one of his earliest uses of his patronage was to award a lordship to a family retainer who had been his tutor.[3]

Albrecht's mother came from a much wealthier branch of the aristocracy, the Smiřický family, but it was her brother-in-law Heinrich Slavata, a prominent member of yet another noble family, who became Albrecht's guardian when his father died. He was thus also related to one of his own later enemies, Heinrich's nephew Wilhelm Slavata, who survived being thrown out of the window of Prague castle in the incident traditionally regarded as the start of the Thirty Years War. Wilhelm was eleven years older than Albrecht, though, and he also turned Catholic at around this time, so it is unlikely that they saw much of each other at the castle of Koschumberg (Košumberk) which now became Albrecht's home.

The religion of Albrecht's own family was the relatively moderate Bohemian Confession, which was derived from both Hussite and Lutheran influences, and his first formative years were spent in an environment which was probably conventionally pious rather than fervently sectarian. Heinrich Slavata, however, belonged to the Bohemian Brethren, a quite different type of Protestantism, strict, zealous, influenced by although not adhering to Calvinism, and with strong national-political links. During his two years at Koschumberg Albrecht will have had instruction in this faith, and while it does not appear to have had a lasting influence on him it did bring him into early contact with the religious divisions which ran through the Bohemian aristocracy, most of whom were Protestants of one form or another, although a few remained Catholic or had converted to Catholicism, including at least one prominent Waldstein.[4]

In 1597 the fourteen-year-old Albrecht was sent off to a grammar school at Goldberg (Zlotoryja), near Liegnitz (Legnica) in Silesia. This was of the traditional type where Latin was the principal language, and it drew its pupils from the sons of the German, Polish and Czech nobility. The rest of the curriculum may be guessed at from that specified by Wallenstein when he founded his own school over 25 years later: the German and Italian languages, arithmetic, riding, dancing and playing the lute or another musical instrument. One document preserved from this period is Wallenstein's own letter complaining to the governor of the province about his treatment in the streets of the town – name-calling, including the epithet 'Calvinist scum', stone-throwing and other forms of hostility – perhaps because he was a Czech outsider or because of religious differences. Goldberg nevertheless provides another example of Wallenstein later recalling a period from his youth with gratitude, which he demonstrated in a practical way by presenting the former head of the school with his thanks and a handsome sum of money when duties as the emperor's commander-in-chief brought him that way in 1626.[5]

After two years at Goldberg Wallenstein moved on to the Nuremberg academy at Altdorf, where he was registered in August 1599, shortly before his sixteenth birthday. His stay at this college was short and tempestuous; after four months the authorities were attempting to expel him and he actually left two months later.[6] Much has been made of the events of this period, perhaps because they are better documented than the rest of Wallenstein's youth, but they need to be put into perspective. Students were then exclusively sons of the well-to-do, away from the discipline of home or a tightly run school for the first time, adequately provided with money and far more inclined to wenching, drinking and brawling than to study. University towns were often riotous places – perhaps why the Nuremberg city fathers had prudently moved their academy some distance away to Altdorf – and like the English universities of Oxford and Cambridge most German seats of learning experienced frequent disturbances in which violence and even murder were not unusual. This was the case in Altdorf before Wallenstein arrived and also after he left. That he seems in his brief stay to have encountered more trouble than the average may as easily be attributed to his Czech outsider status and to falling into bad company when still relatively young as to any innate wildness of character.

The incident in which Wallenstein was most clearly personally culpable was a beating he gave his young German servant, a beating so severe that it came to the attention of the authorities and led to proceedings resulting in a large fine and a larger compensation settlement. As for the rest, he was part of a gang of students, allegedly one of the ringleaders, who mobbed an academic's house one night and broke the door and windows. He was there, too, on the evening when an argument between some students and a junior militia officer led to weapons being drawn and to a brawl in which the latter was killed, although not by Wallenstein, and a little later he himself stabbed a fellow student in the foot. Along the way he spent a couple of nights in the local jail, and in due course he was put under house arrest by the academy pending expulsion. Through a letter to the Nuremberg authorities into which he carefully dropped the names of two of his relatives who were Imperial privy councillors Wallenstein avoided this disgrace, and he was instead allowed to leave of his own accord, at least for public purposes.

After his untimely departure from Altdorf he went off on the grand tour, taking in France and particularly Italy, where he stayed long enough to gain a good grasp of the language and reportedly including a period of residence in the university city of Padua, before heading home to Hermanitz in 1602. By this time he was probably around 5 ft 8 in. tall (171–172 cm according to a twentieth-century examination of his remains), while a portrait suggests that as a young man he was slim and good looking, with a high forehead, dark eyes and dark hair, which he wore short, and he had grown a beard in the fashionable Spanish style. In addition to his native Czech he spoke German and Italian fluently, and he could read Spanish well, French competently and Latin adequately.[7]

Early manhood

What Wallenstein did between 1602 and 1604 is unknown, although his earliest biographers state that he found a place at the lowest level in the court hierarchy of the margrave of Burgau at Innsbruck.[8] While this is not improbable it is also not confirmed, but in 1604, at the age of twenty, he became a soldier. This might suggest military inclinations foreshadowing his subsequent career, but more prosaically he may simply have been casting around for a start in life at a time when a regiment for one of the recurrent episodes of war against the Turks on the Hungarian frontier was being raised by the Bohemian Estates (an assembly with taxation powers and administrative functions, supposedly representing the main social groups – nobility, clergy, townsmen and perhaps other commoners – but in practice dominated by the aristocracy). No doubt his name and contacts helped, as he immediately became an ensign, the most junior officer, rather than starting as an ordinary soldier like many other young gentlemen had to do.

The campaign was short and not particularly glorious but Wallenstein apparently acquitted himself well and learned from the experience. Setting out in July 1604, the Imperial army had established itself in a fortress town on the Danube by mid-September, where it was besieged by a larger Turkish force. Three weeks later the Turks withdrew, battered by artillery fire and after heavy losses in unsuccessful assaults, by which time Wallenstein had attained the rank of captain. Here he may also have met the 45-year-old Johann Tserclaes, Count Tilly, who was to be his principal colleague and rival in the Catholic armies more than twenty years later, as well as Count Heinrich Matthias Thurn, who became a leader of the Bohemian revolt and commander of its forces, and the Spaniard Count Balthasar Marradas, who was successively his superior, subordinate and opponent in the Imperial army in the 1620s and 1630s, all of whom were already colonels.[9]

That was not the end, as a Hungarian revolt replaced the threat from the Turks, and the force on the spot had to combat it. The resulting campaign, running from autumn to well into winter, resembled much of the Thirty Years War, with raids, skirmishing, foraging and looting expeditions rather than pitched battles being the order of the day. During its course Wallenstein sustained a wound in the hand but emerged high enough in the confidence of his superiors to be chosen for an important mission. Not, however, a military one, although it turned out to be dangerous enough. The force had run out of money, the troops were unpaid and refusing to resume campaigning in the spring, and deputations from each regiment had to be sent back to their homelands to beg for funds. Wallenstein represented the Bohemian infantry, another officer acted for the cavalry, and they travelled together with a small escort, suffering numerous misadventures on this hazardous journey, which involved a long detour through the Tatra mountains and Silesia in mid-winter in order to avoid enemy-held territory. On arrival in January 1605 Wallenstein was suffering from what he later described as the Hungarian sickness, not now positively identifiable but which may have been responsible for some of his later recurrent illnesses.[10] His fellow-officer had to cope alone with the plea for cash, but predictably he got nothing.

Wallenstein did not return to the army in Hungary on his recovery. Instead his name appears as one of two put forward by the Bohemian Estates in February 1605 for appointment as a military commissioner to enquire into the strength, readiness and pay of the troops in its frontier areas. Whether he was subsequently appointed and if so how far he got with this is not clear, but a later deterioration of the situation in Hungary led the Bohemians to increase their military strength, in course of which Wallenstein was nominated as colonel of a regiment of infantry which was to be raised. Again events moved on, and before the men could be recruited the campaign was brought to an end by a settlement with the Turks and the Hungarian rebels. Although he may not have achieved much as a commissioner and a colonel the fact that he was put forward for these roles at around the age of 22, and with only one short period of active service behind him, suggests both that he was well regarded and that there was little competition in this field among the Bohemian nobility.[11]

The peace left the young soldier without practical employment, and not until 1607 does the next step in his career appear in the archives. At some point before then Wallenstein had become a Catholic, as by February of that year he was reported to be an attendee at Mass.[12] Joining the Catholic church required no great ceremony, and hence we know neither the date nor anything of Wallenstein's motivation, but many have seen his conversion as inspired by ambition and prospective personal advantage. That possibility cannot be excluded, but two questions arise. Was Wallenstein in fact particularly ambitious at this stage in his life, and if he was, would turning Catholic have seemed an appropriate way to further his aims? For this purpose ambition can be considered in terms of property and of career, and in the former respect Wallenstein probably was ambitious. His estate at Hermanitz would have provided only a very modest noble lifestyle, and for a young man in that position seeking an advantageous marriage was an obvious and indeed expected first priority. However a reported 90 per cent of the nobility in the Bohemian lands were Protestant at that time, so turning Catholic was more likely to reduce than to increase Wallenstein's chances of finding an eligible heiress.[13] It might have been different had there been a specific marriage prospect in the offing but this was not the case, and indeed the husband of the Catholic widow who later became his wife was still alive and well at this time.

The concept of a career is something of an anachronism for an early-seventeenth-century nobleman. Those who could were inclined first and foremost to live off their lands, perhaps spending time on administering, improving and adding to them, or perhaps simply spending the income. Those who could not, whether as landless younger sons where primogeniture was the rule, or as owners of unviably small estates where inheritances had been divided and sub-divided between too many offspring, had to look elsewhere. The church provided opportunities for advancement only for the highest born, and politics in any meaningful sense was also the preserve of the already wealthy. Soldiering, although hazardous, offered prospects of betterment, and many land-poor noblemen emerged as colonels in the Thirty Years War. The remaining possibility was to find a place in some princely court, and by being amenable and useful to progress gradually in the patron's favour in the hope of worthwhile rewards to follow.

Wallenstein's early enlistment suggests that he might have been inclined towards a military career, but employment was uncertain. The wars on the Hungarian frontier were sporadic, and there were few major wars elsewhere in central Europe in the early 1600s. True, fighting continued between Spain and the rebel United Provinces in the Netherlands, and there are indications that Wallenstein was actively considering going there in 1607, but after almost forty years this had become a stalemate and was heading towards the twelve-year truce which was agreed in 1609.[14] However religion would not have been an obstacle had inclination and opportunity been there, as few commanders applied this as a criterion in appointing their officers. Many princely courts were not so liberal, although both Emperor Rudolf II and his brother Archduke Matthias were notably pragmatic concerning the religion of those who could be of service to them. In any case there were princely courts enough of all the main religious persuasions in the Bohemian lands, Austria and the Empire as a whole. Like prospective marriage, a specific opportunity might, in some eyes, have justified a change of religion, but unlike marriage such appointments were not for life and the risks in a conversion of convenience were commensurately greater. In the end Wallenstein did put a foot on a lower rung of a court ladder, but he never appears to have made any great effort to progress further, suggesting that if he was indeed ambitious this was not his preferred route. Marriage probably looked a better prospect, and so it proved to be.

Hence it is far from obvious that turning Catholic would have served the purposes of self-interested ambition. Moreover for Wallenstein it meant joining the religious minority at home in Bohemia just as he had made a start in the military and appeared to stand well in the favour of the Protestant-dominated Estates. Taking a wider view, Protestantism had made such great inroads into the Catholic world during the previous century, particularly in central Europe, that it must have seemed very doubtful whether conversion held out reliable hopes for personal career advantage, even given that the Habsburg monarchy remained Catholic.

The Counter-Reformation changed that, but it was as yet barely under way and no provincial nobleman in his early twenties can reasonably be assumed to have foreseen its progress. Viewed as a matter of personal faith things may have looked different. Ninety years after Luther published his Theses Protestantism was no longer modern, dynamic and progressive. Instead it had split into two major and many minor variants, often more hostile to each other than to Catholicism, and divided by bitter arguments about what to the layman must have appeared abstruse or even incomprehensible points of doctrine. Against that the Catholics offered the spiritual security of the age-old faith and a monolithic establishment in which it was necessary only to believe, not to make difficult choices. At the individual level that was arguably the basis of the Counter-Reformation, and like many others Wallenstein may have been attracted by it. Certainly he was by no means the only young Bohemian nobleman to convert in this period. In his childhood and youth he had been brought up in two different forms of Protestantism, and Goldberg and Altdorf were Protestant establishments, but on the grand tour in France and Italy Wallenstein will have been exposed, perhaps for the first time, to strong Catholic influences. Padua was a centre of Catholic humanism, and if he did in fact serve the margrave of Burgau he will have been in a household which was both Catholic and Habsburg. Some reports ascribe Wallenstein's conversion to the influence of a particular Jesuit priest, but whatever the mechanism it can be said with certainty that he remained a practising Catholic and a generous benefactor of the church for the rest of his life.

When Wallenstein sought a post at court it was to Archduke Matthias that he looked. Given that Matthias was next in line to the Imperial throne this was arguably the best choice he could have made were ambition his motive, although as Matthias was only five years younger than Rudolf this was not an assured or long-term prospect. Possibly equally interesting to the young Wallenstein was that Matthias kept court in the major cosmopolitan city of Vienna rather than in some provincial backwater, but it may also have been a question of the availability of a sponsor highly enough esteemed at that particular court for his recommendation to carry the necessary weight. Matthias was of course a Catholic, but to place the religious question in perspective Wallenstein's sponsor was not, and although the latter mentioned that Wallenstein went to Mass he also noted that it was well known that this would make no difference to Matthias's decision. Not that Wallenstein was aspiring to an important, influential or lucrative post at court. On the contrary he sought no more than to become one of many gentlemen of the chamber, whose main function was to provide a fitting entourage for the prince on progress, in the field or on court occasions. This was a part-time and undemanding role but one in which useful contacts could be made, and as his approach was successful he accordingly went to Vienna in 1607.[15]

His sponsor was Baron Karl Zierotin, who had married his sister Katharina while Wallenstein was at the wars in 1604, and although she had died of tuberculosis during the following year the two men remained in contact. Almost twenty years older than Wallenstein, Zierotin was one of the leading noblemen of Moravia, then attached to the Bohemian crown but a constitutionally separate territory, and he was both well connected and very rich. As a scholar, a leading member of the Moravian Brethren and something of an elder statesman he would not have given a testimonial lightly, so that although his letters say the kind of things that references conventionally do his portrayal of Wallenstein at the age of 23 is probably reasonably accurate: a young gentleman replete with fine and laudable qualities, of excellent family, with good manners, well educated and, considering his youth, sensible and mature.[16] Zierotin also noted that Wallenstein was keen for more military experience and would probably at some point seek leave to serve in Flanders with Archduke Albrecht, another brother of Matthias and Rudolf.

In the following year Wallenstein had his first fleeting involvement in politics. In the early seventeenth century a number of significant flare-ups arose from the underlying and growing tensions within the body politic of Europe at large and the Holy Roman Empire in particular, of which two particular areas of dissension are relevant here. Firstly there was disarray in the Empire at the very top, as both Rudolf and Matthias were not only ageing and childless – or at least without legitimate heirs – but also at constant loggerheads. At best Rudolf was eccentric and at worst verging on madness, while although sane Matthias was scarcely more competent but considered himself far more suitable for the top position. Their personalities and conflict both reflected and exacerbated the pressures on Catholic Habsburg leadership of the Empire, foremost among these being the growing influence of Protestantism in the political as well as the religious sphere. Hence the second important matter was the agitation of the mainly Protestant nobility in the territories of the Bohemian crown, agitation aimed at securing religious liberties in terms which would also politically emasculate their king, a role which Rudolf combined with that of emperor.

Briefly summarised, the progress of these conflicts led first to an armed expedition into Bohemia by Matthias in the spring of 1608, where at Lieben (Libeň), at the gates of Rudolf's capital city of Prague, he and his allies among the nobility forced Rudolf to cede to him the titles of king of Hungary and margrave of Moravia. Then in July 1609 the Estates of the Bohemian lands extorted from Rudolf a 'Letter of Majesty' of their own drafting which granted them the liberties they sought. Finally in March 1611, after much trouble and violence in between, Matthias staged a coup and replaced Rudolf as king of Bohemia, following which he was elected emperor when Rudolf died in early 1612. Wallenstein played a direct if small part in only the first of these events, the armed confrontation of 1608, during which he was recalled to service as a captain in a Moravian regiment supporting Matthias, although he saw no action. Instead he was used as a contact between his brother-in-law Zierotin, who was much more involved, and Matthias, whom he still served as a gentleman of the chamber.[17] It was presumably in this latter capacity that he became one of Matthias's representatives in negotiations with a delegation sent by Rudolf in an effort to resolve the crisis, a small part indeed, but significant enough to make it advisable to seek security from reprisals. As a result Wallenstein was one of those to whom Rudolf had to grant amnesty under the terms of the treaty of Lieben.[18]

Maturity

Nothing came of Wallenstein's prospective military service in Flanders. Instead, probably late in 1608, he went to Olmütz (Olomouc), one of the principal cities of Moravia, to pursue plans for a possible marriage. Aristocratic marriages were then, as long before and long afterwards, principally business arrangements brokered by parents, relatives or influential friends. In this case the link may have been provided by the Jesuit seminary at Olmütz, which had many of the noble rich in its spiritual care. One of these was the recently widowed Lucretia, born a Landek but the last of this line, and owner of large estates which dwarfed Wallenstein's modest property at Hermanitz.[19] The Jesuits doubtless wanted to find her a Catholic husband, not least because she had no children and Protestant relatives had the next claim to her lands. Wallenstein was 25 when they married in May 1609, while Lucretia may have been a year or two older, but this was less surprising than the difference in their financial standing, although even that was not unique; in the relatively small Bohemian and Moravian aristocracy perfect balances of age, wealth, nobility and religion were not always achievable, particularly when the lady was a widow. Nevertheless Wallenstein made a fortunate marriage, as indeed his sister had done, and this existing connection with the Moravian aristocracy in the person of Zierotin probably helped his cause. Even so his success may reflect the 'fine and laudable qualities' and 'good manners' which the latter had earlier ascribed to him; brokered marriages were not forced marriages, and Lucretia was not only rich but independent, so that she had a choice.

As yet Wallenstein had taken no more than a marginal part in affairs of the world. He had made a good start at soldiering but pursued it no further, and he had made an entry into the lower levels of the hierarchy of royal courtiers but had been only briefly involved in political matters. He had, however, become notably rich and a substantial landowner by virtue of his wife, and at the time this seems to have been sufficient for him. His skill and energy in managing still larger estates later in life is well documented, and although equivalent evidence is lacking it may well be that he adopted a similar approach to his Moravian properties at this time. An early account of his life suggests that he also emulated other wealthy country gentlemen by making regular visits to the city, in his case Vienna, and spending lavishly there before returning home to restore his finances for the next visit.[20] This would not be surprising for a young man newly become rich, and anxious to make an impression in the aristocratic company of the gentlemen of the chamber. In the early modern world display was closely linked to status, and kings, princes, nobles and others of the well-to-do were positively expected to maintain levels of spending and ostentation appropriate to their standing, so Wallenstein was not unusual in this respect either as an inconsequential but rich young nobleman or later as one of the leading princes of the Empire.

Even if his new lands satisfied Wallenstein's ambitions, he also had to defend what he had gained. Property rights were often less than clear-cut in this period, particularly where inheritances were involved, and Lucretia's Protestant relatives were not disposed to give up their claims without a fight. Only the smaller part of her estates was unquestionably hers, having been left to her by her father, whereas the position concerning lands which came from her first husband was less certain, and in particular there was a possibility that some were hers for life only and liable to revert to the family on her death. Between 1610 and 1612 Wallenstein and Lucretia made attempts to buy off claimants, and they carried out various transactions to try to secure the legal status of as much of their property as possible. Even so they were involved in two legal actions and they staved off rather than defeated some of the claimants, so that the issue surfaced again to trouble Wallenstein after Lucretia's death.[21]

Other business matters indicate Wallenstein's sense of his own place in the world at this time. In 1610 he sold Hermanitz to an uncle, which was a perfectly logical move as it was small and a long way from his new Moravian interests, but the sale still kept the property within the family. However in parting from it he lost his status as a Bohemian nobleman, and while he had become a Moravian nobleman instead through his new properties he had no personal links to the province. Family meant more to him. It is reported that he had previously increased his sister Katherina's dowry when she married, over and above the modest amount left for the purpose by their father, and also that he sold Hermanitz for a nominal sum both to help out his uncle and because the latter had been looking after his other sister Maria.[22]

Wallenstein's next few years were uneventful and are poorly recorded. In June 1610, during the disturbances accompanying the conflict between Rudolf and Matthias, he appears to have been appointed by the Moravian Estates to command a regiment of musketeers, but during this and the following year its role was to watch the Moravian border and to ensure that the troubles did not spill over from Bohemia, so that his command may have been more nominal than practical. Following Matthias's success Wallenstein, still a gentleman of the chamber, formed part of his ceremonial escort to Prague for his coronation as king of Bohemia in May 1611.[23] Then in the summer of 1612 he went on a trip to Italy, on a pilgrimage to Loreto if an early account by the Jesuit and historian Balbinus is to be believed. A recent researcher has discovered a signature which may be Wallenstein's in the register of German students in the faculty of jurisprudence at Padua university in 1612, so it is possible that he spent some time there.[24] His love for things Italian is amply confirmed, not only by his fluency in the language but by his later choice of Italians as architects and artists for his building works, and indeed as senior officers in his armies. A year later, in August 1613, he accompanied Matthias, by this time emperor, to the Imperial Diet in Regensburg, but again as a courtier rather than having any political role to play.[25] These things apart, he seems to have been content to perform the few duties expected of a Moravian nobleman and member of the Estates, and otherwise to live the life of a well-off country gentleman. If he had any higher ambitions in this period they have not left any evidence in the archives.

Then in March 1614 his wife died, perhaps of the plague, leaving him a childless widower less than five years after their wedding. The extent to which a seventeenth-century marriage was more than a convenient personal and financial arrangement is very difficult to assess four hundred years later, but in Wallenstein's case certain details may be indicative. Firstly there is mention neither of mistresses nor illegitimate children in the records or in the attacks of his later enemies, although doubtless there was plenty of opportunity in Vienna. Secondly, and most unusually for the time, he chose not to remarry for nine years despite being highly eligible. Thirdly he not only gave his wife a funeral appropriate to her standing but also founded a Carthusian monastery on his Moravian estates in her memory and as her resting place. Moreover a dozen years later, approaching the height of his power and fortune, he established another Carthusian monastery at Gitschin (Jičin), the principal city of his duchy of Friedland (Frýdlant), and he named her in the foundation and had her coffin re-buried there.[26]

At first Wallenstein's life followed much the same pattern after his wife's death. At the time tensions were rising between the Protestant majority in the Estates of the Bohemian lands and the pro-Habsburg and mainly Catholic court party, with whom Wallenstein has been identified although he seems to have played little active part in politics. Nevertheless he remained in favour, at least in military matters, so that when in the summer of 1615 the Estates agreed to raise defence forces in response to threatening moves by the Turks and their ally Bethlen Gabor, Prince of Transylvania, Wallenstein was appointed to command the 3000 infantry. Although a quantity of weapons was procured this turned out to be another paper army, but Wallenstein was also taken seriously ill during that September. In the spring of 1616 he is reported to have spent time in a house he had bought in Prague, and in that year he also became a gentleman of the chamber to Archduke Maximilian of Upper Austria, another brother of Matthias, who by that time was chronically sick.[27]

Gradisca

A startling break in this pattern occurred in April 1617, when Wallenstein announced that he was setting out from Moravia with 200 cavalrymen, recruited and equipped at his own expense, to assist Ferdinand, Archduke of Styria, in his local and none too successful war against the republic of Venice.[28] The details of this conflict, known as the Uzkok war and which had already been going on for a year and a half, need not concern us, other than to note that Ferdinand had been unable to persuade the cash-strapped governments of his cousin Emperor Matthias or his Habsburg relative the king of Spain to provide him with sufficient practical assistance, and his forces were by then struggling to hold the fortress town of Gradisca, near the Slovenian border in modern-day Italy. Having failed with governments, Ferdinand issued an appeal for help to the nobility of the Austrian Habsburg lands, but he met with no better response, other than from Wallenstein.

Wallenstein and his cavalry arrived at Gradisca in June. They were too few to make a significant difference to the balance of forces, but they took part in the fighting which lasted through into the autumn, in course of which Wallenstein was twice mentioned in despatches for personal valour and judicious command of his company.[29] At the end of the campaigning season they returned home, while the peace negotiations, which had been going on with Spanish mediation almost as long as the war itself, eventually produced a settlement which departed little from the status quo ante.

The key question is why Wallenstein undertook this surprising and expensive expedition. To many biographers the answer has seemed simple. Ferdinand was the rising star, soon to be king of Bohemia and shortly afterwards Emperor Ferdinand II, while Wallenstein was inordinately ambitious and hence seized the opportunity to earn the gratitude of his prospective new sovereign. Strange, though, that he was the only nobleman in the whole of Austria-Bohemia ambitious and astute enough to see the chance and to act upon it, particularly as he had kept his ambition so well hidden in the past ten years. The truth is probably more complicated than this.

The background was the growing sense of approaching crisis both in Europe at large and in the Bohemian lands in particular. At the turn of the century Sweden had ejected a Catholic king and replaced him with a Protestant relative after a civil war. In 1606–07 sectarian riots in the south German city of Donauwörth had escalated, leading shortly afterwards to the formation of rival military alliances, the Protestant Union and its counterpart the Catholic League, among the princes of the region. In 1610 a dispute over the inheritance of the Rhine duchy of Cleves-Jülich, although initially between two Protestants, had also acquired a Catholic-Protestant dimension, and military intervention by the king of France was only prevented by his assassination. In the Netherlands the twelve-year truce had only five left to run, and both sides, Catholic and Protestant, were seeking allies for a renewed and possibly wider war. In their fraternal strife in the Bohemian lands Rudolf had been backed in the main by the Catholic nobility and Matthias likewise by the Protestants, but since Matthias's accession this position had reversed, and the mainly Catholic court party was becoming bolder and more provocative while the Protestant-dominated Estates became steadily more recalcitrant. Now Matthias was clearly declining, and the question of the succession was on everyone's lips, not least because of the conflict that it might cause.

Adult male Habsburgs were scarce, and most were either old, like Matthias's remaining brothers, or Spanish, which was worse. Ferdinand was almost the only available candidate, but he also seemed the man least likely to pour oil on the troubled waters of the Empire. Jesuit-educated and deeply religious, Ferdinand exhibited a crusading zeal which frightened the more worldly-wise Habsburg practitioners of *Realpolitik* in Spain and the Netherlands. Within a few years of reaching the age of majority and taking up the reins of government in 1595 he had high-handedly and almost single-handedly brought his mainly Protestant archduchy of Styria back to Catholicism, expelling Lutheran pastors, burning their books, and giving the ordinary people three weeks to return to the Mass or to leave his territory. True, there had been little trouble, but in some ways that made things worse. By now approaching 40, Ferdinand showed no sign of a more relaxed maturity, and his earlier success was only likely to encourage him to try again should he become king of Bohemia, this time perhaps with disastrous results. Amid this general Habsburg discomfort about Ferdinand, the king of Spain even considered putting himself forward as a possible candidate for the Bohemian and Imperial crowns, but as this did not seem realistic he allowed himself to be bought off with a land settlement in the family negotiations which eventually concluded that Ferdinand it had to be.

While the Habsburgs debated behind closed doors the most likely outcome was already there for thinking men to see, particularly in the Bohemian lands, where Ferdinand would be the most unwelcome possible candidate for the throne. Trouble could follow from one of two directions. Either the Bohemians would reject Ferdinand, possibly finding another and perhaps Protestant candidate, thus leading to a confrontation with Catholic Habsburg power. Alternatively they could accept him, and Ferdinand might then provoke a rebellion by challenging the Protestant nobility and the freedoms they had extracted from Rudolf in the Letter of Majesty of 1609. Of course some peaceable middle way might be found, but the prospects did not look good.

Where did Wallenstein stand in this? The answer is, potentially out on a limb. His inclinations might have placed him in the court party in any case, but as a Catholic he would probably have had little choice, and unfortunately for him the Habsburgs by no means looked like assured winners. The Austrian branch was under Protestant pressure not only in Bohemia but also in their home lands, while the Spanish had more than enough problems with the prospect of a resumption of war in the Netherlands. Indeed the extent to which the Habsburg powers were overstretched was one reason why they could provide only very limited help for Ferdinand against Venice. Were there to be a revolt in which the Protestants gained control in the Bohemian territories things would be difficult for Wallenstein. At the very least the claimants to parts of his dead wife's lands could be expected to resume their efforts and perhaps extend their claims, which he had fended off thus far only with the assistance of pro-Catholic influence in the legal system.[30] At worst if there were a conflict in which he became involved but on the losing side this might result in him being driven out of Moravia, where he was an outsider and a newcomer, and he could end up as a landless refugee with little to support himself other than his limited experience as a soldier.

Wallenstein was not the man to wait helplessly for his fate, while nothing motivates the *nouveau riche* more than fear of slipping back down the greasy pole. If it came to a revolt his best chance of preserving his position and perhaps prospering might be in the higher ranks of the army. For that he would need friends, as well as more credible military experience than his few months on the Hungarian border thirteen years earlier and his series of temporary and largely nominal commissions thereafter. His appointment as a gentleman of the chamber to Archduke Maximilian may have been a step towards improving his connections, but more was needed. If there were a rebellion in Bohemia it would probably be Ferdinand who would be raising troops and issuing colonel's commissions on the Catholic side, and hence the siege of Gradisca presented a unique opportunity to make a reputation in exactly the right quarters. Renewed combat experience, particularly for the first time with cavalry, would also improve his standing, while raising and equipping the force provided a valuable lesson in the relevant logistics. The whole enterprise may have had an element of investment in furthering ambition, but it looks as much or more like the purchase of a valuable piece of insurance.

3
A Scandal in Bohemia
(Conan Doyle)

The Bohemian revolt, when it came, was a badly bungled affair, and even before it started the protagonists had missed their best opportunity. In the spring of 1617 Emperor Matthias's health was such that he reluctantly acceded to Habsburg pressure to make preparations for the succession, starting with the crown of Bohemia. The Estates were accordingly summoned, and Matthias put forward Archduke Ferdinand of Styria as his nominated successor. The precise legalities of Bohemia's elective monarchy were not clear, but it was at least well established that a candidate had to be approved by the Estates, and had the assembled Bohemian grandees refused to support Ferdinand he would in principle have been denied the succession. In the event they did no such thing, and faced in June 1617 with a candidate who, to the majority, was probably the most undesirable possible choice they voted almost unanimously to accept him. Organisation was not one of the strengths of the Bohemian nobility, and the Habsburg management of the election caught them unprepared, but they were probably deterred principally by the fact that a veto would have been unprecedented and no-one knew what would have happened next. They were soon to regret their lack of determination.

With his family duty done Matthias said farewell to Prague and moved to Vienna to live out his remaining year and a half, leaving Bohemia in the care of a Catholic-dominated council of regents. Matthias's aim in the preceding years had been to claw back in practice as much as possible from the freedoms theoretically granted to the Bohemians, and particularly to the mainly Protestant nobility, in the Letter of Majesty of 1609, so that there had been tensions enough smouldering away before he left. Soon these regents, through a series of provocative decrees and actions, fanned them into flames. One flashpoint was the town of Braunau (Broumov), where the citizens had built a Protestant church, claiming that the Letter of Majesty entitled them to do so. The Catholics and the government denied this, the dispute became protracted, and eventually the regents had a number of the leading citizens arrested and imprisoned.

In a climate of increasing confrontation the defensors, the appointed guardians of the freedoms won in 1609, met in Prague in March 1618 to formulate a petition of protest to the emperor. They received an uncompromising reply from Matthias's government, together with an order to disperse, with which on this first occasion they complied. Matters continued to escalate, and with anger mounting the defensors met again in May. The council of regents again ordered them, in the emperor's name, to disperse, but instead the leading lights held a private meeting at which they agreed on a decisive, albeit theatrical, response. On the following day, 23 May 1618, they marched to the Hradschin palace in Prague, followed by a crowd, and in the council chamber they confronted four of the regents. There, after angry exchanges, they staged an imitation of an event which had occurred at the outbreak of the Hussite revolution two hundred years earlier, hurling two of the principal regents, Jaroslaw Martinitz and Wilhelm Slavata, to their deaths from the high windows on to the paving below. At least such was their intention, and it is a noteworthy comment on the divisions in Bohemia that one of the perpetrators was Slavata's own brother, but this attempt at high theatre ended on a note of farce. Martinitz and Slavata had a soft landing, allegedly on a dung heap, and escaped with little more than bruises.

The meaning of the gesture was nevertheless clear, even if Matthias and his advisers initially preferred masterly inactivity to a military response, despite the more belligerent urgings of Ferdinand's group at court. The Bohemians were less reticent, and once having committed themselves they proceeded to form a governing directorate, to raise troops, and to appoint Thurn, one of the leading figures of the revolt, as their commander. Numerous letters passed between Prague and Vienna, and from each to the rulers of neighbouring territories or prospective allies further afield. In these the Bohemians sought to characterise their revolt as essentially religious, whereas the Imperial side emphasised the secular, political and national aspirations which they saw as underlying this rebellion against law and established authority. There was some truth in both views, but the exchanges were mainly for propaganda purposes and a play for time while the respective sides gathered men and money.

Two developments led to a more active confrontation. Firstly inside a month Thurn headed south with several thousand troops in order to force Bohemian cities which had not immediately endorsed the revolt to come into line. However an advance south could be seen in Vienna as a threat to the Austrian heartland, thus strengthening the position of those calling for military action against the revolt. Secondly in mid-July 1618 Ferdinand, aided and abetted by the emperor's brother Archduke Maximilian, carried out what amounted to a *coup d'état* by having Matthias's principal minister, Cardinal Melchior Khlesl, kidnapped and locked away, after which Ferdinand effectively controlled the government himself. Military preparations were promptly speeded up, and with the aid of Spanish money and generals, Counts Bucquoy and Dampierre, a first Imperialist army entered Bohemia during August and a second one set out from Vienna before the end of the month.

Meanwhile the Bohemians had received covert support from the duke of Savoy, an inveterate anti-Habsburg, who released to them the small hired army he had until recently employed to assist the Venetians in their war against Ferdinand. This army, effectively the property of the freebooting mercenary general Count Ernst Mansfeld, arrived in Bohemia just in time to prevent the Imperialists from making a determined advance on Prague, following which both sides preferred to spend the autumn manoeuvring, skirmishing and ravaging the countryside rather than risk a major battle. In this Thurn fared rather better than the Imperialists, while Mansfeld besieged Pilsen (Plzeň), an important city which had not joined the revolt. Its eventual fall in late November 1618 marked the end of the campaigning season, leaving the troops to find their winter quarters and the governments to pursue the conflict through diplomacy and propaganda until military action could be resumed in the spring.

The revolt had so far been an entirely Bohemian affair, but one watched anxiously in Moravia, Silesia and Lusatia, which also came under the Bohemian crown. Moravia sought to mediate, sending a high-level deputation to Vienna and Prague, comprising two leading Catholics, Prince Karl Liechtenstein and Cardinal Franz Dietrichstein, together with the leading Protestant, Wallenstein's brother-in-law Zierotin. Prudently the Moravian Estates also prepared to defend themselves if necessary, mobilising their establishment of 2000 cavalry and 3000 infantry in the summer of 1618, the latter commanded by Wallenstein with his long-standing commission as a Moravian colonel.[1] There can have been little doubt as to where Wallenstein stood, as a Catholic, a former long-serving member of Matthias's entourage, and only recently returned from active service on Ferdinand's behalf at Gradisca, but although the nobility were predominantly Protestant most of the principal Moravian offices were nevertheless held by Catholics, including two of the three colonels commanding their troops.

Why did Wallenstein, a born Bohemian, become a firm opponent of the Bohemian revolt – a question which has sometimes carried the implication that his position was unpatriotic and dishonourable? Such a view is based on an anachronistic concept of nationalism and patriotism, one which developed later and which did not apply in the early seventeenth century, when loyalties and duties remained personal in a surviving feudal sense. Wallenstein had long since relinquished his position in Bohemia to become a Moravian lord, landowner and colonel, and he owed no legal or moral duty to the Bohemian Estates. The same was true even in Moravia, as the Estates were neither the state nor the government, the head of both being the emperor in his capacity as margrave, and constitutionally the ultimate loyalty was due to him. Many people in the Thirty Years War had to face conflicting loyalties, particularly between their religion and their constitutional duty, but Wallenstein had no such difficulty, as for him they led in the same direction, as did his previous choice of Habsburg service, while his personal outlook was also constitutionalist. Feudal landowners and senior military officers tend to be supporters of established authority and opposed to rebellion, and Wallenstein was no exception. Hence he was bound to reject the Bohemian revolt and to side with Habsburg legitimacy.

Wallenstein's loyalty as a Moravian colonel was thus dependent on Moravia's continued loyalty to the emperor. Internally divided and above all anxious to keep out of the conflict, the Moravians at this stage preferred neutrality. As long as they made no direct break with the emperor Wallenstein's position remained tenable, but he lost no time in preparing for their expected defection. In August 1618 he set about raising money, 20,000 gulden from his own resources and a further 20,000 borrowed.[2] In October he went to Vienna to offer to raise a regiment of 1000 cuirassiers (heavy cavalry) in the Netherlands for service in the spring under his own command. This was a welcome proposition, in response to which Wallenstein received a provisional appointment as an Imperial colonel, confirmed in February 1619 when the regiment was ready, although he was still waiting in May for a receipt for his 40,000 gulden loan to the emperor which had financed the recruitment.[3] Meanwhile despite still being a Moravian colonel he had started to cooperate unofficially with the Imperial forces in

Bohemia.[4] In November 1618, when Bucquoy was hard pressed by Thurn, Wallenstein provided him with provisions and munitions, a clear breach of Moravian neutrality which brought sharp complaints to the Estates from the Bohemians, although with no apparent consequences for Wallenstein.

After a winter of prevarication Thurn resolved the issue of Moravian neutrality in April 1619 by invading with a substantial army. He met with no resistance, and indeed the Protestant nobility were more than ready to join the Bohemians. Most of the Catholics, led by Liechtenstein and Dietrichstein, were also acquiescent, motivated partly by anxiety to save their property and partly by defeatism arising from the poor Imperialist military showing in the autumn.[5] Wallenstein was made of sterner stuff and not inclined to acquiescence even though his own property was equally at risk. On 30 April he and the commander of one of the cavalry regiments made a concerted effort to move their units out of reach of the revolt, intending to transfer them to Imperialist service. Neither succeeded, principally because the troops were not mercenaries recruited from far and wide but mainly Moravians with similar sympathies to the Protestant nobility. The cavalry colonel sought to lead his men out from Brünn (Brno), but his officers queried the source of his orders, and suspecting the true state of affairs they and the men instead displaced him, although they allowed him to make good his own escape.

Wallenstein was initially more successful, and in the middle of the same day nine of his ten companies of musketeers, led by a major, duly marched off from their station at Olmütz towards the Hungarian border. By evening they were back, leading to a confrontation between their major with some 2700 men and Wallenstein coming to meet him with the remaining 300. The officer presumably disputed his orders, and Wallenstein, seeing that he was lost unless the mutiny was suppressed, drew his sword and killed him on the spot. Determined action saved the day, and after appointing another officer to lead the main force away Wallenstein himself returned to Olmütz. That same evening he and his company of soldiers descended on the treasury in the city, seized an official, and forced him to give them access to the money. Almost 100,000 taler in cash, together with a quantity of munitions and supplies, were loaded into wagons before Wallenstein and his men made their escape into the night.[6]

The news soon reached Thurn, who immediately sent his cavalry after him. They caught up with the main force, most of whom were ready enough to return to their Moravian allegiance, but the officers with the wagons and a few hundred men evaded them, so that

Wallenstein and the money reached Vienna. His dramatic exploit was well received privately, and he had an audience with Ferdinand himself (Matthias having died six weeks earlier), but diplomatically it presented something of a problem. The situation in Moravia was still fluid, and although everyone could see how things were going no formal breach with the emperor had occurred, so that there were no legal grounds for confiscation of the treasury funds. Opinion was divided in the penniless Imperial government – it was a lot of money – but in the end it was decided that it had to be returned.[7] The rebels were less hesitant, and Wallenstein was promptly banished and all his assets in Moravia were confiscated. He was not surprised, and he had already provided himself with a newly recruited cavalry regiment, a commission as an Imperial colonel, and the considerable pay and allowances which went with it.

The political history of the Bohemian revolt during its remaining year and a half was principally concerned with the search for legitimacy and allies, problems which were interlinked as Europe's kings and princes were always wary of supporting rebels abroad for fear of encouraging rebellion at home. Having approved Ferdinand's nomination as successor king when they could lawfully have declined, the Bohemians now decided that he must be deposed, a step which was both unprecedented and unconstitutional. They had to find a new king to maintain an appearance of legitimacy, but candidates were scarce, not least because of the very limited powers which the Estates proposed to grant. Several of the princes whose names were canvassed might have been flattered by the offer of a crown but were either unsuitable or unwilling. The duke of Savoy was not prepared to risk all-out war with the Habsburgs and was moreover a Catholic, while John George I, Elector of Saxony, although a Lutheran, was opposed to the revolt and would not contemplate a breach of his own duty to the emperor. The best that could be found was the young, naive and ineffectual Frederick V, Elector of the Palatinate, and even he was both hesitant and a Calvinist. Time was pressing for Bohemia, as Matthias's death had also started the process of an Imperial election, and Ferdinand would be doubly difficult to depose once he had become emperor. The result was an eventful week in August 1619, during which Ferdinand was deposed as king of Bohemia on the 22nd, Frederick of the Palatinate was elected in his place on the 26th, and Ferdinand was elected Holy Roman Emperor in Frankfurt on the 28th.

Allies remained hard to find. A couple of Protestant German princes recognised Frederick's election in Bohemia, but they did no more. The Dutch sent words of support but only a little money and even fewer men.

James I of England, Frederick's father-in-law, made public his disapproval of the whole affair and would have nothing to do with it. The French, anti-Habsburg but also Catholic, were preoccupied with their internal affairs, as were the Protestant Scandinavian kings. Savoy and Venice were too prudent to become further involved, Brandenburg was too poor and too timorous, and John George of Saxony in due course sided with the emperor. The only practical military help came from Bethlen Gabor, the Calvinist prince of Transylvania, in modern terms north-west Romania but then an independent principality, although nevertheless a tributary of the Ottoman Empire. Bethlen had his own ambitions and reasons for becoming involved, which fitted into the long-term pattern of recurrent outbreaks of war between the emperor and the Turkish dependencies on the Austro-Hungarian frontier. To the extent that his interests coincided with theirs Bethlen provided valuable assistance to the Protestant side in the early part of the Thirty Years War, but he proved to be an unreliable ally, prone to concluding truces with the Habsburgs whenever he faced pressures elsewhere or when his own objectives had been achieved.

In the spring of 1619 Ferdinand was almost equally isolated militarily. The forces he had put into the field with Spanish assistance the previous autumn had fared badly, and moreover he was faced with actual or potential rebellion not only in the Bohemian territories but also from Protestant majorities in much of his Austrian heartland, with even Vienna far from reliable. Thurn, following on from his bloodless triumph in Moravia, took advantage of the situation to march into Austria, and by May he had the capital itself under siege. In early June there was a change of fortune. Bucquoy caught Mansfeld and the larger part of his army, defeating him heavily near the town of Záblatí, the first significant Imperialist victory and one which immediately caused the Bohemian Estates to recall Thurn, so that the siege of Vienna was lifted.

The respite was short-lived, as in August Bethlen launched his attack through Habsburg Hungary towards Pressburg (Bratislava), which he captured in October to bring him within striking distance of Vienna. Bucquoy was called back to the defence, and hotly pursued by Thurn he made a hazardous withdrawal over the Danube at Ulrichskirchen, not far from Vienna, but was unable to prevent Thurn and Bethlen joining forces to besiege the city for a second time. Again the siege was abandoned, as towards the end of November Bethlen heard of a diversionary Polish foray into Transylvania, and this and the approach of winter were sufficient to send him home. Thurn, short of money and artillery, his troops ill paid, ill disciplined, and ill from various pestilences, had little choice but to follow suit, bringing 1619 to an end for military purposes.

That was the limit of Bohemian success, as Ferdinand was beginning to gather allies. Spain realised that active help was required to avoid a Protestant defeat of the Empire, and Duke Maximilian I of Bavaria was brought into the conflict by the promise of substantial rewards. Maximilian, who was both Ferdinand's cousin and his brother-in-law, was head of the Catholic League, which like the Protestant Union had become an enduring result of the confrontations in Germany more than a decade earlier, and he controlled its army and its formidable and highly experienced general, Tilly. In the spring John George of Saxony also agreed to support Ferdinand, and the fate of the revolt was sealed. In July 1620 Tilly moved into Upper Austria to neutralise potential rebels there and to join up with Bucquoy. In August an army from the Spanish Netherlands under General Ambrosio Spinola invaded Frederick's Palatinate (which lay on both sides of the Rhine extending from Heidelberg to beyond Mainz), and John George occupied Lusatia, all with little resistance. Tilly and Bucquoy then advanced into Bohemia, finally confronting the combined Bohemian and Palatinate forces under Thurn and Prince Christian of Anhalt just outside Prague. On 8 November 1620 the Imperialists gained a quick, complete and decisive victory at the battle of the White Mountain, and Frederick, henceforth known mockingly as the 'winter king' due to the brevity of his reign, made a hasty and undignified escape the following day.

Wallenstein and his regiment were on active service throughout 1619 and 1620, apart from periods when he had bouts of the ill health which troubled him for the rest of his life. It was during these two years that he really learned his craft as a senior officer and future general, extending his combat experience and adding the grasp of management and logistics which was the basis of his later success. He played no part in the direction of the campaigns, and nor is he credited with any spectacular exploits, either individually or with his regiment. Instead he did what was required of him, and if we have no proof that he did so bravely, reliably and competently we can at least infer this from the additional responsibility that he was given at the end of 1619, and the duties which were assigned to him towards and after the defeat of the revolt late in 1620.

Line officers, colonels included, were expected to lead their men in person when they went into battle, and the casualty list among the higher ranks, both in the Bohemian campaign and later in the Thirty Years War, testifies that they actually did so. Wallenstein had already fought with some personal distinction at Gradisca, and while he was not always with his regiment due to illness and other duties it is clear that he must have seen action during 1619–20. In June 1619 his regiment was with Bucquoy when he defeated Mansfeld at Záblatí, and it was still with him during the retreat to defend Vienna in the autumn of that year. Wallenstein took part in the withdrawal over the Danube at Ulrichskirchen, where his regiment was reportedly assigned to provide defensive cover for the crossing and was one of the last over the pontoon bridge. He was also in Vienna during the siege by Bethlen and Thurn in November. High casualties accompanied so much action, and disease also took its toll, so that Wallenstein had to recruit in the Netherlands over the winter. Campaigning was confined to skirmishing during the early part of 1620, a time when he was ill with gout in April and with a severe fever in July, but he took part in the advance into Bohemia later in the summer. His men fought at the battle of the White Mountain, although Wallenstein himself had been detached for special duties at that time.[8]

Nevertheless the managerial side of a colonel's responsibilities was in many respects more important. A regiment was the biggest functional military entity in this period, and it had to be self-sufficient and able to operate on its own if necessary. Most were business enterprises which for practical purposes belonged to the colonel, and he was engaged by a prince, state or city as a military contractor to supply and maintain his regiment as a fully operational unit. In return he received agreed rates of payment for the number of men, horses and other items provided, as well as allowances for himself and his staff. For a capable businessman there were opportunities for substantial legitimate profits as well as ways of supplementing these by various subterfuges, although there were also financial risks as the colonel might have to make a considerable initial outlay and to provide extended credit to his employer before obtaining reimbursement.

We may assume that Wallenstein quickly proved his organisational competence, as along with authority to re-recruit at the end of 1619 he was shortly afterwards given a commission for a second regiment. Second commissions were not unheard of but they were by no means common, their most likely recipients being those of princely rank and wealth who could advance a great deal of money, or senior staff officers with a track record of success and a purse well lined with the profits. Wallenstein fell into neither category at this time, despite which not only did he receive a second commission, but a double-sized one, for 2000 cavalry instead of the standard 1000. His reputation for loyalty at Ferdinand's court following his actions at Gradisca and Olmütz no doubt helped, but he will still have had to demonstrate his professional skills before receiving a mark of favour of this kind and scale. Wallenstein probably found part of the necessary money from the profits of his first regiment, but he also called in 40,000 gulden which he had placed on loan in Vienna, stating that he required the cash back in order to finance recruiting.[9] This was presumably money which he had previously moved out of Moravia, and he may also have been able to borrow from other wealthy well-wishers, as he already had good connections to the so-called Spanish party at court. These included Ferdinand's first minister, Prince Hans Ulrich Eggenberg, a contact which dated back to the time of Gradisca, the next most influential councillor Baron Karl Harrach, and the Spanish ambassador Count Oñate.[10]

During 1620 Wallenstein was appointed to the Imperial war council, although he excused himself from having to attend in Vienna,[11] and he was also assigned special duties towards the end of the 1620 campaign, leaving his regiments in the charge of lieutenant-colonels, as was the practice of the time. With the military action moving towards a successful conclusion Ferdinand and his councillors were anxious to secure their recovered territory politically. Areas occupied by Catholic forces were safe enough, but their ally to the north posed a potential problem. Lusatia, which bordered on to both Saxony and Bohemia, had been pledged to John George of Saxony as security for his campaign expenses – a pledge which became permanent as Imperial finances never permitted its redemption – and he duly occupied it in the concerted advance on Bohemia. For many of the towns between Prague and the northern border the Lutheran elector might have appeared a much preferable overlord to the arch-Catholic emperor, and hence Wallenstein was despatched to head off any possible defections. Only a handful of troops could be spared for the purpose, so he had to rely on personality and bold pre-emptive action, although backed by the threat of severe punishment once the revolt was over for any who resisted his authority. Thus he went from town to town requiring the citizenry to renew their oaths of loyalty to Ferdinand in his presence, which they duly did. A letter from one mayor describes Wallenstein as 'a very friendly gentleman', who nevertheless left no doubt that he was set on achieving his objective and was not prepared to stand for any prevarication.[12]

Vengeance followed victory. On 11 November 1620, three days after the battle of the White Mountain, the Bohemian Estates made their submission to Maximilian of Bavaria, as the emperor's representative. The highest-placed had already escaped. Frederick, still clinging to the title of king of Bohemia, headed west to Holland, Anhalt went north and took refuge with the Scandinavian monarchs, and Thurn made his way south, eventually to Constantinople, where he tried to persuade the Turkish sultan to help the exiles to continue the war. Many lesser participants also fled but numerous others remained, hoping through their submission to receive mild treatment. Those who stayed underestimated Ferdinand as badly as those who had voted to confirm his nomination as successor to the Bohemian throne, and indeed many of them were the same individuals. Ferdinand had already shown his hand earlier in 1620 by using – or abusing – the legal procedures of the Empire in a move to place Frederick under the ban, making him an outlaw and providing a cloak of respectability for the seizure of his lands. As he showed at later stages in the Thirty Years War, Ferdinand saw victory as an opportunity not for peace and reconciliation but for driving home his advantage to the full.

The blow did not fall immediately in Bohemia. Instead Maximilian promised the Estates to intercede for their lives – which he did not – and then departed for home, leaving Liechtenstein as temporary governor. Three months went by, and it was not until February 1621 that Liechtenstein, acting on orders from Vienna and assisted by Tilly, Wallenstein and their troops, arrested all the members of the former directorate of the revolt who remained within reach, as well as several dozen other participants. They were put on trial for high treason, and of the 40 who were convicted 27 were executed in front of Prague's city hall in a single morning in June, when troops from one of Wallenstein's regiments were responsible for order and security.[13] These killings were accompanied by a wave of expropriations, with property seized not only from those convicted but also from those who had died in arms against Ferdinand, those who had fled, and many others who had been associated to a greater or lesser extent with the revolt. Some were fortunate to have only a proportion of their lands confiscated, and others were even more fortunate to be able to minimise or conceal their involvement, often with the help of influential friends on the winning side. Nevertheless vast areas of land passed into the control of the Imperial treasury and became available for sale to purchasers deemed loyal to the regime, in what constituted not only massive punishment but also a concerted effort to break the economic and political power of the landed Protestant nobility and gentry of Bohemia. And of course the emperor desperately needed the money to meet the costs of the war.

Not that the war was by any means over, even temporarily. In the west there were ominous signs that princes who had been unsympathetic to

Frederick's Bohemian pretensions were nevertheless not prepared to see him deprived of his Palatinate, not least because of the precedent it would set. Mansfeld had spent the winter after the defeat of the revolt occupying Pilsen while unsuccessfully canvassing prospective new employers, but Dutch subsidies had enabled Frederick to re-engage him in the spring of 1621, so that he was in the field again on Bohemia's south-west frontier. In the east Bethlen launched a new attack, to the north there was a rising in Silesia, led by a local nobleman, the margrave of Jägerndorf, and both Bohemia and Moravia were simmering and potentially ready to revolt again. In this crisis Maximilian's Catholic League army had to be deployed against Mansfeld, while Bucquoy headed for Hungary to take on Bethlen and Wallenstein was appointed to lead a force into Silesia.[14]

This was a significant advancement for him, as although it carried no formal higher rank it was his first independent command. Again it was an assignment in which political considerations were as important as military ones. Jägerndorf was to be defeated and his property seized, but at the same time Silesia was to be pacified rather than inflamed, order was to be restored, and the Estates were to be encouraged back to the emperor's side. Events dictated otherwise. Jägerndorf did not wait to be attacked but marched off south-east into Moravia, aiming to join up with Bethlen in Hungary. The Imperialists were already in difficulties following a clash at Neuhäusel (Nové Zámky), east of Pressburg, in which Bucquoy himself had been killed. With Moravia vulnerable and disaffected, Wallenstein was diverted urgently to undertake its defence. He reached Olmütz just in time to secure it and make it his base for the rest of the 1621 campaigning season, during which time he raised more troops and skirmished successfully enough with the Transylvanians to prevent them from making further progress, but his force was never strong enough to mount an offensive and drive them out. Then as winter approached Bethlen once again negotiated a peace with the emperor and went home with his booty.

Letters from this time show the approach to financing war which was one of the fundamentals of Wallenstein's later success. He found a familiar situation in Olmütz, with unpaid and unfed troops stealing and extorting whatever they could from the citizens and peasantry, who in turn were in a state of unrest bordering on revolt. Wallenstein believed in order and favoured the organised and disciplined raising of taxes – later generally known as contributions – from town and country, including the landowners, on something like an equitable basis according to ability to pay. Cardinal Dietrichstein, acting Imperial governor in Moravia, did not agree, probably because he and his friends would have been the largest contributors. When Dietrichstein terminated the levy, Wallenstein, not yet senior enough to override him, could only protest in an angry letter. Good discipline, he pointed out, depended on the troops having quarters, rations and pay. Otherwise they would steal what they could and despoil the countryside. The ordinary people would be better off paying orderly contributions than being ruined in this way, and hence civil disorders would be less likely. With evident frustration he concluded by noting that he had done what he could and would not be responsible if disturbances occurred.[15]

At the end of 1621, with campaigning over for the winter, Wallenstein was in Vienna and moving in elevated social circles.[16] Prince Christian of Anhalt the younger, wounded and captured at the White Mountain and at this time an honoured and paroled prisoner of the emperor, recorded meeting and talking to him, on one occasion during a visit to the Spanish ambassador Oñate. In mid-January 1622 both Wallenstein and the young prince were guests, along with the emperor himself, at the wedding of Maximilian Waldstein, a relative Wallenstein later frequently referred to as 'my cousin Max' and who he both liked and trusted. The bride was Katharina Harrach, daughter of the wealthy and influential privy councillor.

In January 1622 the emperor confirmed Liechtenstein as governor of Bohemia, a position which had not previously existed and with powers which were not possible under the old constitution, but Ferdinand had swept that away, along with the elective monarchy. A day later Wallenstein was appointed commandant of Prague, and hence in practice of the whole of Bohemia, giving him the military equivalent of Liechtenstein's political role, although the latter held the superior status.[17] He was the obvious choice, in part because of his Bohemian origins but more due to his proven loyalty, reliability and competence during the preceding years of war. Moreover he was rapidly becoming one of the most prominent of the emperor's own officers, noting that Ferdinand had so far relied on the Spanish to provide him with generals, two of whom had already been killed in his service. Wallenstein was still some way from achieving that rank, and he had little to do militarily during 1622, as although the war not only continued but escalated, the main campaigning was far away in west and north Germany. There the forces of Spain and of the Catholic League rather than the Imperial army upheld the Habsburg cause, leaving Wallenstein with a little time to attend to his own affairs.

4
Richer Than All His Tribe
(*Othello*)

When Wallenstein clattered into Vienna with the contents of the Olmütz treasury in May 1619 he was himself, if not penniless, certainly landless, apparently with little more to his name than his investment in his new regiment. Less than five years later he was in the super-rich class, the largest landowner in Bohemia and one of the wealthiest men in the Empire. The fortune acquired in this period was the basis of his future success, as it gave him the means to raise, finance and supply armies, to raise further credit, and in turn to extend credit on a vast scale to his massively indebted emperor. How he achieved this is a question which has excited much interest, although without producing definitive answers, and this in turn has prompted speculation that it must have been by dubious means. Examination of the subject is therefore necessary, but it is also undeniably complicated, so that readers of a financially nervous disposition may wish to skip this chapter.

If the answers are not clear the fault is probably not Wallenstein's. His approach to business was orderly and methodical, as is evident from the detailed records and extensive correspondence which have survived both from his career as a general and from the administration of his lands and properties. On the other hand there are large gaps, and documents covering key aspects of his life have disappeared without trace. For example in June 1631 Wallenstein had some five hundred important papers catalogued in Prague and then despatched for safe keeping in the vaults of one of his castles in Bohemia. The documents themselves have vanished but the register has survived, among the items it lists being an official receipt for a very large loan, three and a half million gulden, which Wallenstein advanced to the emperor in January 1623.[1] Some of the files may simply have disappeared through the accidents of history, but it seems likely that many were deliberately destroyed, and certainly the opportunists and adventurers who acquired pieces of Wallenstein's property after his death will have had no interest in seeing too many records preserved. It has also been suggested that efforts were made on behalf of the Imperial court to cleanse the files of uncomfortable material concerning not only Wallenstein's officially sanctioned assassination but also his earlier financial relations with the exchequer. Hence although researchers have turned up many relevant documents the effect created is that of a jigsaw, with just enough pieces in place to produce some tantalising outlines but too many missing to reveal the detail.

Some assumptions can reasonably be made about the first stages of Wallenstein's financial recovery. Firstly, in committing himself to Ferdinand's side and providing himself with an Imperial commission he will certainly have anticipated the possibility of his Moravian estates being confiscated. He advanced Ferdinand 40,000 gulden, 20,000 of his own and an equal amount borrowed, even though he had other liquid assets and was able to place a further 40,000 gulden on loan elsewhere. No doubt he had taken the precaution of transferring as much in cash and valuables as he could raise to Vienna or some other place of relative safety.

Secondly he had his regiments, with an official strength of 1000 heavy cavalry in 1619, increasing to 3000 in 1620 and 1621. This was a very large number for a single colonel, and the opportunity for legitimate profit was commensurately great. During the Thirty Years War a colonel could become wealthy from a single regiment, and heavy cavalry was the most expensive branch and therefore the most profitable. Given Wallenstein's organisational skills and business acumen he seems sure to have made the most of the opportunity. Doubtless he added to his profits through the usual sharp practices, some of which had become so standard as scarcely to be regarded as dishonest. He also benefited from a special allocation of 8000 gulden a year under his commission of 1619, a supplement of almost 50 per cent on the standard colonel's allowance for pay for himself, his lieutenant-colonel and the regimental staff, together with his household and servants. No reason for this was recorded, but it was specifically designated as exceptional and must reflect the favour in which Wallenstein was already held.[2]

Then there were the spoils of war. Looting was the simplest approach, at the lowest level straightforward theft but in its legitimate form safer and more profitable. A town which refused to surrender and was taken by storm was usually given over to the troops for a prescribed period during which they were free to take whatever they could find, this being provided under the 'laws of war' both as a punishment for those who had held out pointlessly and as a recompense for the soldiers who had risked their lives in the assault. Senior officers of the day were certainly not above looting personally, in addition to which they often had a share of what was taken by their men. They also commonly bought valuable items from the finders for a fraction of their true worth, cash being what the soldiers really required. This booty not infrequently changed hands as a result of the fortunes of war, and whether in a skirmish or a full battle the baggage train of the losers, as well as any valuables about the persons of prisoners or the dead, were the first targets of the victors.

Officers had opportunities to extort semi-legitimate payments in cash or valuables from civilians. Safe conduct was one. *Salva guardi* was another, a payment for exempting or protecting a property from looting, increased if a guard was posted to enforce the arrangement. Exemption from billeting likewise had its price. Then there was *Brandschatzung*, a payment for not burning down a property, theoretically only in circumstances where the archaic laws of war would otherwise have allowed it but often more generally applied. These and other payments could relate to an individual or a single property, but they could also cover entire villages or towns, in which case the sums involved were considerable. Technically much of the proceeds should have been paid into the official military treasury, and there were cases in the Thirty Years War where officers were disciplined or even executed for failing to do so, but these were only the most flagrant examples involving particularly large sums. Most of the rest found its way into private pockets, and this was generally regarded not as an abuse but as a perk of the job. Prudent officers transferred their gains to places of safety as often as circumstances permitted, and although it is difficult to quantify them it is known that amounts could be substantial. In the 1630s Sydnam Poyntz, an English junior cavalry officer in Imperial service, recorded having 3000 pounds sterling accumulated from booty with him in the field, an enormous sum at the time, while Augustin Fritsch, then a major in the Bavarian army, noted losing 5000 Reichstaler in cash and a whole sackful of silverware when he was on the losing side at a battle.[3]

Hence Wallenstein had considerable scope to rebuild his finances during the Bohemian campaigns of 1619–21. This is important, as in order to take advantage of the opportunities which subsequently presented themselves he needed a substantial sum of money as his stake and starting point. The collapse of the revolt after the battle of the White Mountain, followed by the restoration of Habsburg authority in

Bohemia and Moravia, also ensured that he would recover his confiscated properties. He had been a substantial Moravian landowner before, not as rich as Liechtenstein, Dietrichstein or Zierotin but nevertheless in the top echelon. By 1621 he was probably significantly richer than he had been before the revolt, and even if his properties were not yet fully restored to him and his military profits were mainly in the form of promissory notes from the Imperial exchequer, they could, given the right contacts, be used as collateral for future business dealings.

Minting money

Next, although slightly ahead of the chronology, we should look at the consortium set up to operate the mints and issue coinage in Bohemia, Moravia and Upper Austria for one year beginning on 1 February 1622.[4] This became a *cause célèbre* both at the time and in subsequent histories, and it has been blamed for the inflation of the period, while the participants were assumed to have made such huge profits that it provoked an Imperial exchequer investigation into Liechtenstein's financial affairs which was still active over 40 years later.[5] The idea was simple enough and may have originated with Paul Michna, head of the Bohemian treasury, who himself became a member of the consortium. With the war continuing the government desperately needed money, but although profit from minting the coinage was a traditional source of revenue this was not going well, with silver in short supply and increasing in price in the prevailing inflationary climate. Nor had a series of debasements (reduction of the silver content of the coins) solved the problem or assured a steady income. Privatisation, as it became known in modern times, looked like an answer, contracting out the sourcing of silver and the minting and issuing of coinage in exchange for guaranteed weekly payments to the exchequer. Financiers were found to run the scheme, the dominant one being Hans de Witte, Bohemia's leading banker, working with Jakob Bassevi, a Prague merchant and silver trader. Impressive names were also required to provide respectability, contacts and influence, first among them being Liechtenstein, together with Michna and Wallenstein, then newly appointed as military commandant at Prague. In the shadows behind them were ten others whose names have not been firmly established, but who were probably well placed at the Imperial court.

The consortium was certainly not principally responsible for the notorious and severe inflation of the period, known as the *Kipper- und Wipperzeit*. This was already under way long before the consortium was formed, as is shown by previous debasements in Bohemia, one under Frederick's short-lived government and no less than three during 1621, which progressively increased the number of gulden minted from a mark of silver (a unit of weight), first from 19 to 27, then to 39, on to 46, and again to 78. Moreover this inflation was rampant far beyond Bohemia and Austria, being well documented across the Empire from Saxony to Strasbourg and all points south.[6] The economic effect of war is a far more credible culprit, aggravated by the actions of governments in adulterating the coinage at a time when the mechanisms of inflation were not fully understood. The new consortium effectively took over the already established minting rate, specified at 79 gulden to the mark, which had to cover payment of six million gulden to the exchequer for the year's contract and to allow the contractors some scope for profit themselves. It has been argued that the consortium stoked inflation by greatly increasing the money supply through the issue of 42 million gulden in the year, 30 million in the first few months, although it has also to be said that the main call for this money came from the Imperial government itself. The consortium certainly had to issue its coins as quickly as possible, because debasement is not only a response to but also a cause of inflation in a classic vicious circle. Hence it drove up the cash price of silver, an increase to which the consortium's own high level of demand will have contributed. As a result de Witte's agents had to seek supplies in financial markets across Europe to meet the requirements. Well before the end of the year the scheme ceased to be profitable, and as renewal terms could not be agreed it came to an end in February 1623. In December of that year the government carried out a currency reform, calling in the debased coins and issuing new ones with something like the original silver content at a rate of one for six.[7]

The official investigation has left only a couple of tables of figures in the archives, and as these are of dubious origin and are not internally consistent no firm conclusions as to the profits made by the consortium can be drawn. It appears that the individual members supplied varying amounts of silver, and were credited for it at very different average prices, with the impressive names being paid much more per mark than the real principals. Their personal profits depended mainly on what the silver had actually cost them, which increased with inflation as the year went on. Calculations based on reasoned assumptions suggest that the contract may have been set up with an expected average silver price of around 55 gulden per mark, as against possibly 40 or less at the outset and apparently in excess of the minting rate of 79 towards the end. However de Witte supplied more than 70 per cent of the silver and was credited an average of 78 gulden per mark, while Bassevi provided over 25 per cent, probably near the beginning and largely scrap, as he was credited only 46 gulden per mark. Nevertheless it may safely be assumed that they made a useful profit. The other thirteen members contributed less than 3 per cent of the silver between them, but Liechtenstein was credited 569 gulden per mark, somewhere around ten times its likely cost, and the ten unknowns only a little less, 440 on average, while Michna received 248.[8] These generous payments obviously related to the recipients' political importance rather than to their practical contribution to the consortium, and they show a clear pecking order. Irrespective of whether the silver cost them 40, 55 or over 79 gulden per mark, most of their credits will have been profit, limited only by the fact that the quantities were relatively modest. Liechtenstein, who contributed only a small fraction of the silver, must have made around 400,000 gulden.

Wallenstein supplied a great deal more silver than the other non-financiers, over six times as much as Liechtenstein and more than the unknown ten put together, but he was credited much less for it, only 123 gulden per mark. This price suggests that he was still relatively unimportant politically, while one possible explanation for the larger quantity is that he actually had silver to sell. Silver tableware was very popular with the well-to-do, both as a portable form of wealth and for purposes of ostentation, and hence it became an equally popular form of war booty, so that Wallenstein may have been able to buy it from other officers in addition to what he had himself acquired. His 5000 marks of silver corresponds to a credit of 615,000 gulden, and after allowing for the relevant share of minting costs and the exchequer's fee this indicates a profit of some 290,000 gulden if he bought his silver at the presumptive average price of 55 gulden per mark. This is broadly in line with one of the enquiry's tables, which indicates that he made 240,000 gulden.[9]

It has been suggested that the consortium actually debased the coins beyond the agreed 79 per mark, but this is highly improbable. That type of fraud was well known, the analysis of the silver content of a coin is a simple matter, the responsible officials would have been watching carefully, and the risk would have been too high for financiers and impressive names alike. It is nevertheless possible that some low-value coins were adulterated, but probably as a smaller-scale fraud carried out at a lower level in the mints. Otherwise it does not appear that the consortium actually did anything wrong, although it has subsequently attracted a great deal of odium. The facts are that the principals entered into a contract with the exchequer, took a risk on the problems of securing enough silver and the inflation of its price, delivered the agreed fee and apparently quite legally made a lot of money over and above. As for Wallenstein, it is unlikely that he played any part in setting up or running the consortium, or indeed delivered any significant political influence on its behalf. He was lucky to be in the right place at the right time, and to have the right contacts, principally Liechtenstein, to be asked to join. Nevertheless it was not, as has been claimed, a major source of his wealth. A profit of around a quarter of a million gulden was a lot of money, but as will be seen the sums involved in Wallenstein's property transactions at this time were an order of magnitude larger.

A man of property

There are three main strands in the complicated history of Wallenstein's property dealings in the early 1620s. Firstly he lent money to the emperor secured on various lands which were liable to confiscation following their owners' participation in the Bohemian revolt. Secondly he pursued and eventually acquired the larger part of the vast Smiřický family estates, by virtue of his claim as one of the best qualified prospective heirs through his mother, who was born a Smiřický. Thirdly he engaged in a huge and frantic but logical programme of purchases, sales and exchanges when the confiscated properties of former rebels were put on the market. All three aspects were bound up with the punitive policy adopted by the emperor, and with the latter's desperate need to raise money as fast as possible to pay some of his debts and continue the war. The proceedings were legally dubious, but the responsibility for that lay with Ferdinand, not Wallenstein.

The first three months after the battle of the White Mountain were deceptively quiet in this respect, but with the arrests in February and the mass execution in June 1621 Ferdinand's approach became apparent. Even so it was not until January 1622 that a special court was set up to investigate those accused of complicity in the revolt, and to confiscate the lands of those found guilty. Its president was Adam Waldstein, often described as Wallenstein's uncle although he may have been a more distant relative, and a long-standing holder of Bohemian offices who had been an Imperial privy councillor while Wallenstein was still at school. Those who had been executed, or had died in arms during the revolt, or had fled the country, were automatically liable to full expropriation. Others less seriously implicated forfeited only a proportion of their property, the most fortunate as little as a fifth, but even in such cases everything was confiscated, and the owners were entitled only to monetary compensation for the balance. The scale was staggering, affecting around a thousand families, two-thirds of them in Bohemia and one-third in Moravia, while half of Bohemia's total land area, or even more according to some estimates, changed hands as a result.[10]

The emperor's financial needs could not await the outcome of the court's work. One quick expedient was to raise loans secured on prospectively forfeit properties, the revenues from which would provide for interest to the lender until such time as the transaction could be converted into a direct sale. Wallenstein was one of the first to come forward, and early in 1621 two loans were negotiated, for 60,000 and 50,000 gulden respectively – although all these figures should be regarded as indicative rather than precise – each secured on estates from the Smiřický holdings. The specification of these particular properties as security was no coincidence, given Wallenstein's separate potential claim on them, as it ensured that they could not be pledged or sold to anyone else. His third loan, in June 1621 and for a further 58,000 gulden, was secured on the estates of Friedland and Reichenberg (Liberec), not Smiřický lands but like them north-east of Prague in the area in which Wallenstein aimed to build up his holdings.[11] Thus in the space of a few months, long before the minting consortium, Wallenstein had advanced the emperor 168,000 gulden, either in cash or by converting into secured loans some of the amounts due to him for the costs and services of his Imperial regiments.

The Smiřický saga is not so easily summarised but is important, firstly because of its size, and secondly because Wallenstein had a legitimate personal interest in the inheritance, albeit only because of the remarkable circumstances both within the family and in Bohemia following suppression of the revolt. The total value of the properties has been estimated at around two million gulden. More significant is that they were reputedly worth four or five times Wallenstein's Moravian estates, which had themselves sufficed to make him one of that territory's richest men. Adding even part of the Smiřický lands would have moved him into a higher league, but by the end of 1622, in his capacity as guardian and sole heir to their mentally incapable owner, he controlled well over half of them.

The story starts much earlier.[12] The Smiřický family property, with its main seat at Gitschin, comprised some seventeen estates to the north and east of Prague. Most of these were freely transferable by sale or inheritance, but some were subject to an entail which prevented this and passed ownership to the senior member of the family for the time being, males taking precedence. Although enormously wealthy, however, the family was gradually dying out, and by 1614 only four surviving children of the deceased Sigmund Smiřický were left in the direct line, together with a couple of more distant relatives, one of whom was Wallenstein. Sigmund left only money to his two daughters, although he had imprisoned the elder one following an embarrassing love affair, a confinement which the family continued after his death. His two sons should have shared the freely transferable property, while the entail should have gone to the elder, Heinrich Georg, but he was permanently mentally incapacitated. Relying on this, the younger son, Albrecht Jan, bypassed the legalities and had the whole inheritance entered in his name in the Bohemian land registry, although it was unclear whether this was claimed to be in his own right or in part as his brother's guardian.

This Albrecht Jan Smiřický later became one of the principal Bohemian rebels, took part in the defenestration, raised a regiment, fell ill and died on campaign. A bitter dispute between the two sisters followed. The elder, having escaped her confinement and married, forcibly seized some of the properties, but the younger obtained orders from the Bohemian courts during the revolt, requiring their return and appointing her as Heinrich Georg's guardian. This ended in a bizarre and widely publicised disaster in February 1620, when during an armed confrontation at the family mansion in Gitschin there was an explosion in a gunpowder store, killing the elder sister and the husband of the younger, as well as a number of other officials, soldiers and servants, some 50 people in all.[13] The thus-widowed younger sister Margareta hence secured control of the entire family estates in her capacity as her brother's guardian, but her success was short-lived. Following the battle of the White Mountain she fled, first to Brandenburg and then to Hamburg, taking Heinrich Georg and as much money as she could with her. Her dead husband Heinrich Slavata had also been a leading rebel and had been there when his own brother Wilhelm was thrown out of the Prague castle window, and doubtless she feared reprisals from the victors.

The legal position following these events was determined by the emperor's confiscation rules. As a rebel who had died in arms Albrecht Jan Smiřický's property was clearly forfeit to the crown and no transfer to his heirs was recognised. Margareta, the surviving sister, had no claim to the property so long as Heinrich Georg lived, and as Bohemian legal rulings during the revolt were invalid thereafter her guardianship was void. Moreover the property of those who fled Bohemia was also forfeit, so that she likewise lost any prospective claim to inherit after Heinrich Georg's death. The outstanding question was whether Albrecht Jan had legally owned his brother's portion or whether he was only holding it as his guardian. If the latter it would not be forfeit, as by virtue of his mental incapacity Heinrich Georg could be deemed neither a rebel nor to have fled, and he would therefore still own the entail and half of the transferable property. Wallenstein, as one of the closest and certainly at that time the best placed of the remaining relatives, applied for his guardianship, which was duly authorised although his efforts to have him returned to Bohemia were unavailing. Some years passed before he could be brought back from Hamburg, following which he lived at one of the Smiřický properties until his death in 1630.[14]

Once appointed guardian, Wallenstein entered a claim for the entire Smiřický family possessions on behalf of his ward, arguing somewhat disingenuously and doubtless on legal advice that as the properties had never been formally divided between the brothers none of them had truly belonged to Albrecht Jan, and hence none of them were liable to confiscation. After having Wallenstein's claim investigated, Liechtenstein advised the emperor that Heinrich Georg's entitlement to the entailed properties was indisputable, and that the part of the claim regarding the other lands might also be arguable in court, so that he advised seeking a compromise.[15] Wallenstein was ready enough to abandon the full claim, an obvious negotiating position, and he settled for the half to which his ward was fully entitled. In return he was allowed to choose which estates to retain, and he was also granted a legal dispensation allowing him to deal freely with his ward's property thereafter.

Although Wallenstein thus controlled more than half of the Smiřický lands he did not own them, and nor was he the only prospective heir on Heinrich Georg's death. The best claim was that of Wallenstein's elderly aunt, his mother's sister. He also had two cousins, sons of his mother's other sister, whose claim was very similar to his own, although one of these was disqualified as he had participated in the rebellion and subsequently fled the country. Wallenstein reached an agreement whereby his aunt and the other cousin gave up any claims, and it seems most likely that this was done amicably on the basis of a cash payment. He had already adopted this approach in dealing with claimants to parts of his wife's Moravian estates, and a financial settlement had the advantage of being above board and legally enforceable. For his relatives cash in hand – an unexpected windfall, given the circumstances – probably seemed preferable to a disputed claim at the time of Heinrich Georg's death, particularly as no-one knew how long he might live or what further upsets there might be in the uncertain political world in the meantime. Wallenstein even sought to reach an accommodation with the exiled Margareta, but this eventually came to nothing.[16]

To round off this story, Liechtenstein purchased the entailed estates, taking advantage of the dispensation which allowed Wallenstein to sell them on Heinrich Georg's behalf, and in 1623 Wallenstein himself purchased his ward's remaining share of the freely transferable Smiřický estates for the sum of 502,000 gulden, the whole of which was then made over to the emperor as a loan.[17] This cleared up the title to the lands and made future dealings legally simpler, while at the same time converting Heinrich Georg's fortune into cash, much of which was secured on the emperor's credit. Insofar as there was any risk in this latter arrangement it was ultimately Wallenstein's, as he was the established sole heir.

Sums of money are very difficult to evaluate in this period, not only because of the normal historical problem of making any equation with modern values but particularly because of the doubt about precisely which coinage is being referred to and what its value was at the relevant moment. Thus gulden can be relatively sound ones, either before the inflation or after the currency reform, or at various stages of debasement in between, and they might also be dubious Bohemian gulden or sounder ones from further afield, Rhine gulden for example. With this caveat it may be noted that in among his Bohemian transactions of 1622–23 Wallenstein sold his Moravian properties for 348,000 gulden, and that his claim for damage to them during the revolt was assessed at 182,000 gulden, so that they were worth 530,000 gulden in total. If it was rightly said that the Smiřický properties were worth four to five times as much, this would confirm their estimated value of two million or more. Wallenstein's share via his ward was thus worth around a million, broadly confirmed by his own purchase of the transferable parts for 502,000 and a report that Liechtenstein paid 433,000 for the entail.[18] Hence from the proceeds of his Moravian estates and the value of his interest in the Smiřický ones Wallenstein owned or controlled assets worth one and a half million. Adding his profits from military contracting and the minting consortium suggests a total of the order of two million, and this is the background against which to examine his other property purchases at this time.

The first of these were the estates of Friedland and Reichenberg, the security upon which Wallenstein had lent 58,000 gulden to the emperor in June 1621. A year later, confiscation completed, they were available for sale, and after some negotiation his offer of 150,000 gulden was accepted.[19] In the following eighteen months, from July 1622 to the end of 1623, Wallenstein undertook an enormous series of land transactions in parallel to the proceedings of the confiscation court. Unlike most of the other purchasers, of whom there were many, he was working to a plan, endeavouring to create a large unified holding based on Friedland and the main Smiřický estates centred on Gitschin. Hence he not only bought but also sold and exchanged properties, retaining those pieces of land which fitted his scheme and using those which did not as trading counters for further acquisitions. It has been calculated that approaching two hundred individual estates were involved and that by the beginning of 1624 Wallenstein had accumulated two thousand square miles of good quality land, stretching from just north of Prague to Bohemia's northern frontier, and east to the Giant Mountains.[20] To indicate the scale, this is about the size of the English counties of Kent and Surrey combined, and nearly as large as Devon, while in American terms it is equivalent to about half of the state of Connecticut or a quarter of Massachusetts.

To carry through a programme of this size at a time when the fastest means of transport was the horse, and there was no postal service or any of the modern means of communication, was a major feat of organisation. Wallenstein must have had not only enormous personal energy and commitment but also agents upon whom he could rely, particularly as he still had his military duties to attend to. Still more important was the availability of financial backers ready to assist him in putting up the necessary money. Who they were is uncertain, although researchers have mentioned not only de Witte but also leading bankers from Hamburg and Augsburg, the principal financial centres in Germany at the time.

Cash was the key. The emperor urgently needed it, and raising it was the main objective of the confiscations and property sales. For would-be purchasers this was a considerable difficulty, as it was one thing to be wealthy in terms of land but another to have large amounts of ready cash available. Wallenstein was far from alone in facing this problem, but he was uniquely successful in solving it. The details are not known, but a few documents suggest the outline. A letter of September 1622 from Emperor Ferdinand to Liechtenstein mentions the possibility of a loan of several million from unspecified persons being advanced to the exchequer against the security of confiscated property. A draft contract prepared in December of that year refers to Wallenstein and the sum of two million gulden, while another draft relates to three and a half million gulden to be provided by Wallenstein and unnamed associates.[21] It seems a safe assumption that these correspond to the item from the catalogue of Wallenstein's papers mentioned at the beginning of this chapter, Liechtenstein's receipt of 13 January 1623 for a loan of three and a half million Rhine gulden provided by Wallenstein against the security of expropriated estates. Although Wallenstein acted as principal, the great majority of this huge sum of money will have been provided by bankers and other lenders, the equivalent of a modern loan consortium, with separate agreements passing on to them rights in respect of the emperor's debt and the properties on which it was secured. However Wallenstein's own estates will certainly also have been put up as collateral for their loan.

This was a remarkably shrewd move. The favour in which Wallenstein was already held at court must have been further enhanced by his part in providing so much cash at so critical a time, and this in turn must have worked to his advantage in his property dealings. No official would have allowed the sale of an estate in the area of Bohemia in which Wallenstein was known to be interested without it having been offered to him, and few would have been prepared to challenge his bid provided that it was within reasonable range of the assessed value. Moreover a sale to him freed the exchequer of one major problem, that of gauging whether a bidder could in fact raise the cash, and if so how long it would take. A cosy relationship of mutual advantage probably developed between the responsible officials and Wallenstein's agents, as one purchase followed another and the transactions became an established routine.

From a late-nineteenth-century study of Wallenstein's property dealings it can be calculated that from 1622 to the end of his life in 1634 he spent seven million gulden on purchases from the exchequer and private landowners. However he also made sales to the value of four million, so that his net investment was three million. Two-thirds of these purchases and sales took place in the first three years, 1622 to 1624, the years of the great confiscations, during which his net outlay was almost two million gulden.[22] While these figures need to be treated as no more than indicative, the general pattern of the business is thus relatively easy to follow. Until mid-1622 Wallenstein was probably lending and spending from his own resources, up to his purchase of Friedland and Reichenberg. In the autumn of that year he put together a very large line of credit and negotiated with Liechtenstein the terms of the three and a half million Rhine gulden loan to the emperor which was made in January 1623. Purchases thereafter may initially have taken up most of this sum, and then as sales began to come through Wallenstein will have been able to make repayments and reduce his debt.

A rough calculation suggests that by 1624 Wallenstein had doubled the value of his gross assets, starting with some two million gulden, including the Smiřický estates, and adding a further two million in net land purchases, giving four million in all, of which about half was funded by debt. In itself that would have been very sound business, but the huge tract of land which he put together was in fact worth far more than twice his original stake. The income was commensurately large, particularly as Wallenstein boosted the prosperity of his own estates by directing as much as possible of his military purchasing to them both before and after he became Imperial generalissimo in 1625. Hence he would have had no difficulty in making interest payments on the debt and could doubtless have paid it off quite quickly had he so wished, and had he not instead been using loans to finance armies in the following years.

How did Wallenstein buy his lands so cheaply? To the envious of the time and to those inclined to conspiracy theories of history the answer lay in shady dealings, influence in high places, crooked valuers, playing fast and loose with debased currency, and other tricks of like nature. More straightforward explanations are available. First among them is the sheer quantity of land put on to the market over a short period by the confiscation process, half of Bohemia and a large proportion of Moravia. At the same time available purchasers were limited in number, as the Catholics were a small minority and few of the Protestants were in a position to buy, while even those Catholics willing and in principle wealthy enough to do so may have had problems raising sufficient ready cash. According to the normal law of supply and demand the price of land would inevitably have fallen sharply. Then there was the way in which the sale process was conducted. The emperor's need for cash meant that it was a question not of securing the last penny but of getting in the quick penny. If the sales had been spread over the next decade much greater sums would have been realised, but that was not a luxury available to the exchequer, and this compounded the oversupply to drive prices down even further.

Currency debasement will have played a part, but not because of financial manipulation by Wallenstein or others. Prices rise in response to devaluation of the currency and thus drive the inflationary circle, but while those of food and basic necessities react rapidly others move more slowly. Rents and agricultural tenancies are among the slowest to adjust as they are commonly fixed over longer periods, so that at the outset the income from property does not keep up with rapid inflation and falls in real terms. Then as now, the income yield was the starting point for property valuation, and hence assessed values will have lagged behind inflation, thus likewise falling in real terms, even before over-supply and the need for quick sales further depressed achieved selling prices. Moreover the assessors were under pressure to produce low valuations for partly forfeit properties, where some compensation was to be paid out, and this will have affected assessments and expectations for properties which were to be sold. We can assume that Wallenstein bought well, and research suggests that his offers were commonly below, but only a little below, the assessed values.[23] Probably his agents used their contacts and knew what prices would be acceptable, and it would have been in his interests to bid at that level in order to maintain relationships for the large number of purchases he wanted to make. That is how business is done.

Resales were an important part of Wallenstein's strategy. Estates rarely consisted of a single block of contiguous land but more often comprised various parcels, some possibly quite distant from the core holding. As in modern property dealing there were often people interested in parts who were unwilling or unable to bid for the whole, but who would pay a relatively higher price for what they wanted. Given that the value of Wallenstein's sales was well over half of his total purchases this effect in itself would have reduced the average price of his retained land considerably, particularly as, unlike the emperor, he was able to wait to get his price. There may also have been a timing effect, with land prices rising to catch up with inflation between purchases and resales.

Currency manipulation is unlikely to have played a part. The receipt for the three and a half million loan to the emperor refers specifically to Rhine gulden, a relatively sound outside currency. Wallenstein's own borrowing would have been denominated in this same currency, and the bankers behind him were far too astute to settle for repayment in debased Bohemian gulden. Likewise the prices of the properties he bought, although valued in Bohemian gulden, will have been offset against his loan account with the emperor at the relevant going exchange rate for Rhine gulden. Hence this was not a source of profit, as both he and the emperor had borrowed sound Rhine gulden and had to repay in the same coin. Nevertheless Wallenstein later made a voluntary additional payment of 200,000 Rhine gulden to the emperor in recognition of their successful business relationship in property dealings and loans. Ferdinand's letter of February 1625 acknowledging this payment made a brief reference to inflated coinage but contained no suggestion of wrongdoing, carefully noting that the exchequer had in fact suffered no loss thereby, so that he commended Wallenstein for his gesture and exempted him from any possible future claims over these matters.[24]

People of the time will not have been aware of even the outline of Wallenstein's financial strategy in the way it is set out above. Instead they will have seen a relatively unknown newcomer quickly become both politically important as second only to Liechtenstein in the control of Bohemia, and also fantastically rich through the purchase of unheard-of amounts of land. They will not have known the extent of his indebtedness and will probably have believed him to be wealthier than he actually was, particularly in the earlier years, while few are likely to have understood the mechanisms whereby he was able to buy so much so rapidly. Hence they assumed the answers to lie in underhand financial dealing and the use of improper influence. Envy and the resentment always present when a new man breaks into the upper levels of the establishment found expression in so many malicious rumours and complaints that after a time they acquired the status of 'well-known facts', to a degree which subsequent historians have often found difficult to resolve.

Doubtless Wallenstein did make use of any influence he had and took advantage of whatever opportunities presented themselves. In this he was far from alone, as there were many other purchasers of confiscated properties, but he was vastly more successful. Among those who were much more influential and initially much richer, it is reported that Liechtenstein bought ten estates and that Eggenberg bought eight. Martinitz and Slavata, the victims of the defenestration, as well as several senior army officers, were also among the purchasers, a number of whom, unlike Wallenstein, also received additional properties or rebates on their purchase prices as rewards for their services.[25] However in contrast to the piecemeal approach of these other purchasers the basis of Wallenstein's rise into the ranks of the super-rich was what in the modern world would be termed a comprehensive and well-thought-out business plan. His key talent was his ability to think on a bigger scale than others. Hence he recognised the unique opportunity created by the confiscation and sale of so much land, in response to which he devised a strategy of buying as much as possible, not at random but in such a way as to create an integral block which could be managed as a territory rather than just a cluster of estates. His boldness was that he committed his resources completely to it, using them not just to fund a few purchases but to create a multiplier effect through very large borrowings. His skill was that he was able to carry through such a large programme in such a short time and in spite of his military commitments, a success which must have relied in considerable measure on his judgement in finding men of ability whom he could trust, and his willingness to delegate power to them to act as his agents.

If his achievement still seems difficult to comprehend it is worth noting that others have done similar things in more recent times when unique opportunities have arisen. The Gettys, father and son, recognised key points in the development of oil, first as a new commodity and then as the basis of the world's biggest industry. Both quickly became super-rich, and the son, John Paul Getty I, went on to become the richest man in the world. However the most comparable example dates from the 1990s after the collapse of the Communist bloc in Eastern Europe, which was followed by a massive sell-off of state-owned property, of which the present author had first-hand experience in what used to be East Germany. A number of super-rich individuals have subsequently emerged, particularly in the countries of the former Soviet Union.

There was, however, a Faustian twist, as in exchange for his new wealth Wallenstein found himself bound irrevocably to Ferdinand. Should the emperor lose in the continuing conflict, or even emerge less than totally successful, a principal condition of any settlement was bound to be the recovery of their lands by the dispossessed Bohemians. Wallenstein and the other purchasers would then in turn be dispossessed, and while they might have a claim on the Imperial treasury to recover what they had paid the chances of securing settlement from this perennially bankrupt source in the wake of a lost war would be slim. The alternatives for Wallenstein were simple but stark: victory for Ferdinand or total ruin for him. Still worse, his salvation depended on the emperor not only winning but making a sustainable peace thereafter, something which Ferdinand was to prove unable or unwilling to do. The resulting dilemma is the key to understanding the rest of Wallenstein's life, and indeed his death.

5
The Fault Is Not in Our Stars
(*Julius Caesar*)

Already in his mid-thirties by the momentous year of 1618, little in Wallenstein's life until then suggested that fate had marked him out for great things. The stars, it seems, thought otherwise, or so astrologers said, while Wallenstein himself was in their thrall – or so tradition and many historians have said. Astrology loomed large among the rumours and legends which accumulated around Wallenstein during his years as the most powerful man in the Empire, tales which lost nothing in the telling in the following centuries, and which found their fullest expression in Schiller's great drama. In this he portrays Wallenstein facing the final crisis of his life, closeted with his astrologer and hesitating to make a decision, until eventually he finds encouragement in his stars:

> ... Now we
> Must act, and quickly, now, before the signs
> Of fortune's favour take their flight again,
> For ever-changing is the face of heaven.[1]

This play had a lasting influence, and just as the historical Richard III has never escaped the image created by Shakespeare so the real Wallenstein tends to be eclipsed by the star-gazer depicted by Schiller. Among twentieth-century biographers, Watson made the point by entitling his book *Soldier under Saturn*, while Mann stated categorically that Wallenstein 'believed in the precision and exact legibility of the nocturnal sky's inordinately fitful writing', and that he had an 'absolute faith in [the astrologer] Kepler's deductions, similar to that which we attach to the skilled analysis of an X-ray picture'. Diwald likewise claimed that 'Wallenstein took Kepler's horoscope as a reliable prediction' and 'laid great weight on every word'.² As this view has frequently been repeated the evidence upon which it is based needs to be examined.

In 1608 the 24-year-old Wallenstein and a former comrade in arms, Lieutenant Gerhard Taxis, decided to have their horoscopes cast by the emperor's own astrologer, the famous mathematician and astronomer Johannes Kepler. Taxis, who made the arrangement, then went abroad, but on his return six years later he wrote several times to Kepler pointing out that while Wallenstein had long since received his analysis he himself had not. The pressing terms Taxis used to persuade Kepler to complete his horoscope indicate his own serious interest in astrology, and he might well have been the moving spirit in the first joint approach.³

Kepler's horoscope for Wallenstein proved to be typical of the genre, containing a number of points which were relatively accurate and some others which were quite wrong, but in the main comprising observations sufficiently general for the subject to discover as much of himself as he cared to within them.⁴ He was not particularly keen to undertake the commission as he was busy with important scientific observations, but payment of official salaries was notoriously erratic so that the fee was probably welcome. As Wallenstein was young, unimportant and not even rich in 1608 it is unlikely that Kepler felt it necessary to exercise more than his normal professional diligence or to do much surreptitious background research before preparing the horoscope. According to convention he was not supposed to know the identity of his subject, but he had two contacts from whom he may have gleaned a little information, Taxis and the Prague doctor who made the introduction. Whatever the sources Kepler used, his mention of problems having arisen between the subject's eleventh and thirteenth years must have suggested to Wallenstein the death of his parents, and he may well have seen reference to difficulties with scholars in the following years as alluding to his escapades at Altdorf, while Kepler's identification of a serious illness in the subject's twenty-first year was accurate enough although a year out. These details from the horoscope are a standard part of the fortune-teller's art, using known or likely events from the past to build confidence in the predictions for the future.

The most striking of Kepler's specific forecasts was that his subject would make an advantageous marriage to a widow, not beautiful but rich, in his thirty-third year. This was not wildly unlikely, as many young noblemen of modest means had aspirations of that kind. Even so Wallenstein was impressed, later writing alongside this passage that he had indeed made the anticipated marriage, and to just such a lady as was described, although Kepler's timing was seven years out.[5] On the other hand the prediction that he would be involved in severe disturbances in or about the year 1613 came to nothing, while the other prognostications were at best a mixed bag, even given that Delphic wording allowed the maximum of scope for the subject to fit his experiences to them.

The remainder of the horoscope is principally a character sketch, the first part of which is a general summary of how many young men would like to see themselves – alert, energetic, enthusiastic, restless, impatient of conventional behaviour, ever looking for new ways, and with more going on in the mind than is externally apparent. Saturn in the ascendant at the moment of birth is then cited as the source of a contemplative, melancholy nature and of unfounded fears – easy neither to confirm nor to contradict – but also of two traits which were clearly incorrect. Even his enemies never accused Wallenstein of being inclined towards alchemy, magic or links to the supernatural, while against the subject's supposed iconoclastic attitude to the works of God and man, accompanied by a disdain for all religions, must be set Wallenstein himself, pillar of the establishment, prop to the Empire, and after his conversion a lifelong Catholic and generous benefactor of the church. Worse followed. Because of the unfavourable aspect of the moon the subject would be cold, merciless, lacking in filial or conjugal love, harsh, covetous, deceitful, usually silent but also often argumentative or violent, as well as capricious and self-centred. Quite apart from being so one-sided as to be almost a caricature, this disparaging portrait does not at all resemble the man Zierotin described at around the same time as 'full of fine and laudable qualities' and with 'good manners', the man who could win over a rich and independent young widow, and the man who was and for years continued to be a gentleman of the royal chamber, a post for which being amenable, likeable and good company were among the main qualifications. However here, as throughout the horoscope, Kepler hedged his bets, noting that as Jupiter followed Saturn there was reason to hope that all these faults would pass with maturity.

The horoscope was summarised by the flattering observation that it was very similar to those of Queen Elizabeth of England and the former chancellor of Poland, both of whom had died in recent years. By implication the subject had the potential to achieve greatness, and Kepler specifically noted that he would have aspirations to honour, rank and power, although warning that the pursuit of these would make him powerful enemies. Nevertheless with a careful regard for the ways of the world wealth and status could be achieved, and once the subject had overcome his faults through maturity his exceptional character would fit him to undertake momentous enterprises. Kepler no doubt anticipated that the recipient would be sufficiently attracted by these prospects to overlook the fact that no details or even approximate timings were provided.

The key question about this horoscope is not what a modern sceptic makes of it but what Wallenstein as the subject might have made of it. The archives provide no answer, as the next substantive reference does not occur until 1624, sixteen years later. We may presume that since he was prepared to commission a horoscope in the first place he was also prepared – like most people of the time – to grant it some credence, but as attitudes to astrology were ambiguous among the more educated classes in the seventeenth century this does not necessarily imply credulity. Wallenstein may have been impressed by the few references to past possibilities which could be approximately correlated with actual events, together with the marriage opportunity which tied in so surprisingly well with what actually transpired – albeit seven years too soon – within a year of his receiving the horoscope. On the other hand he must have had difficulty in recognising himself in Kepler's character sketch, as few people are so self-critical as to imagine faults on this scale. Whatever he made of it, however, it was of little practical help with the business of life, as there were no indications as to how the better prospects were to be achieved or the worse ones avoided. Kepler himself warned in his preamble that it would not be enough to rely on things which were 'simply and solely predicted from the heavens', as 'of all that a man may hope for from the heavens, the heavens are only the father while his own soul is the mother'.[6] In other words if he aspired to the vaguely forecast wealth, status and momentous enterprises he would have to make appropriate efforts on his own account. But he did not, as after his marriage he made no noteworthy progress or impact on the outside world, apart from the brief episode at Gradisca, for almost ten years.

When the horoscope resurfaced in 1624 it was in an entirely different context. Wallenstein's career up to 1618 was unremarkable, but the action-packed six years following the revolution in Bohemia took him from obscurity to the forefront of affairs, bringing him power, fame and fortune, and making him the new man whose name was on everyone's lips, certainly in Bohemia. We do not know what attention Wallenstein had paid to the horoscope in the intervening years, and although biographers have tended to assume, imply or even state outright that he had referred back to it regularly, comparing events as they occurred with those in the forecasts, there is no actual evidence to support this. In one of the most recent biographies Polišenský and Kollmann declared that the horoscope made such an impression on Wallenstein that 'he decided to live in accordance with it', which Diwald echoed in observing that Wallenstein 'made every effort to keep slavishly to it, obsessed with making it come true'. Hence, Diwald added, 'he always had the horoscope readily available by him', while Watson went so far as to describe him 'thumbing the leaves of what had become his gospel', but these are merely fanciful speculations.[7]

What we do know is that in late 1624 Wallenstein wrote to Taxis, who was by that time a lieutenant-colonel and governor of Wallenstein's Friedland estates, and Taxis in turn wrote to Kepler asking him to review the 1608 horoscope. To facilitate this Wallenstein returned the original manuscript, upon which he had made marginal notes of where certain forecast things had happened, but earlier or later than predicted. These notes are the basis for the assumption that he had kept the horoscope to hand as the years went by, but Wallenstein's letter indicates that they were made specifically for Kepler's information and presumably on a single occasion in 1624, as in one of them he recorded not only the date of his first marriage but also of his wife's death and of his own second marriage in June 1623. The notes were only five in number, and Wallenstein ignored those predicted events which had not occurred at all to focus on his marriage and on illnesses which he had developed, but not in the forecast years, and he added that he was neither sick nor given a military command in 1611 but that these things did happen in 1615.[8] Wallenstein also asked Taxis to put a number of additional questions to Kepler, and it is worth quoting the relevant passage from his letter in full:

> Eight days ago I sent you the nativity which Kepler wrote for me thirteen years ago [sic], but because he has placed some things too early and some too late I have set down in the margin when they happened to me. You must seek an opinion from him, but more detailed than was previously the case. If possible I would also like to hear from him what fortune or misfortune I may have each year; also whether or not I will continue in the war, and whether I will have my estates and eventually die in my homeland or abroad. Several mathematicians [i.e. astrologers] agree about that and say that I will live outside my fatherland and also die there, while most say that I will die of apoplexy, and I would like to have his comments on this.

I intend to be in Vienna within fourteen days. N.B. Also what nation or profession will my secret or public enemies come from.⁹

Nothing in this letter and the related correspondence from Taxis suggests that Wallenstein had made any other approach to Kepler in the intervening years, so the question is what prompted him to do so in 1624. One obvious possibility is that the dramatic change in his standing and circumstances had reminded him of the old horoscope with its hints, albeit brief and guarded ones, of great things. An easy inference from his letter is that he had also consulted other astrologers, indeed several, but who had sought out whom is an open question. Kepler may have let slip that he had previously cast the horoscope of the man everyone was talking about, but even without such a hint it is not improbable that the multifarious petitioners struggling to catch the attention of this powerful newcomer included impecunious astrologers, some of whom may have prepared unsolicited forecasts for him in the hope of a full commission or even a post in his entourage. Had the impetus come from Wallenstein it seems more likely that he would have referred in the first instance to Kepler, who had not only already prepared him a horoscope but was also the acknowledged top man in the field. What he did with the forecasts from the others speaks for itself; he referred them to Kepler.

Mann's view that Wallenstein had 'absolute faith in Kepler's deductions' stemmed largely from his supposedly asking 'whether, on the basis of this and that happening at a date earlier or later than anticipated, it were not with hindsight possible to correct the minutes and hour of his birth, especially as "clocks do not at all times go right"'. In fact it was not Wallenstein who asked this but Taxis; the quotation is from the latter's letter to Kepler of 16 December 1624 but there is no comparable point in the instructions from Wallenstein. As noted above, Taxis had his own interest in astrology, and Kepler himself had provided the cue in the original horoscope, where he began: 'Provided that this lord was born at the reported time, day and hour, then it may with truth be said ...'.¹⁰

Kepler was clearly embarrassed by the request to recalculate Wallenstein's horoscope. The unknown young Bohemian nobleman who had commissioned the original work could have been briefly dismissed, perhaps not even favoured with a reply, but the rich and powerful military governor of Bohemia was a different matter. Kepler had to say something – but what? For the sake of his professional reputation he could not simply admit that his previous prognostications were far wide of the mark. Instead he accepted the way out which Taxis had offered him and back-calculated a corrected time of birth, six and a half minutes later than the time he had first been given.[11] To the recipient this might well have seemed credible, as the recorded time of half past four had the air of an approximation quite adequate for the purposes of the midwife and parents but not accurate enough for a horoscope. For Kepler it provided the opportunity to bring at least some of the earlier predictions more closely into line with the actual experiences which Wallenstein had noted, and because the moon was thus moved into the next position he could happily report that the more extreme characteristics of the subject were considerably moderated.[12]

That still left the problem of the further and better particulars that Wallenstein was requesting. Kepler was not inclined to give hostages to fortune by making new specific forecasts for a client in such an influential position in such troubled times, particularly one who had shown himself ready to check them against actual experience and call the forecaster to account. Deciding that attack was the best form of defence, and hiding behind the by then totally threadbare professional pretence that he was working on behalf of an unknown client, he reproached his subject for his superstition and set out a comprehensive repudiation of the idea that astrologers could in fact make precise forecasts of an individual's future from the stars. In fairness it should be said that this fits in with a progressive change in Kepler's attitude to the predictive power of astrology, from faith in his youth to increasing scepticism with advancing age and deeper involvement in astronomy, which he described as a wise mother having astrology as her foolish daughter.[13]

Kepler's beliefs concern us less here than Wallenstein's, but the latter cannot fail to have been impressed by the trenchantly stated warnings given by the leading authority of the day. In his response of January 1625, which was three times as long as the original horoscope, Kepler made the point not once but at least eleven times. It was, he said, a delusion to believe that particular events could all be forecast from the heavens, as they were seldom the impetus and almost never the only one. The subject and others involved did many things of their own free will which they were not compelled by the stars to do, and hence they brought on or delayed the natural course of events so that they could not occur with their due celestial form and timing. Nor was the individual's free will the only thing which might intervene. Were a pregnant woman to fall down the stairs her child might be born notwithstanding that the stellar time was not right. Outside circumstances might frustrate fulfilment, as for example in 1611 when Wallenstein could not have had the forecast military appointment because there was no war in that year. Kepler even pointed out his own errors and demolished his apparent successes. He had forecast that the subject might become the leader of a dissident faction but the exact opposite had apparently happened; since the subject was a native-born Bohemian but was still active in the military it followed that he could not have sided with the malcontents there. Regarding the subject's wife, true enough he had hit the mark, but even so what had happened had its sole basis neither in the subject's nativity nor in his free will but depended also on the counterpart's nativity and free will, which he, Kepler, could neither have seen or known, so that his accuracy here had been a matter of luck and could not be taken as a precedent for other predictions.

Kepler did respond to the particular questions Wallenstein had asked, but only to dismiss them outright or to use them as an opportunity to pour scorn on the other astrologers involved. Nevertheless he consented to calculate the planetary positions for the coming years, the so-called revolutions, not, he emphasised, so that earthly events could be predicted from these celestial configurations, but merely to demonstrate his own diligence. However in setting out the technical data he did also add brief interpretative comments, which read much like horoscopes in modern newspapers. The coming year looked very good and the next was also favourable, but a couple of years later the prospects were more bad than good and for the year after that they were mediocre. One year was disposed towards important actions but also to damaging hindrances. Another would bring honour but also conflict. Almost nothing specific was forecast apart from recurrent gout, a safe prediction as that was the nature of the disease and Wallenstein had already noted that he suffered from it. Only in March 1634 did anything remarkable appear, as all five of the then known planets made a 'wondrous cross', which brought to mind his previous prediction for 1613, 'and the terrible disturbances in the land threatened at that time'. Some commentators have used the March 1634 date and the reference to 'terrible disturbances' to suggest either or both that Kepler had correctly forecast Wallenstein's death in February of that year or that Wallenstein's actions in his last weeks were influenced by fear of some imminent predicted fate. This is simply wrong, as the disturbances were specifically stated to be those threatened for around 1613, not twenty years later. Furthermore, although Kepler's wording here was particularly Delphic, he certainly did not imply that this was the end for his subject, for whom he had previously predicted death at 70, that is in about 1653. On the contrary, having laboriously calculated these revolutions for a full decade he concluded casually in the very next sentence: 'Because the years thus far into the future cause no particular unease of mind, I for my part have no time at present to continue with these toilsome and far-reaching details, so I will let the matter rest there.'[14]

Kepler's revised horoscope has been quoted at some length to show that Wallenstein can have been under no illusions thereafter about the limitations of astrology as defined by the leading practitioner of the age. Equally clear was the latter's view of 'young astrologers who believe in and take pleasure in games of this kind' and 'those who wish to be deceived with open eyes' by referring to them.[15] This has not prevented biographers from writing as though Wallenstein treated Kepler's very cautious new prognostications as his oracle and *vade-mecum*. Diwald claimed that 'he time and again carefully noted the differences in the particulars of his actual life against the astrologically calculated coordinate system of Kepler's'. Mann was categorical: 'Wallenstein disregarded alike the phantasmagoria and the impertinences of Kepler's appraisal. He heeded only the "revolutions", henceforth comparing them year by year with actual events. His notes in the margin of the horoscope prove it.'[16]

There are a number of problems with this interpretation. Firstly there are only seven extremely brief marginal notes, and they deal exclusively with very public matters in which Wallenstein was involved, major events in the war and the pledging to him of the duchies of Sagan (Żagań) and Mecklenburg, things which would have been widely known.[17] Secondly the notes are made only against the astrological data and not against any of the forecasts. Thirdly the manuscript on which the notes are to be found comes not from Wallenstein's papers but from Kepler's. Fourthly the last note refers to January 1630, the year in which Kepler died, although Wallenstein lived another four eventful years. Lastly it is well established that Kepler himself made marginal notes of actual events against the annual revolutions on his own horoscope, which he prepared in 1595, and that he continued this practice to the end of his life.[18] Furthermore in the notes which Wallenstein made for Kepler on the original horoscope he referred to essentially personal matters, his marriages, illnesses and military appointments, none of which are mentioned in these later notes although he had illnesses and military appointments enough. It is also hard to believe that if he was comparing events with the planets he would not have recorded the birth of his only son and heir in December 1627 – probably the most eagerly awaited occurrence in the life of a nobleman and landowner in this period – or the child's death a few months afterwards.

That said, it is nevertheless true that Wallenstein maintained an interest in astrology in later life. In May 1628 he had an indirect approach from Kepler, who was in financial difficulties and uncomfortable as a Protestant amid the zeal of Counter-Reformation Prague, so Wallenstein arranged for him to move to his own duchy of Sagan, which remained his home for the rest of his life.[19] Astrology, however, was very much secondary in Kepler's work, far more important being his standing as the foremost mathematician and astronomer of the age. Wallenstein had in mind founding a university, for which Kepler's prestige would have been valuable, and he also provided facilities for astronomical observation at his palaces in Gitschin and Prague. By that stage in his career he had become not only Imperial generalissimo but a grandee of the Empire, and he was setting out to live as the age believed a great prince should live, including following the example of Emperor Rudolf II as a patron of the sciences.

So far as is known Wallenstein never had his own horoscope cast again, but from time to time he enquired about others. In the 1625 revision Kepler had drawn attention to adverse relationships between the general's nativity and those of the emperor and his son, the king of Hungary, and in 1629 Wallenstein wrote to him with specific reference to the latter, who had by then become a potential threat to his supreme military command. He enquired at the same time about the king of Denmark, recently but not necessarily finally defeated, and the king of Spain, who was a Habsburg ally but not always a friend to Wallenstein. He also employed a Mecklenburg doctor and astrologer to cast the horoscopes of Gustavus Adolphus and the king of Poland, but how much significance he attributed to them is another matter, as in a letter to a senior officer he mentioned the commission but commented 'not that too much rests upon it'.[20] It may be that Wallenstein regarded horoscopes as a form of additional intelligence, not to be taken at face value, but to be considered along with other indicators as to what an enemy might have in mind, noting that even Kepler still allowed that the stars could indicate inclinations, tendencies and the interplay of personalities, even if not forecasting actual events.

In 1631, a year after Kepler's death, Wallenstein took a young Italian mathematician, astronomer and astrologer named Senno (often referred to as Seni) into his service. Whereas the eminent Kepler had been given his own establishment at Sagan, however, Senno merely became part of Wallenstein's entourage, most of which travelled with his headquarters, so that he was in Eger at the time of the general's assassination, following which he was arrested. Although he has had a bad press, such evidence as there is supports neither the theory that Senno was paid to spy on Wallenstein nor the contention that he was a central influence on his policy and actions in the latter years of his career. The official Imperial enquiry came to the same conclusion, as after some fifteen months under investigation he was released on the grounds that 'nothing suspicious' had been established against him.[21]

Astrology was only one aspect of a broad spectrum of seventeenth-century belief in the supernatural, ranging from extremes of religion to outright superstition. Its most sinister manifestation was the wave of witch-hunting which spread across Europe and to the New World, the Salem witch trials in the 1690s being the best known but by no means the worst example. A Thirty Years War soldier recorded in his diary that in the Westphalian town of Lippstadt there were 'evil people. I saw seven of them burned. Among them was a pretty young girl of eighteen, but even so she was burned.' A nun likewise recorded that in Bamberg between 1627 and 1631 'several hundred people were tried and burned, among them many attractive and well-to-do young men and women'. Also among them was her own father, who had previously several times been mayor of the city. Kepler's mother was imprisoned and put on trial for witchcraft, but she was one of the fortunate few who secured an acquittal. Duke Maximilian of Bavaria, a Catholic zealot, criticised Wallenstein's interest in 'fraudulent astrology' but nevertheless believed in witchcraft, as did his brother, the elector and archbishop of Cologne, and there were many witchcraft trials in their territories whereas the supposedly superstitious Wallenstein did not permit them in his.[22]

Magic in various forms was readily accepted. A highly educated German lawyer entered into his diary a report of a Swedish raid under cover of a fog which had been conjured up by one of their soldiers. A monk told of soldiers looting his monastery church but being awed by a picture of the Virgin apparently crying. A soldier recorded visiting a chapel to see a miraculous candle given by the Virgin Mary in the Middle Ages: 'It has, so they say, already been burning for three hundred years and the same candle hasn't burned out yet.'[23] Omens were frequently to be seen, and Protestant pastors were no less credulous than laymen or their Catholic counterparts. Cheaply printed almanacs – the poor man's horoscope – circulated widely, as did pamphlets about portentous comets, unusual bright stars and other phenomena in the night sky, all of which were thought sure to have earthly significance.

The modern world is not exempt. Almanacs are still published and sold, and many popular newspapers print daily horoscopes. A twenty-first-century British national lottery winner told the press: 'I should have known. Three times in the previous week or so I had read in different horoscopes that my finances were about to take a turn for the better.' Even the historians Mann and Diwald were half-inclined to believe in Kepler's horoscope for Wallenstein. 'Were I to say that there were something to the art of astrology, provided that the right man does it, I would no doubt provoke a smile on the part of many a reader. I would happily tolerate that if only I were offered a better explanation.' Thus wrote Mann. According to Diwald, 'almost everything which Kepler predicted was fulfilled', things which 'decades later became reality, mysteriously accurate and almost letter-for-letter true' – a statement which is manifestly incorrect, as can be seen from the foregoing analysis of Kepler's actual texts.[24]

By seventeenth-century standards astrology was rational and scientific. Casting a horoscope required advanced mathematical knowledge and laborious calculations in order to project the positions of the planets back to the subject's time and place of birth, and forward to the times for which predictions were to be made. Interpretation thereafter was not a matter of whim or intuition, but of following the rules and precedents in the vast body of literature on the subject which had been built up over the centuries. Two skilled practitioners should in theory have reached very similar conclusions, although of course not all were equally competent or diligent while some were charlatans. The level of acceptance of astrology among the upper classes of the time can be assessed from the large number of horoscopes prepared by Kepler which have survived, reportedly thousands, although these were not necessarily all paid commissions, and he was only one of many such sages. Moreover astrology had long been embraced by the establishment, with both the papacy and the Empire maintaining official astrologers, although the Catholic church had begun to turn against it after the Reformation. As a result astrology was among the many subjects covered by the rules on prohibited books issued by the pope in 1564, with specific reference to works 'determining destiny by astrology' or attempting 'to affirm something as certain to take place', but many practising Catholics nevertheless maintained their interest. Kepler, a Protestant, wrote to Wallenstein that 'philosophy, and hence also true astrology, is a witness to God's works, and therefore a holy not a frivolous thing', implicit in which is the view that the planets and other heavenly bodies, as God's creations, were capable of revealing as much of the truth as God willed.[25] That this in the end turned out to be a false premise has a parallel in the main astronomical theory of the day, the Ptolemaic view that the earth was the centre of the universe, which was soon to give way to the Copernican heliocentric model.

Like the Ptolemaic system, astrology did not always match up well with practical observation, and to the modern sceptic the half-truths and outright errors demonstrate the falsity of the concept. The educated seventeenth-century mind would have seen it differently. In classical tradition the oracle at Delphi revealed the divine truth, but in a form which was only too readily misunderstood by the human recipients. The stars too doubtless had the truth within them, but human interpretation, even at the highest level, was fallible. Hence one had to be grateful for such insights and revelations as were achieved and not cavil over the errors. There was, however, an important corollary to this. Since one could not know in advance which were revelations and which were errors one had to treat all predictions with caution, at best as indicators as to where one should be careful and where one should look for opportunities. Some people were of course less sophisticated than this and inclined to uncritical credulity, while others were sceptical or hostile, whether on religious or intellectual grounds. A balanced examination of the actual evidence which has survived suggests that Wallenstein was probably somewhere in between, and as such very much a man of his times. His wealth and position allowed him to indulge his interest more than most, and his involvement in astrology is better documented principally because Kepler, as a world-class scientist, kept very precise records and a large proportion of his correspondence has survived.

How much does it matter? Most biographers who subscribe to the traditional Schillerean picture of Wallenstein as obsessively and credulously involved in astrology do not go so far as to say that it had a significant effect on his practical decisions and actions, and some specifically acknowledge that it did not. That leaves a problem of psychological credibility. Rudolf II does appear to have had a blind faith in astrology, but by most accounts he was also unstable, unreliable and incompetent. Wallenstein was a shrewd operator, a brilliant organiser, a successful general, and an all round man of action who knew how to seize the moment when an opportunity presented itself. This is not easy to square with the idea that he was also a star-struck fantast, but fortunately we do not have to do so as the evidence does not support that view. Schiller was entitled to build on the legends about Wallenstein's character for his dramatic purposes, just as he devised a romance between Wallenstein's daughter, in reality then a child, and the totally invented son of Field Marshal Octavio Piccolomini. The historian needs more positive confirmatory evidence before accepting an old tradition.

Was there much truth in the unflattering description of Wallenstein's character in Kepler's first horoscope? Mann observed that 'it remained the accepted portrait of him in his own lifetime and after', which is – to an extent – true, but he went on to imply that it was not only accepted but correct. Kepler, he claimed, 'had cause to be content with the likeness he had drawn', but how, he asked, 'could Kepler *know*?' Nevertheless Mann also noted clear inaccuracies, and he added: 'He oppressed those beneath him rather less harshly than others of his class. He was not a hard-hearted wretch. His conversation ... could be amiable, not to say easy-going and jovial.' The evidence in contemporary accounts is likewise ambiguous. Thus Khevenhüller, an Imperial diplomat and ambassador during Emperor Ferdinand II's reign, of which he wrote a history, described Wallenstein as 'a profound and thoughtful, active, generous, resourceful and magnanimous gentleman, though with a hard and rough nature', which another otherwise critical contemporary observer qualified by noting that 'his customary manner is more artificially than naturally brusque'. Mann suggested on the one hand that Wallenstein took Kepler's character analysis so much to heart that it had a 'formative effect' on him, and on the other that the details of the horoscope may have leaked out and become 'the original of what for centuries was written about Wallenstein'.[26] Both views probably considerably exaggerate its importance. The truth is more likely to be found in the well-known observation that history tends to be written by the victors, in this case Wallenstein's enemies, just as Shakespeare's picture of Richard III was based on the accounts of Tudor historians. No doubt Wallenstein did from time to time display some of the characteristics attributed to him by the traditional picture – as indeed most people do to a greater or lesser extent – but it is wise to be suspicious of such an extreme and one-sided presentation when there is other and arguably better evidence suggesting a more moderate view of his character.

It remains to ask how the idea that Wallenstein was obsessed with astrology became so widespread and firmly entrenched, both towards the end of his life and in subsequent histories. Certainly he himself was not the source. Wallenstein was a prolific correspondent and a large number of his letters have survived in the archives, but the surprising thing is not how often but how seldom astrology is mentioned in them. Most of the significant cases have already been referred to this chapter, and although these have often been quoted by biographers as though they were examples and the tip of the iceberg, in fact there is little more. A modern doctoral study of Wallenstein's astrology identified only four significant references in his own correspondence (some of them involving two letters), together with one briefer item. There are also the dealings with Kepler over Wallenstein's horoscope in 1608 and 1624-25, which were carried out by Taxis on his behalf, and four later letters from Kepler and others which were clearly responding to astrological enquiries from Wallenstein. A letter from one of his officials to another mentions Wallenstein being closeted with Senno during the night hours in December 1631 'in order to decipher the secrets of the heavens', although the German grammatical construction indicates that this was a hearsay report and not the writer's own knowledge. Finally another official noted in December 1632 that Wallenstein had graciously taken in Duke Heinrich Julius of Saxe-Lauenburg's mathematician, possibly as a refugee from the war.[27]

These limited sources are enough to establish that Wallenstein did maintain his interest in astrology, and that he had sufficient personal knowledge to be able to employ the relevant terminology in his correspondence, but they do not suggest that this went beyond what most contemporaries would have considered as normal. He was also far from the only prince who retained an astrologer, others including the Heinrich Julius mentioned above, as well as the emperor's brother, Archduke Leopold, despite the fact that he was the Catholic bishop of Passau and Strasbourg.[28] Nor should it be forgotten that Kepler remained in the emperor's own service until 1628, and indeed thereafter as he retained his Imperial appointment, despite it being common knowledge that he was actively engaged in astrology as well as being a mathematician and astronomer.

Wallenstein's horoscope has attracted considerable attention from modern biographers but it is unlikely that it was known to contemporaries, as it would certainly have been mentioned in the early histories by Priorato and Khevenhüller. Both made much of Wallenstein's links with astrology, but the horoscope itself was not discovered and published until 1852. A public connection between Wallenstein and astrology was probably first established when Kepler went to Sagan in 1628, and it started to feature in the attacks of his enemies at around that time. Later in his life it was certainly common knowledge and camp gossip, as reported by Sydnam Poyntz, who joined Wallenstein's army in 1632 and noted in his memoirs: 'There was an Astrologer in his Court named Signor John Baptista Leni [Seni] a Genoway much esteemed to whome he gave 2000 Rix Dollers for annuall entertaynement and the freedome of the Table of the greatest Cavaliers of his Court.'[29] This and other contemporary observations were relatively matter of fact about the subject, whereas Wallenstein's political opponents set out to characterise his interest as both extraordinary and culpable. Accusations of superstitious belief in astrology featured increasingly prominently among the complaints about him which they repeatedly pressed on the emperor during the later stages of his career, a belief which they equated with atheism in an attempt to play on the religious susceptibilities of the ultra-Catholic Ferdinand. Although the press was still in its infancy its potential as a medium for scurrilous attacks on opponents was soon realised, and hostile pamphlets bolstered the campaign against Wallenstein, as well as spreading the claim that he was dependent on astrologers to guide his military decisions. By the time of his death such claims had been reiterated so often that they had become widely accepted as fact, following which they were quickly taken up by the early historians of the period, from whom they have been successively repeated almost up to the present day. Thus are historical myths created.

6
Some Achieve Greatness
(*Twelfth Night*)

Wallenstein's long-term security in his new lands depended on Ferdinand's success in the continuing war, but by 1623 his immediate position was looking much better than for many years previously. Since the death of his wife in 1614 he had been under threat, first from disputes over her properties, then from the looming revolt in Bohemia, and when that threat became reality he had lost his lands, leaving him dependent on his position as an Imperial colonel and on the outcome of the conflict. Thus it is perhaps not surprising that he did not remarry for much longer than was usual, but with his old lands recovered and important new ones added it was time to re-establish a conventional private life. This time he had no need to seek a financially advantageous marriage. Instead he followed the classic agenda of the *nouveau riche* – first money, then social status – by seeking a match in the higher levels of the old aristocracy. His cousin Max had married a daughter of Baron Karl Harrach, an Austrian grandee and second only to Eggenberg among Emperor Ferdinand's councillors and confidants, and Harrach had to find suitable husbands for two more daughters. On grounds of wealth, religion and political reliability Wallenstein met his criteria, added to which Harrach knew, liked and respected him. Age differences were neither unusual nor problematic in an era of arranged marriages, and Ferdinand himself had recently taken a princess twenty years younger as his second wife. Hence in June 1623, in the presence of the emperor, the 39-year-old Wallenstein married the 21-year-old Isabella Harrach, a move which gave him another link to the inner circle through his new brother-in-law, Harrach's eldest son, who was married to Eggenberg's daughter.

The war was to mean that Wallenstein and his young wife were far more often apart than together during their ten years of marriage.

A series of letters which she wrote to him has survived, and in these the formality of address of the time is combined with evident affection and anxiety about his welfare, suggesting a relationship which was more than merely dutiful. It is known that he replied regularly and that she kept his letters until her own death many years later, although unfortunately they have not been traced, but there are a number of letters to Harrach in which Wallenstein exhibited great concern for his wife's well-being and safety during the turmoils of war, as well as making more personal references indicating a bond between them. Later in 1623, with Bethlen on the advance with a large army and Wallenstein himself besieged in a small Moravian town, he made repeated requests for her to be moved out of harm's way, eventually sending Harrach 'a hundred thousand thanks' for getting her out of Prague, 'so that I am relieved of my greatest worry'. He was certainly a dutiful husband and evidently able to inspire affection, which suggests that he was also able to respond to it, but no more can confidently be said on the basis of the limited evidence available.[1]

During 1623 Wallenstein also found other ways of improving his standing. First he secured an Imperial patent joining many of the Bohemian estates he had purchased to Friedland, and in January 1623 the emperor raised them to the status of a palatinate, conferring on Wallenstein the archaic but prestigious rank of count palatine. Although not carrying with it a formal title this gave him many of the powers of a prince, as well as valuable commercial rights within his territory, and it was a *de jure* recognition of what Wallenstein had achieved *de facto*, the creation of a virtual principality by the acquisition of so much land in a single block. More surprising was the emperor's decision eight months later to elevate Friedland into an actual principality, thus giving Wallenstein the rank and title of *Fürst*, a prince of the Empire.[2] In the complex Imperial hierarchy this was not quite as impressive as it sounded, as *Fürst* was an honorific title applicable to all above the rank of count (*Graf*), but which could also be granted specifically to those like Wallenstein who did not have this automatic right. Nevertheless it was a rare honour and a major step upwards, which may in part have been a reward for Wallenstein's large loans to the Imperial treasury, although political considerations were probably more important. Executions, expropriations and emigration following the collapse of the revolt had left a vacuum in the top levels of society in Bohemia and Moravia, which Ferdinand was seeking to fill through the creation of a new aristocracy loyal to and dependant upon him personally. Even so, titles could not be distributed unless the recipients possessed the lands then deemed essential to sustain the relevant level of dignity. Wallenstein was the first of the *nouveau riche* to accumulate a princely estate, and his loyalty was unquestionable, so it followed that he became a prince.

Ferdinand's policy was not calculated to appeal to the hereditary princes of the Empire, who resented upstarts and opportunists adopting the airs and graces which were the birthright of the ancient aristocracy. Such apparently trivial matters as the entitlement to particular forms of address became bones of contention which dogged Wallenstein in the following years.[3] They mattered to him, as they mattered to the grandees who sought to withhold them, because they encapsulated the distinction between the 'real' aristocracy and those who in their view were merely the creatures and political creations of the emperor. This was a widespread and long-standing attitude. A fifteenth-century chronicler said of peers created by King Edward IV of England that they were 'detested by the nobles because they, who were ignoble and newly made men, were advanced beyond those who far excelled them in breeding and wisdom'. The hostility which Wallenstein later encountered, both at the Imperial court and among the princes of the Empire, was aggravated by this simple but deep-rooted snobbery. Most could have tolerated his power and influence as the emperor's generalissimo, but being forced to treat him as a social equal, or even as a superior, was more than many could bear.

War without end

By the end of 1622 Ferdinand seemed to have weathered the storm created by the revolt in Bohemia, whereas following the defeat at the White Mountain things had gone from bad to worse for his opponent Frederick, the 'winter king' of Bohemia. In January 1621 the emperor placed him under the ban of the Empire on the grounds that he was a 'notorious rebel'. This was a move of sharply disputed legality, as Ferdinand acted on his own authority and without any formal proceedings or trial, but Frederick was effectively outlawed nevertheless. During the same year a Spanish army under Spinola occupied most of his Rhine Palatinate, while Tilly seized the Upper Palatinate, the detached part of his lands on the Bohemian border. Far from helping him, the German princes of the Protestant Union disbanded not only their forces but the Union itself in an effort to keep out of the conflict. The exception, Margrave Georg of Baden-Durlach, did recruit a small army, but in May 1622 he was defeated by Tilly and the Spanish. Frederick's only other help from within Germany came from the eccentric young Duke Christian of Brunswick, administrator of the secularised diocese of Halberstadt and known to his opponents, not without good reason, as the 'mad Halberstädter'. Christian too raised an army but likewise fell foul of Tilly and the Spanish in June 1622, following which he and Mansfeld, who had re-enlisted his army with what little money Frederick had been able to beg or borrow, headed for Holland with the remainder of their forces, and by the autumn they were fighting against the Spanish on behalf of the Dutch rather than for Frederick.

After a winter spent in planning and pipe-dreaming these serial losers were in the field again in the summer of 1623. Their grand strategy was for Christian, supported by Mansfeld, to advance on Bohemia from the west across north Germany, while Bethlen Gabor and some of the Bohemian exiles under Thurn attacked from the east. The indefatigable Tilly foiled the scheme, first interposing himself on Christian's line of march, then catching him as he retreated westward and comprehensively defeating him in early August. A couple of weeks later, and as yet unaware of this disaster, Bethlen belatedly launched his own advance with a large army, said to number 40,000 to 50,000 men, many of them Turks. Against him the emperor could muster only a poorly equipped force of some 9000, of which Wallenstein was appointed third-in-command.[4] Nevertheless Bethlen proceeded cautiously, particularly once he learned of the defeat of his allies and the consequent possibility of Imperialist reinforcements descending on him from the west. Hence he confined himself to raiding and skirmishing in Moravia, while the emperor's little army moved equally cautiously south towards Pressburg, intending to take up a defensive position near Vienna. Bethlen followed, and towards the end of October the Imperialists took refuge in the fortified town of Göding (Hodonín), sixty miles north of Vienna. Bethlen had no siege artillery, so he was forced to attempt to starve them out. After three weeks, closer to success than he realised but with winter coming on and his men wanting to go home with their booty, he gave up and concluded a truce, leaving Ferdinand once again to end the year with no enemies in the field against him.

Some writers have suggested that Wallenstein was the obvious man to command the Imperial army on this campaign, and that therefore he must have been passed over for personal or political reasons. Military seniority is a much sounder explanation. Wallenstein's command in Bohemia was essentially that of a garrison, whose principal task was to guard against any possible renewal of the revolt, whereas leading the only force the emperor could raise against the much larger army of an external enemy was a job for a senior general. Moreover the Imperial war council still believed in the superiority of Spanish training and experience, so that is where they looked for their top two officers, while Wallenstein, recently promoted to major-general, took third place.[5]

The siege of Göding rarely rates more than a mention – and often not so much – in histories of the war. Its main interest here arises from Wallenstein's surviving correspondence, including twenty of his daily letters which were carried by daring messengers to Harrach in Vienna.[6] In these he criticised the inadequate preparations for the campaign, particularly supplies, as well as the wider failure to anticipate an attack and gather forces earlier. He complained that advancing on Pressburg in the hope of protecting Vienna would leave Bohemia, Moravia and Silesia open to the enemy. From inside Göding he commented on the precariousness of their position, particularly should the hungry soldiers decide to save themselves by seizing the officers and surrendering to Bethlen. Nevertheless he sent a stream of advice as to arrangements and troop dispositions which should be made to help secure the Austrian and Bohemian territories should Göding fall. The tone is unmistakeably that of the rising man, not yet at the top but convinced that he could do better than those in command, not only his immediate superiors but the war council itself. He was undoubtedly right, as later events were to prove, but that knowledge usually only serves to make such counsel all the more unwelcome to its recipients. Fortunately Harrach was probably more diplomatic in passing on Wallenstein's opinions.

Despite the relative successes of the previous year the emperor was not in a comfortable position at the beginning of 1624, as other potential threats across Europe were not only emerging but threatening to merge. Spanish resources were increasingly concentrated on their none too successful war in the Netherlands following the end of the truce in 1621, leaving them little scope to offer Ferdinand further help. There was also friction between Spain and France over their respective involvements in northern Italy, and the joint Spanish and Imperialist occupation of the Rhine Palatinate was also a matter of concern to the French, so that despite religious differences they were driven towards the anti-Habsburg camp. The Dutch were inevitably at the centre of this group, and the dispossessed Frederick had long since found refuge with them. The Protestant monarchies of Denmark and Sweden were also nervous about Habsburg and Catholic League successes in northern Germany, uncomfortably close to their Baltic preserve. James I of England, after the collapse in 1623 of a long-running attempt to secure a Spanish marriage alliance for his son Charles, was suddenly more prepared to listen to the anti-Habsburg views of his parliament and the London mob, and to the pleadings of his son-in-law Frederick, while in the east Bethlen Gabor had by no means given up the idea of a further profitable attack on the Empire. Even within Germany there were opponents who might join any campaign which showed signs of success, among them the Protestant electors of Brandenburg and Saxony, who were alarmed by Ferdinand's militant recatholicisation in areas under his control, and by his high-handed transfer of Frederick's status as an elector of the Empire to Maximilian of Bavaria in early 1623. And always in the background was the fear of a renewed revolt in Bohemia and Moravia.

The Habsburgs and their supporters were very much aware of this dangerous coalition gathering against them. Wallenstein in particular, with his new lands and titles at stake, was anxious that adequate defensive measures should be put quickly in hand, leading him to repeat an earlier suggestion that he might recruit a larger military force for the emperor, but this was not a specific proposal and it was not taken up.[7] Maximilian of Bavaria was equally anxious, and for the same reason. He too had done very well out of the war but his new possessions and his impressive status as an elector were also at risk should the tide turn decisively against the Imperialists. Nevertheless he was a reluctant adherent to Ferdinand's cause. On the one hand he was bound to him by kinship and their shared militant Catholicism, but on the other, as ruler of one of the largest territories of the Empire, he had a vested interest in limiting the effective power of the emperor. This led him to maintain a relationship with Catholic but anti-Habsburg France during the Thirty Years War, which although never quite becoming an effective alliance allowed him to avoid total commitment to Ferdinand. Maximilian's diplomatic manoeuvres and contacts with France could not be kept entirely secret, thus increasing the discomfort of Ferdinand's position, as the very limited strength of his own forces left his defence largely dependent on Tilly's army, which although nominally that of the Catholic League was effectively controlled by Maximilian. The latter in turn realised that this army might be insufficient in the event of a concerted attack by the anti-Habsburg coalition, putting not only his gains but also his own security at risk. Hence he urged Ferdinand to raise troops, which he anticipated would be deployed to support Tilly, and would thus come under his own overall control. Ferdinand had no money to recruit or pay new regiments, let alone an army, although he and his advisers recognised the need for additional forces, but preferably under Imperial rather than Bavarian command. In the end it would be Wallenstein who provided a solution to this problem, but during 1624 the Imperialist side were fortunate to gain a respite due to the divisions among their opponents.

The attempts of Frederick and his sympathisers to create a functional military alliance from the loose congruence of interests of the various parties achieved nothing of consequence during that year. James I did reach an agreement with France to make a joint attack on the forces occupying the Palatinate, in which the ubiquitous Mansfeld was to be employed, and the general duly started recruiting English troops, financed with English money. The Dutch and the English, along with Brandenburg, also proposed to support Frederick's cause with an army which was to advance on the Palatinate through north Germany, and they invited Gustavus II Adolphus, king of Sweden, not only to participate but also to lead this campaign. From the Habsburg viewpoint these developments looked very threatening, but differences soon emerged. The Protestant Gustavus would not cooperate with Catholic France, and he made his involvement conditional on his allies providing 40,000 men, of whom he was to have sole command. The new French chief minister, Cardinal Richelieu, then withdrew from the planned French-English joint attack, so that the sole outcome was a small English army under Mansfeld, and even that did not enter service until January 1625.

Perversely it was the hostility between two of the prospective allies which eventually led to action. There was a long history of bitter rivalry and actual war between Denmark and Sweden, so that the Anglo-Dutch invitation to Gustavus Adolphus to lead a joint force had caused great alarm to King Christian IV of Denmark. This was based partly on the fear that a large army under Swedish control and with Dutch naval support would seriously upset the balance of power in the Baltic and might constitute an actual threat to Denmark, but personal prestige also played a major part. Christian was in the unusual position for a monarch of the time of being wealthy enough to act substantially independently of his Estates, and he was not only king of Denmark but also duke of Holstein, in which capacity he was a prince of the Empire and a member of the Empire's Lower Saxon Circle. As plans for the coalition of 1624 faltered Christian proposed to intervene militarily himself, subject to England sending 7000 troops to Denmark and despatching Mansfeld to Holland. Mansfeld was duly sent but James I persisted in trying to involve Sweden, up to the time of his death in early 1625. He was unsuccessful and eventually Christian acted alone, despite the opposition of his own council. In April 1625 he secured election to the vacant post of military commander of the Lower Saxon Circle, and in June he advanced into northern Germany with an army of 20,000 men, which he had recruited and financed from his own resources. By that time almost all his potential allies were wavering or gone. The new English king was less supportive, and Maurice of Nassau, the captain-general of the United Provinces, had also recently died, causing a hiatus in Dutch policy. In the summer Gustavus went off to pursue Swedish dynastic rivalries by renewing his recurrent war with his cousin, the king of Poland, while under internal Catholic pressure Richelieu was forced to distance France from Protestant-led enterprises, shifting over the next couple of years from an anti-Spanish to an anti-English position.

Christian's advance into Germany was not formally an act of war, as it took him initially into the Lower Saxon Circle, where he was military commander and responsible for defence. Although this was a transparent technicality Ferdinand hesitated, but in mid-July Maximilian took the initiative. Acting in his capacity as commissioner appointed by the emperor to enforce Imperial law, he instructed Tilly to put the matter to the test by himself advancing into Lower Saxon territory.[8] This Tilly did with great caution, knowing that he had both Christian and Mansfeld to contend with, as well as other enemies who might take the field. Christian too was cautious, as no such support from his allies appeared, in addition to which he himself had a serious riding accident, the summer weather was particularly bad, and plague also started to affect the troops and the population. Consequently only a limited war ensued, with skirmishing and sieges but no significant engagement in the remainder of 1625.

A general and a duke

Wallenstein watched and waited anxiously throughout 1624, as his own lands were extremely vulnerable in the event of a coalition attack. Not only would Bohemia be a prime target in its own right, but were forces to advance towards Austria from the north-west along the Elbe, and from the Baltic through Silesia, they would be likely to converge in Bohemia, probably aiming to join up with Bethlen Gabor sweeping in from the east through Moravia. Wallenstein had seen enough of Vienna's management of military affairs to know that they were likely to do too little and too late to meet any developing threat, and that even if they had the will they lacked the money to act promptly and decisively. He also knew how badly organised the Imperial war effort in 1623 had been. Never one to wait helplessly for fate to catch up with him, nor lacking confidence in his own abilities, Wallenstein realised that he needed to act, and to goad Ferdinand and his council into acting, if he was to preserve his own property and position. In the latter part of 1624 he renewed his suggestion that he should raise a considerable force, now to be a full-scale army, for the emperor, which as previously he did through his contacts rather than making a formal written proposal, and with Harrach's support he pressed this idea urgently on Ferdinand and his advisers.

The Imperial council was not easy to persuade.[9] Some members agreed that there was a need to raise forces to counter the threat from the north, but others felt that arming against the possibility of a renewed and larger war could make this a self-fulfilling prophecy. It was difficult and expensive to keep a large army idle, so that raising one tended of itself to lead towards war. An inactive army was also a danger to its own side, as its food and fodder requirements quickly stripped any territory in which it was based. This and the notorious indiscipline of the troops could cause severe economic damage and perhaps lead to civil disturbances in the emperor's own lands. Better to wait until an attack was more certain, said some – but that, said others, including Wallenstein, would be too late.

Then there was the man himself. Although he had a number of personal opponents from Bohemia there was no wider hostility towards Wallenstein at the Imperial court. That developed later. His loyalty and military competence were well established and were not questioned in the council discussions. Nevertheless a year earlier he had only been third-in-command of the small force that took refuge in Göding. The military hierarchy in Vienna, mostly Spanish or Italian, could not overlook that, and at 41 Wallenstein was still considered young to command an army. Money was the crux. Whatever the advisability of raising troops the emperor did not have the resources to do so, as the Imperial treasury was already loaded down with debt after the previous years of war. Wallenstein appeared to be willing and able to finance the recruitment and equipping of an army, and perhaps even to fund its subsequent costs, without calling on the exchequer for cash.[10] No-one else was. Thus the issue was simply Wallenstein's army or no army. This too caused uneasiness in Vienna, as 'Wallenstein's army' sounded rather like a private army, calling to mind Mansfeld's, which was well known to be loyal to its general rather than to the ruler employing its services. And how long would it be before Wallenstein's money ran out and the bills came back to the exchequer?

The truth was that Wallenstein could no more afford to maintain an army than could the emperor. His resources and credit could, and in due course did, run to establishing the force, but supporting it for any significant period thereafter was beyond the means of any private person, even one as rich as Wallenstein.[11] Nevertheless he needed an army, not – as has often been said – to serve his own ambition, nor – as some said at the time – because he hoped to make even more money out of it, but because he believed that everything could be lost, for the Habsburg cause and for himself, including all that he had so far gained, if the emperor failed to arm in time. The council were reluctant, and his only hope was to remove the financial obstacle by giving the impression that he could fund the undertaking himself. That would also give him the command, but there is a distinction to be made between mere ambition and Wallenstein's belief that in a dangerous situation he could do a better job than any of the available generals. Put simply, he preferred to take his security into his own hands. When the council eventually decided that the emperor did need an army they chose to accept Wallenstein's offer without dwelling too long on questions of financial practicability. Both parties gambled on the fortunes of war coming up with some kind of solution, and in the meantime they averted their eyes from the problem.

Wallenstein's eventual commission provided for reimbursement of all his necessary expenditure, but no-one at the time had any real idea how this was to be funded. What hopes they had were indicated by another clause, which authorised the extraction of financial support from the enemy territory which it was assumed would be conquered and occupied. Half of the booty from defeated armies and captured cities was also to be converted to cash and used to pay the troops, although the officers and men could keep the other half.[12] Wallenstein, however, wanted to go further than relying on ad hoc levies on occupied country. Regular and systematic contributions, effectively war taxes, would have to be drawn from the Habsburg lands and the Imperial free cities as well as from enemy areas. This near-revolutionary proposal was only slowly, reluctantly and partially accepted, but it was the basis of Wallenstein's future contributions system which funded the armies and sustained the rest of the Thirty Years War. In the short term it was insufficient, as was soon apparent, but this was passed over in the optimistic hope that the war would be short and that the spoils of victory would soon be available to fill the gap.

Nevertheless the matter dragged on for many months, through winter and spring into the early summer of 1625, months during which Wallenstein fretted, lobbied, and wrote anxiously to Harrach, pointing out that the emperor's enemies were not idle and begging him to use his influence to hasten a decision.[13] In April he was informed privately that he was to be appointed to command whatever forces might be required in Germany, although this was only advance notice, not an actual commitment to raising an army. In mid-May the emperor wrote to Maximilian to tell him that he was intending to bring the existing Imperial forces up to strength and to recruit a new army of 21,000 men under Wallenstein's command. This, said Ferdinand, was a response to Maximilian's own urging that he should raise troops, but he took the opportunity to state firmly that these and their new commander were to operate with, rather than under, Maximilian and his League army should an attack from the north require a joint campaign.[14] For Maximilian this was a case of the good news and the bad news, and it was the beginning of his nine years of hostility towards Wallenstein.

Even then the decision was not finalised until a meeting in mid-June, at which it was at last confirmed that Wallenstein was to begin recruitment, now of 24,000 men. It was the end of that month by the time the 'Instruction' which confirmed his appointment as general of all the Imperial armies which were to serve in Germany was signed, a promotion which the emperor matched a fortnight beforehand by raising Friedland to a duchy.[15] Both moves were significant. Armies at this time were normally commanded by lieutenant-generals, rulers maintaining the fiction that they themselves were the supreme commanders. For Wallenstein the elevated military rank of full general was complemented by his new title of duke, giving him a social status the equal of anyone in his armies, among whose officers there were a number of counts as well as several who were themselves dukes.[16] From that time onwards Wallenstein was commonly known to contemporaries by his title, Friedland.

An important question which prolonged the deliberations was the size of the army to be raised. One of the best-known stories about Wallenstein is that he supposedly claimed paradoxically that he could support an army of 50,000 men but not one of 20,000, because only the larger force would be able to hold enough territory in submission to finance and feed itself by the extraction of contributions from the populace.[17] This is apocryphal, but he was certainly seeking a much larger number of troops than the council were initially prepared to sanction. In this their outlook was partly traditional – the emperor had never had such a large army – and partly financial, whereas Wallenstein's reasoning was based on straightforward military logic. Armies were getting bigger. In 1623 Bethlen Gabor reportedly had over 40,000 men, and Wallenstein had learned at first hand what happened to heavily outnumbered units, reduced to trying desperately to evade the enemy, and saved from disaster at Göding only by the lateness of the season. Eventually he settled for authority to recruit the specified 24,000 men, comprising 18,000 infantry and 6000 cavalry, but even then it does not seem to have been clearly agreed whether these were all to be new recruits or whether the total was to include the existing Imperial forces.[18]

Wallenstein did not receive his commission until after Tilly had been despatched against Christian of Denmark, but he had not been sitting idly while Vienna debated and delayed. His preparations were as far advanced as the circumstances allowed – if not further – and in a remarkably short time he began to muster his forces. The place selected was Eger, at the western extremity of Bohemia, where troops were already starting to gather when Wallenstein arrived on 31 July 1625.[19] A month later his new army was in Germany and heading towards Lower Saxony, but the distance was long and marching was slow, so that it was mid-October before he met up with Tilly south of Hanover, by which time the main item on their agenda was winter quarters for their armies. Tilly had made little progress against Christian, so that Wallenstein's arrival with reinforcements was welcome, but the actual number of troops he brought is difficult to establish. It appears that 16,000 men mustered at Eger, but other units, including those of the pre-existing Imperial army, joined them at various stages, while Wallenstein continued to recruit throughout the autumn and winter. Hence he was able to write to the Spanish general Spinola that he hoped 'to take the field in the coming spring with fifty-something thousand men', an impressive number although the quality of some of their officers was another matter, causing Wallenstein to comment that if falcons were not available he would have to hunt with ravens.[20]

The creation of so large a force in so short a time was a major achievement, and one which seems to have surprised the emperor and his advisers as much as it surprised Christian of Denmark, who knew little about it until it was almost upon him. True to his promise, Wallenstein financed its recruitment, which involved cash in hand for every man who signed on, as well as its weapons, equipment, mustering and march into Germany, without recourse to the Imperial treasury. To do this he himself put up a large sum in cash and he borrowed a great deal more, mostly with the help of de Witte, his banker associate from the coin minting consortium. Those he appointed as colonels had to act as subcontractors in funding part of the costs of their regiments, while not only Eger but towns along the way had to pay to avoid billeting and to contribute in cash and kind to the upkeep of the army.

Wallenstein's own contribution to this feat of organisation is evident from the huge number of letters, orders, requisitions and other documents which emanated from his secretariat every day, a large proportion of which he wrote, dictated or originated personally. The archives bear witness to his diligence, the range of his interests, and his knowledge of detail. They also testify to his ability to keep his finger on the business affairs of his own estates, and to think about his wife and her security, despite the pressures of his military responsibilities. As with his land dealings, though, he could not do it all himself, and he knew how to select and delegate to competent staff officers. One who became important at this time was Colonel Johann Aldringer, a Luxemburger from a poor but noble family who had made his way up the military ladder after starting as a pikeman, an impressive although not unique achievement in the Thirty Years War. Aldringer had shown administrative talents early in his career, and in Wallenstein's service he took responsibility both for coordinating the recruitment efforts of the colonels and for negotiating large contributions from towns and cities, Nuremberg for example paying 110,000 gulden at this time for exemption from designation as a mustering place. However Aldringer also continued to correspond freely with his contacts at the Vienna and Munich courts and elsewhere, so that while he was extremely useful he was also something of an irritant to Wallenstein.[21]

The new general was careful in his selection of senior officers, and here he inevitably started to make enemies. The top echelon in the existing army, including the men who had been Wallenstein's superiors at Göding, duly resigned to allow him a free hand. The senior of the two was elderly and probably expected nothing, but Major-General Count Balthasar Marradas was surprised and offended not to be reappointed. He remained in favour at court, and in the event it was not long before he was back in service with Wallenstein's army, but the indignity rankled. Another who was well connected in Vienna and hoped for promotion was Colonel Count Rudolf Colloredo, but he too was disappointed.[22] They were by no means the only ones, as a number of would-be colonels found that recommendations from friends in high places were no guarantee of Wallenstein's approval. His criteria were strictly military, and he had no time for those who did not meet his standards as capable officers, competent administrators and good disciplinarians. On the other hand those he approved of prospered, and in the process of staffing his first army he found many colonels who stayed with him throughout the rest of his career. Not a few of them were Protestants, the first demonstration of Wallenstein's determination to recruit competent officers and soldiers to his armies irrespective of their religion.

In this appointment process Wallenstein demonstrated at the outset both one of his strengths and perhaps his most serious weakness as the emperor's general. Armies of the day were plagued by dilettante officers, men with titles and contacts who were attracted by the status and profit-making opportunities of a colonel's commission, but who lacked the ability, experience and commitment to discharge the responsibilities effectively. Their approach spread to the ranks below them, creating regiments which were ill-disciplined, unreliable in service, and more interested in booty than duty. Wallenstein needed an efficient fighting force and he was not prepared to be burdened with such men, a stance which was quite correct from a purely military perspective. Moreover he was determined to be master in his own house, choosing his men in accordance with his own requirements rather than having officers wished on him by elevated but non-military councillors or courtiers. Gustavus Adolphus adopted the same approach, but he was both general and king, with less need to consider the politics of the situation.

Wallenstein was no politician, and therein lay the problem. Commanders-in-chief have always needed political support, and support drawn as widely as possible, not just from the very top. In Habsburg Austria that meant the emperor's council, the Imperial war council, and the Vienna court at large, whereas Wallenstein was inclined to see himself as answerable to the emperor alone. Rejecting candidates for commissions meant offending not only the individuals, but also those who had supported them and who had expected their recommendations to count for something. Moreover surviving letters show that Wallenstein's reasons for refusing appointments, although generally good, were sometimes very bluntly expressed, and while such correspondence was intended to be private some of the gist doubtless became known, particularly if he spoke as he wrote.[23] The disappointed and the affronted had a common interest with the envious and the antagonistic in seeing Wallenstein brought down, and this was the basis of the hostile faction which started to form in Vienna, and which would become increasingly significant as his career progressed.

7
Go, Captain, Greet the Danish King
(*Hamlet*)

The Dessau bridge

Wallenstein's appointment as Imperial general had come too late for matters to be concluded in 1625, when a conjunction of his and Tilly's forces might have driven the isolated Christian back to Denmark and out of the war. Instead they united in time only for the armies to spend the winter skirmishing, looting the countryside, and eating the peasantry out of house and home, rather than achieving anything of military significance. Meanwhile Christian was involved in two contradictory negotiations, one taking place in Brunswick, where peace with the emperor was discussed, and the other in The Hague, where attempts were made to widen the anti-Habsburg coalition in order to continue the war. The peace conference was the first of many occasions upon which Wallenstein favoured a realistic approach in order to achieve a peace settlement, but the hard-line Imperialist position was determined in Vienna and Munich, and no progress was made. Matters stood little better for Christian in The Hague as most of his prospective allies did not participate, even though they realised that Wallenstein's new army completely altered the balance, and that if as a result Christian were defeated or withdrew from the war their interests would be seriously threatened. However England and the Dutch Republic agreed to provide him with money, Mansfeld's army was despatched to Lower Saxony, and contacts were re-established with Bethlen Gabor. The other Christian, the 'mad Halberstädter', also reappeared on the scene, albeit with a makeshift army of limited military value, while another German prince, Duke Johann Ernst of Weimar, contributed troops to the revived coalition.

There were predictable tensions between the leaders of these diverse forces, at least partly as a result of which their grand plan was based on independent rather than united action. Although this was making a virtue of necessity it was nevertheless a sound strategy, as by separating they prevented Tilly and Wallenstein from combining against them. Mansfeld's task was to draw Wallenstein away by heading east into Silesia, forcing him – so the plan went – to follow because of the threat this would pose to Bohemia, Moravia and ultimately Austria itself. As in 1623 the intention was that this force from the west would join up with Bethlen Gabor invading from the east, when together they would be strong enough to face and defeat Wallenstein. Meanwhile Christian of Brunswick was to bypass Tilly and move south, before turning and threatening his rear while Christian of Denmark confronted him from the north.

It was not a bad plan, and it also exploited the equally predictable tensions between Tilly and Wallenstein, the old, experienced and successful general and the younger unproven leader of a new and unproven army.[1] Rivalry over winter quarters had been the start, but Wallenstein had come off better by moving quickly into the rich lands of the Protestant-held secularised bishoprics centred on Magdeburg and Halberstadt. With Wallenstein thus ensconced by the Elbe, Tilly remained 80 miles to the west on the River Weser, a disposition which determined their respective roles in the campaigns of 1626. There were also differences over strategy. Wallenstein wanted their forces to join up for a decisive attack on Christian early in the year, whereas Tilly preferred to play a waiting game, hoping to trap the Danes between them later in the spring. Wallenstein, closer to Christian's main army, was thus left at risk should the king move first and attack him in strength.[2] The result was that while the generals were arguing the relative importance of possible lines of attack or defence, each seeking support and troops from the other, they lost the initiative and were forced instead to respond to the opening moves of their enemies. Tilly was soon under pressure, and when the 'mad Halberstädter' threatened the city of Goslar Wallenstein was obliged to assist by leading a large force against him, only to find that the enemy quickly disappeared. He then had to turn back to counter an advance south by a Danish division under General Hans Fuchs, which he chased off after a sharp skirmish but without being able to force a battle.[3] Meanwhile Mansfeld was already across the Elbe.

Rivers were of great strategic importance, not only as the easiest line of advance or retreat using the relatively good roads alongside them, but also as supply lines for bringing up heavy guns, provisions and other necessities by water. However major rivers were also potentially dangerous obstacles, particularly to a retreating army, as bridges were few and far between as well as easily fortified or broken down. Hence over the winter Wallenstein had substantial defences constructed on both sides of the Elbe bridge at Dessau, 30 miles south-east of Magdeburg, and he placed Aldringer there with a garrison to defend it. Magdeburg and its bridge were in Protestant hands, while south of Dessau all the way to the Bohemian border the Elbe flowed through Protestant Saxony, so that securing the bridge was a prudent precaution as well as preventing the river being used as a supply line by the enemy. Nevertheless it was a surprise when in April 1626, after taking the town of Zerbst nine miles to the north-west, Mansfeld mounted an attack on the defences around the northern end of the bridge.

Despite the confident accounts given in many histories it is very difficult to describe accurately what happened at battles in the early modern period. Numbers are the first problem. Contemporary reports give large, round and probably exaggerated figures, and for want of anything better these often pass from one history to the next, eventually becoming accepted as though they were established fact. The starting point in the Thirty Years War was to list the units involved, which were known by the names of their commanders and were usually well recorded, and to tot up their nominal strength, 3000 for an infantry regiment, 300 for a company, and 1000 and 100 for the equivalent cavalry formations. The result was the maximum figure, although the one often reported, but units were rarely at full strength even in total, while after deducting the sick, wounded, missing and dead the numbers available and fit to fight could be very much lower, sometimes half or less. This may not matter, as the same applied on both sides, so that the relative strengths quoted may be somewhere near right even if the absolute numbers are wrong, but it helps to explain the frequent discrepancies between different reports of the same event. Numbers of casualties were even more arbitrary, as the dead were mostly buried in mass graves and perhaps not even counted, while those who failed to return for roll-call and were not known to be prisoners were simply struck off the company lists, so that there was no distinction between casualties and deserters. Prisoners were no better accounted for, usually simply being enrolled by the winning side, and here too the numbers represent the loosest of estimates or perhaps simply guesswork. The most accurate figures after a battle seem to have been the number of enemy standards taken – a particular point of military pride – and perhaps the number of cannon captured.

The course of a battle is often as unclear as the numbers involved. Two hundred years later the duke of Wellington noted 'how little reliance can be placed even on what are supposed to be the best accounts of a battle. ... It is impossible to say when each important occurrence took place, or in what order.' There are good reasons for this. Battles were frequently confused affairs, and the participants themselves rarely had a full picture of events, so that subsequent accounts involve piecing together partial, impressionistic and often inconsistent reports to work out what might have happened. The term 'battlefield' is itself misleading, suggesting a conveniently open and something like level discrete area, whereas in fact troops, particularly cavalry, might range widely over territory broken up by streams, ditches, hills, woods, villages and other obstructions to both movement and vision; 10,000 infantry could well be spread out over two miles or more, so that a commander would often not have had a clear view of their disposition. Worse still, once action commenced the guns of the period quickly created 'such an awful smoke ... that we could scarcely see a pistol-shot in front of us', as a Bavarian officer recorded after one such engagement.[4]

The battle for the Dessau bridge is a good example of the numbers problem. Mann, in his biography of Wallenstein, puts Mansfeld's army at 10,000 men, whereas Guthrie calculates less than 7000 in his study of the battles of the Thirty Years War. Of these Mann states that 3000 to 4000 were killed, against Guthrie's estimate of somewhere over 1000. Conversely Mann reports 1500 taken prisoner against Guthrie's 3000, so that according to Mann Mansfeld escaped with 5000 survivors while Guthrie says that it was only about 2000. Neither gives figures for Wallenstein's forces, although Guthrie contends that he had at least twice as many men as Mansfeld, that is upwards of 14,000 by his calculation, whereas Diwald, in his Wallenstein biography, puts his strength at 21,000 infantry and six regiments of cavalry.[5]

The *Theatrum Europaeum*, a major contemporary chronicle, made a speciality of elaborate copperplate illustrations, including detailed plans of battles commissioned from experienced military officers, and these give very helpful pictures of the terrain as it then was, together with such features as earthworks and other defences. A drawing in the *Theatrum* (given as Plate 6 in this book) shows that the Dessau bridge, which was some distance north of the town, spanned both the Elbe and its wide flood plain. It is depicted as a narrow structure built on piers, with small Imperialist forts on the south side and a substantial defensive enclosure around the bridgehead on the north, and with protective wings and trenches securing a strip of land along the river bank in both directions. The whole area to the south was heavily wooded, so that the road along which the Imperialist troops approached was well screened from Mansfeld on the opposite side. The fortifications would have largely hidden the bridge itself from him, and Aldringer had also covered it with tree branches, so that troops crossing could not be seen.[6] The land north of the river where Mansfeld made his camp and positioned his forces was much more open, but he had thrown up temporary earthworks opposite and parallel to the Imperialist defences. To the east a belt of woodland started from the river close to the Imperialist right wing, extending northwards and then westwards so that it effectively bounded the whole of Mansfeld's left flank.

Mansfeld's initial probes in early April and a more substantial attack a week later showed that although Aldringer had only a small garrison the position had been too well prepared to be easily taken. Mansfeld accordingly brought up guns and set his men to digging approach trenching for a full-scale storm of the bridgehead. His reasons are not well established, but if his plan was to draw Wallenstein after him into Silesia he would have needed a head start so that he could reach Bethlen Gabor before Wallenstein caught up with him. Taking the bridge and leaving a rearguard to defend it would have helped to prevent the Imperial army following too hard on his heels. Christian of Denmark was also worried that Mansfeld's departure would weaken his own position, so that he wanted him first to hamper Wallenstein by cutting his supply line along the river and opening up a potential threat to his rear.[7] Fuchs was charged with supporting the action, but he was still recovering from his own clash with Wallenstein, so that he did not appear on the scene. Hence Mansfeld launched the attack on his own, perhaps tempted by the opportunity of an easy victory over the heavily outnumbered Aldringer. His career had been remarkable more for his ability to recover from setbacks and survive disasters than for any achievements in the field, and he may have wanted a triumph to register with Christian. Successive failed attacks seem only to have made him the more determined to persevere, and to have made him oblivious to the changing balance of forces around the bridge.

Mansfeld's perversity was Wallenstein's opportunity. It had been a frustrating winter, and he was well aware that critics in Vienna were saying that in the six months since the novice general set out with his new army nothing of consequence had been achieved. Now there was a chance of action. He could not move too early in case the attack on the bridge was a diversion as part of some larger plan, but once Mansfeld brought in artillery and his main army Wallenstein was ready to respond. The first step was to move up enough reinforcements to prevent Mansfeld gaining a quick success, and Colonel Heinrich Schlick was swiftly despatched with the necessary troops. Schlick managed to get his men over the bridge and into the northern defences either unobserved or with their numbers sufficiently hidden by the screening, so that when Mansfeld attacked on 23 April he encountered much stronger resistance than he had expected and he was obliged to withdraw. Meanwhile Wallenstein moved up his own artillery and a large force of both infantry and cavalry.

The key point in his plan was the wood on Mansfeld's eastern flank, where the latter had not placed troops either for lack of men or because he did not think it important. On 24 April Wallenstein moved more units over the bridge, including heavy cavalry. Then under covering fire from an artillery battery south of the river, and assisted by a diversionary sally from the west side of the bridgehead defences, his men occupied the wood. Presumably Mansfeld again underestimated their number and strength, as he pressed on regardless, launching a heavy frontal attack on the fortifications early the following morning. Reports indicate that he made several unsuccessful assaults over the next three hours before Wallenstein ordered a counter-attack, which was followed by heavy and evenly balanced fighting on the open ground. At the critical stage Wallenstein sent infantry reinforcements over the bridge, and the issue was then decided by a flanking cavalry attack from the wood. To add to the confusion of Mansfeld's men some of their gunpowder wagons exploded in the rear, so that retreat quickly turned to flight. Mansfeld managed to escape back to Zerbst with many of his cavalry, but most of his surviving infantry were captured.[8]

Wallenstein's battle plan was well conceived and well executed, following a central principle of military strategy by concentrating superior forces before engaging the enemy. Nevertheless it was a bold undertaking, as getting large numbers of men and horses over a narrow bridge and into a small defended area in the face of the enemy had its own risks, while fighting with their backs to the river left little scope for an orderly retreat had Mansfeld proved the stronger. Wallenstein's own report was brief and to the point:

> Mansfeld and his entire army moved up to the fortifications at the Elbe bridge near Dessau, besieging and bombarding them, to counter which I led the majority of the Imperial army entrusted to me out to meet him, advancing against him from the aforementioned

fortifications. Yesterday God gave us the good fortune to defeat him, cutting through his forces and putting them to flight.

He sent an officer to provide a fuller account to the emperor, who was delighted with these 'impressive and knightly deeds', as he enthusiastically wrote in congratulatory letters to Wallenstein and his principal officers.[9]

1626: A campaign and a conference

What was Wallenstein to do next? Mansfeld took refuge only briefly in Zerbst before hastening off into the neutral but pro-Protestant territory of the elector of Brandenburg. Following him would not only risk turning its wavering prince into an enemy, contrary to Wallenstein's orders, but would also be pointless. Mansfeld's cavalry would be hard to catch and harder to pin down to a fight, and – a key point of seventeenth-century logistics – Wallenstein had no fodder available for his horses. Moving ahead of him, Mansfeld would take whatever was to be found in the barns, while it was too early in the year for the horses to find much to eat in the fields. Moreover the very purpose of such a pursuit was questionable. The armies of the Thirty Years War were hydra-headed; cut one down and another swiftly grew in its place. Mansfeld was an expert in raising armies and if deprived of one he would soon replace it, provided that his employer still had the money. For the moment he had been neutralised, but Christian of Denmark's much more formidable army was still in the field. Wallenstein went back to his station in Magdeburg-Halberstadt territory.

A stalemate ensued, as Christian could not break out but neither could Tilly and Wallenstein agree united action against him. Wallenstein was becoming increasingly frustrated and depressed by the lack of progress. His original concept had been to raise his army in early 1625, to campaign against and defeat Christian in that same summer, and to make peace before the end of the year, a timescale which offered some hope of financial viability. Instead approval had been delayed so long that nothing was achieved militarily in 1625, and nor had he been able to secure Tilly's agreement to a joint attack on Christian in early 1626. Even after Dessau Tilly preferred a war of attrition, laying siege one by one to cities far to the west of where Wallenstein's large but inexperienced army confronted Christian at uncomfortably close quarters.

Little by way of provisions and even less money came from Vienna, so that Wallenstein's debts mounted and his troops were unpaid, hungry and potentially mutinous, to add to which he himself was often ill. He wrote several times to Harrach about the possibility of resigning his command, but that would have left him massively indebted and with little hope of securing repayment from the emperor in the foreseeable future. Victory or peace were the only ways out. In May he initiated contacts with the Danish king through intermediaries, and in June he advised the emperor to reopen peace negotiations before Christian strengthened his forces further and perhaps secured additional allies. Ferdinand and his advisers were reluctant, saying that the initiative should come from the other side, but when Christian did make a direct approach they still temporised and it came to nothing.[10]

Wallenstein had forgotten neither Bethlen Gabor nor Mansfeld. For months he had been urging Vienna to recruit troops to guard against an attack from Bethlen, and to strengthen garrisons in Silesia to deter Mansfeld from making an incursion. Little had been done in response, and the victory at the Dessau bridge was seen as justifying doing even less, causing Wallenstein to comment ironically that 'once a couple of flies have been killed they cease recruiting in Vienna'. In mid-1626 a peasants' revolt broke out in Upper Austria, setting a large if amateur army on the rampage, while to the east Bethlen was making unmistakeable preparations for a further campaign which only Wallenstein had the forces to counter. Consequently his command, initially limited to Germany, was extended to include the Habsburg hereditary lands, and he despatched troops to Silesia to prepare its defences.[11]

Mansfeld rapidly rebuilt his army in Brandenburg territory, despite Wallenstein reminding the elector that allowing this was incompatible with his neutrality, and on 10 July he broke camp and moved swiftly east, passing to the north of Berlin and then across the River Oder into Silesia. Christian sent troops under Duke Johann Ernst of Weimar to support him, although for most of the following campaign the two forces moved independently, albeit in parallel, while serious differences over strategy later arose between the two commanders. Wallenstein was in a dilemma. To follow them would leave Tilly exposed, outnumbered and facing Christian of Denmark alone. Not to do so would leave the Habsburg territories undefended against Mansfeld and Bethlen. As a first step he despatched cavalry to follow them and to harass their rear, but a brief attempt at interception had to be abandoned in order not to be drawn too far away from Christian. Hence he watched and waited for almost a month to see how events developed, by which time Mansfeld was already approaching the northern borders of Hungary and threatening Moravia. Wallenstein could delay no longer, and on 8 August he too headed towards Hungary, but taking a shorter, more westerly route in an effort to catch up with Mansfeld.[12]

This was exactly what Christian and his allies had intended, but the outcome was not what they had hoped. Once Wallenstein was out of the way Christian in turn broke camp, heading south towards the rich and undefended territories of central Germany. Tilly followed, and only then did Christian learn that Wallenstein had left a substantial part of his army to bolster Tilly's strength.[13] Anxious and probably now outnumbered, Christian wanted neither to confront Tilly nor to be cut off by him, so he turned and hastily tried to retrace his steps. Too late. With Tilly in hot pursuit Christian was eventually obliged to turn and fight, and on 26 August 1626 he was heavily defeated at the battle of Lutter, an event which he recorded in his personal diary only with the terse entry: 'Fought with the enemy and lost. The same day I went to Wolfenbüttel.'[14] Like Mansfeld a few months earlier, though, he was down but not out.

Wallenstein made rapid progress, marching his men as hard as they could go into Moravia. On the other hand Mansfeld had come almost to a standstill waiting for Bethlen, whose troops were part-timers, farmers who brought in the harvest before reporting for military duties, so that he had been late off the mark and was still making his way across Hungary. Moreover his army was weaker than he had expected, as the Ottoman sultan had his own problems and did not want to be involved in the war with the emperor, so that Bethlen had been able to secure help only from a few local lords. A period followed in which four armies, those of Wallenstein, Mansfeld, Johann Ernst and Bethlen, marched hither and thither, trying either to find or to avoid one another. All were suffering from shortage of supplies and the hardships of long forced marches, so that illness, deaths and desertion were rapidly eroding their numbers. At one point Wallenstein and Mansfeld were not far apart, but after Dessau Mansfeld had learned to treat his opponent with more care, and he had no intention of trying the issue without his ally, instead moving smartly away. At another stage Mansfeld considered breaking off the campaign entirely and marching his army across Bohemia and Germany to regroup over the winter in Alsace. That plan was rejected by his own officers, as well as by Johann Ernst, who insisted that his orders from Christian were to join up with Bethlen.[15]

Wallenstein too was looking for Bethlen, the most important of the enemies, and when he received word of his approach he moved cautiously into Hungary in preparation for a decisive engagement. On 30 September his vanguard made contact with Bethlen's outriders, and that evening the main armies met and took up positions. It was then too late to fight, but by morning Bethlen had gone, as he too was not willing to risk a direct challenge. Wallenstein was ready for a battle but not for a chase, having left his baggage train and supplies well to the rear.[16] In any case Bethlen's lighter and more mobile forces would have been hard to follow, difficult to catch, and probably impossible to pin down to a battle. A wild-goose chase across the Hungarian plains offered Wallenstein little prospect of success but a fair chance of disaster if Bethlen led him too far from his base and supply lines.

In fact Wallenstein had achieved precisely the objectives of a good general. He had protected the Austrian heartland, neutralised the emperor's enemies, and in the end driven them from the field. Within a fortnight Bethlen was making peace overtures and ready to go home, while Mansfeld, ill and out of money, was dead by the end of the year, a fate which had overtaken the 'mad Halberstädter' earlier in the summer. Bethlen too was ill, and although he survived a couple of years he did no more campaigning, leaving it to his successor to resume the role of thorn in the Habsburg side.[17] Nevertheless Wallenstein had to keep his sick and starving army in the field well into December until Bethlen had withdrawn, increasing his bitterness at the failures in Vienna and in Hungary to make adequate arrangements, indeed scarcely any attempt, to provide them with food, supplies or pay.

A thorn in the side for Wallenstein personally was the persistent criticism from armchair strategists in Vienna, 'women, clerics and various rascally Italians', as he called them.[18] Most of the courtiers understood little of the realities of war and were impressed only by spectacular victories, while the unemployed officers and the Imperial war council, the 'rascally Italians', the envious and the place-seekers, took every opportunity to feed these prejudices and to undermine the general. Angry and resentful at their sniping, Wallenstein was feeling the strain of his first year in high command. The military situation had been difficult, and his hesitations suggest that he was not yet fully confident in his new role, a problem exacerbated by a divided command and differing opinions in dealing with a common enemy. Nor had he had time to find and establish his own senior staff officers, so that he was desperately overworked in trying to do himself all that needed to be done. For provision of a field marshal (then one rank below lieutenant-general) as his deputy he was dependent on Vienna, although the old school of lordly, leisurely, Spanish-trained cavaliers which held sway there was neither to his taste nor in tune with his robust approach to organisation and duty. The first, Count Rombaldo Collalto, who was president of the

Imperial war council both before and afterwards, managed well enough for three months before resigning in a huff over a row about discipline. Wallenstein's nomination for his successor was turned down because he was a Protestant, a fact which mattered to the court but not to their general, who already had many Protestants, and even Protestant princes, among his colonels.[19] The replacement eventually sent from Vienna was none other than the Spaniard Marradas, who had been second-in-command at Göding. Again he managed well enough, but without providing Wallenstein with the full level of support which he needed.

Wallenstein complained repeatedly of being tired, overburdened and ill, chiefly with gout, a painful and debilitating condition. There are reports of him flying off the handle in public and carrying reproof over what he saw as deficiencies beyond the normally accepted limits. His correspondence contains caustic assessments of officers whom he regarded as incompetent or more interested in unscrupulous self-enrichment than in military duty, which while possibly true were certainly immoderate, particularly as in some cases he later reversed his opinions. The symptoms of stress are easy to see, even without the repeated statements of his wish to give up the command, at the latest at the end of the 1626 campaigning season, which he made in his letters to Harrach.[20]

His biggest worry was money, as the imprecise financial arrangements which had enabled him to secure approval for the creation of his army quickly came back to haunt him. 'It is sufficient for the emperor', wrote Wallenstein, 'that I have provided him with an army the like of which no-one has had before, and for which he has still not laid out a single farthing.' He had fulfilled his side of the bargain in raising the army and putting it into the field without making any call on the treasury, but he had not intended to finance it indefinitely thereafter, and nor was he capable of doing so. That was beyond the capacity of any private individual no matter how wealthy. Unfortunately it was also beyond the capacity of the emperor and his exchequer, and the result was that there was frequently no money to pay the troops. This had military significance, as Wallenstein complained: 'It is not possible to do with an unpaid army what a paid one will do.' It also had a direct significance for Wallenstein himself, as it appears that by the end of the 1626 campaign he was near exhausting not only his own credit but also that of his banker and collaborator Hans de Witte. His lament that his time in the emperor's service would leave him a pauper was doubtless an exaggeration, although possibly not very much of one.[21] But he was effectively trapped. He had raised the army with the defence of his own possessions in mind, but now these were pledged to such an extent that he could not withdraw again.

Nevertheless by the late autumn of 1626 his position as the emperor's general was precarious, not because there was any serious wish to remove him, although there were rumours and gossip, but more because he might be driven to turn resignation from a private threat into a public reality, whether because of his own temperament or as a result of the increasing volume of criticism at court. There the credit he had gained from the victory at Dessau was soon overshadowed by Tilly's success at Lutter, while detractors ignorant of or determined to ignore the strategic realities complained about Wallenstein's delay in following Mansfeld south and his failure to bring either him or Bethlen to battle. And why, they asked, could a winter offensive not be mounted to finish both off once and for all, a prospect unfeasible at the best of times but out of the question with an army exhausted from long marches, wasted in strength by illness and inadequate provisions, and unpaid into the bargain. With all the main enemies off the scene some even started to wonder whether the army was necessary.

Wiser heads looked further and saw Sweden, France, England and Holland waiting in the wings. First Harrach and then Eggenberg came to realise that Wallenstein might actually withdraw from his command, a prospect which could entail the disintegration of the army, which was held together principally by his credit as both its general and its paymaster.[22] A meeting was arranged between the three men, for which Eggenberg, making a considerable gesture, travelled out from Vienna to Harrach's castle at Bruck an der Leitha, some 30 miles east of the city. A private conference took place on the evening of 25 November, the exact substance of which no-one other than the three principals knows or knew – although many thought that they did.

The reason for that was an anonymous memorandum purporting to describe the discussions, which was sent within a few days to Maximilian of Bavaria. Historians have concluded that the author was Count Valeriano Magni, an aristocratic Italian-born Capuchin monk who had been raised in Bohemia and had long been acquainted with Wallenstein. Magni seems to have been fascinated by intrigue for its own sake, and he had earlier been Maximilian's emissary in his clandestine contacts with France, but by 1626 he was the confessor and trusted adviser of Cardinal Harrach, archbishop of Prague and Wallenstein's brother-in-law.[23] It is possible that the cardinal may have been at Bruck at the time of the conference, and that Magni may have acted as secretary for part of the discussions. On the other hand he may have learned something of them indirectly, perhaps from conversations in a coach travelling back or subsequently in Vienna, but certainly his knowledge was only partial and his reporting was selective and slanted. However his central thesis corresponded sufficiently to one possible interpretation of the observed facts to alarm not only Maximilian but also the other Catholic princes to whom he promptly circulated the report.

According to Magni, Wallenstein's – and by implication the emperor's – intention was to maintain a large army not so much to defend the Empire as to oppress it, so that power would shift to the centre at the expense of the princes and their cherished freedoms. Exactly this apprehension underlay the duality evident in Maximilian's policies throughout the Thirty Years War, a duality in which loyalty to the Empire and its institutions conflicted with the fear that it might acquire real power and subordinate the principalities to an incipient centralised state. Although by no means its sole source the memorandum played on this anxiety, conditioning princely attitudes, particularly among the Catholic League, to Wallenstein and his Imperial army. Their resulting hostility largely explains the paradox that Wallenstein's most influential long-term opponents were not the Protestant but the Catholic princes of the Empire, foremost among them Maximilian himself.

The matters actually discussed at Bruck can be deduced from subsequent events, and from the new appointment document which was eventually issued on 21 April 1627.[24] They were clearly important enough for Eggenberg to need to consult the emperor, as Wallenstein's letters after the conference show him waiting impatiently for their formal confirmation. Strategy will certainly have been on the agenda, but the practical issues were men, money, and Wallenstein's own authority. Military expectations for the following year required more, not fewer men, Wallenstein evidently argued, so that his depleted forces were not merely to be rebuilt but expanded by new recruitment. Moreover he could no longer fund their pay, so that a formal tax levy on the hereditary lands was required. To ensure a unified strategy he should command not only his own army but all Imperial forces wherever they might be. This latter point was not accepted for another year although some concession was made, as Wallenstein began to sign colonels' commissions in his own right rather than referring them to Vienna for confirmation. The tax levy took longer and was inevitably obstructed by the self-interest of leading figures in Bohemia and Moravia, causing Wallenstein to comment to Harrach that he would welcome some such pretext for withdrawing his head from the noose and relinquishing his command.[25]

1627–28: Denmark and Stralsund

Wallenstein spent most of the winter in the palace he was having built in Prague, but although at home and with his wife he was far from idle, as the interlude amounted to little more than a shift of his headquarters while the business of quartering, recruiting and re-equipping the army went on. Come the spring, he had to seek approval for his campaign plans for 1627, necessitating a trip to Vienna and a spell among his detractors which Wallenstein viewed with undisguised gloom. Then, as was often the case in times of particular stress, he fell ill. To what extent psychological causes underlay these recurrent flare-ups of his gout can only be a matter of speculation, but such illnesses are none the less real, painful and incapacitating. He delayed his departure for three weeks, and when he eventually set out he had travelled only a short distance before a worsening of his condition confined him to a village inn for almost a month, so that he eventually reached Vienna in a litter in late April. There he remained in bed for a further month, able to receive visitors although not to go out, despite which he managed to transact his essential business. On 23 May, after a single brief audience with the emperor, he left Vienna, and he never visited the city again.[26]

The strategic situation at the beginning of 1627 looked very similar to a year earlier. Christian of Denmark was rebuilding his army and could be expected back in the field in Lower Saxony, where Tilly was still stationed but with insufficient troops to confront him alone. Mansfeld himself was gone but his army was likewise rebuilding in Silesia, while Transylvania appeared to present the usual threat, as at that stage Wallenstein could not know that Bethlen would not fight again. The Dutch had pinned the Spanish down on land and established clear superiority at sea, so that no help was to be expected from that direction. On the more positive side France had internal problems with a major Huguenot revolt, while England was not only unwilling to commit further support to the war against the emperor but had instead become actively involved in assisting the Protestant Huguenots against France.

More than offsetting this limited good news, in Wallenstein's view, was the growing threat from Sweden.[27] Having declined to join the anti-Habsburg coalition previously, Gustavus Adolphus had been happy to leave the burden to Denmark while he pursued his own interests in Poland. There he had been very successful, establishing control over what are today the Baltic states and much of their hinterland, as well as over most of the ports along the Polish coast. This was not only militarily and politically significant, but also provided him with a valuable income from trade and tolls with which to finance further campaigning. During 1626 he had landed an army in Prussia, ignoring the neutrality and protests of his brother-in-law, the elector of Brandenburg, to whom Prussia belonged, although it was a part of Poland and not of the Empire. Nevertheless his presence there was a potential threat to Pomerania, and hence to Germany, as well as to the Habsburg territory of Silesia, presenting two possible directions in which a Swedish attack might be launched in support of the emperor's enemies. Gustavus's incursion was intended more to further his Polish campaign than to position him for such an attack, but Wallenstein could not ignore the risk, for if Sweden were to enter the war before Denmark could be driven out of it the threat to the Imperialist position would be grave. Moreover both countries were havens for Bohemian refugees, and indeed Thurn, who had commanded the forces of the revolt, was serving as a field marshal and third-in-command of the Danish army. These exiles were waiting eagerly to join any advance into Habsburg territory, where their first aim would be to recover their confiscated lands, Wallenstein's purchases foremost among them.

Despite his illnesses and frustrations Wallenstein prepared thoroughly for the campaign of 1627. Central to his planning was to ensure that when he eventually confronted Christian he would have the superior force at his disposal, while still having enough other troops to deploy against threats elsewhere. Hence he set out to build his army up into the largest early modern Europe had thus far seen, of the order of 100,000 men in total.[28] His growing reputation also enabled him to attract outstanding officers to strengthen his higher levels of command. Notable among them was Hans Georg Arnim, a Protestant and a Brandenburger by birth, a soldier by profession and something of a diplomat by temperament. He had already served ten years as a colonel with Gustavus Adolphus, as well as briefly with the king of Poland and even more briefly with Mansfeld, a progress which was not then unusual for a career officer. Although he appeared an unlikely applicant to join the Catholic Imperial army he quickly became not only a key officer but also Wallenstein's trusted confidant. Highly capable as well as highly educated, and noted for his probity, piety and sobriety, he was far from typical of the officer corps of the day, which may well explain his high standing with Wallenstein. It was to prove a fateful relationship.

Wallenstein's first concern was to reduce the risk of intervention by Sweden, or at least to delay it. The most promising approach was to keep Gustavus entangled in his Polish war, and to prevent him from bringing this to a successful conclusion. Hence Wallenstein despatched a regiment to Poland early in 1627, as the first instalment of more substantial assistance which was to follow.[29] The second requirement was to limit Danish freedom of movement. Christian's options were already closed off to the south and west, as after Lutter he was unlikely to risk battle with Tilly unless he had clear superiority of numbers, but to his east the two dukes of Mecklenburg were among the few German princes who remained actively supportive of his campaign, while the elector of Brandenburg hid his sympathy under a cloak of nervous neutrality. The most feasible route to the Habsburg heartlands lay across these territories into Silesia, where the rebuilt Mansfeld army, now under Danish command, was waiting. Wallenstein needed both to pen Christian in and to prevent a conjunction of his two armies. In April he sent the regiments which he had left with Tilly the previous year to take control of key places along the Havel river, a tributary of the Elbe which flows through Brandenburg west of Berlin. Next he despatched Arnim with a section of his main army to march north along the Oder through Silesia and into eastern Brandenburg. There Arnim quickly occupied strategic points on that river and on the Spree, a tributary which joins the Havel near Berlin, thus securing the lines of march and potential crossing points against Danish movements.

With these preparations completed it was time to begin the main campaign.[30] In early June Wallenstein moved north-east from Prague into Silesia, where the Danish forces had established themselves in a number of fortified towns. Against them he deployed the largest section of his army, reportedly 40,000 men and more than twice the strength of the opposing forces. Not surprisingly the latter preferred to remain behind their defences rather than risk taking the field, so that a systematic reduction of one place after another was quickly carried through, with surrender in most cases followed by the enrolment of the defenders in the Imperial army. Only the cavalry got away, but with Arnim's forces blocking escape to the west they too were soon trapped, defeated and mostly captured. Among them were a number of prominent Bohemian exiles and the Danish Colonel Heinrich Holk, who became one of Wallenstein's own principal officers a few years later. Though relatively easily gained this string of successes was just what the Vienna court was looking for, so that with the usual fickleness of public opinion Wallenstein soon became the object of general admiration instead of the earlier criticism, at least for the time being.

Christian was still in Lower Saxony, so while Arnim moved into Mecklenburg the main force, in two divisions under Schlick and

Wallenstein himself, advanced on him from the south-east. Tilly too was on the march, crossing the Elbe from the west and driving between the principal sections of the Danish army, which were commanded respectively by Christian and his lieutenant-general, the ageing margrave of Baden-Durlach. All but deserted by his allies, Christian had been on the defensive throughout the year, and now he had no choice but to retreat. At the end of August Wallenstein and Tilly met at Lauenburg, twenty miles east of Hamburg, where a brief peace negotiation took place, but the Danish representative was offered severe and unacceptable conditions. The campaigning season was not over, the Imperial and League generals were in a very strong military position, and their armies would soon need winter quarters. Where better to find them than in Denmark.

The advance continued under joint command, but Tilly was wounded during a siege, putting him out of action and leaving the campaign and the glory to Wallenstein. Baden-Durlach retreated to the small offshore island of Poel, east of Lübeck, but under pressure from Arnim he evacuated this refuge by sea, landing on the Holstein coast. Here he was confronted by Schlick's division, at which point his men hastily surrendered and joined the Imperial army, although he himself managed to get away to Denmark. Christian and his remaining forces had already withdrawn into Holstein, and with Wallenstein following they retired further northwards. The garrisons of individual fortresses resisted for a time but there was no major battle, and the retreat continued into Schleswig and the Jutland peninsula, part of Denmark itself. The main campaign took only six weeks, and by the end of October Schlick had advanced to the northern tip of the peninsula, thus leaving only the Danish islands (and Norway) in Christian's possession. The king himself, with the remnant of his army, was already in Funen, the island on which the city of Odense stands, safely out of Wallenstein's reach.

Wallenstein's success was total, but at the same time limited. Although defeated on land, Danish strength at sea meant that the Imperialists could advance no further, and hence Christian could neither be forced to make peace nor be prevented from rebuilding his army. Worse still, he would be able to land a force for a new campaign at any point on the Baltic coast from Jutland to Pomerania, just as Gustavus had appeared without warning in Prussia the previous year. There was little Wallenstein could do except watch and wait, guarding as much as possible of this extended coastline in readiness for whatever the campaigning season of 1628 might bring.

Wallenstein himself went home in the late autumn, and it was early summer 1628 before he took the field again. As before he maintained his control over the army throughout the winter, as well as making significant progress with the next stage of his private ambitions, a subject which will be discussed in the next chapter. He also turned his attention to the question of sea power in the Baltic, which would be essential if it proved necessary for him to pursue Christian on to his islands.[31] The Spanish also had a plan to develop trading links into the Baltic, hoping to undermine the profitability of the long-established Dutch business there as a form of economic warfare. The cities of the Hanseatic League were envisaged as partners in this enterprise, and a naval presence would be necessary to provide protection.

The idea was to establish a joint Spanish-Imperial fleet in the Baltic, but ships and a suitable port proved difficult to find, while for the Hanse the attractions of the prospective business opportunities were outweighed by the threat to their existing trade if they incurred Danish, Swedish and Dutch hostility. Even had the Spanish been able to transfer warships to the Baltic – which was doubtful because of Dutch naval superiority in the North Sea – they could not safely have passed through the Sound, as this narrow passage controlling the access was effectively closed by Danish guns. Wallenstein's thought of bypassing this obstacle by digging a canal was more than 250 years ahead of its time (the Kiel Canal opened in 1895), although work was actually started. The Hanse cities were unwilling to risk selling ships to Wallenstein, and although a few were eventually obtained from Poland this was not enough, so that his only alternative was to build first a shipyard and then the vessels. A base was set up at the Mecklenburg port of Wismar, but he soon realised that a navy could not be constructed in the short period in which he had built his army. The project lingered on for a couple of years, until the small fleet and its port were captured by the Swedes in 1631, but it never matched up to the impressive title of 'General of the Oceanic and Baltic Seas', which Wallenstein had acquired from the emperor in order to ensure that any navy actually established would be under his rather than Spanish control.[32]

As soon as Christian's forces had been driven back to Jutland Wallenstein began pressing the emperor to make peace, but in Vienna they were still insisting on punitive conditions which the Danes were certain to reject. He also floated the idea that if peace were made in the north his army could be released for a campaign against the Turks, a concept to which he returned a number of times over the next couple of years. In part this may have reflected the romantic attachment to the idea of a new crusade which lingered on in some European circles, while there is no doubt that Wallenstein would have preferred war elsewhere to continuing conflict in the Empire. He also believed that the Turkish occupation of the Balkans presented a long-term strategic threat to the Habsburg lands of Austria and Hungary, which indeed it did and continued to do for the rest of the century and beyond. 'I rate this task as highly', he wrote to Arnim, 'as anything else in the world.' Nevertheless his proposition cannot be taken at face value, as some historians have been inclined to do.[33] Wallenstein was prone to introducing into his prolific correspondence ideas which appealed to him conceptually, but this did not mean that he viewed them as current practical courses of action. It is also noteworthy that his subsequent returns to the subject were at times when he was trying to avoid some other military commitment of which he disapproved, notably sending troops to Italy in 1629–30. He had no wish to campaign in the Danish islands in 1628, and he may have hoped that the idea of a campaign against the Turks would appeal to the ultra-Catholic Ferdinand on religious as well as strategic grounds, thus inclining him more to a peace settlement with Denmark. Moreover Wallenstein continued to fear an attack on the Empire by Sweden, as he repeatedly stressed, and this in itself makes it unlikely that he was seriously contemplating the early despatch of his army to the most distant corner of Europe.

Other strange things went on during that winter and the spring of 1628. Wallenstein even had exploratory contacts with Gustavus to see if there was any basis for an accommodation between Sweden and the Empire. Arnim was probably the instigator and certainly the principal line of communication, but it is unlikely that either side had any serious intentions or expectations.[34] Elsewhere Maximilian of Bavaria was organising intrigue and espionage with contacts in Vienna and in Wallenstein's own circle, arising from which he received two further alarming memoranda about the general's character and intentions, from the same probable source but in even more lurid terms than that describing the Bruck conference.[35] With these he frightened both himself and his fellow Catholic League princes, but with Wallenstein's stock standing high after the successes of 1627 they could make little progress towards their objective of having him removed from his command and his army all but disbanded. Meanwhile a little local difficulty was gradually developing into one of those curious incidents, like the War of Jenkins' Ear or the Agadir Crisis, which achieve a fame both at the time and in subsequent histories which is out of all proportion to their actual significance.

Stralsund was not the largest or most important port on the Baltic coast, and nor, like Lübeck, was it a free city of the Empire. Instead it belonged to the duke of Pomerania, who had previously had difficulties enough with its faction-ridden council. Hence when Arnim reached agreement with the duke to place Imperialist garrisons in Pomerania's towns and cities late in 1627 it was perhaps not surprising that Stralsund was the one which objected most vociferously. More surprising was the city's decision to resist by barring the gates and looking to its defences. Arnim was willing to negotiate, and a payment of 100,000 taler for exemption from billeting was agreed, with a first instalment of 30,000 actually paid over. Nevertheless the city still refused a garrison and continued to build fortifications, recruit militia, and bring in weaponry, establishing itself in a warlike state which could only be regarded as a provocation. Arnim countered by landing troops on the tiny island of Dänholm, which straddles the entrance to Stralsund's harbour. The council responded first by mounting guns to threaten the island, and then by using their much superior shipping to blockade it, so that in April 1628 Arnim was forced to withdraw his men. Prestige was now involved, and in a further escalation Arnim besieged the city from the landward side and started to make threatening moves against its defences, hoping to frighten the citizens into adopting a more compliant attitude.[36]

Opinion in the city was divided, with the rich, who had most to lose, generally inclined to a settlement, while the radicals and have-nots favoured further resistance. Help from Denmark had initially been declined, but now their military supplies were accepted, while Gustavus sent a gift of munitions and an offer of further assistance. These moves were noted by Arnim's observers and informers, so in mid-May he increased the pressure on the city by means of gunfire and sallies against its fortifications. At Whitsun he proposed a truce, but the city council instead sought further help, and in early June 1000 troops commanded by Holk, who was now back in Danish service, were landed in the city from the sea, and 600 Swedes soon joined them. This converted what had begun as local recalcitrance, irritating to the authorities but by no means unheard of in this unruly age, into an act of war. It also deprived the city of control over its own destiny, as inviting foreign forces in was one thing, but persuading them to leave again would be quite another. Before his men landed Gustavus specified a formal twenty-year alliance, albeit one supposedly not directed against the Empire, but in the event Stralsund remained under Swedish control until 1815.[37]

Wallenstein had followed the reports of the developing confrontation, although in the main leaving it as a local problem for Arnim to deal with, but following the arrival of Danish and Swedish forces he headed for Stralsund himself, hoping by means of an even larger show of force coupled with an offer of clemency to achieve a settlement with the city. When no positive response was forthcoming on his arrival in early July he had little choice but to make good his threat of a full-scale attack, particularly as he had a considerable army tied down by this relatively insignificant city. Stralsund, however, was extremely well defended, being almost an island and even on the landward side protected by large stretches of water which hindered an assault. Bombardment and fighting continued for two full days and nights, with heavy casualties on both sides, leaving the Imperialists in possession of most of the defences but not yet inside the city. Another day would probably have finished it, but the council asked for talks and Wallenstein agreed, stopping the attacks although maintaining pressure with artillery fire, despite which the city's negotiators went back and forth to consult, dragging out the discussions over an extended period. Their prevarications were heavily influenced by the Danish and Swedish commanders, and when the Danes used the opportunity to bring in reinforcements Wallenstein realised that he was either going to have to give up or to renew the assault, this time carrying it through to the bitter end. He preferred to avoid that, so after making a face-saving agreement whereby the duke of Pomerania accepted responsibility for bringing his own city into line, he withdrew.

Many have questioned his motives for abandoning the siege, but there seems little reason to doubt his own statement, made in a letter to the emperor, that he wanted to avoid 'the inevitable bloodbath' which arose when a city was taken by storm, particularly when the attacking troops had themselves suffered heavy losses. As a soldier Wallenstein was accustomed to doing what was necessary in accordance with the standards of the times, but gratuitous bloodshed, terror tactics or reprisals were not a part of his approach. He also added that such an outcome would have been seen as 'a great act of tyranny', causing 'massive embitterment', exactly what happened two years later when Tilly took Magdeburg by storm in the most notorious event of the entire Thirty Years War.[38] Storming Stralsund, itself a Hanseatic city, would also have destroyed the good relations Wallenstein was trying to establish with the Hanseatic League, while Christian's fleet was offshore looking for somewhere to land his army, so that the city was becoming an increasingly unwelcome diversion from the main threat. The intention throughout had been to oblige Stralsund to submit, not to destroy it, and it is to Wallenstein's credit that he was prepared to accept a tactical set-back rather than sacrifice many more lives in order to gain an objective of little practical importance.

His enemies of course saw it differently, both in the anti-Habsburg camp and in Vienna and Munich. The Protestant side had had little enough cause for rejoicing over the past years, and now they made the most of this first defeat for the great Wallenstein, celebrating Stralsund's heroic resistance in a flood of mocking pamphlets. Their satisfaction did not last long. On 11 August Christian landed with some 7000 men on the offshore island of Usedom, little more than 30 miles south-east of the city. What exactly he hoped to achieve with this small force, even had they been able to join up with the Stralsund garrison, is far from clear, and in the event he achieved nothing apart from seizing the town of Wolgast, on the mainland opposite the island. Wallenstein and Arnim were soon there, and on 2 September 1628 they stormed the defences and comprehensively defeated the Danish force, although the king himself escaped again by sea.

Christian was still not ready to give up, but in the end the decision was effectively taken out of his hands. Peace negotiations had been under way in Lübeck for many months, but negotiations after the fashion of the times, whereby each side made wildly unrealistic demands, responded to proposals only after the maximum possible delay, and preferred to argue over protocol rather than substance, all the while hoping that some success of their commanders in the field might improve their negotiating positions. Manoeuvres of this kind in Westphalia lasted for five years before finally bringing the Thirty Years War to an end in 1648. In Lübeck the parties to this stately quadrille were theoretically Wallenstein, Tilly, Christian, and his Danish council, but in practice diplomats representing them. Wallenstein was well aware that the severe terms being sought by Vienna and Munich were unlikely to produce a settlement, as despite Wolgast Christian was as secure as before on his Danish islands, and moreover his allies were belatedly rallying round in an effort to keep him in the war.[39] The Danish council, on the other hand, particularly those members with lands in occupied Jutland, were tired of what they regarded as Christian's personal war in his capacity as duke of Holstein, rather than Denmark's affair. Hence Wallenstein used the lack of progress in Lübeck to press a more realistic approach on the emperor, and he initiated secret diplomacy in parallel to the formal negotiations.[40] In these private contacts an agreement was reached whereby Christian would keep his lands in exchange for a promise to take no further part in German affairs, together with the renunciation of his family's claims on the territories of various secularised north German bishoprics. This the Danish council successfully pressed upon Christian, despite his last-minute attempt to reactivate the war by launching a series of seaborne raids on the Holstein coast, while Wallenstein likewise persuaded the court at Vienna. Even so the peace was finally ratified only at the end of June 1629.

Wallenstein's military strategy had been fully justified. Rather than seeking out the enemy at the earliest opportunity in 1627 he had waited until his army was completely ready and the necessary advance positions had been established. Even then he had not rushed into a direct confrontation with Christian, instead methodically reducing stronghold after stronghold in Silesia until the smaller Danish army had been eliminated and most of the men enrolled in his own regiments. Only then had he turned on Christian, ensuring by joining up with Tilly that the king was boxed in by a vastly superior force, and leaving him no choice but to retreat to the safety of his islands. The events of 1628 had been mainly a mopping-up exercise, in which Wallenstein had again been able to concentrate his forces at the right place and time to overwhelm the Danish king at Wolgast. There had been fighting enough in the campaign, but the war had been won by superior strategy rather than being hazarded on the fortunes of the battlefield.

The peace was as much Wallenstein's achievement as the victory. In a manner which was to become familiar in the following years he had seen each military success as an opportunity for negotiations, which he had repeatedly urged on the emperor. He knew only too well that the resources of the anti-Habsburg powers greatly exceeded those of the Imperialists, as he wrote in 1626: 'The emperor does not have the means to wage war, and without money this is something which cannot long be sustained.' Later in that year, with the military position bolstered by the victories at the Dessau bridge and at Lutter, he wrote to Ferdinand: 'With the advantage and the renown, you now have the best opportunity to negotiate a peace', adding that no reliance could be placed on that situation continuing. In late 1627, with Christian effectively defeated, he renewed the appeal: 'The great strength which Your Majesty has will enable a good and lasting peace to be made in the Empire, which I respectfully advise.' Although Wallenstein himself briefly considered imposing punitive terms on Christian he soon recognised that these were unrealistic, and that no quick or enduring peace settlement would be reached on that basis. While Vienna persisted with a hard line at the formal negotiations in Lübeck, and made no progress, he looked for an alternative. His more generous and flexible approach through the Danish council undermined Christian's domestic political position, and hence Wallenstein reached an agreement which not only took Denmark out of the war but removed any further threat from that quarter for the foreseeable future. Nevertheless it was not entirely popular with his critics at court.[41]

8
At the Parting of the Ways
(Ezekiel)

Mecklenburg was one of the great hereditary duchies of the Empire, significantly exceeded in size only by the electorates of Bavaria, Brandenburg and Saxony. Its dukes could trace family ownership back eight centuries or more, but the joint incumbents had been rash enough to side openly with Christian of Denmark, and – unlike others in the Lower Saxon Circle – imprudent enough to delay an ostentatious show of renewed loyalty to the emperor until after it became clear that Christian was going to be the loser. With victory in sight Ferdinand moved to place them under the ban of the Empire and to begin the process of expropriation. As a first step he granted a lien on their territories to Wallenstein, who took possession in April 1628, while in the same month he also extended the general's authority to all Imperial forces, promoting him to the unheard-of rank of *General-Oberster Feldhauptmann*, usually abbreviated to generalissimo.[1]

Mecklenburg was the private business which had been Wallenstein's main concern after the 1627 campaign. He was already a duke, as Friedland was indeed a duchy, but a very recent and much smaller one. Mecklenburg had history and class. Moreover its duke stood directly beneath the emperor, whereas in Friedland the king of Bohemia came in between, and although Ferdinand occupied both offices this was nevertheless an important difference, affecting both the status and the legal scope for independent action of the ruler. Wallenstein behaved from the beginning as though he were outright owner – and with good reason as there was a private agreement behind the public arrangement – but he had to wait until June 1629 for the last step in his elevation, the formal document from the emperor which confirmed him in full and hereditary possession.[2] Only then was he able to style himself Albrecht,

Duke of Mecklenburg, and to proudly initial his future correspondence 'AHzM' (Albrecht, Herzog zu Mecklenburg).

The expropriation of Mecklenburg's dukes was controversial at the time and has remained so in histories, with Wallenstein often cast as the villain of the piece. It needs, however, to be put into context. Ferdinand never had enough cash to pay for the crippling costs of the war, and so he turned to property, first his own and then that confiscated from others, which he used initially as security and later as outright payment for his debts. Of his own lands, Lusatia went to the elector of Saxony, first as a pledge and then in perpetuity, and Upper Austria was pledged for some years to Maximilian of Bavaria. The estates of the Bohemian rebels and anyone even loosely associated with them were confiscated and sold for cash, with Wallenstein the largest but far from the only purchaser. Frederick, the 'winter king', was deprived first of the Upper Palatinate, then of his electoral title and his heartlands on the Rhine, which were used mainly to satisfy further debts to Maximilian. The emperor, not Wallenstein, was the originator of these measures, which in the case of Frederick were of disputed legality in respect of the confiscations and almost certainly beyond his powers regarding the transfer of the title, while although a front of judicial procedure was established in Bohemia the basis of the unprecedented seizures was more despotic than legal.[3] Ferdinand was prepared from an early stage to manipulate the strict forms of Imperial legality in order to override property rights, and Mecklenburg fits into that pattern.

Hence it is not surprising that with the emperor's debts mounting ideas of expropriation emerged almost as soon as the first signs of success in the field in 1626. The initial targets were members of the lower aristocracy who had taken military service with Christian of Denmark, but due to the inadequacies of the bureaucracy in distant Vienna progress was slow.[4] Nevertheless ambitions escalated, and the possibility of confiscating the duchy of Brunswick was considered following the death of the 'mad Halberstädter' in June of that year. At the time Wallenstein warned that such a provocative action would lead to prolonged war, an objection which has been viewed as hypocritical in the light of his later acquisition of Mecklenburg.[5] This overlooks the fundamental difference in the military situation. In mid-1626 Christian of Denmark, Bethlen Gabor and Mansfeld were all still powerful enemies, and the emperor could not afford to make any more; by late 1627 they were defeated, departed or dead, and thoughts of plucking the fruits of victory to pay for the war were more realistic.

Eyes then turned to Christian's own lands, with aspirations increasing parallel to the military advance of 1627, first envisaging the confiscation of his German duchy of Holstein, then adding the captured Danish territories in Jutland, and finally seizing upon reports that the Danish council were contemplating depriving him of the crown itself.[6] In a letter of January 1628 Wallenstein confided to Arnim that people at court, including the emperor, had offered him the opportunity to seek the Danish throne, 'but I declined with thanks, as I would not be able to maintain it'. He wondered whether the Danes might instead be persuaded to choose the emperor as their king, while for his own part he preferred to proceed with 'the other', that is Mecklenburg, as it was more secure.[7]

Money was desperately needed for the army, both to meet immediate needs and to pay off some of the accumulated debts, which in turn was essential in order to obtain further loans, so that Wallenstein was constantly pressing the court for action to improve funding. One result was a more determined effort to enforce confiscations. In the latter part of 1627 commissioners with sweeping powers were appointed for the purpose in Lower Saxony and Westphalia, while the court itself moved against Mecklenburg. In June of that year Tilly had protested to Vienna about the hostile activities of the dukes, demanding that they be given an official Imperial warning and an order to desist. Ferdinand's advisers then concluded that the dukes were 'notorious rebels', which in their view justified the emperor in acting against them without formal legal proceedings.[8] In September Imperialist forces took Mecklenburg as they advanced towards Denmark, so that confiscation became a real and immediate possibility. That left the problem of whether a buyer or buyers able to finance so large a purchase could be found, a problem which both then and later hampered the progress of smaller confiscations in north Germany. Wallenstein resolved this difficulty by proposing to take Mecklenburg himself.

The first report of his interest is in a letter from late October 1627, but this also indicates that the subject had been raised before. So too had the duchy of Sagan, a minor principality in Silesia belonging to the emperor, which had been offered to Wallenstein.[9] About this he hesitated, changed his mind, and finally accepted, but Mecklenburg he wanted, and he was prepared if necessary to buy only a part although he preferred to have it all, with the price to be offset against the emperor's debts to him. Such a transfer was highly contentious politically, with some of the Imperial councillors arguing that the hereditary dukes of Mecklenburg could not be treated in the same way as minor noblemen, and warning of widespread opposition in the Empire.[10] These reservations were accentuated by the thought that the beneficiary was to be the Bohemian upstart Wallenstein rather than, as had been the case with Frederick of the Palatinate, the ancient and prestigious line of the duke of Bavaria, but when all was said and done financial realities prevailed, so the general acquired the duchy.

Why did Wallenstein want Mecklenburg? The most pressing reason was his need of money. Trying to drum up cash, whether from contributions or elsewhere, was a permanent struggle as he juggled with expenditure priorities, loans and repayments. In part this was his own fault, as he was spending increasingly extravagantly on his large retinue and ambitious building plans at Friedland, but personal expenditure was very much secondary to the burden of funding a vast army with little help from the Imperial exchequer. The emperor had no cash with which to pay his debts, so if Wallenstein was to get anything at all, property it had to be. Mecklenburg would at least bring in a future income, and whereas the emperor's promissory notes were by now almost worthless as collateral the lands of the duchy might be used to raise further loans. To this pressing current need we can probably add a hard-headed assessment by Wallenstein that if he was ever to secure settlement from Ferdinand he had to take what was available, and while it was available. Should the war end, repayment might well be indefinitely deferred.

Security was a likely second consideration for the perennially insecure Wallenstein. Additional and geographically separate lands reduced the chances of losing them all in some future reversal of military or political fortune. Military security was also relevant, as the safety of the Empire was also Wallenstein's own security in possession of his estates. Mecklenburg in his hands would not offer Gustavus Adolphus the support its dukes had given to Christian of Denmark, and its ports would be closed to him, whereas they would become available for the Habsburg Baltic navy Wallenstein was trying to establish. This was also a consideration for Ferdinand, who had no friends among the Protestant princes of north Germany, so that substituting the loyal Wallenstein for the hostile dukes of Mecklenburg had the same attraction as his policy of replacing Bohemian rebels with a new nobility of his own creation.

Putting ambition for personal aggrandisement in third place may not conform to the traditional interpretation, but although Wallenstein doubtless had such aspirations he was first and foremost a practical man. Money and security were necessary before ambitions could be achieved and enjoyed, but the weight he attached to the title and status of Mecklenburg should nevertheless not be underestimated. Certainly he played the part once in full possession, employing the relevant titles and forms of address, living in the appropriate style, issuing coinage bearing his own head and motto, and generally behaving in the way expected of a ruling prince.

That point is worth noting. Such behaviour was indeed expected and was the norm for the times. In an age when sumptuary laws carefully graded the apparel of the citizenry even of minor towns Wallenstein would have seemed decidedly odd had he not acted like a great lord. Historians have frequently drawn attention to the grand manner in which he lived and travelled, quoting contemporary descriptions to support an implicitly critical stance. This, however, is a modern attitude, as the seventeenth century was more inclined to admire than to censure ostentation. In 1600 Maximilian of Bavaria took 1200 horsemen with him to escort his sister to her wedding to Ferdinand, who was then only a junior scion of the House of Habsburg, and by the time they arrived the cavalcade had grown to 3000.[11] In Wallenstein's case his retinue was often also the travelling headquarters of Europe's largest army. Any contemporary disapproval is likely to have been directed not so much at the display itself as at the fact that a minor Bohemian nobleman had risen so far as to warrant it, an exaltation which many regarded as running against the natural order of things. This is perhaps also a clue to Wallenstein's attitude, that of the parvenu ever sensitive to real or imagined slights and seeking to compensate by climbing still higher up the social scale. Mecklenburg may have been welcome to him from that point of view, although it inevitably also fed the hostility of his enemies, but Wallenstein was never the man to be deterred by that.

In the autumn of 1627 there was one other reason why Mecklenburg may have seemed particularly well suited to Wallenstein's ambitions. His wife was pregnant and he was hoping for a son to add to their daughter Maria Elizabeth. A male heir was central to the aspirations of a man of wealth, lands and titles, giving a sense of enduring purpose to the accumulation of all three. A boy, Albrecht Carl, was indeed born at Gitschin on 22 November 1627, to the great joy of the family, but the baby was premature and lived less than two months. Worse still, it was evident that Duchess Isabella could have no more children, so that the prospect of an heir was both fulfilled and dashed within a few short weeks. Such personal tragedies were by no means uncommon, although no less bitter for that, but life had to go on. Wallenstein returned to work, resigned himself to the situation, and in due course appointed his cousin and brother-in-law Max as his heir.[12]

The Edict of Restitution

After defeating Christian of Denmark at Wolgast in September 1628 it might have been expected that Wallenstein and his vast Imperial army, said to number 150,000 men, would have had little to do, and indeed there were voices enough in the Empire loudly expressing this opinion and calling for drastic reductions in the number of troops. Emperor Ferdinand was deaf to them, as he had plans of his own in Germany for which the army would be needed, while his Spanish cousins were busily embroiling him in their problems in Holland and Italy. Wallenstein was convinced that the principal danger was Swedish intervention, so he stepped up his help to Poland in order to keep Gustavus tied down there. Hence 1629 was to be a busy and eventful year.

The emperor had already shown that his response to military success was to exploit it to the full rather than to seek reconciliation. In Bohemia the political side of this had been the wave of expropriations which provided him both with money and with a purged and renewed aristocracy upon which he could depend. For Ferdinand, however, religion was more important than politics, and he had used this position of strength to drive through a wholesale recatholicisation reminiscent of his early days in Styria, and with the same consequence of large-scale emigration as ordinary people were forced to choose between their Protestant religion and their homeland.

Success in the Danish war provided an opportunity to implement another measure which had long been an objective for the Catholic church in the Empire, and which the three ecclesiastical electors, supported by Maximilian of Bavaria, pressed upon Ferdinand. This was the recovery of church lands which had been secularised and transferred into Protestant ownership over the past three-quarters of a century, specifically since 1552, the base date agreed at the peace of Augsburg of 1555, which had established an uneasy *modus vivendi* between Catholic and Protestant territories in the Empire following the Reformation. Secularisations had nevertheless continued, affecting some 500 monasteries, convents and other foundations, as well as a dozen entire bishoprics. This involved extensive areas of land and their populations, together with commensurately large revenues, much of which passed into the hands of Protestant rulers, particularly in north and central Germany. Technically illegal though these secularisations may have been, most had occurred long enough ago to seem hallowed by time. Some of the properties had been sold or had been passed on through inheritance, perhaps several times, while the monks, nuns and clergy in possession at the time of original transfer were long gone, many having themselves turned Protestant and left their orders. Lawsuits had been brought seeking return of individual properties to the church, but this piecemeal approach had achieved little, so the prelates looked to the emperor for more sweeping measures.

Ferdinand was far from unwilling. As early as autumn 1627 he had informed the Catholic hierarchy that he considered the opportunity of recovering church lands to be the principal benefit gained from success in the war, and that he saw it as his responsibility to pursue all possibilities to their limits.[13] Practical action nevertheless had to wait until the final defeat of Christian of Denmark, but with that accomplished a draft of the proposed measure was produced in the autumn of 1628. Consultations within the Catholic camp followed, but Ferdinand dismissed any reservations, including the contention that the matter ought to be considered by an Imperial Diet, and in March 1629 he went ahead, promulgating his Edict of Restitution entirely on his own authority as emperor.[14] Whether he had any such authority is extremely questionable, even though he disingenuously claimed that he was doing no more than setting out to enforce existing law. Despite this, two points certainly went beyond the Augsburg settlement of 1555, and hence beyond existing law. Firstly the right of secular princes to determine and enforce the religion of their subjects was extended to ecclesiastical princes – all of course Catholics – from whom it had been specifically withheld at Augsburg. Secondly the edict was applied in many Imperial free cities, which had been guaranteed freedom of religion at that time. Moreover the official date of 1552 was by no means scrupulously observed in practice, with many longer-standing secularisations unceremoniously clawed back at the same time. With these resumptions, a measure which affected only the wealthy, went compulsory recatholicisation of whole populations, the closure of Protestant churches, and the expulsion of those who would not conform, reportedly 8000 from Augsburg alone. Added to that, the rights which were allowed to Protestants were limited to Lutherans, thereby excluding Calvinists and others, a restriction which had been in the Augsburg settlement but which had lapsed in practice since.[15]

The resulting uproar in the Empire showed only too clearly why Ferdinand still needed the army. Imperial commissioners seeking to enforce restitutions often met resistance, and on many occasions troops were used to support them, although mainly from Tilly's League army. Wallenstein largely prevented the employment of his men for this purpose, at least in the earlier stages, but the mere existence of his army, stationed as it was mainly across the Protestant north of Germany, had great coercive force, as well as preventing any serious thoughts of an organised rebellion. For the time being Ferdinand and his fellow zealots carried the day, regardless of the bitter hostility they were arousing and oblivious to what it was to cost them when Gustavus Adolphus finally invaded. Nor was the opposition confined to Protestants. Many of the lay Catholic nobility were more inclined towards class solidarity with fellow men of property, albeit of a different religion, than to aligning themselves with the vindictive acquisitiveness of their own higher clergy, and those appointed as commissioners often found excuses or simply neglected to carry out their tasks.[16]

Wallenstein made no secret of his disapproval, repeatedly commenting sharply on the edict and its consequences. In June 1629 he complained that mobs were creating disturbances and attacking property south of Hanover, noting that 'the edict causes it'. In September representatives of the Hanse cities met Wallenstein at Halberstadt and reported him as saying that 'the edict cannot be sustained. ... One cannot simply scrap the religious peace [of Augsburg].' In October he informed Collalto, the president of the Imperial war council, that he saw no possibility of dissuading the Hanse from supporting the Swedes and the Dutch, all because of 'the untimely and drastic reformation [recatholicisation], and the emperor's Edict of Restitution of church property and proscription of the Calvinists'. In November the elector of Saxony's envoy reported from Halberstadt that Wallenstein's chancellor had told him of the general's 'strong disapproval' of the edict and that he had no intention of allowing himself to be used to enforce it. In the same month Wallenstein wrote to Collalto that 'the emperor's edict has turned all the non-Catholics against us', a point which he repeated in February 1630, adding that 'their embitterment is so great that they are all saying that if only the Swede [Gustavus] would come they would gladly die with him, even if he cannot help them'. In April he complained of wishful thinking at the court, where 'they believe the situation to be what they would like it to be, and think about recatholicisation and not about recruitment'.[17] In a nutshell, Wallenstein saw what Ferdinand and his party could not or would not see, namely the folly of giving hostages to fortune by creating new internal enemies on a large scale at a time when there were still more than sufficient external enemies to be faced. Unfortunately for the Empire and its people the emperor paid more attention to his confessor than to his general. Not, it may be added, that Ferdinand was entirely unworldly in his approach. A planned side benefit of the edict was the restitution to the church of the wealthy archbishopric of Magdeburg, where the new prince-bishop was to be none other than Ferdinand's own twelve-year-old son Leopold.[18]

An Italian entanglement

The Danish peace was formally concluded in July 1629, but how far from peaceful things were is revealed by Wallenstein's own figures. He had, he told Collalto, sent 15,000 men into Poland and 17,000 to the Netherlands, at least 12,000 were needed to guard against hostile moves in Brandenburg and Pomerania, while 6000 were tied down around Magdeburg, which was proving as recalcitrant as Stralsund had been the previous year. The wider Empire required a large number of garrison troops, and men were also needed in other places, while the possibility of a further attack by Bethlen Gabor had always to be kept in mind. He was already short of troops, and now he was being asked for 14,000 men for a proposed campaign in Italy.[19]

The details of the war which developed there need not concern us, but the outline is as follows. In December 1627 the duke of Mantua died, leaving his possessions to his distant but nevertheless closest relative, the French duke of Nevers. His two separate territories, Mantua and Montferrat, both adjoined the Spanish duchy of Milan, and these, together with Savoy and Venice, were the only parts of north Italy not under Habsburg control. There had been wars over the succession a decade earlier, in which Savoy, with French support, had opposed Spain, so that a pro-French duke in Mantua was now highly unwelcome to the Spanish. An alternative claimant was found, and with the emperor's help archaic Imperial procedures were invoked to declare Nevers in breach of the law, as he had taken possession of his duchy, both parts of which were Imperial fiefs, before the succession had been formally established. He was ordered to quit the territories at once, which he did not, so that a facade of legitimacy was provided for military enforcement.

The Spanish had already sent forces from Milan to seize Casale, a powerful fortress in Montferrat, but instead of the expected quick victory a protracted siege followed, lasting throughout 1628. In October the French Huguenot stronghold of La Rochelle fell, ending a fourteen-month siege, so that after a long period of internal troubles France was able to turn to international affairs again. In February 1629, despite the winter snows, a French army marched over the Alps and relieved Casale. The Spanish renewed their attack on the fortress in the summer, at the same time appealing to the emperor for help in return for the assistance that they had given him against the Bohemian rebels. Ferdinand agreed, and in the late summer a large Imperial army moved into Italy, led first by Collalto and later by his deputies, Count Matthias Gallas and Aldringer, but it was not until July 1630 that they finally took Mantua and expelled Nevers from his duchy. Less than a year later he got it back – or what was left of it after the armies had fought and looted across it – as with Spain and the Empire under pressure from events elsewhere peace had to be made in Italy.

Wallenstein had been against the war from the outset, both in principle and on strategic grounds. As early as March 1628 the bishop of Mantua, sent by Nevers on a diplomatic mission to the Imperial court, reported back what he had heard from no less a person than the emperor's chancellor, Count Verda Werdenberg; Wallenstein had told the council and the Spanish ambassador that 'if they wanted to wage a war against Mantua and the duke of Nevers they should not let the thought enter their heads that they would get a single soldier from him, even if the emperor himself gave the order. It would be an unjust war, as all the laws of the world supported Nevers.' Wallenstein benefited from lands taken from others, both in Mecklenburg and Bohemia, but the dispossessed were undeniably rebels however dubious and vindictive the emperor's proceedings may have been. Nevers was not a rebel, and the legal grounds invoked for action against him provided scarcely a fig-leaf to cover the expropriation of his property for nakedly political reasons. Wallenstein also feared – quite correctly – that a Spanish attack would bring a French response, and that Imperial support for Spain would renew French hostility to the Empire, adding a threat in the south and west at a time when there were threats enough in the north and east. As the situation developed he found a series of reasons for delaying sending troops to Italy, at some times citing the need for men in other theatres of war, at others referring to the possibility of a war against the Turks, and at yet others claiming to be preparing to lead an army to Italy in person. Throughout he advised against the campaign, but he could not evade Imperial orders indefinitely. When troops were eventually despatched he wrote to Ferdinand begging him to ensure that the artillery and supplies promised by the Spanish were forthcoming, as otherwise 'the army will quickly be ruined, as a result of which Your Majesty would lose more than you have won in all these wars, and the damage would be irreparable'.[20]

Although Wallenstein retained overall command of the Italian campaign he limited himself to the strategic disposition of forces, remaining in Germany and focusing his main attention on the problems in the north, while delegating operational control in Italy to Collalto and his deputies. His view of the situation remained gloomy, as 'all the enemies of the House of Austria have made peace among themselves and united to defend Nevers.' He blamed Spain: 'If the Spanish had not attacked Nevers then France would not have become involved, and nor would the Venetians', adding that in addition to hostility from Protestants because of the Edict of Restitution the war in Italy was turning even Catholics against the Habsburg side. In February 1630 he pleaded that 'if it can actually be composed let no-one refrain from doing so, as both Majesties [the emperor and the king of Spain] would gain far more by turning the armies against the Dutch'. In April he declared that he could not send any more men to Italy and told Collalto that he should try to recruit locally there instead: 'I cannot undertake any more recruitment in the Empire, as I get reprimands from the court by the hour on that account, while all the electors and princes are opposed to it. The most important thing is that peace is made in Italy.'[21]

The Mantuan war also diverted resources from the Netherlands, as Wallenstein pointed out. Here his attitude fluctuated, sometimes favouring attempts to negotiate a new truce and at others looking to increase military support to enable Spain to keep the Dutch on the defensive, hence limiting their ability to provide assistance to other enemies of the Empire. Both were attempted. Once Christian of Denmark was in full retreat Wallenstein transferred a number of regiments to the Netherlands, while soon afterwards Spain began to explore the idea of a truce. Had they achieved a quick success at Casale this might have been more feasible, but as the siege dragged on the Dutch realised that their best opportunities lay in the field rather than at the negotiating table. Also in 1628, the Dutch navy captured the entire Spanish treasure fleet bringing silver from America, both depriving Spain of the vital bullion and making it available to finance Dutch military advances in 1629. Early in that year they besieged the major city of Hertogenbosch in the Spanish Netherlands, and although in response Spanish and Imperialist forces invaded United Provinces territory the Dutch had the best of the campaign. The Habsburg armies were forced to retreat, and the Dutch not only took Hertogenbosch but also moved into north-west Germany, where over the winter of 1629–30 they drove Spanish garrisons out of many key places.

Wallenstein's own priority in this period continued to be the threat of Swedish intervention. This was a danger about which he had repeatedly warned, but which had not so far materialised other than on the margin at Stralsund, perhaps one reason why it was dangerously underestimated in Vienna. Wallenstein's efforts to keep Gustavus Adolphus bogged down in his Polish campaign had helped to contain him, but by 1629 the Poles required further help, so he despatched Arnim with an army.[22] The joint campaign went surprisingly well, although not without constant friction which eventually drove the frustrated Arnim to resign, claiming ill health. Wallenstein had reluctantly to let him go, but not before the combined forces had inflicted a heavy defeat on the Swedes at Honigfelde in late June, a defeat in which Gustavus himself had a narrow escape, one of a number in his adventurous career.

One other significant effect of the war in Italy was to direct French diplomacy to creating problems for their Habsburg opponents wherever possible, which they did nowhere more successfully than in Poland. After Honigfelde the Swedes retreated to the fortress of Marienburg, but the Poles too were at the limit of their resources, so that both sides were glad of an opportunity to extricate themselves. French mediation was instrumental in brokering an extended truce, and although Gustavus had to make significant concessions of conquered territories he kept important parts of his gains, as well as securing valuable rights to tolls on shipping to Polish and Prussian ports for the duration of the truce. This was to last six years, from September 1629 to 1635, and this is what freed him to turn his attention to Germany, while the tolls were to prove an important source of finance for his forthcoming invasion.

The limits of power

In 1629 Wallenstein's standing was at its peak, and many thought him the most powerful man in the Empire. Not only did he command the largest army the times had yet seen, with unprecedented authority over all Imperialist forces wherever they might be, but he also had the prerogatives previously reserved to the emperor of commissioning colonels and authorising new recruitment. Only for appointments of officers at the highest levels of command did he need Imperial approval. His personal status too, as hereditary duke of Mecklenburg, Friedland and Sagan, was second only to the six electors, while the size and value of his combined territories placed him amongst the greatest princes of the Empire. Diplomats, echoing wider gossip, hinted that the emperor himself took good care not to offend his general, and even that he would like to dismiss him but was afraid to do so.

Certainly Wallenstein was a powerful man. In his own three duchies he had the powers of a ruling prince, on a par with others in the Empire, who if not as absolute as they became a century later nevertheless had few constraints on their authority within their own realms. In the army too his word was law. Regiments moved on his command, and only on his command, officers were appointed, promoted, cashiered and on occasions executed, campaigns were begun and ended, quarters taken up or left, supplies and equipment purchased, contributions demanded and extracted, cities besieged or left in peace, all on the strength of his orders. Small wonder that ordinary people and even other princes were inclined to see him as omnipotent, and to attribute all that happened, good and bad – but especially the bad – to his favour or malevolence.

Nevertheless there were constraints, even in the army. Discipline is a case in point. Wallenstein, like Gustavus Adolphus, sought to maintain good order, and in particular to protect the peasantry and townsmen from the worst excesses of the soldiery, whose collective inclination towards theft, rape and violence was notorious. Both generals issued streams of ever sterner orders prohibiting such behaviour, and both had frequent exemplary punishments and executions of offenders carried out. Partly this was because both saw that war brought enough suffering with it, unavoidably in their view, without it being unnecessarily increased by licentious troops. Partly it may have been the natural antipathy of professional military officers to disorder in the ranks. Certainly both generals recognised that their armies had to live off the country and the local economy, and that this would not long be possible if their soldiers stole the seed corn, the draught animals and the breeding livestock, drove the peasantry from the land and disrupted the business of the towns. Nevertheless all these things happened frequently and on a large scale, as numerous eyewitness accounts testify, and if the horrors may often have been embroidered in the telling the reality was certainly terrible enough.[23] The mechanisms and resources of military discipline were simply insufficient to exercise effective control over a rootless and footloose soldiery, largely divorced from the civilising influences of society, and who were often unpaid, hungry, and with hungry dependents to provide for. Most of their officers were little better, at best adventurers and at worst out-and-out scoundrels, more interested in what they themselves could steal than in preventing theft by their men. The further from headquarters the less effective were the generals' orders in this respect, but despite their own endeavours they inevitably bore much of the odium.

Although it may seem an obvious point it is worth mentioning that in time of war the freedom of action of the supreme commander is also limited by the enemy. In particular the movement and stationing of army units has to anticipate or respond to the threats or opportunities presented by the tactics of the opposing forces. Any general who fails to do this adequately not only hazards the lives of his own men but also risks the security of the ruler or state he serves. To the ordinary people, however, and even to many of their princes, who had little information concerning the wider military situation and even less knowledge of strategy and logistics, the movements of the troops were inscrutable but their presence was always unwelcome. Even the better-disciplined units caused damage and consumed all the food, drink and fodder they could lay hands on, so that the passage of a regiment was frequently likened to that of a swarm of locusts. And the longer they stayed in one place the worse it became.

At the time Germany was divided into a large number of individual territories, ranging from the major to the very minor, and at any given moment most were desperately seeking to avoid involvement in the war. Military necessity and geography often combined to prevent the generals from respecting the supposed neutrality of any but the most substantial principalities, and not always even them, but those affected were inclined to suspect political or financial motives, or to ascribe troop visitations to the punitive intent or simple ill-will of the commander. Sometimes there was an element of truth in this, as there may have been more than one route a march could take or more than one place in which a unit could be based, allowing other circumstances to influence the choice, but more usually strategic considerations, supplies and practicality were the decisive factors. Of necessity protests and pleas commonly fell on deaf ears, but again the commanders, and the supreme commander in particular, were held to blame.

If the passage of troops was unwelcome, billeting them was doubly so, and providing winter quarters was worst of all. This was a relatively recent innovation other than on a small scale, as until around the turn of the seventeenth century it had been normal practice to disband armies at the end of the campaigning season and to re-recruit if necessary in the spring. Winter quartering meant the presence of large numbers of soldiers, their families and other dependents in billets for three months or more, and sometimes significantly longer. Although these unwelcome and usually non-paying guests were as widely dispersed as possible, thus spreading the burden for the local population, the economic effect on the territory as a whole was severe. Inevitably the choice of location for winter quarters became highly political. The ideal solution from a general's point of view was to pass the season in enemy country, but in practice this was only occasionally achievable. Where neutral or friendly territory had to be used protests, pleas, complaints and criticism invariably followed, along with allegations of mismanagement or malice on the part of the commander. Princes and landowners led the outcry, horrified by the loss of revenues from their estates which winter quartering would cause, and they bombarded the Imperial court with their grievances over Wallenstein's choices of location. Again, however, military considerations usually left little real choice. Armies had to winter close to where the end of campaigning had left them, as marching them off somewhere else was rarely feasible. The hardships of a long march cost many lives at the best of times, and the later in the year the greater the death toll, with provisions and shelter from the cold hard to find *en route*, while wounds and illnesses were even more frequently fatal than in the summer.

Money was always a constraint, but as lack of funds from the Imperial treasury meant relying on enforced contributions from the populace the burden and limitations imposed on Wallenstein were greatly increased. The sums required were too large to be raised by the initiatives of local commanders, so that a systematic approach and an organisation to match were necessary. That in itself consumed resources, as some form of coercion was almost always required. A company of soldiers and the threat of more was often enough to persuade the local mayor and council to cooperate in collecting cash in defenceless country areas, but even so the number of men who had to be allocated to these duties quickly multiplied as large areas were brought under contribution. The wealthier towns and cities could pay more but were less easily intimidated, often requiring protracted negotiations and a significant military presence to ensure that any agreement was subsequently honoured. Not infrequently cities with walls simply closed their gates, leaving the responsible commander the choice of undertaking costly and time-consuming countermeasures or of moving elsewhere in search of an easier target. Occasionally the situation escalated into a crisis, as at Stralsund and Magdeburg, not only involving a major commitment of troops but requiring Wallenstein's personal intervention. As a matter of routine he had to deal with a stream of complainants and petitioners from places where contributions were being levied, as well as parallel pleadings passed on from and endorsed by the Imperial court. The need for money left little scope for favourable replies, at best a slightly reduced assessment as part of the negotiation, but usually the answer had to be no. Wallenstein's characteristic response implicitly recognised this reality, not a deterministic 'no' but a fatalistic *'es kann nicht sein'* – it cannot be.

The ultimate constraint on Wallenstein's freedom of action was political, as for all his supposed power he had surprisingly little influence on Imperial policy. As long as it was a matter of confronting opponents with strong armies who had invaded the Empire this made little difference, as the policy was necessarily survival and survival was essentially an operational matter for the commanding general. It was in this phase of the war that the impression of Wallenstein as all-powerful developed, but the image lingered on long after the defeat of Christian of Denmark had changed the situation, following which the realities gradually reasserted themselves.

The image had also been fostered by the considerable latitude available to a general at this time, particularly one with as wide a command as Wallenstein. Even in the modern era politicians have had perforce to leave much of the conduct of hostilities to the generals, and this was much more the case when a despatch from the front in northern Germany could easily take a week to a fortnight to reach the court in Prague or Vienna, with a reply taking at least as long. Naturally the commanders, Wallenstein included, exploited this, sending back regretful notes pointing out that the situation had changed, the operational realities were not fully appreciated at court, the number of men available was insufficient for the proposed action, and a dozen other variants of a politely dressed-up refusal. Sometimes the court attempted to redress this balance by sending their own envoy, even an Imperial councillor, to assess the situation on the spot. These gentlemen, though, travelled at a more leisurely pace than military despatch riders, so that there was even more scope for the situation to have changed, and not infrequently they ended up as advocates for the general and his strategy back at court rather than vice versa. Hence Wallenstein enjoyed a high level of operational autonomy, particularly while he was still seen as being the proprietor of the army he had financed and recruited, and which he was sustaining largely independently of Imperial funds.

Nevertheless he was not an Imperial councillor, still less the emperor's principal adviser, and indeed his personal audiences with Ferdinand were increasingly rare after he ceased visiting Vienna, although they did occur from time to time in Prague. He kept his own representative at court, but in the main his communication with the emperor was in writing and principally concerned with military matters. Wallenstein was simply not consulted during the preparation of the Edict of Restitution,[24] nor in any meaningful way about the developing entanglement in Italy over Mantua. Hence he was no more than a disapproving voice on the periphery of the most important events of 1629, and moreover his disapproval was ignored. If this illustrates his lack of political power, it also shows the limits of his power in the military field. In both cases he started with the clear intention of keeping himself and his army out of the resulting operations, but in both cases he was eventually forced to give way. In assessing this reality the elaborate style of the correspondence of the day can be very misleading. The emperor's letters to his general were often exquisitely polite, omitting none of the courtesies of title and form due to one who was not only commander-in-chief but also among the foremost princes of the Empire in his own right. Even so these were orders, not of the kind requiring instant and unquestioning execution, but also not of the kind which, when repeated and persisted with, could be indefinitely evaded or ignored. Wallenstein recognised this situation in a letter of August 1629: 'I have received four different strict orders from the emperor to lose no time in despatching troops to Italy, and even though I do not think it advisable I have obediently complied, because His Majesty has commanded it.'[25] Ultimately Wallenstein was a soldier, and ultimately he had to obey the emperor's orders.

By the middle of 1630 it was becoming increasingly obvious to Wallenstein that he was no longer directing the strategy underlying the operations of the army he commanded. Meanwhile the voices of his enemies were becoming louder and more influential, gaining strength from the widespread hostility created by troop movements, licentious soldiery, billeting, contributions, and all the other evils stemming from the war which were increasingly laid at Wallenstein's door, as though he personally were their source. For a time this had been useful to the emperor, acting as a lightning conductor in diverting attention from their real root causes, but as pressure mounted so did the possible advantages of sacrificing the scapegoat. Wallenstein's own successes meant that he no longer seemed militarily indispensable, and when his most influential opponents, the Catholic electors, attacked him by pressing Ferdinand at his weakest spot, the position of the supposedly all-powerful general suddenly looked very vulnerable. Wallenstein had a good intelligence system and he could probably read the writing on the wall. When in mid-1630 he moved his personal headquarters south to Memmingen, officially to be nearer to the operations in Italy, he may already have had a suspicion that he might leave the town still a prince but no longer the emperor's generalissimo.

9
The Wheel Is Come Full Circle
(*King Lear*)

Dismissal

Maximilian of Bavaria and his fellow Catholic electors had worked and waited a long time for the chance to secure Wallenstein's dismissal. In 1624 Maximilian had urged the emperor to raise troops to counter the threat from the anti-Habsburg coalition, but he had envisaged these being attached to Tilly's Catholic League army, and hence ultimately under his own control. The outcome had been quite different, a separate Imperial army which freed the emperor from his military dependence on the League, hence considerably diminishing Maximilian's political influence on Ferdinand. Wallenstein was the cause, as only his offer to finance the raising of an army had made it possible. By the time the new force reached north Germany in late 1625 Maximilian's hostility to its general was already apparent in his correspondence, and in the following years this developed into something approaching paranoia.

As far as is known, neither Maximilian nor any of the other electors, Catholic or Protestant, had actually met Wallenstein in person by 1630.[1] Hence their view of him was based mainly on gossip and rumour, collated and passed on by self-seeking informants or by retainers anxious to match their accounts to their masters' prejudices. It is easier to demonise someone who is not known personally, and hence Maximilian and his fellows were only too ready to give credence to many of the lurid and not infrequently contradictory reports which were in circulation concerning Wallenstein's character, motives and intentions. Moreover these leading members of the German aristocracy viewed the Bohemian upstart with the distaste and suspicion traditionally accorded to *arrivistes* by those who consider themselves their betters.

Even so there were some real issues. For the Catholic electors one was Wallenstein's open opposition to the Edict of Restitution, which had also turned Father Wilhelm Lamormaini, the emperor's Jesuit confessor, against him, while the burden of supporting his army was resented much more widely.[2] Since the defeat of Christian of Denmark at Wolgast in September 1628 there had been no enemy in the field against the Empire, and thus arguably no need for an Imperial army, certainly not one as large as Wallenstein's. The wars between Gustavus Adolphus and the king of Poland, between the Spanish and the Dutch, and between Spain and France over Mantua, were none of them concerns of the Empire, opponents contended, but the Empire was paying for involvement through the contributions levied to support Wallenstein's army, as well as suffering from all the other problems of garrisoning, billeting and a licentious soldiery outlined in the previous chapter. Protestants raised the same objections to Tilly's army, which had also been maintained at full strength in north Germany although it had done almost nothing militarily in the two years since the end of the Danish campaign, but for Maximilian and his colleagues that was not an issue.

The electors also had a deeper political concern. They and their fellow princes traditionally regarded themselves as the guardians of the so-called 'German liberties', which in practice meant their own liberties to rule their territories much as they pleased, with only the limited and largely formal constraints exercised by the weak central institutions of the Empire. This meant that the emperor had prestige and perhaps influence but little real power. Wallenstein intended to change that, or so it was reported in the colourful and imaginative analyses of his supposed thinking which Maximilian had circulated to the other Catholic electors following the Bruck conference in late 1626, and again in 1628. Maximilian was an eager, not to mention credulous, recipient of this alleged inside information, with its claim that the generalissimo planned to use his vast number of soldiers to oppress the territories of the princes both physically and financially, until the emperor, and behind him Wallenstein himself, became the principal powers in the land.

The electors' fears may have had some justification, but they were misdirected. Wallenstein was no politician and not the man to contemplate such a grandiose and Machiavellian plan. According to Khevenhüller his enemies claimed in 1627 that he had been heard to speculate that it might be a good thing if the Empire were more like the monarchies of Spain and France, but this is a far cry from establishing that he actively intended or even considered it possible to bring this about.[3] Ferdinand was another matter. While it is unlikely that he had any express centralising intentions he showed strong absolutist tendencies which if left unchecked could have led in much the same direction. The Catholic electors welcomed the Edict of Restitution, and Ferdinand's confiscation of Frederick's Palatinate and electoral title benefited Maximilian, but they were nevertheless dangerous precedents, while the expropriation of Mecklenburg and involvement in the Dutch and Italian wars were much less acceptable to them. But whoever was the real threat, Ferdinand's increased power rested on Wallenstein, so as far as the electors were concerned he had to go.

Despite the eleven years of crisis and war since his election as emperor, Ferdinand had never felt it necessary to convene an Imperial Diet or to attend a meeting of the electors, in itself a significant indication of his attitude. There was, though, one matter which he could not resolve on his own. In 1630 he was 52 and not in the best of health, so he wanted to secure the succession for his son rather than leave the risk that an alternative candidate might come forward were he to die unexpectedly. Other names had been canvassed in 1619, and there were rumours that Maximilian of Bavaria might be interested, which would present a significant threat given that not only Maximilian but also his brother, the archbishop of Cologne, were themselves electors. Election to the honorary position of King of the Romans had long been regarded as designation as the emperor's successor, and it was this which Ferdinand sought for his son, Archduke Ferdinand. The electors saw this as an opportunity to extract concessions from him, and more than two years earlier the elector of Mainz, in his capacity as Imperial chancellor, had pointedly informed Ferdinand that he could not guarantee his son's elevation while Wallenstein remained in command of the army.[4] In 1628 the emperor could afford to wait and to ignore the complaints about his general which came from an assembly of the Catholic electors; in 1629 he still felt able to disregard renewed protests from two meetings of the Catholic League; by 1630 his personal and political needs had become more pressing, and he had to meet and listen to the electors.

In March 1630 the elector of Mainz summoned his colleagues to attend an electoral meeting at Regensburg that summer, but by the time they arrived it seemed that everybody who was anybody in the Empire, as well as a large number of nobodies, were converging on the little city. Ambassadors and envoys also came from outside, prominent among them those from the pope, from Spain and from France, including Richelieu's own confessor and *éminence grise*, the Capuchin Father Joseph. Many of this multitude came to present petitions and complaints, while others, particularly the more elevated, came principally to attend what promised to be the social event of the year. Ferdinand himself arrived on 19 June, with a huge escort befitting the Holy Roman Emperor, and the Catholic electors also came in person. On the other hand John George of Saxony refused to attend, fearing that the Protestant electors would come under heavy pressure, outnumbered five to two, as the king of Bohemia – that is Emperor Ferdinand – was also an elector, and he persuaded the elector of Brandenburg to do likewise. The most talked-about prince of the Empire and the centre of the meeting's attention also did not come to Regensburg, but Wallenstein chose that moment to move his headquarters three hundred miles south. He arrived at Memmingen, a hundred miles from Regensburg, ten days before the emperor reached that city.[5]

Wallenstein was well aware of the princely animosity towards his army and himself, and that the objective of the Catholic electors at the meeting was to secure his dismissal. Like Maximilian, he made it his business to be well informed, and as early as 1623 he had an established network of representatives and informers, 'for which I have certainly already laid out several thousand gulden'. The Catholic electors started complaining bitterly to Ferdinand about Wallenstein's recruiting activities early in 1627, and they kept up a constant campaign thereafter. In late 1628 he did make some concessions towards limiting his forces, consolidating or disbanding under-strength units, only to be faced with demands for troops in Italy and the Netherlands in 1629. The consequence of maintaining his army, as he wrote in October of that year, was that 'I have had to make enemies of all the electors and princes, indeed everyone, on the emperor's account. ... That I am hated in the Empire has happened simply because I have served the emperor too well, against the wishes of many.'[6]

Wallenstein was not the only item on the electoral meeting agenda. In fact he was not on Ferdinand's agenda at all. Instead the emperor's opening paper of 3 July addressed first the question of a universal peace, but implicitly assuming that this could not be achieved went on to consider war against the Dutch, war against the Swedes should they invade, and war against the French in Italy.[7] A final reckoning with Frederick of the Palatinate was also mentioned, as was – almost as an afterthought – the possibility of improving the Empire's military organisation, but there was no suggestion of replacing Wallenstein. Nor was the election of Archduke Ferdinand as King of the Romans overtly proposed, so that both the emperor and the Catholic electors had principal objectives of their own underlying the formal agenda.

There were other parties at Regensburg. The envoys representing the elector of Brandenburg had instructions not to participate in any moves against Wallenstein which might increase the influence of the Catholic party over the Imperial army, while the Saxons argued that were the question of peace to be properly addressed then problems with the army would become irrelevant. Paradoxically, although Wallenstein's view of the Spanish had become steadily more jaundiced, culminating in his opposition to their attack on Mantua, Spain supported him diplomatically.[8] To the Spanish, attacks on Wallenstein were attempts to weaken the emperor and hence the Habsburg party, while without him the Imperial army would certainly be reduced in strength and effectiveness. Worse still, control might pass into the hands of Maximilian and the Catholic League, which was particularly undesirable as Maximilian was not only anti-Spanish but also prone to dangerous dalliances with France. Conversely French diplomats worked to undermine Wallenstein, and in this they were supported by the papal representative, whose master's aim was to weaken Spanish influence in Italy, hence making him a supporter of French policy.

Nevertheless the Catholic electors were the driving force in the discussions, which for all their seriousness proceeded at a stately pace. On 17 July the electors responded to the emperor that while the other subjects could be discussed their priority was Wallenstein. They reiterated the complaints previously made about him, laying at his door all the evils associated with the wars and the army, and urged the emperor to remove him forthwith. Their stipulations about a replacement left little doubt that they had Maximilian in mind, although without naming him. On the other side the emperor and his advisers, though somewhat taken aback by the strength of the attack, were not prepared to abandon their general without a fight, still less to have Maximilian foisted upon them. It took a mere three days for them to issue a sharp reply, only slightly softened by a generalised promise of improvements in military discipline in the future. The Catholic electors were not to be fobbed off, however, and they spent ten days preparing their next missive.[9] This time they delivered it in person, all four of them placing it in Ferdinand's hands on 1 August and waiting while he read it. If not new their litany was comprehensive, starting from the creation of what they deemed an unnecessary army in 1625 and proceeding to date. The religiously confrontational Ferdinand was less good at personal confrontations, so rather than the electors being sent away with a polite flea in the ear their paper was referred to the emperor's council.

Six weeks after the participants had arrived in Regensburg positions were beginning to shift, and the councillors were in two – indeed several – minds. Many of the claims made by the electors were demonstrably incorrect, but on the other hand the determination with which they were pressing their opposition could not be lightly brushed aside. 'What if' scenarios started to be aired. What if Wallenstein were to be dismissed? Would he go quietly? What if a Swedish invasion gained a foothold in the Empire? Could the army, with its large number of Protestant officers and men, be relied upon? The emperor was left to ponder a response from his disunited council which was more discursive than helpful. Meanwhile a holding reply was sent to the electors on 7 August, taking a generally firm line on military topics but studiously avoiding the real question. By now, though, it had become apparent that as long as Wallenstein retained his command Ferdinand would secure electoral support neither for the wars in Holland and Italy nor for the election of his son as King of the Romans. At times of crisis Ferdinand was inclined to prefer his religious to his political advisers, foremost among them Lamormaini, who may in turn have been influenced by Father Joseph and the papal nuncio. Whether their opposition to Wallenstein gave the final push cannot be said, but on 13 August Ferdinand gave way and agreed to replace him.[10]

He got little in return. Even though the electoral meeting continued far into the autumn no election of a King of the Romans took place, no support for the war in the Netherlands was forthcoming, and although there were diplomatic excitements over the war in Italy these soon became irrelevant as the Swedish invasion, which had taken place earlier in the summer, gained strength. Both Ferdinand and the Empire emerged significantly weakened just as this new crisis was thrust upon them, while the Catholic electors were soon to pay a heavy price for their victory. The Spanish, having failed to prevent Wallenstein's dismissal, at least managed to block Maximilian's ambition to succeed him, although for want of anyone else and after a long delay the choice fell on Tilly, Maximilian's own general. A thankless task faced him, as once Ferdinand had abandoned Wallenstein he also agreed to reduce the size of his army drastically, in principle by as much as two-thirds, and as soon as possible, while Tilly was not provided with adequate finance for even such troops as were to be retained.[11]

The news of his dismissal was not communicated officially to Wallenstein until 22 August, by which time he had probably long since learned of it from his own informants at Regensburg. Nevertheless there was anxiety among the councillors as to how he would react, and the emperor's message was so politely, guardedly and diplomatically expressed as to require reading between the lines to fathom its true harsh meaning. The unenviable task of conveying it to the general was allocated to two of his better friends among the emperor's councillors, and from a letter written by one of them, Baron Gerhard Questenberg, to his brother we know that they were in fact received courteously and without recrimination. They had brought, said Wallenstein, the best news he could have had; 'I thank God to be freed from the net.' The following day he wrote to Collalto: 'I am glad to my innermost soul about what they have decided in Regensburg, as it means that I can escape from this great labyrinth.'[12]

Contemporaries were astonished by this mild response, which many saw as a calculated dissimulation intended to hide the anger and resentment which they assumed Wallenstein to feel. Biographers have long taken the same view, often asserting that he was largely motivated thereafter by a desire for revenge on those who had brought about his downfall, and on the emperor who had sacrificed him to them. Khevenhüller, the chronicler of Ferdinand's reign, found an explanation in astrology, which he and other early historians credited with not only forewarning Wallenstein of his dismissal but also with foretelling his reappointment. Hence Khevenhüller presented an alternative account of Wallenstein's meeting with Questenberg and his colleague:

> The duke received them graciously and politely, and as they sought to deliver their message in the best manner they could think of he broke in. Taking a Latin document from the table, which he read out, and in which his own, the emperor's and the elector of Bavaria's horoscopes were set down, he responded: 'Gentlemen, you can see for yourselves that I knew your mission from the stars, and that the elector of Bavaria's spirit dominates the emperor's. Hence I cannot place any blame on His Majesty, although it pains me, and I will obey.'[13]

Biographers, even the relatively recent Diwald, Polišenský and Kollmann, have repeated this story uncritically, although it is well known that historical writers from Thucydides until the early nineteenth century considered it perfectly acceptable to invent such scenes and to place appropriate speeches into the mouths of the principals.[14] Had there been any truth in this version it would have been the talk of Regensburg, but it does not feature in any of the gossip assiduously gathered and reported back by the various diplomats. Nor, of course, does it square with Questenberg's own account, but it is interesting as an example of the legends, particularly in connection with astrology, which attached themselves to Wallenstein, and which became accepted by virtue of constant repetition despite the lack of any supporting evidence.

In truth Wallenstein's reaction as reported by Questenberg is entirely credible. Over the past year he had increasingly been obliged to employ his army to pursue policies of which he disapproved, while at the same time his repeated warnings about the danger from Gustavus Adolphus were ignored. He was fully conversant with the complaints and criticisms of his enemies, but he had been neither willing nor able to defend himself effectively against them. On the one hand he lacked the political skills required for successful in-fighting, while on the other he believed, to judge from his correspondence, that his services should have spoken for themselves, disdaining as a result to make regular appearances at court in the undignified position of defendant and his own advocate. Nor had he had the time to do so, constantly burdened down as he had been with the massive workload of generalissimo and paymaster of a vast army operating in widely separated theatres of war. He suffered from persistent ill health, with stomach problems as well as gout necessitating a three-week cure to take the waters at Karlsbad (Karlovy Vary) *en route* to Memmingen, although the benefit must have been doubtful as he continued to work throughout. Above all there was the problem of money, the endless struggle to raise the cash needed to keep the army functioning, which by mid-1630 had reached crisis point. The net in which Wallenstein felt himself to be enmeshed was largely financial.

The chief victim of the cash crunch was not Wallenstein himself but his principal banker, Hans de Witte, who by 1630 was at the centre of large-scale international funding operations, which advanced money to the Imperial army in exchange for the rights to the agreed contributions from cities and territories of the Empire as they came in. Wallenstein even depended on a monthly cash shipment from de Witte to finance his headquarters and his personal outgoings.[15] The problem was that agreeing contributions was one thing, collecting them quite another, and the longer the war went on the more difficult it became for Wallenstein's officers in the field to enforce punctual payment of what had been promised. Ready cash was drying up, and local officials could not themselves lay hands on the necessary sums. Arrears mounted. De Witte could not meet his commitments to his business partners and

The Wheel Is Come Full Circle 131

he faced bankruptcy. His letters became increasingly desperate. It was probably coincidence that the last was written one day after the decision to dismiss Wallenstein was reached at Regensburg, although de Witte may have guessed which way the wind was blowing, and in it he included not only a summary of the full extent of his problems but also a note that he was unable to continue even the general's own monthly advance. News of this last financial blow reached Wallenstein a few days before the official messengers from the emperor, and with this added to everything else he had reason enough to be glad to leave the problems to his successor, and to accept his discharge with some relief. De Witte committed suicide soon afterwards.[16]

The most amazing aspect of the whole Regensburg saga is that it was played out with total disregard for the threat presented by Sweden. The emperor sent his opening agenda to the electors on 3 July, and three days later Gustavus Adolphus landed on the Baltic coast with an army of 13,000 men, quickly joined by a further 4000 from the Stralsund garrison. On 17 July the electors sent their initial reply to Ferdinand, and three days later the city of Stettin (Szczecin) opened its gates to the invaders. In the following four weeks, while the parties at Regensburg kept their sights on Wallenstein, Gustavus consolidated his position in Pomerania and frantically recruited soldiers. For reasons unknown the commander of the large Imperialist forces Wallenstein had placed in the area to guard against a landing did not stick to the plan to make an early attack on the Swedes, preferring a passive strategy of containment. By the time this news reached Memmingen the decision to dismiss Wallenstein had been taken but no replacement had been appointed, so that there was no commander-in-chief to direct the campaign for the remainder of the season. The emperor notified senior officers of Wallenstein's discharge on 13 September, whereupon some officers began to break up their regiments of their own accord, while men deserted in large numbers from others.[17] Many of them were only too glad to obtain alternative employment with the renowned Gustavus, and by the late autumn, when the emperor and the electors went home from Regensburg, the Swedes had over 40,000 men and were secure for the winter.[18] Despite the threat, and then the fact, of the Swedish intervention, the emperor yielded to the pressure to dismiss his generalissimo and disperse his army. No doubt the Catholic electors calculated that the war would continue to be fought out in the north, far from their own domains – as indeed did Gustavus – but a year later the Swedes took Mainz and six months after that they were in Munich.

Intermezzo

Talk of Wallenstein's recall began even before the ripples caused by his dismissal had died down. Within two months Ferdinand began writing to him again, and he did not hesitate to ask his ex-general's advice on military and political developments. Wallenstein responded in a professional manner from his Bohemian retreat, but he ignored hints that he should come to Vienna, which Questenberg attributed to his 'infirmity, lack of inclination, and apprehensions about being pressed to serve again'. Rumours nevertheless abounded, and many senior officers maintained a correspondence with Wallenstein which assumed that his career was not over. In January 1631 his cousin Max wrote to him that 'Prince Eggenberg tells me that His Majesty and all the councillors already recognise what they have lost in you'. By the spring Questenberg was writing to him frankly: 'We realise the wrong that we did, and we regret it. ... Now people are seeing whether or not you were right with your extravagant recruitment, and what we have come to in such a short time with our penny-pinching economy.' After Gustavus stormed Frankfurt an der Oder in April he added that 'we have made our own bed, and now we must lie in it'. In May Ferdinand wrote to Wallenstein personally, asking him to come to Vienna, where matters could better be discussed, but still he made no move.[19] In the summer the military situation deteriorated alarmingly, Saxony reluctantly threw in its lot with the Swedes, and on 17 September Gustavus led their combined forces to a spectacular victory over Tilly at Breitenfeld, near Leipzig. Still Wallenstein remained deaf to the increasingly desperate messages from Vienna. Within two months the Swedes were in Mainz and the Saxons were in Bohemia, and on 15 November they took Prague. Two days later Wallenstein agreed to meet Eggenberg, and a month afterwards he was once again the emperor's general, although he would accept only a three-month appointment to reorganise the army.

Sixteen months between dismissal and reappointment briefly summarised, but several questions left to answer. Why was Wallenstein apparently so reluctant to return? Why in the end did he do so? What was he doing in the meantime? The conspiracy theory has it that he was biding his time, enjoying his revenge, and waiting for the situation to become so bad that he would have to be re-engaged on his own terms. Certainly, glad though he may have been to lay down the burdens of command, he would have been less than human had he not felt some bitterness. Nevertheless nothing in his extensive correspondence or in any reliably reported statements betrays any resentment over his dismissal or how relatively easily Ferdinand had been persuaded to let him go.[20] There are more rational explanations for his behaviour than mere vindictiveness.

Firstly we need not doubt that Wallenstein was tired and ill, disillusioned and dispirited. *En route* from Memmingen to Bohemia he had been forced to extend the journey by several weeks due to severe attacks of gout, and these continued to trouble him in the following year. It is hardly surprising that he was in no mood for a recall which would have involved not merely starting again where he had left off, but having to rebuild the army and to confront a military situation which had rapidly deteriorated once he was off the scene. Furthermore the political situation did not change as rapidly as the military one, and while Ferdinand would soon have been glad of his return the Catholic electors, as yet unaffected by the war, remained as hostile as before. Nor had the financial position improved.[21] Wallenstein's own resources were stretched almost to breaking point, the emperor was as penniless as ever, and with de Witte bankrupt and gone there were scant prospects of large-scale borrowing from financiers, while after Regensburg the collection of sufficient contributions would be even more difficult than before.

Secondly Wallenstein may initially have felt that his own return would not be necessary in order to contain the Swedish threat. Gustavus was a formidable general but he had suffered his defeats, whereas Tilly had never lost a battle in a lifetime of campaigning. He also still had a large and battle-hardened army, with the Catholic League core supplemented by units returning from Italy, whereas although the Swedes had increasing numbers, including a leavening of seasoned troops, many of their regiments were newly formed and far from fully prepared for a major contest of arms. Gustavus himself recognised this and he proceeded cautiously, but instead of pressing him in the spring of 1631 Tilly instead committed much of his army to a protracted siege of Magdeburg. This had been the first and indeed the only major territory to declare for Gustavus after his landing, and Tilly's intention was to draw the Swedes deeper into Germany in an attempt to rescue the city before forcing them into battle. The Swedish king was not to be drawn, although he deferred his expected advance into Silesia to avoid appearing to abandon his co-religionist allies. Magdeburg was taken by storm on 20 May 1631, and in the sack and the terrible fire which followed the majority of the citizens and a considerable number of Tilly's men died.

Even then Tilly did not move against Gustavus, apart from one short thrust which he had to abandon when the Swedes dug themselves into an impregnable position at Werben, on the River Elbe. Instead he turned on Saxony, where the elector had been building up a significant if raw army of his own in order to be able to defend a position of armed neutrality. Seeing this as a threat, the emperor had demanded that he either disband his forces or join them with the Imperialist armies, and Tilly now issued an ultimatum. Quite why he took this hard line is uncertain, although it may have been forced on him by the need to move his army into unspoiled country where his men could find food, but whatever the reason the outcome was predictable. Tilly's forces moved into Saxony in the first days of September, the elector almost immediately allied himself with the Swedes, and two weeks later the battle of Breitenfeld put the Imperialist cause into full retreat. Wallenstein may justifiably have felt that he could have handled things better, but during the time he had kept himself on the sidelines neither he nor anyone else had expected such a startling Swedish success.

The course of the war also affected Wallenstein personally. First to go was Mecklenburg, most of which had fallen to the Swedes by May 1631, while Gustavus presided over a triumphant reinstallation of the previous dukes in July. The resulting loss of income further strained Wallenstein's resources, and his correspondence with his officials in this period shows him concerning himself anxiously with sums of money which previously he would scarcely have noticed.[22] He knew that Sagan would probably be next, although in the event Gustavus's decision not to march into Silesia provided a respite. Instead the Saxon invasion of Bohemia brought with it raids on Friedland properties by returning exiles. By then it was obvious to Wallenstein that unless there was a rapid revival of Imperialist fortunes he was likely soon to become a landless refugee, the same danger which had threatened him in 1624–25 and which he had actually experienced in 1619. His response was the same. He re-entered Ferdinand's military service.

Before tracing the course of this renewed commission it remains to consider what Wallenstein was doing during his period of unemployment. Although he long declined the blandishments of Vienna he by no means distanced himself from the situation. On the contrary he kept himself very well informed. His correspondence was as voluminous as before. Senior officers wrote to him, sent him reports, grumbled about the handling of the war, and expressed their eagerness to serve under him again should he resume the command. Moreover his household, whether in Gitschin or in Prague, retained the capacity to resume the functions of a military headquarters and secretariat. This has been seen as indicating that he intended all along to regain his position, but more likely is that at the back of his mind he never entirely ruled out the possibility, while after being at the centre of affairs for so long he could not easily have turned his back completely on them, even had others been prepared to allow him to do so.

That they were not is shown not only by the emperor's eagerness to seek Wallenstein's advice and the efforts of the court to entice him back into service, approaches which progressed during 1631 from hints to requests to supplications, but also by the secret diplomacy which they entrusted to him. In view of the long-standing rivalry and tension between Sweden and Denmark, war with the former suggested that there might be benefits in seeking improved relations with the latter. Who better than Wallenstein to explore the possibility, given that he was known to the Danes as having been a moderating influence on the final terms offered at the peace of Lübeck in 1629? Vienna was happy enough when he proposed to offer King Christian the opportunity to buy sections of his own Mecklenburg territories – no great concession on his part as the duchy was at that time already threatened by the Swedes – but the emperor objected to Christian regaining the north German bishoprics which he had been forced to give up at Lübeck.[23] Ferdinand's opposition, ostensibly on religious grounds although he also had his eye on one of the bishoprics for his son, proved to be the stumbling block, and in the end nothing came of the contacts.

After the defeat at Breitenfeld the court turned to Wallenstein again, recalling his friendship with his former field marshal Arnim, who was by then commanding the new Saxon army. The Saxons had only joined Gustavus as a last resort, and it therefore seemed worth trying to entice them away with the offer of a separate peace. Again Wallenstein accepted the commission, and he obtained a safe-conduct for Arnim to visit him, but the plan was overtaken by events when the latter unexpectedly marched his army into Bohemia. Wallenstein did not wait in Prague to receive him, but a private meeting did take place nearby at the end of November, following which he reported on the discussions to Eggenberg, although the details are not known. The Saxons duly notified their Swedish allies of the meeting, but naturally they made no mention of a separate peace, saying only that the possibility of an overall settlement had been debated.[24]

Contacts with the other side also took place earlier in 1631, a time when the Bohemian exile groups, ever optimistic but rarely realistic, thought that they saw a chance to involve Wallenstein in their schemes. They were not particularly hostile towards him, apart from those whose own properties he had acquired, as he had done no more than many others following the defeat of the Bohemian revolt, and he had usually treated exiles who had been taken prisoner while fighting for the enemy generously. Now, like most contemporaries, they assumed him to be nursing his grievances against the emperor, so they sought to bring him over to the Swedish side. Despite Wallenstein having neither men nor money to contribute they imagined that Gustavus might be persuaded to provide troops, to which Wallenstein would add his name, reputation and leadership, to create a Bohemian army of self-liberation. Wildly improbable. Gustavus was not the man to detach a substantial number of soldiers from his personal command and hand them over to an unknown quantity at a critical point in his campaign, even had he had them to spare, which he did not. The cautious Wallenstein was not the man to burn his boats in Bohemia, where confiscation of his properties would immediately have followed, even had he been ready to abandon his loyalty to the emperor, which he was not. Nor would a successful return of the Bohemian exiles have been in his interest, as claimants to his lands would have been in the vanguard. Wallenstein's only hope of retaining his domains lay in an Imperialist victory. Before Breitenfeld that still seemed feasible, and indeed at that stage Gustavus himself was looking no further than securing Pomerania and the Baltic coast for Sweden.

Nevertheless an attempt to suborn him was made, although details are scarce, as plots by definition leave few traces in the archives. The main participant in Wallenstein's circle was his young brother-in-law Count Adam Trčka, an Imperialist colonel who had married the third of Harrach's daughters a couple of years before. The Trčkas had always been rich but had, like Wallenstein, grown richer through cheaply bought confiscated Bohemian lands, but even so they had close connections with the exiles, one of whom was Adam's own brother. Their main contact in Gustavus's camp was another Bohemian, the ubiquitous Thurn, who was serving as the Swedish representative to the electorate of Brandenburg. The go-between was an exiled minor Bohemian nobleman, Sezyma Rašin, and almost all the information about this strange episode stems from the highly suspect testimony he gave to the Imperial investigation into Wallenstein's affairs in 1635.[25] In return he received a pardon, and he was allowed to return to Bohemia and to recover his properties, as well as being paid an indemnity for his losses while in exile. Slavata, one of Wallenstein's principal enemies, made the arrangements, and he admitted that he had prompted Rašin to add various things 'in order that his report should be more complete'.[26]

Rašin went back and forth between Trčka and Thurn in the spring of 1631, and Thurn informed Gustavus of an alleged connection with

Wallenstein. The king, it may be recalled, had been in touch with the general through Arnim back in 1627, and once again he was probably curious to see where, if anywhere, this might lead. Hence he gave Thurn an authorisation to pursue the approach, together with a letter of accreditation, although in it he referred only to 'a certain cavalier'. Later Thurn asked Gustavus for an army of 12,000 men and eighteen guns for his contact, who he then described as 'this princely person'.[27] The matter ended, according to Rašin, when he and Thurn met the king on the march south after Breitenfeld, but were bitterly disappointed to be told bluntly that he had no substantial number of men to spare for Bohemia.

It is possible that Wallenstein had some contact with Gustavus, whether through Rašin or otherwise. As duke of Mecklenburg and an independent prince he was entitled under the constitution of the Empire to do so, just as Maximilian had his long-standing contacts with France and at around this time was also in touch with Sweden. Likewise Wallenstein was as free to deal with Bohemian exiles as John George of Saxony was to give them shelter in his territory. Virtually every prince in north Germany whose lands lay within reach of the Swedish armies had exchanges with Gustavus, and Wallenstein had the same legitimate interests to protect. That of course is different from seeking to borrow an army to use against the emperor, but Rašin apart there is no evidence to connect Wallenstein himself with this chimera, and it may be that the whole thing was conducted by Trčka without his knowledge. At most if he learned of it at some point he may have been content to let it run once started in order to see what response it elicited. Had he been more actively involved in this hare-brained scheme it would certainly have been better thought out.

One other story from this period which requires comment is the claim that Wallenstein deliberately undermined the Imperialist war effort by refusing food and other supplies to Tilly from Mecklenburg and Friedland. This is a very naive proposition, implicitly assuming that the resources of these territories belonged to Wallenstein himself and that he was in a position simply to order their despatch. In fact the peasants who produced the food and the artisans who manufactured the other goods would have had to be paid for them. Tilly had no money, but nor at the time had Wallenstein. It was different when he was in command, as then he also controlled the funding of the armies and was able to ensure that supplies ordered from Friedland, Mecklenburg or elsewhere were paid for in cash, albeit with money borrowed against contributions yet to be collected. This system, already tottering, collapsed after

Wallenstein's departure, and Tilly's hungry soldiers were the victims. The truth is that no-one supplied the Imperial or any other army without expecting to be paid, and even if Wallenstein had been willing to do so he could not have financed it.

Resumption

Once Wallenstein decided that he could no longer afford to stand aside the response from the court was predictably prompt, and at the beginning of December he set out for Znaim (Znojmo), about 50 miles north of Vienna. There he met Eggenberg, and after some initial sparring about arrangements the matter was quickly settled, with Wallenstein's appointment to date from 15 December 1631.[28] It was he who stipulated that it was to be for three months only, and for the specific purpose of reorganising the army over the winter. Some have seen this as a tactical manoeuvre on his part, but this would have been pointless as he could have named his own terms from the outset. Instead it reflects his continuing reluctance to return to the command, accepting a limited commitment only because of the increasingly desperate military situation. No doubt a sense of duty to the emperor, whom he had first volunteered to help as Ferdinand of Styria in 1617, and whom he had loyally served for most of the intervening years, counted for something, particularly in view of the latter's personal appeals.[29] Whether this would have sufficed had not Wallenstein also been in straitened immediate personal circumstances, and facing much worse should a victorious enemy restore the status quo ante in Bohemia, is another matter.

Whether he really believed that he would be able to withdraw after three months must also be questionable, despite him repeatedly stressing the temporary nature of his assignment in his correspondence. Perhaps this was wishful thinking, closing his eyes to the likely longer-term burden he was reassuming, or perhaps he was seeking to leave a way out if the task proved impossible or his health deteriorated further. The problem of financing the army remained intractable, and such promises of funds as Eggenberg had been able to bring were barely enough to make a start. His critics had been temporarily silenced by their own fears and need for help, but he had experience enough to know that they would soon be back. Tilly's relieved response to his discharge from the Imperial appointment spoke for itself, echoing Wallenstein's own at Memmingen.[30] Then Tilly had been the only feasible candidate to replace him. Now there was no-one. Three months looked a forlorn hope.

10
Once More unto the Breach
(*Henry V*)

During the sixteen months between Wallenstein's dismissal and reappointment the wider political situation became increasingly complicated. Although Gustavus Adolphus was hailed as a prospective saviour by many of the ordinary Protestant people of Germany his arrival was far from welcome to most of their princes. They could see well enough that a new outside intervention could only renew and prolong the war in the Empire, and that they and their lands were likely to suffer heavily in consequence. Sincere though Gustavus assuredly was in his desire to assist the Protestant religion, his record of seizing and holding territories along the Baltic coast of Poland left them in little doubt that he had similar ambitions in Germany. Moreover with the examples of Mecklenburg and the Palatinate fresh in mind the princes feared Imperial retribution should they assist Gustavus, only for him, like Christian of Denmark, nevertheless to be defeated. Neutrality was their preference, but realistically this was only tenable from a position of strength. Hence the electors of Brandenburg and Saxony convened a meeting to discuss the situation, at which almost every significant Protestant ruler in Germany was present or represented, as well as delegates from a number of Imperial free cities. The resulting Leipzig Manifesto of April 1631 provided for the creation of a force of 40,000 men, which was to be used strictly for self-defence if attacked, thereby preserving its legality under the Imperial constitution. Nevertheless there was an implicit threat to resist any further pressure from the emperor, while the agreement also served notice on the Swedish king that he could not expect willing support from the Protestant princes. John George of Saxony rather reluctantly became head of the association, and initially he was the only one to recruit a significant number of troops, whereas the unfortunate elector of Brandenburg soon discovered that Gustavus had no time for neutrals. In June he was coerced by a show of force into a nominal alliance with the Swedes, after which they commandeered the important fortresses and other resources of his electorate.

Meanwhile Gustavus found support elsewhere, paradoxically from Catholic France. At Regensburg, in parallel to the contest over Wallenstein, negotiations had taken place between France and the emperor over a number of issues, including the war in Italy. When news arrived that Mantua had actually fallen the French representatives panicked, and in the absence of fresh instructions from Paris they concluded a peace on their own authority, but the king of France angrily refused to ratify the treaty and the war went on into the following year. This left the French looking for other ways of putting pressure on the emperor, so leading them back to the Swedes. The result was the treaty of Bärwalde in January 1631, by which France agreed to provide financial support for the Swedish war effort over a period of five years. The amount of money was relatively modest, but it came at a point when Gustavus's finances were most severely stretched, and he also strengthened his position by publicly announcing the alliance, even though Richelieu would have preferred to keep it secret. In return he agreed to maintain freedom of Catholic worship as he advanced, willingly enough as he was in any case tolerant about this, and also to respect the neutrality of Catholic League lands provided that they themselves remained neutral.

Maximilian of Bavaria was also engaged in feverish diplomatic manoeuvring. He had done very well out of the war, but as the Swedes gained strength he became more and more anxious about being able to hold on to his spoils, particularly as restoring Frederick to his Palatinate was one of the aims which Gustavus was trumpeting abroad. Maximilian had no friends among the Protestant princes, and he was all but openly hostile to Spain, so he had to look elsewhere for allies, leading him to renew his long-standing but intermittent contact with France. This time dalliance progressed to something more substantial, the secret treaty of Fontainebleau, which was concluded in May 1631. In this the French not only recognised Maximilian's new lands and electoral title but also promised to assist him should he be attacked, while he in turn agreed to give no help to the enemies of France. The two treaties, Bärwalde and Fontainebleau, were inherently incompatible, but they served the French purpose of creating further problems for Ferdinand. Maximilian's position was similarly contradictory, duty bound to the Empire on the one hand, but on the other in alliance with the emperor's enemy France, and thereby linked to the Swedes, who were in process of invading the Empire. The position was only tenable, if at all, as long as Gustavus could be confined to north Germany, well away from Maximilian's domains. Before Breitenfeld this seemed feasible; afterwards it was not. The unfortunate Tilly, with his dual command, was also left in an impossible position, required by one master, Maximilian, to keep his distance from the Swedes, and by the other, the emperor, to take energetic measures to defeat them. His decision to turn instead first on Magdeburg and then on Saxony may have been in part a result of this dilemma.

After Breitenfeld Maximilian's anxiety turned into panic, and he sought to go yet further in the attempt to preserve his lands from Swedish attack. With Gustavus virtually on his borders and Tilly, distraught after his defeat, bereft of ideas as to how he was to be contained, a separate peace with Sweden and withdrawal into neutrality seemed his only hope. A forlorn hope. Gustavus, rightly perceiving Maximilian as one of the principal opponents of the Protestant religion and a prime mover behind the Edict of Restitution, was not inclined to sympathy. Despite French mediation he was prepared to offer him nothing other than virtual surrender, a principal condition of which was the reduction of the Catholic League army to a mere garrison force a fraction of its fighting size. This was scarcely a serious offer, as it would have left Bavaria defenceless and dependent on dubious Swedish goodwill and ineffectual French influence. Even though intercepted letters had revealed to Vienna Maximilian's attempt at what amounted to desertion of the Imperial cause, by early 1632 he had no choice but to creep back, vociferously asserting his loyalty to the emperor, and begging for assistance from Wallenstein's new army against the coming Swedish storm.[1]

Gustavus was more interested in pursuing his military advantage than in negotiating, although he also had to take political factors into account. At Breitenfeld the raw Saxon army had fared badly, and it had been the Swedes who had won the day, so that the king had to view his reluctant ally as both militarily and politically unreliable. Consequently Gustavus did not, as had been expected, exploit his success by marching through Silesia or Bohemia towards Vienna. Instead Arnim's Saxons made an independent but essentially diversionary advance in that direction, although this at least prevented the Imperialist forces still in those territories from joining Tilly as he tried to regroup his army. Gustavus's own immediate priority was to move into prosperous and unspoiled territory where he could find winter quarters and exact substantial contributions to support his campaign. Hence he split his forces, sending some west to extend his control in north Germany, while he led the main army into the rich bishoprics of Franconia and on to Frankfurt and Mainz. There he celebrated Christmas in 1631, and only the onset of winter and strong Spanish garrisons prevented him from pressing on to Heidelberg, the capital of Frederick's Palatinate.

He had already driven the Spanish out of a number of places *en route*, and the French also moved troops towards the Rhine, further threatening the Spanish hold on the Palatinate. The Catholic electors of Trier and Cologne, the latter Maximilian's brother, then prudently placed themselves under French protection and denied use of their territories to the Spanish. Faced with these additional pressures the king of Spain was in no position to help the emperor, other than with a little money, and that only a drop in the ocean compared to what was needed. Gustavus, on the other hand, suddenly had allies enough, as some of the bolder spirits among the Protestant German princes responded to his success by plucking up the courage to join him in arms, while others had their minds made up by a Swedish army at their gates. The Dutch too offered him money to add to the French subsidy, although by now Richelieu was finding that paying Gustavus was one thing, controlling him quite another.

Wallenstein's second army

'The sinews of war are unlimited money', wrote Cicero in the time of Julius Caesar, and this was equally true in the Habsburg lands 1700 years later, as Wallenstein set out to reconstruct his army. When he had done so Arnim commented that 'the duke of Friedland has laid out money on 130 regiments, but not the emperor, not the Empire, not half of Europe will be able to pay them'.[2] An accurate summary. Gustavus reportedly had 100,000 men, and if he were to be defeated a force of like size was essential. Somehow the money was found to create it, but how to pay for it thereafter was a question no-one was inclined to ask, let alone able to answer. To drum up enough cash to make a start the Estates of the Habsburg hereditary lands were coerced into making grants, and special commissioners of the highest standing set about collecting the money with a great deal more than the usual expedition. Some help came from Spain, and even the pope felt obliged to make a modest grant, needled by accusations that his pro-French stance was effectively putting him on the side of the arch-Protestant Gustavus. Colonels and captains were expected – as was usual – to make advances towards raising and equipping their regiments and companies, advances which they anticipated recovering with considerable interest both from official payments during service and from the less official profits of war. Other loans were raised wherever possible, although offers were less easy to find than before. When everything was added up it was still not enough, but it had to suffice.

Men too were getting more difficult to come by. Successive waves of recruitment had reduced the pool of potential volunteers, while the unprecedentedly large armies now being raised greatly increased the demand. Moreover many parts of the Empire were no longer available to Imperial recruiting officers because they were controlled by Gustavus or his Protestant allies and sympathisers. As a result Wallenstein's regiments had an average of well below half their official complement of men, although this at least had the advantage that the colonels' and captains' advances went a bit further. Offsetting this was the rise in price caused when demand exceeds supply, not here in terms of subsequent pay but in the amount of cash in hand which had to be offered to men as a signing-on inducement. This was the only payment of which a recruit could be sure, and during the rebuilding of Wallenstein's army it rose to as much as three or four times the traditional level, substantially increasing what was in any case one of the larger outlays in the process. Nevertheless Wallenstein got his 100,000 men, or possibly rather more, so far as can be judged from the sketchy, unreliable and not infrequently fraudulent figures of the period.[3]

Organising and equipping this number of men – huge by the standards of the time – was a formidable task and one which Wallenstein led personally, although equally essential was his ability to find, select and delegate to staff officers with the right talents for the job. They were not, of course, starting from scratch, as many units from the old army still existed and were drawn into the rebuilding process. Even if sadly depleted in numbers and lacking in adequate or even basic equipment, these and their officers and sergeants still provided a nucleus and a structure which permitted more rapid progress than a completely fresh start. There were professionals of every kind and at every level to help, men who knew how to specify artillery and munitions, and knew where they could be obtained, others who knew how to order and issue boots, picks and shovels, still others experienced in recruiting wagoners and arranging fodder for their horses, or in organising supplies of bread from civilian bakers, finding charcoal for the blacksmiths, running the regimental secretariat, and a thousand and one other necessary jobs. Tough, experienced sergeants knew how to drill raw recruits, and to set them to building their own encampments or digging latrines, and there were chaplains, field surgeons and even whoremasters to attend to other needs. Not least, there were specialist military policemen to manage discipline in army camps which often rivalled the larger cities of the day in population, as wives, children, soldiers' boys, servants and other camp followers usually brought up the total to something like double the actual number of enlisted men.

How it was all achieved cannot be related in detail, even were the details known, but the letters Wallenstein wrote and received in these few months ran into thousands.[4] Among other things he did was to establish a new general staff structure, with an appropriate range of largely new ranks for the senior officers required. Among their names were some already familiar and others newly prominent which became well known later. Collalto was dead, but his deputies in the Italian campaign were there, Aldringer, who had held the bridge at Dessau, and Gallas, who was a little later to become Wallenstein's second-in-command and eventually his successor. Newer men, and apparently closer to Wallenstein himself, were Baron Christian Ilow, a Brandenburger who had progressed rapidly from colonel to the higher ranks in the Imperial army, and Holk, the Dane who commanded the garrison at Stralsund but switched to Imperial service after Denmark's defeat. Both appealed to Wallenstein because they were efficient, capable, reliable and down to earth. There was enough for them all to do, but Wallenstein's three months had extended to five before he considered his new army ready for serious action.

As that time slipped by the court at Vienna exhibited increasing anxiety. By February Eggenberg himself was writing plaintively to Wallenstein that 'should Your Grace have decided irrevocably to resign after these three months it would be the death of me, as in that case I can clearly envisage our total ruin'.[5] Not, it seems, that he gave them any additional cause beyond his original stipulation, and relevant passages in his correspondence shifted progressively from stressing the temporary nature of his appointment to making references to the forthcoming campaign. Nevertheless there was considerable relief when at the end of March 1632, having ignored earlier hints and approaches, Wallenstein agreed once more to meet Eggenberg. In mid-April both travelled to Göllersdorf, halfway between Znaim and Vienna, where they settled the substance of the matter in a relatively short time, leaving the details to be resolved with the assistance of the ailing minister's factotum, Bishop Antonius of Vienna.[6] The whole procedure was reminiscent of the meeting at Bruck in 1626, and once again a secret informant claiming inside knowledge swiftly provided Maximilian of Bavaria with a full, lurid and fundamentally inaccurate account of the agreement.[7] A few of the points he noted were both obvious and valid, such as that Wallenstein retained his right to Mecklenburg or some compensation for it at any peace settlement, and he did in fact receive the small Habsburg duchy of Glogau (Głogów), in Silesia not far from Sagan, as a surety in the meantime.[8] Most of the alleged terms, however, were either extremely unlikely or demonstrably untrue, although this did not prevent them from passing into the common knowledge of the day and subsequent histories. Here we will confine ourselves to the facts, insofar as they can be ascertained.

The first point to note is that there was no formal agreement, or at least one has never been found although the court archives would certainly have held a copy, and nor is there even a written report of the meeting or the decisions reached. Some argue that the relevant papers were destroyed after Wallenstein's assassination, which is possible, although it must be noted that references to them in the general's own correspondence are also lacking, whereas the emperor's original negotiating instructions for Eggenberg have survived.[9] As Wallenstein had previously been very particular about precise documentation of his appointment the lack of such formality in this case makes it unlikely that anything extraordinary or any new far-reaching powers were demanded or granted. As far as can be deduced from his subsequent behaviour he was essentially confirmed in the position and with the powers which he previously held, as well as being authorised to continue his negotiations with the Saxons, but with no significant additions. He was also promised more regular and reliable payments towards the army's costs from taxation in the Habsburg hereditary lands, nothing like enough to fund them in full but at least more than was forthcoming previously. Doubtless he was also given assurances of full Imperial support in the future, that he would not have to contend with interference in his command from the court, that credence would not be given to his enemies as it had been in the past, and so forth. He was experienced enough to know that these were pious intentions rather than bankable guarantees, and that the second honeymoon would not long outlive the danger from the Swedes. It was as much as he could expect, so he let it delay him no longer and turned back to the conduct of the war.

In looking at Wallenstein's achievement in re-creating such a large army in such a short time it is worth asking whether the Imperial court's almost hysterical anxiety to have him undertake it was justified.

Could not someone else have done much the same thing? In 1625 there had been one factor which was unique to Wallenstein; he was the only one who had the necessary financial resources and was prepared to commit them to the undertaking. In 1632 this was not the case, as Wallenstein was no longer in a position to make a major personal contribution, and nor was de Witte on hand to facilitate raising loans. That apart, in some ways the job may have been a little easier in 1632, as there was a larger nucleus available upon which to build, while having done it all once before Wallenstein was in a position to gain from his own experience. His knowledge of the key officers and specialists was much greater, as many, if not most, will have served under him in the intervening years, and his grasp of the sourcing of supplies, weapons and munitions had developed commensurately. In other respects the task may have been harder than in 1625. Morale was an obvious problem in the remains of an army which had been abruptly dismembered, added to which some units had only recently straggled back from the ultimately pointless campaign in Italy, while others had been with Tilly at Breitenfeld. The knowledge that the next opponent was to be Gustavus Adolphus, who was rapidly becoming a living legend, cannot have helped. Above all there was the pressure of time, the awareness that Gustavus would be in the field early in the year with a large, successful and now battle-tried army, while on the Imperialist side there was so much to do before he could be faced at all, let alone with confidence.

Other generals had also demonstrated proficiency in raising new armies quickly. Mansfeld had been something of a specialist, although with forces one tenth of the size. On the other hand the track record of such generals was not encouraging, as their hastily gathered hosts were not infrequently effectively destroyed at their first serious test. The notable exception was Gustavus himself, the only other early modern commander up to that time to have raised an army of 100,000 men. Even he, however, had taken much longer to build up to this number from the core of 17,000 well-organised troops he started with in north Germany. Wallenstein's achievements in this respect are therefore unique.

So, it can be argued, were the circumstances, so could someone else have done it? No-one seems to have thought so at the time, and although there were would-be generals on the Imperial war council none of them commended themselves to the emperor and his closest advisers. Gallas later went from bad to worse as a commander in less challenging circumstances, although he inherited the army rather than having to create it. Arnim achieved a lot in a short time for the elector of Saxony, but his army was not able to stand its ground at Breitenfeld, even with Swedish support. Some of Gustavus's protégés became outstanding generals, but they never faced the challenge of building an army in the 50,000 to 100,000 man class. Perhaps they could have done it. The one sure fact is that Wallenstein did. Twice.

Towards confrontation

The central contest of 1632 pitted Gustavus Adolphus against first Tilly and then Wallenstein, but as the campaigning season approached the latter could not focus his attention solely on the king and his army around Mainz. Many more forces and theatres of war were involved. Gustavus had so many men that he was able to detach units to operate independently across Germany, and indeed he was obliged to do so, as no one area could for long feed the number of mouths, human and equine, involved when all were together. By this time he had no fewer than six such subsidiary forces, several of them armies in their own right, two relatively close by in Franconia and Hesse, and the others further north near Weimar and Magdeburg, as well as in Mecklenburg and Lower Saxony. Moreover several of the Protestant princes who had declared for him had raised armies of their own, which although smaller were still militarily significant. To add to Wallenstein's problems the French sent troops into Alsace, an Imperial territory, the Dutch were steadily gaining the upper hand in the Netherlands, and in Transylvania the new ruler, Georg Rákóczi, showed ominous signs of having inherited not only Bethlen Gabor's principality but also his anti-Habsburg warlike inclinations. Closer to home the Saxon army continued to occupy northern Bohemia and might resume its advance should the opportunity present itself.

To counter and contain these threats Wallenstein too had a number of subsidiary forces, the remaining parts of the old Imperial army, in addition to the new one he was raising in southern Bohemia. Even the former Catholic League army, now essentially a Bavarian force, was in two parts, as while Tilly was rebuilding in the south his deputy, Count Gottfried Pappenheim, had remained in northern Germany after Breitenfeld, where he was engaged in a hit-and-run contest with Swedish and allied units. It was the commander-in-chief's job to evaluate and prioritise the multiple calls on his army's resources, and to judge what steps to take in the light of the overall strategic situation. Maximilian behaved in 1632 as though Bavaria were the only theatre of war. Wallenstein could not afford to do likewise.

Perversely it was Maximilian and Tilly who opened hostilities in southern Germany in 1632. Gustavus had left one of his generals, Gustav Horn, to hold captured territories in Franconia around Würzburg, and over the winter Horn had also occupied the neighbouring bishopric of Bamberg. Although well away from Bavaria itself this was close to the Upper Palatinate, which Maximilian had acquired from the dispossessed Frederick, and this in turn bordered on the western edge of Bohemia. Despite the weakened state of Tilly's army Maximilian decided to go on to the offensive, aiming to secure not only Bamberg but the link to Bohemia, where he hoped to receive support from Wallenstein, although he had not obtained his prior agreement.[10] Surprisingly, Tilly succeeded in driving Horn out of Bamberg during March, thereby making a small dent in the Swedish record of success, but it was one which Gustavus would not allow to go unrepaired. By attacking the Swedes Maximilian had abandoned his neutrality, thus freeing Gustavus from the limited constraints of his Bärwalde treaty with France. The king immediately changed his original plan for 1632, which had been to move southwards from Mainz, through Swabia to the Danube, and then east along the river towards Austria. Instead he marched back towards Bamberg, joining up with Horn at nearby Schweinfurt. Tilly did not wait for him, hastily abandoning his conquest and retreating to the Bavarian fortress city of Ingolstadt, which he reached at the beginning of April. Gustavus followed at a more leisurely pace, pausing to make a triumphal entry into Nuremberg on the way, but he now clearly had Bavaria in his sights.

Gustavus decided to cross the Danube upstream at Donauwörth and to approach Bavaria from the west, from which direction the border was defined and protected by the smaller but still substantial River Lech. The Bavarians had destroyed the few bridges, so the nearest feasible crossing point was a little south of the town of Rain, 25 miles west of Ingolstadt, and here Tilly, accompanied by Maximilian himself, quickly established a strong defensive position. His intention was to delay Gustavus by forcing him to march further south looking for an alternative crossing, difficult because of the seasonally high level of the river, fed by melting Alpine snows. Twenty miles in that direction would bring him to the important free city of Augsburg, Protestant in sympathy but garrisoned and under Catholic control, so that the Swedes would be further delayed by the need to capture it. Gustavus, on the other hand, was well aware that Wallenstein was rebuilding the Imperial army, although he did not know how far he had progressed or when he would be ready to take the field, but he had to take into account the possibility that strong reinforcements might be on the way to Tilly. Hence he decided, not for the first time, to ignore the conventional military wisdom of the age, and to force a crossing of the river in the face of Tilly's defences. It was a risky venture, as Horn, second-in-command of the army, pointed out.[11]

On the morning of 13 April 1632 Gustavus drew up his army in battle order along the river opposite Tilly's positions, as though about to make an assault, but this was merely a diversion while his engineers constructed emplacements for three powerful artillery batteries. This work continued into the night, during which bridging materials were also brought up. On the following day an artillery battle across the river ensued, in which the Swedes were better placed because of the much larger number and heavier calibre of their guns. Nevertheless this too was essentially a diversion while preparations for bridging the river continued a little further to the south, unobserved by the Bavarian commanders. Early on 15 April elite Finnish troops crossed by boat to a small island in the middle of the river, a bridge to which was quickly constructed, and a strong force followed. Tilly noted the activity and moved up reserves to counter it, but the Finns crossed the second part of the river in their boats under cover of a massive smokescreen and an artillery bombardment, with the bridge being rapidly extended to follow them. Heavy fighting followed into the afternoon, during which the Swedes could make little progress from their bridgehead but the Bavarians were unable to dislodge them.

Meanwhile Gustavus sent cavalry units in both directions along the river to try to find places to ford or swim across. Both were successful, but the smaller body to the north was quickly pinned down by the defenders. To the south a substantial force crossed late in the afternoon, but it was immediately attacked by Tilly's cavalry reserve, and a similar situation to that at the bridgehead developed, where they neither made ground nor were repulsed. As evening approached both Tilly and Aldringer, who was commanding a body of Imperialist troops attached to the army, were wounded and put out of action, leaving the non-soldier Maximilian in command. At this stage the Bavarians were by no means defeated, but as darkness fell it was obvious to Maximilian and his colonels that they could not prevent Swedish forces crossing in strength at their bridgeheads during the night. Rather than face a renewed onslaught from the much larger army on the following day they quietly evacuated their men and made for Ingolstadt, an operation conducted so skilfully that the Swedes discovered it too late to mount an effective pursuit.[12]

Well beforehand Maximilian had begun making plaintive appeals to Wallenstein for help, professing his personal friendship and his loyalty to the Imperial cause as though he had taken no part at Regensburg or in earlier moves against the general, still less tried to desert the emperor and take refuge in French-protected neutrality.[13] Wallenstein sent him sound military advice but no more troops, and this Maximilian, most contemporaries and many subsequent historians have attributed to his vindictive desire for revenge on his principal political opponent. Whatever Wallenstein may have felt, however, his decision was unquestionably correct from a military point of view. One need only consider the opposing forces at Rain. According to Guthrie, Gustavus had 38,000 men and 72 guns, Tilly 22,000 men and only 20 guns, and over half of Tilly's men were partially trained recruits or militia, while his guns were of lighter calibre.[14] To redress this balance Wallenstein would have had to send not a couple of regiments but a full-scale army complete with artillery train. He did not have it. His operational forces were already deployed far and wide countering other threats to the Imperialist position, while his new army in Bohemia was not ready. A more political general might have despatched a few thousand men as a gesture, while privately recognising this to be pointless. Wallenstein was gathering his strength for a decisive campaign against Gustavus, and he did not intend Maximilian, or even Gustavus himself, to divert him from his preparations, still less to induce him to squander his resources before he was ready.

Gustavus took the opportunity to capture Augsburg, which he did a few days later rather than following hard on Maximilian's heels, and given this respite the Bavarians not only strengthened their position at Ingolstadt, where Tilly died, but also occupied Regensburg and dug in most of their army around it. These two important fortress cities controlled the Danube and threatened Gustavus's proposed route into Austria, and by the time he reached Ingolstadt at the end of April, and Horn reached Regensburg shortly afterwards, it was too late. Neither place could feasibly be taken by storm, nor induced to surrender without a siege which might have lasted months. Although Gustavus had another of his lucky escapes while he was assessing the situation personally at Ingolstadt, when a cannon ball from the defences killed his horse under him, his campaign was not going well. He had intended to inflict a heavy defeat on Tilly's army at Rain, thus eliminating it as a factor to be reckoned with in the future. Instead it had not only slipped away, but had secured itself and two key strategic points against him. Nor had Wallenstein been induced to move before he was ready in order to bring reinforcements. Frustrated, Gustavus turned on the undefended Bavarian hinterland and the city of Munich, ravaging the former and plundering the latter during the month of May. Profitable enough in terms of loot, this contributed nothing to his military position, and while he was making himself at home in the electoral palace in Munich and playing tennis on Maximilian's court Wallenstein was starting to move.

The generalissimo had maintained his contacts with the Saxon commander during the spring, but his repeated peace feelers had elicited no positive response from the elector.[15] Hence his first priority was to secure his rear by driving the Saxons out of Bohemia and Silesia, a task readily enough accomplished by confronting Arnim with twice as many men as the latter could muster. Starting in the middle of May, Wallenstein's forces were in Prague late in the month, and by mid-June the reoccupation of the two Imperial territories was completed with a minimum of serious fighting. Elector John George fully expected him to press on to attack Saxony itself, and Gustavus became very anxious about his ally. He had been kept informed of the contacts with Wallenstein, and naturally he suspected that there was more to them than Arnim reported, while the latter's brisk evacuation of Bohemia and Silesia added to his concern. Was Saxony on the point of making a separate peace, or was it about to be invaded and occupied by Wallenstein? Either way Gustavus had a problem, as Wallenstein, together with Pappenheim's army in northern Germany, would then threaten his lines of communication and possible retreat to the Baltic. Although his armies elsewhere were still making progress, especially on the Rhine, Gustavus seemed uncertain what to do next himself. With problems in his rear, advancing along the Danube into Austria was no longer feasible, particularly as in addition to Ingolstadt and Regensburg being in enemy hands Wallenstein had taken the precaution of reinforcing the border city of Passau. Instead Gustavus first turned west from Munich to Memmingen, but in view of Wallenstein's threat to Saxony and John George's appeals for help he divided his forces in mid-June, leaving part to hold his conquests in the south while he turned north and marched back towards Nuremberg with the remainder.

But Wallenstein did not invade Saxony. That was not his objective. Instead he gathered together a large part of his reconstructed forces into a formidable army and headed south-west from Bohemia to seek out Gustavus. The Bavarians took the opportunity to break out from Regensburg, and although the Swedes attempted to intercept them they slipped past and met up successfully with the Imperialist army, providing the occasion for the first personal meeting between Wallenstein and Maximilian. Khevenhüller gives a dramatic description of this scene in his *Annales*, and many histories have eagerly repeated and embroidered it, but in fact there are no reliable contemporary accounts and even the exact place and date are unknown, so we can only imagine what they said to each other.[16]

At this point Gustavus recognised the danger he was in. Wallenstein, approaching with his much larger army, threatened any move north towards Saxony. Retreating to the south or west, where he had other forces, would have been possible but would have taken him further from his Baltic base, leaving Wallenstein blocking his emergency escape route. This would also have enabled the Imperialists to recapture much of the territory previously conquered by the Swedes, and from which they were drawing the contributions to finance their campaign. Moreover retreat would have been politically damaging, encouraging wavering allies to defect, and it would have meant abandoning the loyal Protestant city of Nuremberg, just as Gustavus had been forced to abandon Magdeburg to its fate barely a year earlier. Hence he decided to return to Nuremberg, dig in and stand his ground while sending for reinforcements. He reached the city at the beginning of July 1632, just in time to make his preparations, as Wallenstein arrived within striking distance only a few days later. Shortly afterwards the Saxons took their opportunity and invaded Silesia, but if this was intended to assist Gustavus by diverting Wallenstein the attempt failed, although it later provoked him to despatch a force under Holk to carry out a retaliatory invasion of Saxony itself. That remained in the future. For the moment the stage was set for the confrontation outside Nuremberg between the two greatest generals of the age, leading up to the final act, at least for Gustavus, a few months later at Lützen.

1. The old image: 'Seni predicts Wallenstein's death'. Illustration from an 1877 edition of Schiller's play. In fact the astrologer was no more than 32 years old at the time, and certainly nothing like as influential as Schiller suggests.
(bpk Berlin)

2. Wallenstein, aged about 30, c.1614, before the start of his public career. (Muzeum Cheb)

3. Wallenstein, aged about 46, c.1630, as Imperial generalissimo. (Muzeum Cheb)

4. Emperor Ferdinand II, aged about 55, c.1633. (bpk Berlin)

5. Elector Maximilian I of Bavaria, aged about 60, *c*.1633. (bpk Berlin)

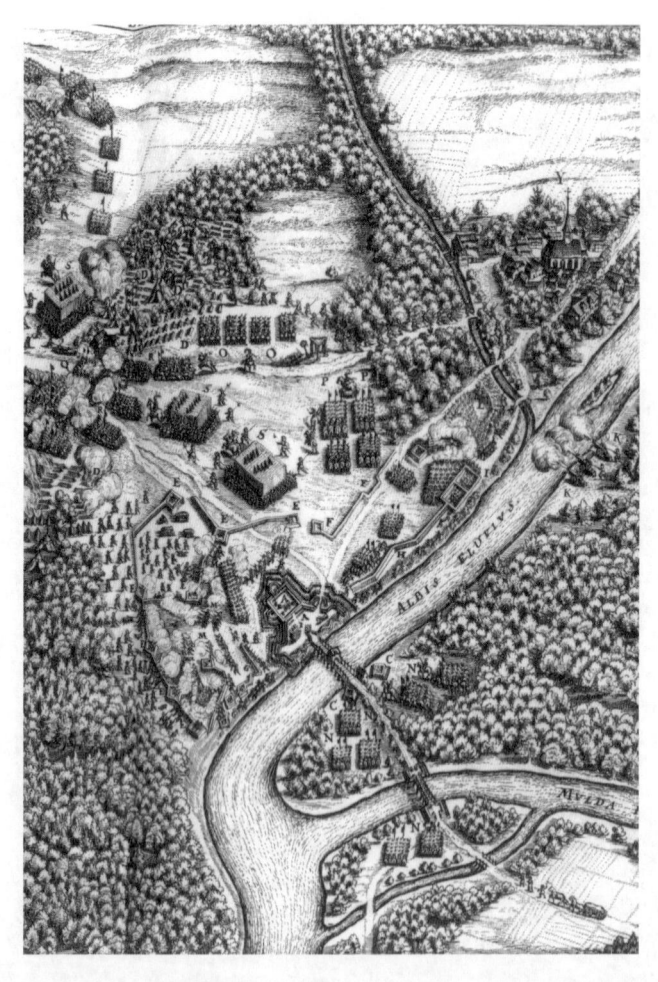

6. The battle for the Dessau bridge in 1626, from the *Theatrum Europaeum*
The legend to the small letters on the plan reads: A. Imperialist fortifications;
B. Elbe bridge; C. Imperialist redoubts; D. Mansfeld's camp; E. Mansfeld's fortifications; F. Mansfeld's approach trenches; G. Imperialist approach trenches and redoubts; H. Aldringer's approach trenches; I. Position held against Mansfeld; K. Imperialist artillery; L. Mansfeld driven off; M. Imperialist sally; N. Friedland's cavalry on the near side of the river; O. Mansfeld's cavalry; P. Friedland's cavalry; Q. Mansfeld's flight; R. Friedland commences pursuit; S. Schlick's and Aldringer's infantry; Y. The village of Rosslau.
(bpk Berlin)

7. Cross-section showing typical construction of the defences at the Alte Veste camp. (© Jane Turner)

8. The murder of Trčka, Ilow, Kinsky and Niemann, Eger, 25 February 1634, from the *Theatrum Europaeum*. (bpk Berlin)

11
From the Fury of the Norsemen Deliver Us
(Medieval Prayer)

The Alte Veste

Wallenstein had already won round one of the contest by the time his army came face to face with the Swedes outside Nuremberg. His move against the Saxons had not only covered his own rear by driving them out of Bohemia, but had also brought Gustavus hurrying northwards to counter the threat to his ally. Wallenstein had not fallen into the trap of making a hasty and ill-prepared foray with an insufficient number of men in an attempt to relieve Bavaria, but Gustavus had walked right into its counterpart. He had neither moved fast enough to evade Wallenstein, nor brought sufficient forces to fight him. Unable to reach Saxony and join up with Arnim's army, nor to prevent the Bavarians joining up with the Imperialists, he found himself isolated and outnumbered by more than two to one. According to Guthrie, Gustavus had 18,500 men to Wallenstein's 41,000, although others have said 48,000, while Wallenstein himself referred to 40,000 men before the Bavarians reached him and 50,000 thereafter.[1] Whatever the precise numbers, the disparity was far too great for Gustavus to contemplate a battle, and instead he was forced to run for cover.

Nevertheless it was only round one, and there was a long way to go before the final bell. Gustavus had at least found himself a strong defensive position. Nuremberg was sympathetic, well provisioned and already fortified, and he had arrived in time to extend and strengthen the protective earthworks around the city and his army. Wallenstein would have preferred to catch him in the open where he could be forced to battle, but he was probably not surprised by the situation he found. Despite his superior numbers he also knew that there was little chance of quick success by a direct attack on the Swedish camp.

Experience had repeatedly shown that relatively small garrisons in well-fortified cities could hold off full-scale armies for prolonged periods, Stralsund and Magdeburg being two prominent examples. Positions defended by a force the size of the Swedish army would be still more difficult and costly in terms of attackers' lives to take by storm. Tilly had withdrawn rather than make such an attempt against Gustavus's camp a year earlier at Werben, while Gustavus himself had recently marched impotently away from the fortifications of Ingolstadt and Regensburg.[2] On the other hand Wallenstein could not simply lay siege to Nuremberg and the Swedish camp. He knew that Gustavus would send for reinforcements, but he did not know from which direction or in what strength they would come, nor how long they would take to arrive. History offered too many examples of besieging forces defeated by surprise attacks from the rear for him to make such a simple error.

Wallenstein's answer was to build a heavily defended encampment of his own, from which he would be equally safe from attack while he watched and waited. Gustavus could not escape until he had accumulated reinforcements, but he would then have to stand and fight, or else retreat ignominiously back to Saxony with the Imperialist army hard on his heels, and he might well be driven back to his Baltic base. Wallenstein also had another reason to be patient. Storming the camp and defeating Gustavus's relatively small army, even were it possible, would not be final. The king himself would probably escape – generals usually did – to rally the much larger balance of his forces and fight again. Waiting for him to bring in his reinforcements offered the chance of inflicting a much more decisive defeat, particularly as he would then be able to force Gustavus to take the initiative simply by staying behind his own defences. In the meantime the spectacle of the Swedish king trapped at Nuremberg could cause second thoughts among some of his more uncertain recent allies.

Wallenstein chose his position carefully. The River Rednitz flows northwards past Nuremberg four to five miles west of the city centre, and although it is not large it provided protection for the camp which he established beyond it. The road from Nuremberg to Rothenburg crossed the site, running due west somewhat above and parallel to a tributary river, the Bibert, from which the land rises gradually to a ridge which became the southern boundary. At one end of this ridge a small hill, the Hainberg, overlooks the Rednitz, while at the other a strong artillery fortress was established on the high ground of the Petershöhe, outside the main defences and standing above the more open territory to the west. From the Bibert valley the land rises higher to the north, culminating in a heavily wooded ridge, beyond which the ground falls away steeply again. Here the perimeter ran just short of the crest, west to east and on to the Weinberg, a hill forming the end of the ridge a little way back from the Rednitz. Strong defensive outworks were constructed at the top, including another substantial artillery battery as well as fortifications around the Alte Veste (Old Fortress), a ruined medieval castle at the summit from which the whole camp takes its name.

Much more than usual is known about this camp, because after the armies had moved away the Nuremberg authorities commissioned cartographers to make a detailed plan, which is still in the archives.[3] Perhaps the most striking thing about the layout is its size, which contrasts sharply with the usual image of such camps as small and hopelessly overcrowded. Although not neatly rectangular the enclosure was some three miles long, north to south along the Rednitz, and a mile and a half wide, with ten miles of perimeter fortifications enclosing an area of almost four square miles. To put this in perspective, this is approximately half the area inside the modern city of Nuremberg's ring road, within which lives most of its population of half a million. Looked at in another way, the three or four villages which were inside Wallenstein's camp have grown into the spacious modern communities of Zirndorf and Oberasbach, with a combined population of 44,000, the great majority of whom live inside the camp area, despite which a significant part of it is still open farmland. For two months in 1632 the camp housed something like this number of soldiers, together with a similar number of dependants and camp followers, as well as a great many horses, so that while it was no doubt a bustling place it was probably not unmanageably congested. The Rednitz, the Bibert and another stream, the Asbach, provided water, while for most of the time the camp was not besieged so that there was relatively free access to the countryside beyond.

The standard construction method for the fortifications (see Plate 7 in this book) was to drive in large stakes and weave a six-foot-high fence from saplings and the smaller branches of felled trees. Immediately outside this a ditch was dug, the earth from which was piled up against the front of the fence, while more stakes with their ends sharpened into spikes were driven into the bottom. Inside the fence a step was built to provide a platform for the musketeers, enabling them to fire over the top but to reload in relative safety at the lower level. A local historian has calculated that the ten-mile perimeter would have required the felling of 13,000 trees and the excavation of 64,000 cubic metres of earth (about 80,000 tonnes), and the whole task is said to have been completed in three days.[4] Formidable though this sounds, with some 40,000 men available it reduces to two tonnes of earth per man and one tree between three, without allowing for women and boys pressed into service for the work. Once finished, the fortifications on the north and east sides supplemented the already strong natural defences provided by the steep wooded slope and the River Rednitz respectively, and while the ridge to the south was somewhat less daunting it was still challenging enough for an attacking force. Only to the west were the fortifications largely unsupported by nature, but this weakest side was furthest from Gustavus's position in Nuremberg, while from the top of the Alte Veste not only the city and the Swedish camp but also the entire countryside around could be seen.

When the digging and building were complete the long wait began. Outside the camps patrols probed, foraged, escorted their own supply trains or attempted to seize those of their opponents, and they skirmished from time to time. Although the Swedes had some significant successes the Imperialists were in the stronger position, not only because of their greater numbers at Nuremberg but also as a result of their hold on much of the surrounding territory. Roads were crucial both for supplying the camps and for bringing up relief forces, but they were few and poor, and Wallenstein set out to control them. Strategic towns and castles along most of the routes radiating out from Nuremberg were occupied, and although their garrisons were not strong enough to prevent reinforcements from eventually reaching Gustavus they considerably hampered his movements of men and supplies in the meantime.[5] Nor was the attempt to blockade the Swedish camp completely successful, but its effect was cumulative in reducing the availability of food and fodder for the troops and for the city. Wallenstein himself remained busy, not only as general of the army on the spot but also as generalissimo responsible for the Imperial forces in all other theatres of war, in addition to which he found time for his own lands, sending out a stream of enquiries and instructions to his governors.[6] Maximilian fretted and criticised the military inactivity as the summer wore on, but Wallenstein knew what he was trying to achieve, and he had the last word.

The waiting took its toll on both sides. Disease was endemic in army camps of the time, even ones as spaciously constructed and relatively well supplied as Wallenstein's, but he was at least able to move some of the sick out to recuperate elsewhere, helping to limit the spread of infection in his camp.[7] Conditions for the Swedish army were worse, as although Nuremberg was well provisioned at the outset it could not feed so many for so long, and the blockade soon started to pinch.

Soldiers and their dependants fell sick and died. Horses died or were slaughtered, although mostly draught animals rather than cavalry mounts. The citizens, also besieged, suffered most of all, both from disease and from hunger, as they took second place to the troops in the queue for food. According to the *Theatrum Europaeum* 29,406 people died in Nuremberg during 1632, many times more than in a normal year, indicating the scale of their tribulation.[8]

During this time reinforcements were assembling. Wallenstein brought in some himself, but the Swedes were busily gathering all their available forces, principally from the Rhine and southern Germany. Count Axel Oxenstierna, the Swedish chancellor and Gustavus's confidant, headed the operation, slowly but surely gathering together a reported 30,000 men before starting to move on Nuremberg in the latter part of August. It has been suggested that Wallenstein could have intercepted this army, but this is an unrealistic view. Intelligence was poor and armies had been known to slip past one another, so that interception was by no means certain, as demonstrated by Gustavus's own recent failure to catch the Bavarian army. Moreover had Wallenstein moved to meet the reinforcements the king would have been able to follow and to attack him from the rear as they engaged him from the front. The general was not inclined to such risky undertakings, and he preferred to confront the full Swedish force from the strength of his carefully prepared position.

When all were assembled they constituted the largest armies to face one another during the Thirty Years War, estimated to number around 45,000 on each side, although Gustavus had significantly more cavalry and correspondingly fewer infantry than Wallenstein. Both sides also had a formidable array of guns, but the Swedes had the larger number, having seized many in Munich which had been captured by the Bavarians earlier in the war. Still Wallenstein made no move, but Gustavus did not have the option of blockading him until he was forced into the field to offer battle. His men in Nuremberg were already far too short of supplies, and the arrival of 30,000 reinforcements had made the position still more critical. As Wallenstein had anticipated, he was forced to take the initiative, and quickly. Oxenstierna's relief army arrived on 27 August, but they were granted only three days respite after their long march before being ordered into action.[9]

Gustavus had had six weeks to study Wallenstein's finished camp, and given his habit of carrying out often risky reconnaissances personally it would be surprising if he had not looked at it very closely. He will have known the western side to be the weakest, but to attack from that direction involved a long march around the Imperialist encampment, particularly difficult for the artillery over poor roads, and with his columns at constant risk from sallies out of the defences. The alternatives were little better, as the other three sides of the camp had stronger natural defences, and thus Gustavus found himself in the same position as Wallenstein almost two months before, facing a well-prepared fortification occupied by a large army and with no obvious way of attacking it successfully.

Hence Gustavus's first move can be seen more as a probe for weaknesses than as an all-out attack. Early on 31 August 1632 the Swedish forces moved out of their encampments and took up position some distance back from the east bank of the River Rednitz, opposite the eastern defences of the Imperialist camp. The whole army was then drawn up in battle array in what amounted to a challenge to Wallenstein to come out and fight. It was a challenge which no competent general would have accepted, as it would have meant leaving a superior defensive position, crossing the river under Swedish gunfire, and then fighting with the river behind cutting off the line of retreat. Later in the day Gustavus moved his troops up closer and began to build emplacements for his guns in positions where they could fire right into the Imperialist camp. Wallenstein sought to hinder this both with his own artillery and with sallies from his defences, so that some skirmishing took place, in course of which one of the Swedish generals, Johan Banér, was severely wounded by a musket ball. Dusk brought this action to an end, but during the night the Swedes installed their heavy guns in the prepared batteries ready for the morning.

The following day, 1 September, opened with an artillery battle, and it was soon clear that the better-equipped Swedes had the advantage. Wallenstein countered this by moving his own guns back from the perimeter to new positions in which they were out of effective range of the Swedish batteries but still able to strike at troops attempting to cross the river. The Swedes then bombarded the camp for much of the day in an attempt to drive the Imperialists out, but Wallenstein's men and guns were well dug in and survived with little serious loss. More probing and skirmishing followed, but by evening it was clear to Gustavus that the fortifications were too strong and well defended to be taken by storm across the river, so he broke off the action.

At dawn on 2 September Wallenstein was probably not surprised to find that the Swedish army had moved during the night. Gustavus had marched four miles north to Fürth, where he had been able to cross the Rednitz and draw up his forces in defensive array in case of any

159

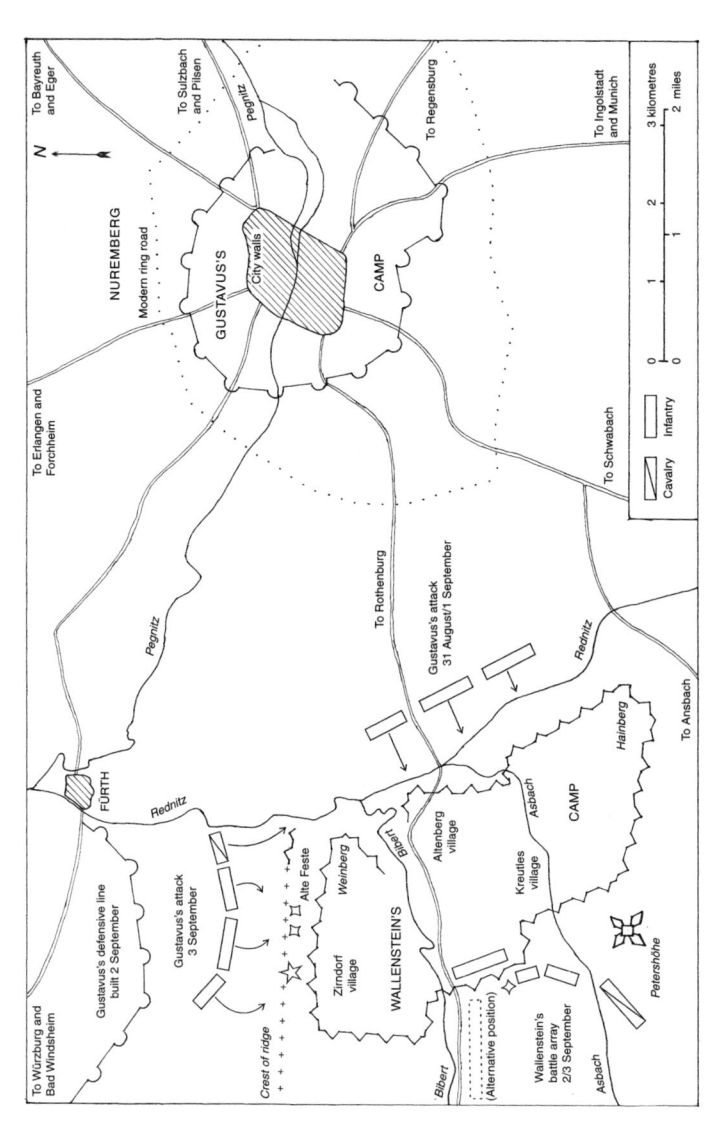

2. The battle at the Alte Veste, 31 August to 4 September 1632

counter-attack. Wallenstein assumed that his intention was to move on around the Imperialist camp in order to attack from the west, and he made his own preparations accordingly. This time he was ready to give battle, both because his weaker defences on this side made it advisable and also because the ground here was to his advantage. According to the contemporary Nuremberg plan he arranged his forces on a north-south line in front of the southern section of his camp, with the left (south) flank secured by the high ground of the Petershöhe and its artillery fortress, and the right by the Bibert river. A smaller artillery fort outside the perimeter was included in this line, while a third battery inside the camp was so placed as to be able to fire between or over the Imperialist formations. Cavalry were stationed to the left on the Petershöhe, as well as within the perimeter ready to emerge where needed, while the main infantry reserve was also kept behind the defences. This was a strong position, as the ground, although not steep, slopes steadily upwards towards the camp, while both wings were well secured and the perimeter fortifications provided shelter for an orderly retreat should it be required. However the historians of the Swedish General Staff show a different configuration, with the Imperialist army arrayed on an east-west line above the south bank of the River Bibert, and with its right flank on the camp defences.[10] It is possible that both are correct. Wallenstein may well have stationed an advance guard along the Bibert in order to hamper a Swedish crossing, or to threaten their flank should they have attempted to attack the camp on the rising ground north of the river. If so this advance guard could have been intended to fall back as the battle progressed, joining or withdrawing behind the main body positioned as previously described.

Much to Wallenstein's surprise the Swedish army did not appear, although he kept the Imperialist forces in the field ready for battle for the whole of 2 September and through the following night.[11] Instead Gustavus spent the day constructing a defensive position at Fürth, on an east-west line parallel to Wallenstein's northern perimeter and about a mile and a half back from the ridge which led up to it. At the same time he was making preparations and giving orders for the quite different plan he had for 3 September, an unconventional surprise attack on the strongest part of Wallenstein's defences around the Alte Veste. This was a major error, as will be seen, but first we need to consider the reasons for it.

It has often been claimed that Gustavus was misled by information from prisoners or his own scouts into believing that Wallenstein's move out of his camp was not to prepare for battle but to make a hasty retreat, so that he decided to attack from the north, expecting that the fortifications would be defended at most by a small rearguard. This tale probably stems from contemporary pro-Swedish sources which preferred to blame faulty intelligence rather than the king's judgement, but it is not credible. Gustavus was noted for his careful reconnaissance, and it is inconceivable that he or his scouts could have mistaken an Imperialist army standing in the field all day in battle order for one hurriedly making its escape. One of those best placed to know, Oxenstierna, wrote an account of the battle for the Swedish council, and he does indeed mention reports of an Imperialist retreat and a prisoner who confirmed them on 2 September, but he goes on to say that Gustavus immediately set out with an escort to make a personal assessment, that there were skirmishes, and that 'the enemy was thus forced to battle, and had to bring back his guns and look to his defences'. The king himself, in a letter to the elector of Saxony, also refers to information that Wallenstein was withdrawing, leaving only a few regiments as a rearguard, but he immediately adds that the report of the retreat was found to be false and that the enemy had only changed position somewhat. Hence when he launched his assault Gustavus was well aware that Wallenstein and his army were still drawn up for battle outside the western perimeter. If not there would have been no point in attacking an almost empty camp on its strongest side. Nor was the plan an impromptu response to an unforeseen development. Robert Monro, a Scottish colonel in Gustavus's army, states in his memoirs that the king's plan was to capture the high ground to the north in order to drive Wallenstein out of his camp, and hence 'we marched in the night through Furt, towards the other side of the enemies Leaguer, of intention to take in the hill'. Furthermore the coordinated attacks at multiple points early on 3 September had clearly been carefully planned, while the only apparent reason for building the defensive line at Fürth the previous day was to cover a retreat if they did not succeed.[12]

The truth was probably simpler. As an experienced general Gustavus knew that Wallenstein would expect him to attack the camp next on its weakest side, but he also knew that if it came to a battle there between armies of similar size Wallenstein would have the advantages of the ground, of being in position first, and of having his defences to fall back upon, whereas the Swedes would have no ready line of retreat. Faced with this unattractive prospect Gustavus decided, as he had at Rain, to do the unexpected and to attempt what others thought could not be done. Had a commando-style attack from the north succeeded quickly, he could have captured Wallenstein's camp behind him, together with most of his munitions and supplies, completely turning the tables and forcing him to withdraw. However Wallenstein had anticipated the possibility of an attack from the rear, and he had left Aldringer with a complement of guns and six regiments of infantry – probably of the order of 6000 men – to defend the camp if necessary until reinforcements could be sent.[13] Gustavus also underestimated the difficulty of the uphill assault through the woods, and the strength of the Alte Veste fortifications, while he was too confident of the ability of his veterans to overcome such problems. It was a gamble which did not pay off.

The fighting on 3 September was bitter and prolonged. The Swedish plan was to attack early and simultaneously at points across the northern perimeter of the camp, but this quickly fell behind schedule. Wallenstein had stripped the top of the ridge of trees, as well as clearing part of the way down the slopes to provide lines of fire for his defenders, but lower down they remained thickly wooded, while some of the felled timber had been left to lie there to act as a further impediment. The Swedish troops were hampered by long, heavy pikes and muskets, difficult to carry at the best of times but particularly unsuitable for traversing steeply sloping woods, and they found the going hard and slow. Soon they came under fire and started to take heavy casualties, but although they persevered bravely valuable time was lost and the attacks were no longer coordinated. Wallenstein quickly learned of the assault, but he was confident of Aldringer's ability to hold the fortifications for some time, so that he waited until he was sure that this was the main attack rather than a diversion. Once convinced, he sent his army flooding back into the camp to reinforce the northern defences.

The battle continued all day, and the Swedes managed to capture the artillery emplacement on the ridge as well as various other defensive outworks, but not the Alte Veste itself. Here Monro found the fighting 'cruell hot ... the Hill was nothing els but fire and smoke, like to the thundering Echo of a Thunderclap, with the noise of Cannon and Musket'. Wallenstein had the advantage of being able to relieve his men on the front line with fresh ones from the camp at regular intervals, and there are reports of him in the thick of the fray throwing handfuls of coins to encourage them.[14] Whether fact or fanciful rumour these confirm that he took personal command at the Alte Veste, as did Gustavus only a few hundred yards away on the Weinberg. Here the Swedes more than once pushed right up to the camp perimeter, but each time they were driven back by sallies from the defences, while both on this wing and on the river bank below there were sharp cavalry clashes during the afternoon.

As the fortifications seemed to be impregnable an alternative idea was developed, that of dragging Swedish heavy guns to the top of the hill, where they could be mounted in a position to bombard most of the camp below, thus forcing the Imperialists out. Duke Bernhard of Weimar, a German prince but one of Gustavus's generals, was in command of the troops holding the top of the ridge west of the Alte Veste, so he set men about trying to haul the necessary artillery up a steep track through the woods. The idea may have been good but the execution proved difficult, carried out under fire and harassed by Imperialist light cavalry, and it became impossible when it started to rain late in the afternoon, turning the track into mud. Night fell, leaving both sides standing at their posts on the ridge, but although there was a pause in the fighting it continued to rain. By the morning of 4 September it was clear that there was nothing to be gained from continuing the attack, and Gustavus ordered a retreat.

Wallenstein did not attempt a pursuit, as his own men were exhausted, having been in the field or in action for 48 hours. Moreover the Swedish defensive position at Fürth had been prepared for just such a contingency, and he had no wish to allow Gustavus to salvage something of his reputation by fighting a successful rearguard action. As it was, the aura of invincibility which had built up around the king during eighteen months of successes in Germany was severely damaged by this failure, while from the Swedish ranks Monro criticised him for relying on inadequate intelligence about the strength of the defences, and for continuing the attack long after it was apparent that it had little chance of success. Casualties were high as a result, and it is estimated that the Swedes lost of the order of 1000 dead and 2000 seriously wounded, while the Imperialist losses were no more than a third of this level. In his report to the emperor Wallenstein gave generous credit to Aldringer for his part in the engagement, adding that 'all officers and soldiers, infantry and cavalry alike, behaved as bravely as I have ever in my life seen in a battle'.[15]

While Wallenstein went back to his waiting game Gustavus looked for ways to extricate himself from the situation. He suggested peace negotiations, offering to send Oxenstierna to Wallenstein or even to meet him face to face himself, to which the general courteously but firmly replied that he had no authority to discuss such matters but that he would forward the king's proposal to the emperor in Vienna.[16] Even had there been any prospect of success in that quarter Gustavus could not afford to wait. Autumn was coming and his army was starting to melt away. Disease and casualties had already made inroads, but now hungry men, demoralised by a long period on the defensive followed by two failed attacks, started to desert. Many simply slipped away to the Imperialist camp, where they found food, a welcome and often a reward. By 15 September they were 'running away in droves', Wallenstein reported, noting that his own recruitment was going well as a result. On one occasion an entire company of cavalry, 80 men, killed their own captain and came across. 'More will follow them', he concluded. Within a fortnight of the failure at the Alte Veste Gustavus is believed to have lost a third of his army, leaving him with no choice but to withdraw.[17] Wallenstein noted with professional approval that 'he sent six cavalry regiments in advance, their strongest company only twenty horse, before he himself made a fine retreat silently in the night', adding that he could see 'from this as from all his campaigns that unfortunately he understands his calling only too well'.[18]

Much to Maximilian's annoyance Wallenstein did not immediately follow. His reasons, given in his report to the emperor, were firstly that he had dispersed his own cavalry widely in order to conserve supplies of food and fodder in the camp, and secondly that the Swedes retained possession of the route by which Oxenstierna had approached, so that they could retreat safely from one strong point to the next. Instead he was waiting for Pappenheim's army, which he understood to be marching towards him from the north, in order to trap Gustavus between them, 'and then he will be done for'. Although better off than the Swedes, Wallenstein's own army was also suffering from the effects of the long stand-off over the summer, including illness and shortage of supplies, so that, as he added to the emperor, 'I do not want to place at risk what I have made certain of'.[19] He stayed five more days in the camp, but as nothing was heard from Pappenheim he then marched off in a different direction. To begin with neither army went very far, Gustavus moving some 30 miles west to Bad Windsheim while Wallenstein headed 20 miles north to Forchheim, where both detached substantial parts of their forces for other purposes while they considered their next moves.

Lützen

Gustavus was at a loss to know what to do. He had planned to use the summer of 1632 to make a decisive strike east along the Danube into the Austrian heartland, putting himself in a position to dictate terms to Emperor Ferdinand. Instead he had been outmanoeuvred by Wallenstein and forced to sit idly in Nuremberg while the campaigning season slipped away. By the end of September it was too late for any major strategic initiative, and time instead to think about shortening his lines of communication, consolidating his position and finding winter quarters. Logically this suggested withdrawing at least to the River Main, which is what Wallenstein expected him to do, but that would have meant ending the year back where he had started it, and effectively abandoning most of his conquests further south. Such a prudent approach was not to Gustavus's liking, but he could find no clear alternative.

In the last week of September he left Bad Windsheim, but intelligence was so poor that for the next two weeks Wallenstein did not even know in which direction he had gone, still less exactly where he was. In fact Gustavus went south, where he spent a month marching back and forth, first through Swabia and beyond, then to the Danube and on into Bavaria, before finally hastening back to Nuremberg in the last week of October. During this time he undertook nothing of military significance, and such objectives as he appears to have had were at best of minor importance, although he doubtless collected some useful financial contributions. If nothing else his presence denied this source of funds to Wallenstein, who was as short as ever of money for his army, as his many letters show.[20]

For a time Wallenstein hesitated, perhaps waiting for some firmer indication of Gustavus's intentions to emerge. Nevertheless his own underlying strategy was clear. Firstly, although he was alert to the possibility of catching Gustavus for a decisive battle, it is evident that he regarded this as principally a problem for the following year, given the lateness of the season. Secondly he continued to view detaching Saxony from the Swedish alliance as central to improving the Imperialist position. Matters had escalated since the failure of his attempted peace negotiations with Arnim, and following the latter's invasion of Silesia in July Wallenstein had sent Holk to make a retaliatory raid, hoping by taking the war on to Saxon territory to persuade Elector John George that it would be more prudent to return to his allegiance to the emperor than to rely on Swedish help. As that had not succeeded Wallenstein decided to occupy the whole electorate, and on leaving Nuremberg he despatched Gallas with a large force to commence an invasion, intending to follow himself to complete the operation, and at the same time to solve his perennial problem of finding winter quarters.

Wallenstein was also still anxious to add the elusive Pappenheim to his strength. His own army was by this time becoming uncomfortably small, weakened not only by casualties and the losses through disease and desertion which affected all armies during a summer in the field, but also by the number of units he had detached for service elsewhere. Throughout 1632 Pappenheim had been operating on a roving commission in north-western Germany, and even for a time in the Netherlands, and he liked his independence. Where possible he ignored higher orders which did not suit him, and where not he returned evasive replies, leading Wallenstein to send off increasingly peremptory instructions that he should come to join him.[21] Pappenheim eventually replied that he was heading for Thuringia, and in early October Wallenstein marched north via Coburg in order to meet him *en route* to Saxony. Maximilian, anxious that Gustavus was still in the south and hence a threat to Bavaria, decided to depart for home with his army, aggravating Wallenstein's shortage of men, but he at least agreed that Pappenheim – as and when he could be induced to return – should come under Imperialist command. In exchange the general lent him a strong force under Aldringer to counter Gustavus's activities in Bavaria.[22]

Pappenheim did not arrive, but news of Wallenstein's move north reached the king by mid-month and set his alarm bells ringing. Thuringia meant two things to him. Firstly the rough, hilly, heavily wooded territory lay between him and the north German plain, with its access to the Baltic. There were few feasible routes across it for an army, and if Wallenstein held them his own principal line of retreat would be blocked. Secondly, beyond Thuringia lay Saxony, reviving Gustavus's fears of earlier in the year that his most important ally might be detached from him, whether by defection or defeat. Were Saxony to desert him Brandenburg would follow, and then others. The prospect at least resolved his uncertainty. From Nuremberg he embarked on a forced march north, passing Maximilian's army going south but without making contact, and on 3 November he was joined at Arnstadt by forces under Bernhard of Weimar. Pappenheim was ten miles further north near Erfurt, but Wallenstein was already in Saxony, where Holk had captured Leipzig two days earlier. Gustavus moved on to Erfurt, but Pappenheim headed for Leipzig to join up at last with Wallenstein's army, and on 10 November the king advanced to Naumburg, 27 miles south-west of Leipzig, where he rapidly built himself a defensive encampment based on the town's walls.

Wallenstein had anticipated that Gustavus would respond to his thrust into Saxony, but the speed of his advance caused him some surprise. The force he sent to take Naumburg arrived too late; the Swedes were already there. The general reacted swiftly, moving his army up to Weissenfels, a few miles from Naumburg, on the following day, but Gustavus stayed firmly behind his defences. In a letter of 12 November he explained to his Saxon ally that it had been his intention in coming north to attack Wallenstein immediately, but now, finding himself 'a good deal weaker than the enemy', particularly in cavalry, he needed to wait for reinforcements. Another of his allies, Duke Georg of Brunswick-Lüneburg, was heading towards him from Lower Saxony, and his cavalry had reached the fortress of Torgau, on the River Elbe 60 miles to the north-east, while his infantry were two days march behind. Lüneburg's forces, 8000 strong, so Gustavus hoped, although other sources say 6000, should reach him soon, but in the meantime 'we intend to stay here in Naumburg and strengthen our position'.[23]

At this point, so historians have commonly stated, Wallenstein concluded that Gustavus would do nothing more that year and that he intended to winter in Naumburg. Hence he immediately started to disperse his own men into their winter quarters, thus giving the king the opportunity to attack his remaining forces at Lützen shortly afterwards. These writers do not, however, offer any credible explanation as to why the habitually cautious Wallenstein should have made such a careless mistake. The fact is that he did not, as although he was undoubtedly planning his winter dispositions both these and the more immediate moves he made were calculated responses to the military situation, albeit in so doing he made a near-fatal error.

Gustavus was in a difficult position, one quite similar to his first encounter with Wallenstein. Again he had moved hastily but in insufficient strength, had failed to head off the Imperialist reinforcements, and had been forced to take shelter in a fortified position. As at Nuremberg this was too strong to be taken by assault, but his refuge was nevertheless a potential trap. This time it was too late in the season to gather reinforcements from far and wide, while despite his optimistic letter to the Saxons it would be difficult for Lüneburg to reach him from Torgau, with Wallenstein's much larger army directly in between. Wintering in Naumburg was scarcely an option. The town, with a population of only a couple of thousand, was too small for his army of 19,000 men and their dependants over an extended period. Nor could he disperse his troops into the towns and villages across a wider area – the usual practice for winter quarters – as long as the Imperialist army remained within striking distance. Wallenstein was sure to occupy and place strong garrisons in all the surrounding towns he did not already hold, both denying them to the Swedes and enabling his cavalry to control the territory over the winter. Were he to be blockaded in Naumburg,

Gustavus could expect his army to start to melt away as it had after the failed attack on the Alte Veste.

Nevertheless Wallenstein could not contemplate a prolonged siege of Naumburg, with his army in an undefended position, in the open and the cold. Nor was constructing a camp, as he had done at Nuremberg, feasible with the weather already bad and winter at hand. Men and their families needed proper shelter, or sickness, death and desertion would soon start to take their toll on his own army. Although his forces were temporarily superior to Gustavus's, he too was aware that Lüneburg at Torgau would soon have enough men to redress the balance, and precautions would have to be taken to prevent him reaching Gustavus. Then there was Arnim with the main Saxon army in Silesia. Wallenstein did not know accurately where he was, although at a probable distance of 150 miles or more he was not an immediate threat, but he might have been able to send some cavalry to join Lüneburg at Torgau. Wallenstein had summoned Gallas, but he was 100 miles away, south of Dresden, where he was making slow progress trying to haul his artillery through the hills in bad weather. Meanwhile Aldringer lingered on in Bavaria with some 8000 men in response to Maximilian's pressing appeals, despite the general's summons and Gustavus's departure.[24] However reinforcements would not solve the immediate problem that the Swedish position in Naumburg could not feasibly be taken by storm. The Imperialist army would have to move.

Wallenstein recognised that Gustavus would probably break out as soon as he himself withdrew, but where would he go? He had an urgent need of both winter quarters and reinforcements, but to the east lay not only the occupied city of Leipzig, controlling the road to Torgau, but a series of towns across southern Saxony which had been taken by Gallas and Holk, while Wallenstein also had forces facing Arnim in Silesia. On the other hand there was no substantial Imperialist army to the north-west, so that it seemed more likely that the king would head in that direction, instructing Lüneburg to move west to join him. If so his first destination would probably be the city of Halle, twenty miles to the north, which – unknown to Wallenstein – was the rendezvous Gustavus had originally given Lüneburg, although his order had not been received.[25] Halle lay not in Saxony but in the territory of the archbishopric of Magdeburg, and beyond and west of the city were a number of prosperous towns, among them Quedlinburg and Halberstadt, in an area in which Wallenstein had himself wintered in 1626–27. Halle was Protestant, it had a strong castle, and it was the only large fortified place within a day's march of Naumburg not already in Imperialist hands.

It was a logical target and intermediate refuge for the Swedes, if they could secure it. Wallenstein made his plans accordingly.

On 14 November he drew back to Lützen, a little town with a small castle, sixteen miles from Naumburg, eleven from Leipzig, and on a direct line between the two. There orders were given for what was to follow, and Holk, acting as Wallenstein's chief of staff, drew up a long list of troop dispositions and a memorandum of the instructions the general had given him.[26] These plans included both immediate actions and arrangements for the winter, and they covered not only the regiments at Lützen but also those with Gallas, which were to be stationed at towns and castles stretching across southern Saxony from Zwickau to the Bohemian border, hence securing Wallenstein's communications, supplies and line of retreat in case of need.

In his account of the battle of Lützen Holk recorded that Wallenstein had waited several days at Weissenfels to see if Gustavus would take the field.

As that did not happen, he ordered Pappenheim to march to Halle with nine regiments, and he wanted to follow himself in order to do battle with the king should he attempt to relieve the city, but because the duke was plagued by gout he halted, contrary to some advice, beyond a crossing over a small river, Rippach by name, at Lützen. He sent four regiments under Hatzfeld to Eilenburg, in the direction of Torgau, and two to Altenburg to guard against the possibility that the enemy might threaten the route to Zwickau and Chemnitz, the link to Bohemia. Consequently we were reduced by fifteen regiments, among them some of the strongest in the army.[27]

Wallenstein's plan, as outlined here by Holk, was to send a strong force to occupy Halle before Gustavus could do so, while despatching other units to prevent Lüneburg from advancing and to protect his own line of communication. Anticipating that Pappenheim would have to besiege Halle, and that Gustavus might therefore try to relieve the Protestant city, Wallenstein was preparing to march there himself in order to confront him. His further orders specified that were that not to happen Pappenheim was to send some of his regiments on to the bishopric towns, which were to be made to pay contributions, and their walls were to be destroyed to prevent future resistance. These troops were then to winter in that area, but the short-term objective was to deny it to Gustavus. For the same reason garrisons were also allocated to a number of towns between Naumburg, Halle and Leipzig, including a strong contingent for the latter city, so that in the event of an attack on one a large relief force could have been quickly assembled from the others. However these units did not leave Lützen in the first instance. Holk himself was to go further afield over the winter, to Westphalia and beyond, in order to secure important towns, raise contributions and recruit new men for the following year. The numbers of men he required to garrison each place were listed, and regiments were allocated for the purpose, but they likewise remained at Lützen at this stage.

Less certain is why Wallenstein waited at Lützen. The troops who stayed were presumably those he intended to take to Halle in order to attack Gustavus, and it may be that he delayed his departure, as Holk said, because of his own illness. However he may also have deemed it advisable to wait for the Swede to show his hand before moving, and he despatched a senior officer, Major-General Rudolf Colloredo, back to Weissenfels with 300 infantry and some light cavalry, so-called Croats, probably to watch and keep in touch with the king's movements. In the meantime he evidently felt strong enough to stay at Lützen. It was his first, indeed his only, major mistake in his duel with the king, as he had not anticipated how quickly Gustavus would act. Nevertheless he took precautions, including withdrawing to Lützen, at a safer distance from the Swedes, before despatching forces elsewhere, and he left troops to guard the Rippach crossing. It has also been argued that a surviving battle plan for Lützen which Pappenheim had with him the following day was prepared beforehand by Wallenstein as a contingency measure, rather than being hastily sketched after warning of Gustavus's approach was received. On the morning of 15 November the whole army was drawn up in battle order from seven until nine in the morning to cover the departing units against any possible attack, and the light cavalry were kept in the field for the rest of the day just in case.[28] Pappenheim reached Halle the same afternoon, where he was able to occupy the city immediately without meeting any resistance.

Gustavus was on the move even earlier on that mid-November morning. On arriving at Naumburg he had sent orders to Lüneburg to come to join him, prescribing a circuitous route to avoid Leipzig, via Grimma, fifteen miles south-east of the city, and then Altenburg, twenty-three to the south.[29] As the Imperialists withdrew Gustavus saw his chance. Hoping by moving immediately to be well on his way before an interception or pursuit could be organised, he set off eastwards towards Grimma to try to meet Lüneburg. Wallenstein had guessed wrong. Nevertheless the king could have had no idea of the Imperialist dispersals, as they had not yet begun, and still believing himself to have the weaker army he was not 'intending to do battle with the enemy, but to advance towards and join up with [Lüneburg's] Saxon troops'. Hence Gustavus moved very cautiously, slowly and in full battle order, in case the withdrawal was an attempted trap. His route took him to the south of Weissenfels, and although sources are not clear on the details it seems that cavalry outriders protecting his left wing clashed with Colloredo's Croats moving up to the town.[30] Prisoners were taken, from whom Gustavus learned of Pappenheim's despatch, but conversely Colloredo learned that the Swedish army was on the march. The king took stock of the situation. With the element of surprise gone he could no longer hope to slip by the Imperialist army towards Lüneburg. He had to change his plans, but his options were limited to retreating back to Naumburg or preparing for battle with Wallenstein. Gustavus was temperamentally inclined to the bold and unexpected course of action, but he also realised that with Pappenheim on the way to Halle he would have the Imperialists outnumbered until he could be recalled. It was a brief window of opportunity, so he decided to attack at once.

This was about mid-day. Colloredo hastily withdrew, harassed by Gustavus's cavalry, but at the Rippach, a mere four miles from Lützen, his men and the troops Wallenstein had left on guard, around 1000 in all, staged a spirited and effective delaying action. Despite bringing up their artillery the Swedes were unable to force a crossing until it was already dusk and too late for an attack that day. Meanwhile despatch riders sped out from Lützen after the recently departed units, and hasty preparations for a battle were put in hand. Pappenheim could not be expected back until the following day, but some of the others arrived in time to take up their positions by torchlight.[31] Wallenstein had the night to complete his defences and array his forces.

The country around Lützen is almost flat, with few natural features helpful in positioning an army for battle. Instead Wallenstein stationed his troops along the northern side of the road which runs north-east from Lützen towards Leipzig. This road had ditches on either side, and during the night the troops were set to work deepening them and raising the road, while whatever timber could be gathered was sharpened into spikes to hinder a cavalry attack. Although the road from Naumburg along which the Swedes were advancing would have brought them up on to the Imperialist right wing, this was protected by the town itself, while marshy ground along a stream, the Mühlgraben, ensured that they could not easily move round to the west of Lützen and attack Wallenstein's flank and rear, but would instead have to pass the town to the south and east, bringing them up to face his line of battle.

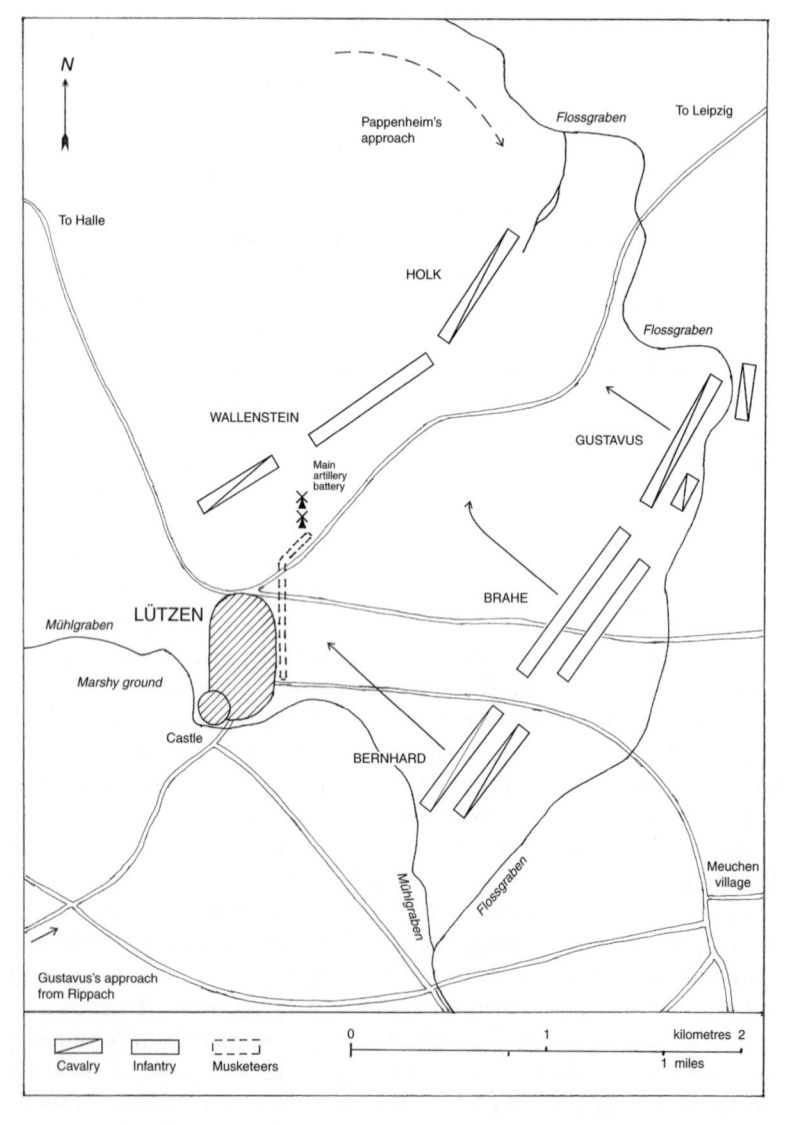

3. Disposition of forces at the commencement of the battle of Lützen, 16 November 1632

This alignment also meant that the road from Halle was to the Imperialist rear, so that when Pappenheim arrived his men would readily be able to take up their allotted positions. On Wallenstein's right some windmills stood on slightly elevated ground just outside the town, and here he stationed his main artillery battery, while smaller batteries of lighter guns were also placed towards the centre and left of the line. The battle array followed the conventional pattern, with cavalry on the wings flanking the main infantry force in the centre, with the reserves behind, but the heavy cavalry was mainly on the right, leaving a more numerous but mostly lighter contingent to hold the left. This was the weakest point, with no flanking defence apart from another stream, the Flossgraben, which was not a major obstacle, and it was hoped that Pappenheim would arrive in time to remedy this deficiency.[32] The sources are vague on the command arrangements, but it appears that Pappenheim was to take over on the left as soon as he reached the field, freeing Holk, who was initially posted there, to move across and take over on the right, which Wallenstein himself commanded at the outset, together with the whole of the centre.[33]

Wallenstein moved swiftly, and the end result was probably as good as could have been achieved on this ground even given more time, but the main problem remained; when the battle began he was outnumbered and outgunned. In total numbers the deficiency did not appear too great, as Guthrie estimates 19,000 on the Swedish side against 16,800 Imperialists. Wallenstein actually had rather more cavalry, although some of these were lightly armed Croat skirmishers, so that there may have been a rough equality. However Gustavus had 13,000 infantry to his 10,000, a superiority of 3000 men or 30 per cent, and the Swedes had half as many guns again as the Imperialists.[34] Hence Gustavus was able to arrange his men in a double line facing Wallenstein's, with the main force supplemented by a reserve across its full length. A Swedish general, Count Nils Brahe, commanded the infantry in the centre, Bernhard of Weimar and Gustavus himself commanded the forward cavalry units on the Swedish left and right respectively, and the artillery was distributed between several batteries along the line.[35]

The Swedes halted for the night a mile or two short of Lützen, and their attempts to move up early in the morning were hindered by fog. Hence they had to wait for the light to improve before they could take up their battle positions, but by the time they had done so the fog had thickened, further delaying their attack. Gustavus could only wait anxiously, knowing that Pappenheim could arrive at any time. The fog also made it difficult for both sides to assess the strength and positions of the enemy units, a situation which continued during the battle as recurrent swirls of mist worsened the already poor light of a short mid-November day. The same problem also affected subsequent reports of the battle, which are more than usually tendentious, and they make an undoubtedly confused situation the more confusing in the telling. No attempt will be made here to give a spuriously authoritative account of the action, instead picking out only a few points which are both central and relatively reliably recorded.[36]

It was around eleven before Gustavus could begin the attack, but his cavalry on the right soon ran into trouble against Wallenstein's defences, while those on the left made little progress in trying to reach the artillery battery by the windmills, coming under heavy fire from Imperialist musketeers stationed among the houses of Lützen. The town either caught or was set on fire, the smoke adding to that of the guns in further reducing visibility on the battlefield. After regrouping, the Swedes started to make progress, particularly on their right, but around noon Pappenheim arrived with some 2500 cavalry, and although men and horses were tired after their long ride he set about preparing a counter-attack, which he launched at about one in the afternoon. He himself was almost immediately shot down, dying of his wounds a few hours later, but with the arrival of his men the numbers on both sides were now similar. In this era evenly matched forces often resulted in battles which were prolonged and bitterly fought, with advantage swinging first one way and then the other, and frequently varying at different places on the field. This was the case at Lützen on the afternoon of 16 November 1632. As the day progressed the course of events emerges less and less clearly from the reports, but it is evident that rather than the generals being able to exercise effective control or execute any overall strategy the battle became a series of localised thrusts, defences and counter-thrusts, dependent on the initiative of the officers on the spot. One who particularly distinguished himself on the Imperialist side was the young Italian colonel, later general, Octavio Piccolomini, who rallied the left wing after Pappenheim had fallen, despite himself being several times wounded. Wallenstein, some say, commanded for much of the day from the confines of a litter, as the pains of gout meant that he could sit only briefly on a horse. Others report him in the thick of the fighting, where Holk says he was wounded, while another account says that he was shot in the hip by a musket ball, but it did not penetrate his thick coat.[37]

At some stage in this conflict the 37-year-old Gustavus Adolphus was killed, which is almost as much as can be said with certainty on the subject, as contemporary accounts vary and owe more to hearsay than to eyewitnesses. The generally preferred version is that during the early afternoon, seeing a force of his infantry cut off and under heavy pressure on the Imperialist side of the road, Gustavus gathered together a body of cavalry and charged to the rescue. In the resulting mêlée, perhaps in the mist, he became detached from most of his escort, and as because of an old wound he wore only light protection rather than full armour a shot disabled him, following which he was surrounded and killed. Who knew of his death and when they learned of it is also uncertain, but a story that his chaplain quelled panic when the news arrived by setting the Swedes to singing a psalm may well be taken with a pinch of salt.[38] The king's absence was noted and Bernhard of Weimar took command, following standard procedure were Gustavus to be incapacitated in any way, but although rumours began to circulate his death was only confirmed when his body, stripped of his valuable clothes and effects, was found later in the afternoon and taken to the small church at the village of Meuchen, in the Swedish rear.

Battles usually ended when one side gave way under pressure and men started to flee the field, while the victors gave pursuit and set about plundering the enemy baggage train. This did not happen at Lützen. Despite several changes of fortune and although Wallenstein's main artillery battery had been captured, as the last light faded at five in the afternoon both sides were holding substantially their original positions. The issue could still have gone either way, but by then the exhausted armies had fought themselves to a standstill. At that point Pappenheim's infantry, around 3000 men, finally reached Lützen, still capable of fighting even after their long march, but although their commander was keen to launch a final attack it was too late. Some 2000 men from each army already lay dead, probably more on the Swedish side, with perhaps twice as many seriously wounded, large numbers of whom would die of their injuries. It was dark, units were scattered and disorganised, ammunition was in short supply, and nothing more could be attempted that night. The question was what to do next.

Once again the poor visibility and limited information about exactly what had taken place influenced the outcome. Neither side had any clear idea of the remaining strength and fighting capability of the other, although they were better informed about their own deficiencies. Sydnam Poyntz, an English captain in Wallenstein's army, gave a graphic picture of the situation:

> The night beeing farre in, both Armies retreated the space of one half English mile and refreshed themselves beeing wonderfull weary

> man and horse, so many of both as were left unkilled: wee were scarcely laid downe on the ground to rest and in dead sleep but comes a commaund from the Generall to all Coronells and Sergeant Majors to give in a Note how strong every Regiment was found to bee. ... I could give hym but account of 3 Officers of my Companie which lay there downe by my side. It seemes hee found most of his Companies as weake as myne, for presently that night the Army was commaunded to march away without sound of Drum or Trumpet.[39]

Bernard of Weimar, young, ambitious, and for the first time in overall command, preferred to hold his position rather than risk being thought over-cautious, besides which retreat had its own dangers. Wallenstein, older, more prudent, and himself ill, was not inclined to take a chance on what the morning might bring, particularly with the safety of Leipzig within marching distance for his army. Moreover he was worried that help might be on its way to the Swedes from Torgau or even from Arnim's Saxon army, so he withdrew that evening.[40] The newly arrived regiments from Halle provided a rearguard, but the Swedes made no attempt at pursuit, and the following morning they themselves retreated back to Naumburg.

As the Swedes were left in possession of the field they were able to claim victory under one of the established conventions of the day. Using another common measure Wallenstein counter-claimed that he had won, as he had captured far more of the enemy's standards than vice versa. This propaganda battle has been going on ever since between the protagonists of the two sides, while neutrals usually describe the outcome as a draw. Certainly neither side can be said to have won in any wider sense, as both suffered heavy casualties and were unable to proceed with their original intentions, while neither was able to eliminate the other as a force to be reckoned with, or even to inflict enough damage for the setback to outlast the winter.

Those who had certainly lost still lay where they had fallen. Lieutenant Augustin Fritsch, arriving in the evening with Pappenheim's infantry, was sent to reconnoitre under cover of darkness around the captured Imperialist artillery battery. He found the big guns which had been the centre of so much fighting standing unguarded, 'with not a single man there from the enemy'. Instead 'the whole field, as far as we could see, was full of lights, which I took for musketeers' slow matches, causing me some alarm, but when we came down from the windmills and went further I saw for the first time that they were only torches, which the soldiers had in their hands as they went looting among the dead on the battlefield'.[41]

12
Of Peace and Other Demons
(After Marquez)

In January 1633 a small group of Imperial councillors prepared a memorandum for the emperor on the progress of the war.[1] Circumspectly phrased, and with all the obligatory references to the righteousness of the cause and the emperor's duty to the church, their assessment was nonetheless gloomy. After years of fighting, bloodshed and devastation of the emperor's lands, the position of the Catholic church was less, rather than more secure. Indeed, it was worse than it had been at any time since the Reformation. There were far more Protestants than Catholics in the Empire, a regrettable fact which assisted the emperor's enemies, as the success of the Swedish campaigns had shown. Prior to Gustavus's intervention the Catholic side had won many battles but had not been able to achieve an enduring victory, but the loss of one battle, Breitenfeld, had cost them most of Germany. A number of Protestant princes of the Empire had allied themselves with the Swedes, while others, including Catholics, had taken refuge in neutrality. The emperor's only reliable external ally, Spain, could provide little practical help due to the continuing war in the Netherlands, while on the other side France was assisting Sweden and had its own designs on Imperial territory, while England and Holland were also actively hostile, and Denmark was at best uncertain.

It was not realistic to think, they went on, that the situation could be fundamentally altered by one or two successful battles, or to imagine that the Catholic side could be restored to its former position by force of arms quickly or even in a few years. The resources in the hands of the enemy were far greater than those of the emperor's hereditary lands, where to impose further hardships on the population could provoke another revolt, and even the Habsburg succession to the Imperial crown could be called into question if the Estates of the Empire were further alienated by a continuing war. The military efforts of the previous year had not been able to force the centre of the conflict away from the emperor's lands and deep into enemy territory, but they had at least restored a balance, for a time, in which neither side could feel certain of victory. That was precisely the situation in which peace negotiations had the best chance of success, and the kings of Denmark and Poland had both offered themselves as mediators, as had Landgrave Georg of Hesse-Darmstadt. These opportunities should be pursued now, before campaigning started again in the spring, and a truce should be sought for the duration of negotiations in order to spare the emperor's lands further burdens of war.

The authors of this appraisal were Count Maximilian Trauttmansdorff, a senior and increasingly influential councillor, Baron Peter Stralendorf, the vice-chancellor, and Bishop Antonius of Vienna, while Eggenberg and Questenberg, who were known to hold similar views, were also among the 'peace party' in Vienna. Wallenstein, never a politician and for years absent from Vienna, was not one of their number, but his analysis was identical. Lützen had been, as Wellington said of Waterloo, 'the nearest run thing you ever saw in your life', and Wallenstein realised more clearly than anyone else that had Gustavus lived and won, it would have been disastrous for the Imperialist side.

As it was Wallenstein had achieved his own minimum objectives for 1632. He had prevented Gustavus from invading and occupying the Habsburg hereditary lands, he had stemmed the tide of Swedish victories, depriving them of their reputation for invincibility, and he had inflicted, if not a decisive defeat, at least two severe setbacks on the enemy. It was not enough. His own losses had not been so heavy that his army could not be rebuilt over the winter, but he could not afford to risk it again in a major battle with an opponent of comparable strength. Were the army to be destroyed neither he nor the emperor had money enough to raise another, and nor were sufficient men readily to be found within the limited area still under Imperialist control. The Swedes were not so constrained. They and their supporters held much of Germany, giving them scope to raise contributions and troops much more widely, and they had external allies with deep pockets and further territories for recruitment at their disposal. Even without Gustavus they had able generals, while Oxenstierna had taken over the political control and was intent on continuing where his king had left off. An Imperialist victory, Wallenstein saw, was not achievable in any real and sustainable sense, and although it was necessary to rebuild and maintain a strong army the principal effort had to be directed towards finding a basis for peace.

'I long for peace as much as for my own salvation', he told a Danish representative at this time, 'but nevertheless I am now making greater preparations for war than I have ever done.' This time, however, his efforts were to be directed first and foremost against 'those who spurn the offer of peace negotiations and want yet more bloodshed'.[2]

There was another reason for his desire for peace. At 49 Wallenstein was past his prime by the standards of the time, and his health, never good, was deteriorating rapidly. His gout, a progressive and debilitating condition for which there was then no effective treatment, was steadily crippling him. At Lützen he could still ride, if only for a time, but thereafter a coach or a horse-litter were his principal means of transport. He had increasing difficulty in writing, sometimes unable even to sign his name due to the pain in his finger joints, and he suffered from other recurrent illnesses, given names such as Hungarian fever and perhaps stemming from his early days as a soldier. Precisely what they were has not been established but is in any case irrelevant. What is clear is that he was constantly unwell and frequently more severely ill, a fact which became common knowledge as 1633 progressed. Wallenstein knew it best of all. The war had dragged on for almost fifteen years already, but he could not command for many more. Even had it been winnable he did not have time to win it, so peace became his priority, even his obsession. Peace too for himself, freedom from the crushing burdens of command which he had reluctantly resumed a year earlier. Peace to enjoy for the little time remaining to him the lands and palaces of his duchy, which, as his correspondence shows, were never far from his thoughts even at the most hectic periods during his campaigns. Mecklenburg was gone for as long as the Swedes held north Germany, while Sagan, like the rest of Silesia, was threatened or actually occupied by Arnim's army, but he still had Friedland. Even that would go if the Swedes and Saxons resumed their advance, allowing the Bohemian exiles to return. There were many reasons to long for peace.

The twists and tangles of the ensuing contacts between the warring parties, in most of which Wallenstein was the central figure, are not easy to understand. Mann went so far as to claim that efforts to do so have been in vain, as 'a description of the last year of Wallenstein's life cannot be based upon pure reason', because this 'presupposes what did not exist'. Fortunately this is too pessimistic a view. It may indeed be difficult, as Mann argued, 'to create reasoned order from what he said, what his authorised, half-authorised, or completely unauthorised self-proclaimed friends said that he said, or what they said of him', but if attention is focused upon what little Wallenstein himself can be shown with reasonable certainty to have said, and even more upon what he actually did, the picture becomes sharper.³

After Lützen Wallenstein did not remain long in Leipzig, or indeed in Saxony. Seeking winter quarters for his battered army in hostile territory, and with Arnim, Lüneburg and Bernhard of Weimar still at large, no longer seemed feasible. Security was necessary to allow for rebuilding, and this was only to be found in Bohemia, albeit this meant wintering again in the Habsburg hereditary lands, much to the dismay of the court. His army withdrew, and Wallenstein himself went to Prague. There he wrote a letter of condolence to Pappenheim's widow, and a few days later he sent her a significant sum of money to tide her over, 'as we are not unaware that in current circumstances the lady is unable to get anything from her lands'.⁴ He also distributed generous rewards to officers and men who had acquitted themselves well at Lützen, together with payments to the wounded. There were those, however, who had conducted themselves differently. The unexpected appearance of the Swedes had not allowed some to prepare themselves mentally for battle, the shifting fortunes of the day had misled others into thinking at various times that the battle was lost, and the unusually prolonged fighting had frayed the nerves of still others. There had been deserters, some of them officers, even a colonel. One captain fled so far that he met Pappenheim's men on the march towards Lützen, telling them that the battle was lost and advising them to head back to Halle as fast as they could. Some of the runaways had taken their entire units with them, although Wallenstein blamed the officers, 'for if they had stood their ground then the troopers would also have remembered their duty'. Military justice had to follow, 'for just as the good are rewarded, so must the bad be punished'.⁵

The result was the so-called Prague blood tribunal, arising from which twelve officers and five other ranks were executed, while some thirty junior officers who had prudently disappeared and evaded capture were sentenced to death in their absence. Some historians have presented this as Wallenstein seeking scapegoats for his failure to achieve a clear victory at Lützen, as well as claiming that this turned many of his officers against him, but this is improbable.⁶ Holk was responsible for the process, a large and widely drawn bench of judges carried out the court-martial, and the evidence was carefully examined over a period of three weeks. Some of those who had been suspected initially were cleared without being brought to trial, others were acquitted, and one was sentenced only to a dishonourable discharge, but for the proven deserters, and particularly those who not only fled but first robbed their own army's baggage train, military law prescribed death.

Wallenstein's duty as commander-in-chief was to confirm the sentences, despite representations from high places on behalf of the aristocratic colonel who was the most senior of those condemned, while an eighteen-year-old cavalry captain attracted particular sympathy, reportedly including a plea for clemency from Piccolomini, which Wallenstein also refused. They were harsh times, and war then, as later, was a harsh business. Eighteen-year-olds were still being executed for cowardice in the face of the enemy during the First World War almost 300 years later. As for the proceedings turning hard-bitten career officers against Wallenstein, they will have expected nothing less, as such measures were deemed necessary to ensure that men did their duty in combat. Moreover they were normal practice. Three months earlier a colonel in Swedish service who surrendered the town of Rain was court-martialled and executed after Gustavus Adolphus re-took it a few days later, and the Saxon officer who surrendered Leipzig to Holk was executed at Dresden.[7] Nevertheless the numbers involved after Lützen were unusually high, reflecting the exceptionally hard-fought nature of the battle, while the fact that the sentences were carried out in the same Prague square where leading Bohemian rebels had been executed twelve years before has given the event a particular notoriety.

In military terms 1633 was a year in which neither side achieved much of consequence, as although the war did not by any means come to a standstill it was effectively relegated into second place by a convoluted series of attempts to find some basis for peace. Nevertheless Swedish progress in both political and military matters early in the year confirmed the fears so recently set out by the peace party in Vienna. Oxenstierna became head of the regency government, with 100,000 men still in Swedish service in Germany, and in order to provide a sounder basis for continuing the war he concluded a new alliance with France, as well as pursuing a scheme already initiated by Gustavus for forming a tighter union of Protestant German princes and cities. Hence the Heilbronn League was formally constituted in April 1633, with its members drawn mainly from the Franconian, Swabian and Rhine circles of the Empire, and with Oxenstierna as its director, although it did not include the important electorates of Saxony and Brandenburg, neither of which he could regard as fully reliable. His personal diplomacy was required to secure their commitment to campaigning in 1633, and then only on condition that the main focus was to be Silesia and that the Swedish commander there was to be nominated by Saxony. The elector's strange choice was the Bohemian exile Thurn, who was then serving as a Swedish general. Such compromises were necessary, but by spring 1633 the Swedes had re-established their political position after the death of Gustavus, and they were set to continue the war.

Militarily too they held the initiative. After Lützen Georg of Brunswick-Lüneburg had retired from Saxony into Westphalia, and in the spring he consolidated his position, occupying important cities and keeping the opposing Imperialists on the defensive until he was able to defeat them at Hessisch Oldendorf, west of Hanover, in early July. Bernhard had moved south to the River Main, and in the early spring he joined forces near Augsburg with the Swedish marshal Gustav Horn coming up from the south-west. Aldringer, with the Imperialist contingent still attached to the Bavarian army, retired ahead of them, while Maximilian again sent frantic pleas for help to Wallenstein and to Vienna. However the Swedes also had difficulties. The Heilbronn League had been more forthcoming with promises than with money, and hence it had not solved Oxenstierna's immediate problem of how to pay his soldiers some of their long-standing arrears. This led first to unrest and then to outright mutiny by the Swedish forces in south Germany in the spring of 1633. As Monro put it: 'our Armie did settle themselves in a close Leaguer at Donavert [camp at Donauwörth] for three months together, ... resolving to enterprise no exployt or hostility against the Enemy, till such time as they should know, who should content them for their by-past service.'[8] By the time enough expedients had been found to pacify the troops and their officers at least temporarily it was August and much of the campaigning season had slipped away. Meanwhile Wallenstein's peace initiatives and accompanying truces had effectively neutralised Saxony and Brandenburg, as well as his own main Imperialist army, so that nothing more of military significance happened until well into the autumn.

Exile intrigues

One of the principal obstacles to any peace with the Protestant German princes remained Ferdinand's determination, influenced by his confessor Lamormaini and the ultra-Catholic party at Vienna, to press on with his efforts to roll back the Reformation. In their January memorandum Trauttmansdorff and his colleagues had noted that one argument put forward for continuing the war was that the Edict of Restitution could scarcely be implemented by peaceful means, but they had gone on to recommend at least its moderation. Instead Ferdinand and his advisers chose that moment to proceed further against non-Catholics, stipulating that even the ambassadors of Protestant princes must appear before a commission and convert to Catholicism 'or quit the hereditary kingdom and lands within the short space of three days or even 24 hours', as one of those affected wrote. This was the inauspicious background to the first peace contacts of 1633. In March, after first conferring with Wallenstein, who emphasised to them and to the court that no opportunity should be neglected, Imperial delegates met Georg of Hesse-Darmstadt, who was acting as an intermediary for the Protestant electors, but the discussions did not proceed beyond non-committal explorations of position. Brandenburg and Saxony held somewhat different views, although they agreed on such fundamentals as the repeal of the Edict of Restitution and equal treatment for Calvinists, concessions which remained unacceptable to the emperor and the zealots around him. Danish mediation was accepted in principle, but the talks became bogged down in arguments about procedure.[9] Although it was eventually agreed to meet in Breslau (Wroclaw) the delegates were still waiting in the autumn, and the conference never took place. That was the official way of conducting peace diplomacy at the time, and for most of the next fifteen years.

Two decidedly unofficial approaches to Wallenstein personally followed. In April Thurn, ambiguously both a Swedish officer and a Bohemian exile, sought to renew the contacts made in 1631 following the general's Regensburg dismissal. This time Wallenstein agreed to a meeting, specifying that the envoy should be Johann Bubna, a long-standing Bohemian acquaintance serving as a Swedish major-general, and this took place at Gitschin on 16 May 1633, following which Bubna wrote an account of the discussion.[10] Thurn's contention, which he delivered to Wallenstein, was that the Swedish side had concluded that there was no possibility of negotiating with the emperor because of the clerical influences which dominated him, but that if Wallenstein were to take the crown of Bohemia there would be better prospects of peace. Wallenstein responded that any attempt on the crown would be 'gross villainy', but that those who had the armies in their control could negotiate and reach a conclusion which others would perforce have to accept. This was not the answer Bubna was looking for, but he agreed to take it back to his principals. He was then sent to report to Oxenstierna, who pointed out the lack of clarity about what Wallenstein meant and the inconsistency of his implied position, as he had either to be a loyal Habsburg officer or a rebel. Were he willing to seek the Bohemian crown through the old electoral procedure, and thereafter to restore Bohemian political and religious liberties, as well as being prepared to acknowledge Sweden's legitimate claims in a settlement to the war, then he could count on Swedish support. Otherwise not.[11] This reply reached Wallenstein at the end of June, but it elicited no further response from him.

At around the same time another scheme was being concocted to persuade Wallenstein to break with the emperor. This time one of the prime movers was a French roving ambassador, the Marquis de Feuquières, who spent some weeks at the Saxon capital. There he met the wealthy Bohemian exile Count Wilhelm Kinsky, who was then living in Dresden, and who was married to the sister of Wallenstein's young brother-in-law Adam Trčka. Kinsky had been peripherally involved in the exile schemes to link Wallenstein with the Swedes in 1631, together with Trčka, Rašin and Thurn. Now, claiming to be well connected to Wallenstein, he tried again. In May he met the Swedish ambassador, and he asked him whether Sweden was still interested, but it seems that the response was cautious. A few days later Feuquières showed more interest, helping Kinsky to draft a letter to Wallenstein from 'loyal friends', noting his difficult situation with an ungrateful court in Vienna, drawing attention to the strength of the gathering military alliance against the emperor, and urging him to consider an attractive alternative personal opportunity which could carry him to a yet higher position. The text of the letter is in Feuquières's memoirs, but whether Wallenstein actually received it is unknown, although it seems certain that he did not respond. Nevertheless the French persevered, and having drawn the conclusion that no direct contact was to be expected from Wallenstein unless there was a specific offer they formulated one, which Louis XIII himself signed on 16 July. The central points were that Wallenstein was to become king of Bohemia and an ally of France, which would provide him with a subsidy of a million livres a year to maintain an army of 35,000 men in order to join in the war against the emperor. There were a variety of other promises and conditions, but they were all irrelevant as once again Wallenstein did not respond, even when, according to Richelieu's confessor, the cardinal wrote personally to him. Kinsky was forced to admit to his contacts that he did not in fact know what was in Wallenstein's mind, but that perhaps he was more interested in an alliance with the Protestant electors than with either France or Sweden.[12]

These two approaches are important only in that they are the basis for rumours at the time and various claims subsequently that Wallenstein aspired to the Bohemian crown. In both cases the suggestion came from the other side, and the proponents relied on the completely unproven assumptions that he was both boundlessly ambitious and still bitterly resentful of his earlier dismissal from command. These are understandable in the context of the standards of the age, and they were already the stuff of common gossip, but they are not supported by any evidence in Wallenstein's own actions or letters. To sustain them analytically one has further to assume – as indeed many contemporaries did – a Machiavellian degree of cunning and dissimulation. That Wallenstein could be persuaded to abandon most of a lifetime in Habsburg service, and induced to undertake an unparalleled and dishonourable betrayal of trust and duty, may have been within the bounds of the imagination of daydreaming Bohemian exiles, or of Feuquières, carried away by the cleverness of his own scheming, but Oxenstierna's scepticism was more realistic.

Two of Wallenstein's most pronounced personal characteristics also speak against it. Firstly he was perennially cautious, and far more inclined towards preserving what he had than to risking everything on his next move. Defecting to the enemy and reaching for the Bohemian crown would have been appallingly risky undertakings, quite out of keeping with one who had already turned down the half-offer of the crown of Denmark on the grounds that he would not have been able to maintain it.[13] Secondly Wallenstein was essentially a practical man, whereas seeking election as the king of Bohemia was a wildly impractical idea. The emperor and the Habsburg party would have had to be defeated and driven out before any election could have taken place, and even then the outcome would have been unpredictable. Moreover if, as Oxenstierna suggested, Bohemian political and religious liberties were to be re-established, then resumptions of forfeit property would inevitably also have been involved, thereby depriving Wallenstein of his remaining possessions. Hence even if he could have secured election he would have been a penniless puppet king entirely dependent on Swedish or French patronage. How long that would have lasted once the political convenience of the moment had been served is a question Wallenstein could not fail to have asked himself, but it is unlikely that he got that far. As in 1631, and as with the contacts with Gustavus Adolphus through Arnim back in 1627, it is possible that he saw no harm in seeing what the other side had to say, but improbable that he took it at all seriously.

The only reasonably authentic statement that we have from Wallenstein on the subject of the Bohemian crown is Bubna's report that he described any attempt upon it as gross villainy. A more public action hardly suggested that he was trying to conciliate the Bohemian exiles in order to become their king. Also in May 1633, Wallenstein set up a commission to investigate and punish those whose behaviour during the Saxon occupation of Bohemia from late 1631 to mid-1632 had implicitly allied them with the rebels of 1618.[14] During that period the skulls of those executed in 1621 had been removed from display and interred, the Jesuits had been chased away and Protestant pastors brought back, some former landowners had reoccupied their forfeit properties, others had incited peasant riots on confiscated estates, and all concerned had acted as though the defeat of the Bohemian revolt had been permanently reversed. The leaders were mostly returning exiles, many of whom held Swedish army commissions and hastily departed when the Saxons withdrew, but there were others still with property in Bohemia. These now found themselves facing similar proceedings to those of ten years earlier, and some two hundred confiscations eventually followed. Wallenstein's motive was his army's need for money, but his long-established dislike of rebellion may also have played a part. The action was at least consistent with what had been done previously, and on this occasion the losers were less able to argue that they had not known what to expect.

Fruitless endeavours

Wallenstein's initial military plan for 1633 was as cautious as that of the previous year. He would make no move until his army was properly prepared, and he then intended to secure his rear by recovering the Habsburg territory of Silesia before turning his attention to the Swedish armies in the Empire. Arnim was still in Silesia with the Saxon army, with Duke Franz Albrecht of Saxe-Lauenburg as his second-in-command. Although a Protestant, Franz Albrecht had been an Imperialist officer for ten years, five of them under Wallenstein, who knew and liked him, but he had resigned his commission in 1631 before joining the Swedes and fighting at Lützen, where he was in Gustavus's immediate entourage when the king was killed. Despite this he was distrusted by the Swedes, and Oxenstierna regarded him as essentially Wallenstein's man. Alongside the Saxons in Silesia, and cooperating closely with them although nominally independent, was a detachment from Brandenburg under Colonel Burgsdorff, and there was also a small Swedish army of around 6000 men, including many Bohemian émigré officers and with Thurn in command. Opposing them were a number of Imperialist regiments commanded by Gallas, but over the winter and into spring 1633 neither side made any move against the other.

In mid-May Wallenstein was ready. His army, some 35,000 strong, had been mustered at Königgrätz (Hradec Králové), 60 miles east of Prague, and it now advanced into Silesia, halting near Schweidnitz (Świdnica), 30 miles south-west of Breslau. The Saxons and their allies had a far smaller number of men, but instead of attacking them Wallenstein sent Trčka to Arnim with an invitation to meet him to discuss the possibilities for peace. Arnim accepted, and on 6 June he arrived in Wallenstein's camp, accompanied by a colonel from each of the three Protestant forces, where they met Wallenstein, Gallas and Trčka out in the open, the generalissimo in a litter because of his illness.[15] Lurid reports soon circulated about what Wallenstein is alleged to have said in this small and private soldierly gathering, about the machinations of the Jesuits, about Maximilian of Bavaria, and about his intention to oblige the emperor to make peace by force if necessary, although these were probably considerably exaggerated versions of anything he may actually have said.

As Arnim was to report on the meeting to the electors of Saxony and Brandenburg, he made a note of his interpretation of its substance and sent Franz Albrecht to Wallenstein with it the next day to seek confirmation. The generalissimo's opinion was, he wrote, 'that hostilities between the two armies should be suspended, and that the forces should be used in combined strength against anyone who should attempt further to disturb the state of the Empire and to impede freedom of religion. Which I [Arnim] construe as meaning that everything in the Holy Roman Empire should be restored to its previous condition, in respect not only of honour, dignity, privileges and immunities, but also and above all of religion, as it was in the year of 1618.' Wallenstein's reply was careful, and made on his behalf by Trčka rather than personally. He commended Arnim for preparing his memorandum and wished him well on his journey to the electoral courts. He for his own part would keep without fail to what he had promised. Thus he did not specifically endorse the points which Arnim had attributed to him, still less the inference which he had drawn from them, and indeed shortly afterwards, in writing to Vienna, Wallenstein denied having agreed the latter.[16] Doubtless it suited Arnim's purpose to phrase his summary in a way which went rather further than the discussions themselves; doubtless it suited Wallenstein neither to confirm nor to contradict his interpretation. This is part of the process of negotiation.

Before departing Arnim wrote again to Wallenstein, telling him that he had shown the memorandum to those of the commanders on his side who needed to know the position, 'as I do not want to come under suspicion all over again'.[17] Here he was referring to the Swedes, who knew of the initiative through Thurn and were watching the conduct of their allies very carefully. Wallenstein was similarly careful to keep Vienna informed of the discussions, which were within his established authority dating as far back as his contacts with Arnim at the court's request in 1631. The Saxon general's consultations took three weeks, during which an uneasy truce was maintained in Silesia, and Wallenstein took the opportunity to entertain both Franz Albrecht and Thurn in his camp, the latter invitation causing particular annoyance in Vienna. When Arnim returned on 27 June it was with evasive answers and references to Danish mediation at the planned conference in Breslau. Privately he had been told of Swedish concerns about the truce, while the imprecise nature of Wallenstein's proposition allowed many detailed problems to be raised by those who did not wish to pursue it. Hostilities resumed, but only briefly. Wallenstein despatched a force to mount a surprise attack on the nearby town of Schweidnitz, but the Saxon garrison was ready and held out until Arnim arrived to relieve it. Both armies then went back to their well-defended camps, and an informal truce replaced the previous official one, a situation which lasted for over a month. Wallenstein did not give up hope of an agreement, but in order to apply more pressure he repeated his tactic of the previous year, sending Holk's troops back into Saxony at the beginning of August to remind the elector – or more precisely his unfortunate subjects – of the horrors of war which only a more constructive move towards peace could end.

Meanwhile in the early summer of 1633 a new plan for Spanish intervention had been developed in Madrid, involving sending a large army over the Alps from Italy to the Tyrol and thence to south-western Germany. Its ambitious objectives were to secure Burgundy against the French, to expel the Swedes first from Alsace and then from Swabia and Franconia, to free the road to the Netherlands, and to link Germany with Italy through a chain of garrisons. Some of the men were to come from Italy, with others to be recruited in the Tyrol or elsewhere *en route*, 24,000 in all, and support from the Imperialist army was also envisaged. Wallenstein was firmly opposed to the idea, seeing it as a repeat of the Spanish confrontation with France over Mantua which had caused so much trouble in the latter years of his first command. In early June he informed all concerned that he was not in a position to provide any troops. Nevertheless planning continued, and a month later Wallenstein warned the emperor that such a campaign would not only bring the full power of France into the war against the Imperialists but also destroy the prospects of the current peace contacts. The councillors in Vienna were at first inclined to agree with him, but as concerns mounted about lack of progress with either peace or war in Silesia they became more receptive to proposals for action elsewhere. In late July the emperor agreed to the duke of Feria leading an army into Germany, and Wallenstein had to accept Aldringer and his Imperialist detachment being sent to assist him.[18] Although they made little progress towards their main objectives the joint forces did achieve some limited successes in south-west Germany, including relieving the Rhine fortress of Breisach, 30 miles north of Basle, the long-running siege of which had made it something of a *cause célèbre*. However that was not until 20 October, and the effect was offset by French seizure of the duchy of Lorraine, although winter prevented the fuller involvement of France which Wallenstein had feared.

The parallels between this new Spanish venture and the Mantua campaign, in both of which Wallenstein's objection and initial refusal to send troops were overruled, were all too obvious, and they marked the beginning of a similar decline in the court's confidence in the generalissimo. On 12 August Count Heinrich Schlick, president of the Imperial war council, was sent to visit Wallenstein's headquarters in Silesia, with official instructions to review the general's negotiations with Arnim, to encourage a more active approach to the war, and to press for further help for the Spanish intervention force. He also had secret instructions to make contact with Gallas, Piccolomini and other senior officers, and to seek to ensure their loyalty 'in the event that a change should ensue concerning the duke of Friedland on account of his illness or otherwise'. By the time Schlick arrived negotiations for a second truce were already under way, and he himself attended one of the subsequent meetings. On 22 August the accord was signed, providing for a four-week cessation of hostilities not only in Silesia but in Saxony, Brandenburg and the surrounding areas, during which positions were not to be reinforced while negotiations took place.[19]

At this point it starts to emerge that two quite different concepts of the objectives of these negotiations were circulating in parallel. The official Imperialist view was summed up by Hermann Questenberg, brother of the better-known Gerhard, who spent this period at Wallenstein's camp, waiting with Trauttmansdorff to represent the emperor should the peace conference at Breslau ever take place. Writing to a third brother on 22 September, he noted that religious affairs were to be restored to their state under Emperor Matthias, and that the armies of Wallenstein and the Protestant electors were to unite and to march into the Empire against anyone who would not consent to the settlement. Piccolomini, reflecting the view current among senior officers, wrote to a correspondent that an agreement was about to be made on those terms, but he added that there were to be no negotiations with the Swedes, 'as they will not be persuaded amicably to give up their power, but no foreign nation can be tolerated with an army in the Empire'. 'We hope', he went on, 'to strike at them before going into winter quarters, as both His Excellency [Wallenstein] and Arnim intend.' A similar view was reported to the emperor from Saxony and Brandenburg by Duke Franz Julius of Saxe-Lauenburg, brother to Franz Albrecht but a Catholic in Imperial service, who was in Dresden during the truce and met not only the electors but also Arnim and Franz Albrecht. The electors, he said, were minded towards reconciliation with the emperor, and the generals were only waiting for agreement on certain key points before they would proceed with uniting the armies under Wallenstein's command. These included that 'everything should be returned to its state before the Bohemian unrest', but also that thought should be given to 'how foreign troops may be removed from the Empire', which might be either by peaceful means with reasonable compensation, or failing that by force of arms. All three reports are essentially the same. Peace between the emperor and the Protestant electors was to be followed by the ejection of the Swedes, by agreement if possible but by force if not.[20]

Not surprisingly, there was a different version for Swedish consumption, and this involved a change of sides not by the Protestant electors but by Wallenstein. This time there was no mention of the Bohemian crown for him, as he was presumed to be willing to act solely out of animosity towards the emperor. At the end of August Thurn gleefully wrote to Oxenstierna that Wallenstein was proposing 'the expulsion of the Jesuits from the whole Roman Empire, which will vex the emperor to death. He will have to go to Spain.' A few days later he repeated that 'your Excellency should not have the slightest doubt that it has been decided to chase the emperor out to Spain'.[21] Arnim gave the Swedish chancellor a fuller account in person on 12 September, which Oxenstierna relayed to Bernhard of Weimar. Arnim, he wrote, had discussed Danish mediation and the proposed Breslau conference, observing that the emperor was said to be inclined towards peace with Saxony, Brandenburg and others in the Empire, but that he would not hear of negotiations with Sweden and France. Wallenstein, however, still nursed a grievance over his 1630 dismissal, was on bad terms with the court, was further offended by Feria's Spanish army being allowed into the Empire but not under his own overall command, and would gladly seek his revenge if assured of Swedish help. The generalissimo, so Arnim had said, thought that he could count on the support of most of his officers, and he had plans to neutralise those of whom he was unsure by posting them to distant places. He would ally himself with the Swedes and then proceed personally against Austria, while Bernhard and Holk were to occupy Bavaria and Horn would deal with Feria. Oxenstierna was extremely dubious, commenting that it would be a great opportunity 'were it genuine, but it seems to me much too suspicious'. He had, he said, probed further 'in order to find out the real motive, but he [Arnim] was decidedly reticent, as is his manner and temperament', although when pressed he had conceded that he himself had some doubts as to Wallenstein's designs. Nevertheless Oxenstierna had told him to assure Wallenstein that 'if he proceeds with his intentions we will not abandon him', commenting to Bernhard that come what may 'this business can do us no harm'.[22]

Wallenstein, on the other hand, had everything to lose and nothing to gain from such a scheme, apart from the satisfaction of an assumed obsessive desire for revenge, which however does not feature in his voluminous correspondence and is not supported by any confirmed action of his. Therefore the proposition has to be presumed to be a deception, necessary to allay Swedish anxieties while attempts were made to reach a peace settlement with their allies. Thurn, neither the most astute of politicians nor the most competent of soldiers, was easy to deceive. Oxenstierna, more worldly wise, was right to be suspicious. More difficult is to say who was carrying out the deception, a question to which we will return.

As well as Oxenstierna, Arnim also met the electors of Saxony and Brandenburg during this second truce, and they furnished him with responses to Wallenstein's proposals which went only slightly further than in June. These envisaged an 'arrangement' between the Imperial and Saxon armies, a term as ambiguous in the German original as in English, accompanied by polite references to the interests of Sweden and lofty phrases about the desirability of working towards a general peace.[23] Arnim appears to have believed – or he sought to persuade others to believe – that this might suffice to draw Wallenstein into a 'German third party' with the Protestant electors in order to coerce the emperor into making peace on terms acceptable to them. To Wallenstein himself it was becoming apparent that little progress was being made but a lot of campaigning time was being wasted. On 14 September he said in a brief note to Trčka that nothing was going to come of the negotiations. On the same day he ordered another officer to start preparing supplies for renewed campaigning, 'as from various information we have received we perceive that the enemy is not inclined towards peace'. On 21 September Trauttmansdorff was still enthusiastic and optimistic about the negotiations, but three days later he too saw the writing on the wall, noting to Wallenstein that 'I fear that the business with Oxenstierna will have to be carried out by Your Princely Grace with the sword, and not by us with words or the pen'.[24]

Wallenstein was disappointed and angry, but although accounts of his conduct at this and other crucial points suggest uncontrolled outbursts of rage there was nevertheless an underlying logic to his approach. On this occasion he decided to bring matters to a head by declaring his objective in unmistakeable terms. Franz Albrecht was again Arnim's emissary, and he wrote an account of his discussions with Wallenstein of 25 and 26 September 1633 (although he did so seven months later, after the general's death and when he himself was a prisoner of the Imperialists).

> The duke of Friedland asserted that all troops of foreign potentates, whether Spanish, French, Swedish or from Lorraine, and all foreigners who did not belong in the Empire, must be expelled in order to restore it to its state during the time of the Emperors Rudolph and Matthias. ... When I asked to know and write down the specific terms of the peace he would not agree, instead insisting that both armies should march immediately into the Empire, directly against the Swedes, who at that time were the nearest, to remove them.

Franz Albrecht took this message back to Arnim, returning on the following day to say that the latter had no authority to make peace on those terms, but proposed instead that they should make a separate peace and leave the question of Sweden to be settled afterwards. To this Wallenstein replied 'with great vehemence that it could not be, and that his sole condition was that we should join with him to march into the Empire and attack the Swedes, and likewise the French and Spanish should we encounter them there. Moreover he absolutely insisted that he should have the command.' Finding no agreement, Wallenstein politely took his leave of Franz Albrecht, commenting that he would honour the remaining days of the truce, which had previously been extended, but would then know how to proceed.[25]

The Protestant side viewed this as flagrant bad faith on Wallenstein's part. Oxenstierna and John George of Saxony complained that he could not be trusted, and that no reliance could be placed on anything negotiated with him, while Arnim expressed the same opinion to the elector of

Brandenburg. He also hurried to clear himself with the Swedes, writing to both Oxenstierna and Thurn that he had rejected Wallenstein's demand that the Saxons should join in an attack upon them.[26] 'That would have been a fine piece of villainy, to show ourselves so ungrateful to those who have shed their blood, even laid down their lives, to help us.' He would not have taken part in the negotiations, he said, 'had not our situation made it necessary', adding that 'I do not see what the duke of Friedland has gained from the truce, but it has been useful to us in that we have preserved our army'. Painfully aware of this, Wallenstein felt equally deceived, writing to Trauttmansdorff: 'I cannot conceive that God's justice will leave this falsehood unpunished. ... This deception is indeed not the first which I have experienced from them, but it will certainly be the last.'[27]

Even so he wasted little time on recriminations, promptly despatching Gallas into Saxony with an army, at the same time appointing him as lieutenant-general and second-in-command of all Imperialist forces. Arnim responded by withdrawing to Saxony, leaving Thurn with his small Swedish army and the Brandenburg contingent to hold Silesia. In early October Wallenstein caught them on the defensive at the town of Steinau (Ścinawa), on the River Oder ten miles east of Lubin. He had a reported 30,000 men, Thurn around a quarter of this number. Not surprisingly, although much to Arnim's annoyance as Steinau was well defended, Thurn surrendered immediately, and in exchange for his own freedom and that of the other Bohemian exiles he ordered the surrender of all strongholds under his command. At a stroke Wallenstein thus recovered the whole Imperial territory of Silesia, restoring for the moment much of his waning credit in Vienna and delighting the emperor in particular, even if there was some anger about him freeing Thurn, one of the ringleaders of the Bohemian revolution.

Despite everything Wallenstein had still not given up hope of detaching Saxony from the Swedish alliance, so that his tactics were to increase the pressure rather than joining with Gallas to trap and destroy Arnim's army. His troops advanced threateningly towards Saxon territory, but at Crossen (Krosno Odrzańskie), twenty miles east of the border, he halted, and there on 20 October he met Franz Albrecht yet again. The outcome was a short draft agreement drawn up and signed by Wallenstein, the only time he committed himself in writing during these negotiations, and hence probably the clearest indication of his underlying aim throughout.[28] This treaty was to be made between the electors of Saxony and Brandenburg of the one part, and Wallenstein in his capacity as Imperial generalissimo of the other, 'who seeing the present comprehensive devastation and decline of the Empire have considered ways and means by which this may be remedied, and the Empire and its constituent parts rescued from despoliation by foreign troops and restored to their former prime and well-being'. Hence both electoral armies were to join with the Imperialist forces and be placed under Wallenstein's command, 'in order to achieve the above objectives and through their combined might to restore the stability of the religious and secular peace as it was during the Imperial reigns of Rudolph and Matthias, and under his present Imperial Majesty before these troubles which have arisen, and to maintain the same against anyone who persists in further disturbing it'.

The electors' replies reached Wallenstein three weeks later, on 13 November, their refusals presented as delicately as possible by Franz Albrecht, and with a hint that the generalissimo's poor health contributed to the problem, as it could not be assumed that he would be able to remain in his post to see the matter through.[29] Their responses were negative because at root the electors were not ready to abandon the Swedes, not least because they still looked to be the stronger party. John George of Saxony was a stubborn and conservative man who had only very reluctantly been induced to break away from his duty to the emperor and the Empire, which he saw as the natural order of things, but once having done so the same conservative sense of honour and duty held him bound to his new alliance. George William of Brandenburg was an altogether weaker character, but as a Calvinist he found the emperor's religious policy even more threatening, and he had always been more inclined towards the Swedes than his Saxon counterpart. For both, the withdrawal of the Edict of Restitution was fundamental, but the Imperial delegation's position during the attempted mediation earlier in the year, and the emperor's increased anti-Protestant measures in his own lands, gave them no encouragement, while Wallenstein's reference to the old religious peace was far too vague.

Therein lay the central problem. Wallenstein was looking for an act of faith based on trust in himself, effectively asking the electors to burn their boats by breaking with the Swedes, but to leave negotiation of settlement terms with the emperor until afterwards. He himself said, in sending a copy of his draft treaty to Trauttmansdorff, that he had not sought to specify any details, as that would fall to the emperor and the other parties to determine later. Never was Wallenstein's political naivety more clearly exposed. Two months earlier the emperor's councillors had drawn up negotiating positions for the delegation to the prospective Breslau peace conference. The efforts of the devious minds in Vienna take up 34 pages of modern printed text, Wallenstein's proposals a bare half page, of which all the points of substance have been quoted in full above.[30] Naive but at least consistent. Wallenstein's objective throughout 1633 was the same as it had been since his first contacts with Arnim in 1631, to induce Saxony not merely to break with the Swedes but to resume allegiance to the emperor. John George, Arnim and Wallenstein all shared a deep dislike of foreign interventions in the affairs of the Empire, and to Wallenstein a return to their former loyalty by Saxony and Brandenburg automatically implied a switch to active hostilities against the Swedes or other invaders. The electors and Arnim, on the other hand, were seeking to find refuge in a face-saving neutrality, so that, joined by Wallenstein to form a German third party, they could negotiate peace terms with both the emperor and Sweden from a position of strength. The two sides misunderstood these essential aspects of each other's intentions, and hence both felt deceived when Wallenstein's eventual forcing of the issue brought out into the open that the electors were not prepared to join a military united front against the Swedes, while the generalissimo had no intention of being detached from the emperor.

In looking for explanations for this misunderstanding a useful starting point is to note that there is no evidence that Wallenstein ever intended either to act independently of the emperor or to coerce him into making peace, whatever others claimed that he had said at various times. Gallas took part in the first meeting with Arnim, other senior officers were aware of the progress of discussions, Imperial councillors were in Wallenstein's camp for much of the late summer and attended at least one of the meetings, while the emperor himself wrote to express his approval of the proceedings.[31] If Wallenstein was playing a double game it was very cleverly done. Nevertheless he may have spoken and conducted himself with sufficient ambiguity in the early stages of the parleying to allow Arnim to draw his own erroneous conclusions. It is also possible that his position changed over the course of the discussions. Early in the summer he might have settled for neutrality from the electors, if this could have been agreed quickly, thus leaving him free to use the campaigning season against the Swedes. Later in the year, with the best months already wasted, he needed more. He needed active participation in order to force the Swedes to withdraw to the Baltic coast, thus laying the basis for real peace negotiations over the winter. Wallenstein's problem was that the longer the talking went on the poorer his chances became of achieving a substantial improvement in the Imperialist military position during 1633, and hence the lower his own standing became at the Imperial court.

Arnim was equally sincere in seeking peace, but in his case the contacts were worthwhile in their own right, because the longer the truces lasted the further the day of military reckoning for Saxony and his army was postponed. Thus it probably suited him to interpret Wallenstein's words and manner in a way which allowed him to convey to the electors a more flexible interpretation of where the generalissimo stood. In this there may have been an element of self-deception and an effort to play the honest broker, hoping by maintaining the contacts to encourage the sides to move closer to a mutually agreeable conclusion. Arnim's problem was the Swedes, mistrustful from the outset and increasingly suspicious of him as matters progressed, to the extent that they were inclined to believe that he had deliberately abandoned their force under Thurn to enable Wallenstein to capture it at Steinau.[32]

Arnim had to tell the Swedes something about the contacts, but he could hardly tell them the truth, that he was trying to bring the Protestant electors and Wallenstein together into a German third party, which they would inevitably have seen as detrimental to their interests and probably as actively hostile to them. Hence the claim that Wallenstein was willing to turn against the emperor in a spectacular act of revenge, a story which may have been credible to those who knew him only from the rumours and legends in popular circulation, although Arnim, who knew him well, was forced to admit under pressure from Oxenstierna that he himself had his doubts. As well he might. Hard enough to believe that Wallenstein, having fought for the emperor through 1632, including placing his own life at serious risk at Lützen, should in 1633 be so resentful as to be prepared to change sides in what would universally have been seen as an unprecedented and dishonourable betrayal. Harder still to believe that such a step would be condoned and imitated by his senior officers, most of whom were noblemen and had a strong if limited sense of their personal honour. Hardest of all to credit that in months of negotiations a plan to move across to the Protestant Swedes would not have come to the ears of, and been actively opposed by, loyal Imperialists such as Gallas and Piccolomini, who not only had no grounds for hostility towards the emperor, but were Italians rather than Germans, and good Catholics into the bargain.

Nevertheless it is difficult to imagine that Arnim simply invented the story, although equally difficult to imagine that its source was Wallenstein himself. Nothing can be proved, but the best guess is that somewhere in the middle of this thicket Trčka was lurking. Trčka, who according to the later testimony of a senior officer was at this time with Wallenstein almost every evening from seven to eleven.[33] Trčka, who during Wallenstein's ever more frequent indispositions spoke and wrote on his behalf, as he did to Franz Albrecht after the first 1633 meeting with Arnim. Trčka, the link with the Bohemian exiles Rašin and Kinsky in the manoeuvrings around Wallenstein in 1631 and 1633. Trčka, who loved intrigue but lacked the wisdom to separate the realistic from the fantastic in his schemes, or to judge the ends which they were to serve. Trčka it may have been who suggested to Arnim that Wallenstein might be ready to change sides if assured of Swedish support, and Arnim may have been willing to grant him sufficient credence to allow him to use the story for his own ends in dealing with the Swedes.

Mention of Trčka provides a timely reminder that many of the people involved in the contacts of 1633 had interests of their own to pursue. Thurn and many other Bohemian exiles were serving in the Swedish army, but most had no wish to replace Habsburg with Swedish hegemony in their homeland, and in this they were closer to Trčka in Wallenstein's camp or Kinsky intriguing in Dresden than to the Swedish leadership. Necessity had made Saxony and Brandenburg Swedish allies, but although they had as little wish as the Bohemians to see the Swedes establish an enduring presence in north Germany they did not share the aims of the exiles in other respects. Arnim, despite serving Saxony, had his own independent view of what was required, similar in substance to Wallenstein's although his approach differed. The Swedes themselves had few illusions about their allies, and they were concerned primarily with their own military and political interests, to which those allies were purely secondary. Consequently most of the participants had both overt and covert objectives, and in the best diplomatic traditions nothing they said or wrote can necessarily be taken at face value.

Suvanto's 1977 study is useful in providing Oxenstierna's perspective on these tangled negotiations.[34] This shows how even those at the centre of events were dependent for their information on rumour and hearsay gathered by diplomats and informers, and also how they set out to manipulate such sources in order to confuse their enemies – and posterity in the process. Thus Oxenstierna's agents sought to undermine Wallenstein's peace proposals in Dresden and Berlin by representing them as ruses, while characterising Wallenstein himself as mercurial and untrustworthy. Similarly they put pressure on Arnim by insinuating that he was too close to Wallenstein, and they endeavoured to undermine the generalissimo's own position in Vienna by spreading rumours about his putative contacts with France and his supposed interest in the Bohemian crown. The exiles too put their own slant on the stories going around, and it is worth noting that reports linking Wallenstein to the

Swedes and the French all involve Bohemian intermediaries who were themselves the source of most of the surviving information. Against this background it becomes easier to see how even the more fantastic stories about Wallenstein could gain credence in some quarters. 'The first casualty when war comes is truth', said an American senator in 1917, and his remark would have been equally valid three hundred years earlier.

13
Decline and Fall
(Gibbon)

As the peace negotiations in Silesia ground on towards their ultimate failure there was still time for a flurry of military activity in late 1633 before the winter closed in. At the end of September Aldringer and his Imperialist troops joined the duke of Feria's army, finally arrived from Italy, near Constance, and a few days later they relieved the besieged city. Shortly afterwards Wallenstein took Steinau, and with it Silesia, while Feria and Aldringer headed west to the Rhine at Breisach. This provided the Swedes with the opportunity they needed to counter-attack elsewhere, and with the defending forces out of the way Oxenstierna directed Bernhard of Weimar to move against Bavaria.

By 20 October, the day that Breisach was relieved, Bernhard was on the Danube at Ulm. Maximilian appealed frantically for help, and his pleas were endorsed by the emperor, who was no less frantic about the threat to his own lands which might follow. Wallenstein judged the matter differently. Bernhard, he thought, planned to attack Bohemia from the south-west in order to divert him from Saxony and Brandenburg, hence relieving the pressure on the electors to make a positive response to his final peace initiative.[1] Consequently he moved his main army south-west on to the border between Saxony and Bohemia, from where he could either attack the former or defend the latter should the need arise. Bernhard advanced east along the Danube, until on 4 November he reached the strategic fortress city of Regensburg. From there he could have followed the river south-east towards Passau and Austria, or turned north-east and headed for Pilsen and Prague.

On 13 November Wallenstein received the final refusal of his peace proposals. At first his anger and intended military response were directed at the electors and Arnim, while he continued to discount the threat to Regensburg, but on reflection he decided that it was necessary to move against Bernhard. On 16 November he set out towards the Danube, but too late, as Regensburg had already fallen. Wallenstein had assumed that Bernhard would not waste time so late in the year on a lengthy siege of the city, just as Horn had been deterred by its formidable defences the previous year. The mainly Protestant citizenry, however, sympathised with the Swedes, while after ten days the Bavarian garrison decided that honour had been satisfied and quietly surrendered. It was a considerable blow to Wallenstein's standing at court, seen at best as a major error of judgement and at worst as a deliberate abandonment of his known enemy Maximilian. In military terms it was of no significance. Wallenstein quickly reinforced Passau, thus blocking the route into Austria as he had in the previous year, while Bernhard had time only to advance slightly further east before winter caught up with him.

Wallenstein himself continued southwards, reaching Pilsen on 26 November. There he met Trauttmansdorff, who found him angry over letters he had received from Vienna. People at court, including leading ministers, were denigrating his efforts, he said; his successes were being attributed to mere luck while setbacks were blamed on his negligence; orders had been sent from the court directly to Aldringer and other officers; never in his life had he been more offended, to the extent that he no longer wished to retain his command. Tactfully Trauttmansdorff allowed the storm to blow itself out, and afterwards Wallenstein went on to talk about the emperor's situation, which he summed up forcefully: 'If there is no peace, then all is lost.'[2]

The approach of winter meant that no major campaign could be contemplated, and a siege to recover Regensburg was out of the question. Moreover Arnim was in Saxony with three times as many men as Gallas, who had been left to guard the Bohemian border. Hence Wallenstein left most of his infantry and artillery at Pilsen to be on hand to reinforce him if necessary, while he continued towards the Danube with the cavalry in order to harass Bernhard. It soon became evident that this was too little to be of much value, and too late in the year to be prudently undertaken. By the beginning of December Wallenstein's force was in hilly, heavily wooded country with no forage for the horses, little shelter for the men, and the weather, already cold, threatening to deteriorate further. He held a council of war, but although a majority of his senior officers were prepared to press on he overruled them. He had always regarded winter campaigning as unwise and impractical, and like a year earlier after Lützen he preferred to withdraw rather than to risk a disaster.[3] On 4 December his force set off back to Pilsen, arriving a week later.

Maximilian was furious, the emperor was furious, even Eggenberg, long one of Wallenstein's principal supporters, was furious. The credit gained from the success at Steinau vanished as quickly as it had come, destroyed first by Wallenstein's misjudgement over Regensburg, and then by him moving against Bernhard but dashing the hopes this raised at court by withdrawing without firing a shot. The prospect of his removal from command was once more the talk of Vienna. Wallenstein himself, Piccolomini wrote to Gallas on 2 December, 'would like to conclude a peace in any way possible, because he has fallen under so much suspicion at the court that he wonders if there may be some action from there. The negotiations at Schweidnitz are more than ever on his mind, and remembering them makes him severely depressed.'[4]

The gathering storm

The need for winter quarters always exacerbated the problems caused by the burdens of war. At the beginning of 1633 the proponents of peace had pointed out the exhaustion of the Habsburg hereditary lands, and by the end of that year the position was still worse, so that the prospect of sustaining the army during the winter caused dismay among the emperor's councillors and despair among his subjects. Wallenstein's men were unwelcome in Bohemia, Moravia and Austria, while Aldringer's detachment was equally unwelcome in Bavaria when it returned from campaigning with Feria. Even the princely courts, including those of Maximilian and Wallenstein himself, were strapped for cash and unable to pay their officials.[5] Some of Wallenstein's senior officers were also growing restive, as the prospects of profit from their regiments depended largely on the spoils of war, but truces and long marches without action brought only costs, in the form of illness, desertion and death among the men who were their stock in trade.

Indications that Wallenstein intended to winter the army yet again in the hereditary lands caused alarm in Vienna, and Questenberg was despatched to meet him with something between a plea and an order to look elsewhere. The suggested places, Brandenburg, Lusatia, Saxony and Thuringia, were widely spread out and all in the hands of the enemy, a point glossed over with the optimistic claim that the presence of Imperialist forces in these areas would give hope to those worthy citizens who remained loyal to the emperor. Questenberg's instructions ended on a stern note. He was to dissuade Wallenstein from going against these express wishes of the emperor, as this would 'diminish our high authority, and could give rise to thoughts among foreign potentates that we have a co-regent on hand, and no longer have free disposition over our own lands'. Against this background of concern over winter quarters Wallenstein's abandonment of the move against Bernhard and his return to Pilsen created an open breach between the emperor and his generalissimo. This change of plan, Ferdinand wrote, had come to him as most unwelcome news, and he reiterated his view of the military threat to his lands. Rather than his previous polite approach he issued a blunt order. 'It is my express wish and demand that Your Excellency should immediately turn the army round and proceed towards Passau and the duke of Weimar, march against him, follow him and drive him out, and this is my final decision, upon which I am completely firm and immovable.'[6]

In his reply Wallenstein noted that he had advised against both a further march to the Danube and an attempt to find winter quarters in enemy territory, but on receipt of the emperor's so clearly expressed wishes he had not taken it upon himself alone to respond, but had sought the advice of his generals. This he attached in the form of a memorandum prepared at a conference in Pilsen on 17 December, with the request that this be approved, and that the army should remain where it was for the winter in order to be in good shape for the forthcoming summer campaign.[7] In their advice the officers stated that to move the army to seek quarters elsewhere 'in this winter period is not only difficult, but with the army in its present condition quite impossible'. As soon as they left the emperor's lands they would have to contend 'not only with the enemy, but especially with the cold, lack of provisions, money and all the other indispensable necessities, so that the remaining soldiers would either die or be driven to desperation'. Should those who had given the emperor such advice have to try to carry it out, they would soon discover the impossibility for themselves, particularly as most of the suggested places could not be taken without artillery and sieges, whereas in this season even shovels could not readily be employed. The same applied to the order to advance against Bernhard of Weimar, the only result of which would be that 'horse and man would be laid low and must inevitably perish'. They went on to complain that pay and provisions had not arrived as promised in the past year, and that there seemed little better hope for the coming one, 'on account of which we have to keep these things completely secret from the NCOs and ordinary soldiers, for fear of a general mutiny'.

These exchanges indicate not only the growing tension between the court and the generalissimo, but also the disaffection which was developing in the army. Reports from Trauttmansdorff and Questenberg, both of whom were in Pilsen at this time, show Wallenstein himself in two minds, alternately talking about resignation and about the prospects for the next year's campaign.[8] To Trauttmansdorff's chiding that putting the emperor's orders up for debate by his officers was bad for discipline he responded that 'the authority he exercised over the army was, thank God, so great that he could at any time pull on the reins'. On the other hand he complained that he was treated dishonourably by the court, where all kinds of dangerous things were being said about him. He hoped that the intention was not to drive him to resignation out of disgust, as there were other means should it be deemed in the emperor's interest, but he did not himself intend to do anything precipitate.

Nevertheless he kept coming back to the subject. Trauttmansdorff had brought a proposal for Wallenstein to meet Eggenberg, which he declined. He anticipated that the latter would suggest to him that he should share the command of the army with the emperor's son, the ambitious king of Hungary, but, he said, the king was his master and much too good to be his fellow. He would rather give up his command, provided that this could be done with honour and a modest payment. He would be glad to be relieved of the burden, and he would hand everything over to His Majesty in good order, advising him to the best of his ability on what was to be done, but he would not remain with the army himself. He cautioned, however, that the matter would have to be handled carefully or a mutiny might follow, as the majority of the colonels had been recruited on the strength of his personal credit, and were he to depart without their debts having been satisfied, for which the means were not to hand, considerable difficulties could arise. He ended with his usual refrain: 'Peace must be made, otherwise everything will be lost for our side.'[9]

Some historians have suggested that Wallenstein made a practice of offering his resignation, but that this was merely a stratagem intended to apply pressure to the court in Vienna. As discussed in Chapter 7, he certainly referred repeatedly to the possibility of giving up his command in his letters to Harrach during 1626, but this changed after the Bruck conference in November of that year, and the issue did not feature again until late 1633. There are important differences between the two periods. In 1626 Wallenstein was clearly feeling the strain of his first year in command, and he used his frequent letters to Harrach as a kind of safety valve. There was some ambiguity because of Harrach's position as an Imperial councillor, but nevertheless these were private letters from Wallenstein to his father-in-law, and although he talked of resignation this is quite different from actually offering it, which he never did.[10] From late 1633 onwards his references to the subject were no longer confined to private correspondence with a close relative, but were made openly to senior councillors such as Trauttmansdorff, who did not number among his particular friends, while by early 1634 he progressed to making specific offers of his resignation to the court and the Imperial war council. This difference of approach also reflects a difference of substance. In 1626 Wallenstein was temperamentally inclined to resign but could see no practical way of doing so without seriously endangering both his fortune and his position in Bohemia. From late 1633 onwards he began to realise that he had little alternative, given his poor state of health and the deterioration of his relationship with the court. Again resignation was not an easy option, despite which his offers appear to have been increasingly serious rather than a protracted ruse, while those in the latest stage of his life give every indication of having been genuine.

As winter approached another matter also developed into a sharp dispute between the emperor and his general. On 9 December Ferdinand wrote to Wallenstein that he had ordered Colonel Suys to advance from Upper Austria to the River Inn near Passau 'as I deem it more useful for his regiments to be moved forward to join our other troops facing the enemy than to remain in their present position, where they are only consuming supplies and may cause a new rebellion among the peasants'. This, he added, was a provisional order, which he had no doubt that Wallenstein would immediately confirm. Ferdinand was no soldier, and the impetus for this move undoubtedly came from his advisers, but he was sensitive about his authority, to which the military question was purely secondary. For Wallenstein both issues were important. Suys had been stationed where he was for good reasons and he was not needed on the Inn, while direct orders to officers from the court were contrary to the terms of his own appointment. Wallenstein had always lacked political skills, and by this time he was less than ever inclined to defer tactfully, contrary to his military judgement. Far from confirming the order, although he was diplomatic enough not to refer to it, he instructed Suys to stay where he was, carefully setting out his reasons and emphasising that these were in the best interests of the emperor's service. The unfortunate colonel thus received contradictory orders from his emperor and his commander-in-chief. Much to Ferdinand's annoyance he chose to obey Wallenstein. More orders from the court and countermands from headquarters followed, but Ferdinand shrunk from confronting Wallenstein directly. Instead on 24 December he wrote peevishly to Questenberg in Pilsen, instructing him to remonstrate with the general, who should either immediately issue the necessary order to Suys or replace him with another suitably qualified officer, 'who will know how to obey our Imperial commands with more discretion'.[11]

On the same day Ferdinand also replied to Wallenstein about his officers' advice that further moves against Bernhard or into enemy territory to seek winter quarters were impossible at that time of year. In a letter clearly drafted by the military advisers at court he both denied that it was ever intended to leave the troops without proper winter quarters and at the same time justified the order to attack the Swedes around Regensburg. Indeed, he went on, it was still necessary to despatch Suys to the Inn and to send more troops from Bohemia, 3000 infantry and 1000 cavalry, to reinforce the Bavarians. Wallenstein's response was prompt but evasive. He had just heard from Aldringer that he and his men had arrived back in Bavaria, while he himself was moving regiments in Moravia closer so as to have them readily available should the enemy actually make a threatening move. As regards the cavalry in Upper Austria, he continued, but without mentioning Suys, it would be better to be patient until the spring, when they would be up to strength and in sounder condition to do good service. Surprisingly but ominously Ferdinand gave way, opening the new year with a mild acknowledgement, and conceding that in the changing circumstances and as winter was advancing he was prepared to be guided by Wallenstein's opinion.[12]

The reason for this change of tone was a closely kept secret, but Bartholomäus Richel, the Bavarian vice-chancellor and representative at the Imperial court, was nevertheless able to report it to Maximilian on 31 December. His Imperial Majesty, he wrote, had secretly decided to remove the duke of Friedland from his command, and was already at work winning over and making sure of the leading officers in the army. What to do with the duke himself was as yet undecided; to let him go free was problematic, while to arrest him, which His Majesty himself thought the safest and best suggestion, also had its difficulties.[13]

Wallenstein's enemies had at last convinced the more important of his former friends, and most significantly the emperor himself, that the generalissimo had to go. These enemies were in three groups, the Catholic die-hards, the long-standing personal foes from Bohemia, and the disappointed officers without senior posts on active service, including some who Wallenstein had dismissed or pushed into retirement. Most influential among the first group were the Jesuits Wilhelm Lamormaini, the emperor's confessor, and Johannes Weingartner, the court preacher, both determined advocates of continued counter-Reformation and full enforcement of the Edict of Restitution. Prominent in the second were Cardinal Dietrichstein and Wallenstein's cousin Wilhelm Slavata, chancellor of Bohemia, while a more recent addition was Heinrich Schlick, one of Wallenstein's principal commanders during the Danish campaign and by this time president of the war council. These were able men and formidable opponents, well capable of using the embittered failures among the soldiers in the third group for their own purposes, in order to give a veneer of professional military credibility to their criticisms of Wallenstein. The fiasco of the latter's advance against Bernhard at the end of November enabled his opponents to move from whispering in ante-chambers to shouting in the streets, almost literally, in the form of a number of virulent anonymous pamphlets which circulated during December.[14] Their authors almost certainly included Weingartner and Slavata, and it may be assumed that they reached the emperor's eyes, as well as being avidly read by Maximilian, who was once again seeking to orchestrate the chorus of complainants.

Perhaps more important than this round-up of the usual suspects, however, was a shift in the Spanish attitude to Wallenstein. They had supported him unsuccessfully at the time of his earlier dismissal, and Count Olivares, the chief minister, continued to see in him the best chance of bringing the war in Germany to a successful conclusion, thereby freeing joint Habsburg resources for the war in the Netherlands, which remained the principal Spanish priority. The ambassador at the Imperial court, however, was of a different opinion, and in order to investigate his negative reports Olivares despatched Count Oñate, a previous ambassador and regarded in Madrid as the expert on Germany, to Vienna in the autumn of 1633. Oñate was startled to discover the extent to which Wallenstein's standing had declined, even among his former principal supporters, and under pressure of events and the criticisms of the general's enemies his own support wavered at the critical moment.[15]

One factor which helped to confirm his doubts was a visit to Wallenstein by the Capuchin monk Diego de Quiroga, who arrived in Pilsen on 4 January 1634. The regent of the Spanish Netherlands, the aged Infanta Isabella, had recently died, and there were fears that a power vacuum could provide the opportunity for a rebellion favouring the Dutch, so that the Spanish court were anxious that her successor, the king's younger brother, known as the Cardinal Infant, should reach Brussels as soon as possible. This was no simple matter, as the Dutch controlled the sea, while Feria's recent campaign had failed to secure the land route along the Rhine, so a circuitous journey through Austria and Bohemia, and then west across Germany, was proposed. Quiroga's mission was to ask Wallenstein to provide an escort of 6000 cavalry for this last stage. The general received the envoy politely but pointed out the military impossibility of the proposal. From Bohemia to Brussels was some 500 miles, and almost every place of importance on the way was in the hands of the enemy. The Swedes would first have to be defeated, which could not be done until the spring, otherwise the escort might be intercepted and destroyed, and the Cardinal Infant captured. By this time, however, the atmosphere of suspicion was such that these logical arguments fell on deaf ears, and Wallenstein's refusal was assumed to be motivated by malice and obstructionism rather than by sound military reasoning.[16]

The general's health was continuing to deteriorate, so that he spent much of the time in bed, even to receive important visitors such as Quiroga, and he was able to attend to business for only short periods at a time. Surviving apothecaries' bills show that he was taking large quantities of medicines, probably principally for pain relief but with unknown side effects. Questenberg's doctor, who became aware of what was being prescribed, expressed the view that such a patient did not have long to live, although Wallenstein's own doctors reportedly gave him up to two more years.[17] In this condition he became increasingly dependent on the two men holding the key positions around him. One of these was Christian Ilow, field marshal and chief of staff since the death of Holk during the previous autumn, but the most influential was the ubiquitous Adam Trčka. The latter was not only colonel and owner of half a dozen regiments, but also occupied a position akin to adjutant-in-chief, often writing and speaking on the general's behalf as well as largely controlling access to him. Unlike the reliable Holk, however, these were not men who merited Wallenstein's confidence, and the degree of latitude which they acquired reflected his own decline. He had always liked Trčka, but in the past he had kept him well in check, whereas now this fantasist and intriguer had freer rein, while he and Ilow were united in recognising that their own positions and prospects were entirely dependent on Wallenstein. Any threat to him was a greater threat to them, and they were determined to preserve his power, even against his own inclinations should this prove necessary.

This was the background to the strange, even bizarre, meeting of senior officers held from 11 to 13 January 1634.[18] Summoned in late December, almost all the general officers and colonels of the Imperial army, 49 in total, assembled at Pilsen, the only notable absentees being Gallas and Aldringer, respectively commanding forces in Silesia and Bavaria.

Whether Wallenstein initiated or merely agreed to the meeting is unknown, but Ilow organised and conducted it. His first aim was to unite the officers in opposition to the policy towards the war and the army emanating from Vienna. He drew their attention to the demands for winter campaigns, one against Bernhard, another to secure winter quarters, and a third to escort the Cardinal Infant across occupied Germany to Brussels, all proposals which the assembled officers unanimously agreed to be impossible. Moreover, Ilow continued, the court never provided the money which was due to the army, although it had enough to spare for other purposes, while ingratitude, criticism and slander rather than thanks were the generalissimo's rewards for all his efforts. Wallenstein, he said, intended to resign, unless they, his officers, were able to persuade him to change his mind.

Virtually all of those present agreed with Ilow's analysis of the attitude of the court to the army, and most wished to see Wallenstein retain the command, but one topic which united them completely, reflecting the general's remarks to Trauttmansdorff a few weeks earlier, was anxiety over money. The officers had all made substantial investments in their regiments, for which Wallenstein personally was the guarantor, and without him they would be at considerable financial risk, as the emperor's perennial shortage of cash was well known. A five-man delegation led by Ilow was duly appointed to call on Wallenstein, but when he met them he remained firmly set on resignation. The delegation retired, deliberated, and returned, and at this second meeting Wallenstein finally agreed that he would retain his position a little longer, in order to secure the officers and the army their dues, and to try once again to bring peace. Some people, both at the time and since, have seen this as an elaborate charade, and so it may have been. On the other hand it may have reflected Wallenstein's own indecision, torn between a wish to be free of the burden of command and a desire to do his duty to his officers, and to seek peace as his final achievement.

This, however, was only a step on the way to Ilow's real objective, to secure a ringing declaration of loyalty to Wallenstein in order to deter the court from any move to dismiss him. The generalissimo had committed himself to them, he told the officers, and they should therefore reciprocate by swearing an oath to support him. Dinner followed, a veritable banquet given by Ilow in the Pilsen city hall, and a thoroughly drunken affair which is magnificently presented in a key scene in Schiller's *Wallenstein* play. Among the carousing, horseplay and occasional drawn swords, the document containing the oath was passed around to the officers, some signing it readily, others more hesitantly, but in the end all appending their signatures. Schiller makes much of a trick in which the original document contained a proviso that the officers' loyalty to Wallenstein was subject to their duty to the emperor, but after the wine had done its work another without this clause was substituted for signature. This story was in circulation soon after the event but is most unlikely, not least because this was not the final version. An oath which some appeared to have signed reluctantly, while others could claim to have been drunk at the time, was not sufficient for the principals. The following afternoon Wallenstein himself received the full assembly of officers, and the result was that a new document, known as the Pilsen oath, was signed in all sobriety by each of them, with copies made for retention by the senior generals of the three sections of the army, and two more to be sent to Gallas and Aldringer for their signatures.[19]

The text emphasised that the officers' only prospect of honourable recognition for their loyal service was Wallenstein, upon whose word and in hope of future recompense they had hazarded their fortunes and their lives. The general, in response to their entreaties, had consented to remain with them to see what funds could be procured for the support of the army, and had agreed not to leave without their explicit prior knowledge and consent. They in turn swore to stand by him honourably and faithfully, and neither to part from him nor to allow themselves to be parted from him, but to offer their all with and for him, down to the last drop of blood. Stripped of the grand phrases, however, this oath was essentially a symbolic gesture, a warning shot to Vienna rather than an actual threat, and it was neither kept secret nor formally transmitted to the court. As such it had little practical significance, but it did allow Wallenstein's enemies to resurrect and exploit the old fear, dating back to 1630, that he would not go quietly if dismissed, but would turn the army against the emperor and the court. Hence more drastic measures would have to be considered in order to get rid of him.

Hope springs eternal

While Ferdinand was preparing the ground for Wallenstein's dismissal, and Ilow and Trčka were trying clumsily to prevent it, other contacts, negotiations, and attempts to make peace or to make mischief were also taking place. As before there were two separate strands, Wallenstein's own efforts to find some basis for a settlement with Saxony and Brandenburg through Arnim, and Trčka's intrigues with Kinsky, both still pursuing their old aim of involving the generalissimo in a liaison with France and Sweden. It is difficult to establish what knowledge, if any, Wallenstein had of these latter manoeuvres prior to the last week of his life, as the reports are scanty and often second or third hand. A good example is Franz Albrecht's note to Arnim in mid-January, based on information from the Saxon colonel Anton Schlieff, recently returned from Pilsen, that 'the general is greatly offended because he has been censured by the court on account of Regensburg, and because they are planning to take the army out of his hands. He wants to revenge himself on the emperor, that is certain.'[20] There is no mention of this in the record of Schlieff's own account to the Saxon court of his conversation with Wallenstein, but it is safe to assume that he, like Kinsky, also had discussions with Trčka and Ilow.

This illustrates the biggest problem, that people usually assumed that what Trčka, Ilow and later Kinsky said genuinely emanated from Wallenstein and had his full authority, hence recording it as though the general himself had said it, whereas much of the time they were probably usurping that authority to press forward their own schemes. Few of those directly involved – including the emperor and most of his advisers – actually saw Wallenstein in the latter stages of his life, and it is evident that most still took him for the commanding personality he had previously been, rather than realising the extent of the deterioration caused by his illness. A better indication was provided by Ilow, who was reported in mid-December as saying that Wallenstein was able to receive visitors only when strictly necessary, and even then a proper discussion was scarcely possible as the general cursed terribly throughout because of his great pain.[21] At key moments Wallenstein could and did still make the effort to intervene personally and exercise his old authority, but increasingly such occasions were the exception rather than the rule, as his progressive decline put him ever more under the influence and virtual control of the cabal around him.

At the end of December Trčka wrote to Kinsky, urging him to come to Pilsen because Wallenstein had decided to make agreements not only with Saxony and Brandenburg, but also with Sweden and France, adding in an oft-quoted phrase that they 'were now determined to take the mask right off' in order to make a start.[22] What exactly he meant by this is a matter for speculation, but it certainly did not mean that contacts with Sweden and France were to be brought out into the open, not least because it is unlikely that Wallenstein himself had authorised them. It was, after all, only three months since he had insisted that Arnim join him in attacking these foreign interlopers, the condition upon which the peace negotiations had foundered, and the final crisis which was to force him to reconsider was still almost two months away. Trčka was not the man to let such details stand in the way of his grandiose schemes, and with his encouragement Kinsky hastened to contact the French emissary Feuquières, to propose a revival of the proposition discussed the previous spring. The latter's response was cordial but he was privately dubious, and initially he did not even report the approach to Paris.[23] Nevertheless Kinsky, after a meeting with the elector of Saxony, and accompanied by his wife, set off to Pilsen, where he attached himself to the Imperialist headquarters. On 9 January Wallenstein duly reported his arrival to Trauttmansdorff, as one of a number of accredited representatives of Saxony who had come to renew efforts to find a settlement, a move which Ferdinand himself not only approved but assisted by despatching his leading lawyer to Pilsen to help.[24] Thereafter Kinsky was ever present alongside Trčka and Ilow, playing a central part in their manoeuvres and the contacts with the Saxons.

His other schemes made little progress. Feuquières did eventually notify the contact to the French government, receiving a better reception than he had expected, but the matter progressed so slowly and cautiously that Kinsky's representative was still awaiting a definitive answer after both his principal and Wallenstein were dead.[25] As for the Swedes, Oxenstierna was as sceptical but even blunter than before, telling Bubna that he would respond only to actions, not words, from Wallenstein. Kinsky fared no better with Bernhard of Weimar, who did at first agree to receive him, but then refused outright when Kinsky, pleading illness, asked him instead to send a representative to Pilsen.[26] The only results of these contacts were to increase Bernhard's distrust of approaches from those around Wallenstein, and to cause Oxenstierna to intensify his efforts to nullify the general's negotiations with the Saxons.

These latter contacts too had been renewed, and their most enthusiastic proponent was the indefatigable Franz Albrecht of Saxe-Lauenburg. The elector of Saxony was wary but nevertheless willing, whereas by this point Arnim was disillusioned with the whole process, despondent about its chances of success, distrustful of Wallenstein, and determined not to be used again. He was only persuaded by the recognition that the sole alternative to negotiating with Wallenstein was to remain tied to the Swedes, to whose long-term involvement in Germany he was even more strongly opposed than the generalissimo himself. Faced with these unpalatable options, he observed that 'the first holds great danger, yet some little hope; the other contains still greater danger, and to my mind no hope at all', adding that 'one must have great anxiety about negotiating with the duke of Friedland, but without him all negotiations are in vain'. Nevertheless he procrastinated. He insisted that he must have precise instructions before going to meet Wallenstein, so that all possibilities which might arise in the course of negotiations had first to be examined. This detained him in Dresden until the beginning of February, even though Wallenstein had issued a safe conduct for him on 10 January.[27]

Arnim's anxieties were increased by a Swedish campaign to discredit him, claiming that he was too close to Wallenstein and resurrecting the story that he had deliberately abandoned Thurn at Steinau the previous October. Moreover the Swedes were attempting to detach Brandenburg and to persuade its elector to join the Heilbronn League. Action had to be taken to prevent this, Arnim argued, in order to maintain a united front when it came to negotiations with Wallenstein. Consequently he was himself despatched to Berlin, while Wallenstein waited for him and fretted. Instead Franz Albrecht was sent to Pilsen to excuse the delay, where he spent the first half of February writing repeatedly to Arnim and Elector John George urging haste, while Wallenstein sent to him daily, sometimes more often, to enquire whether there was any news of Arnim's approach.[28]

From 6 to 10 February Arnim was in Berlin, where he found the electoral council not disposed towards further negotiations with Wallenstein, and certainly not without Sweden being party to them. He persisted, and he obtained an audience with the elector himself, later summarising their discussion in a letter to John George of Saxony, a missive striking for its anti-Swedish tone.[29] He had, he reported, pointed out that the Swedes had waged war for decades against the Russians and the Poles, and were now on course to do so in Germany. They had no interest in peace, as not they but Germany were the losers from continuing the conflict, while they were determined to secure Pomerania for themselves. This last shot struck home with the elector of Brandenburg, who expected to inherit Pomerania when its duke died, and he conceded to Arnim that he did not want to be separated from Saxony but to seek peace together. Arnim thought that he had made progress, but once this was put in writing the council's proviso that any peace would have to be acceptable to Sweden had reappeared. It was the best he could get, and on 12 February he was back in Dresden.

All the while Wallenstein continued to consider resignation, and to sound out Vienna on the possibilities. Richel reported to Maximilian that he had learned from no less a person than Schlick, president of the war council, that on 17 January one of Wallenstein's officials, Count Hardegg, had brought a message that 'His Princely Grace is minded to resign the command, provided that His Imperial Majesty will guarantee his personal safety and arrange for him to be paid a sum of 300,000 Reichstaler'. This would have been no more than a down payment on the huge Imperial debts due to Wallenstein, and indicates how short of cash he was by this time. On 24 January Richel heard that Wallenstein had written to the court that 'after four months he would voluntarily resign, meanwhile putting the army back on to a sound footing and equipping it for the field. Thereafter he would present it to the king, the emperor's son, hand it over completely, help His Majesty into the saddle, kiss the stirrup, and take himself off into retirement.' Richel did not name his source on this occasion, but it is known that Count Max Waldstein, Wallenstein's heir and often his confidential messenger, was in Vienna at that time, although the flowery style, untypical of Wallenstein's usual correspondence, suggests some embroidery of what he may actually have written. On 8 February Richel reported hearing from Eggenberg himself that Wallenstein 'had sent for his cousin Maximilian, through whom he had recently offered the emperor his resignation'. This series of reports from the well-connected Bavarian vice-chancellor is clear evidence both that Wallenstein was indicating his willingness to resign and that this message had been received at the highest level in Vienna.[30]

Condemned unheard

At court they were too busy planning how to dismiss Wallenstein to give any consideration to his offers to resign. At first, however, this was not treated as a matter of great urgency, and on 9 January Richel reported despondently to Maximilian that things were going badly and slowly, as key ministers were talking only of limiting the generalissimo's powers, while sharing the command between Wallenstein and the emperor's son was also being mooted as a solution. For Maximilian and for Wallenstein's enemies at court this was not enough, but their agitation for more radical measures made little progress until two developments brought about an abrupt change of approach. First Piccolomini reported secretly that Wallenstein planned an all-out attack on the House of Austria, and then news of the Pilsen oath came at just the right moment to appear to confirm this threat. In the resulting atmosphere of crisis in Vienna ready credence was also given to rumours such as those reported by Richel some days later, to the effect that Wallenstein was in weekly correspondence with Richelieu, and that his representative had had a seven-hour meeting with the cardinal and the French king in Paris, tales which may have been a distorted echo of Kinsky's vain attempts to establish such a contact.[31]

Piccolomini, highly ambitious and a field marshal at the age of 34, had his eye on still higher things, including ultimately Wallenstein's command, together with any status and possessions he could gather on the way. On 3 January 1634 he met Gallas and Colloredo on official business in Silesia. Privately he reported to them that Wallenstein had taken him into his confidence, as something of a favourite, and told him of his intention to take the army across to the enemy.[32] The general, he said, proposed to use the combined forces to attack the emperor, and to capture not only the hereditary lands but also the other Habsburg possessions in Germany and beyond, notably in Italy, Alsace, Burgundy and the Low Countries. These territories would then be distributed, partly to appease neighbouring powers, including France, Poland, Savoy, the Papacy, and perhaps Venice, as well as granting freedom to the Netherlands, and partly to reward Wallenstein's loyal supporters. The three officers themselves were included. Gallas was to have the duchies of Glogau and Sagan, Colloredo the Italian province of Friuli, and Piccolomini the duchy of Teschen and other lands in Bohemia and Silesia. The king of France was to become King of the Romans, and hence successor to the Imperial crown, while Wallenstein himself would become king of Bohemia, and – according to another report of Piccolomini's claims – archduke of Austria too. There are many such differences of detail in the contemporary accounts.[33] One version says that Franz Albrecht was to have the electorate of Saxony, Bernard of Weimar would take Bavaria, Arnim and Horn would become electors of Mainz and Trier respectively, while Mecklenburg would go to Gallas, Milan to Piccolomini, Moravia to Trčka, Teschen to Ilow, and so on. Yet another gives Saxony to Bernhard, Brandenburg to Franz Albrecht, and Pomerania to Arnim. No doubt the tale grew in the telling, but even at its most basic level it would have been a gigantically ambitious enterprise.

Elements of this story are familiar. Wallenstein was certainly prone to talk and write loosely about what might be desirable – not of course the same thing as his practical intentions – including in the earlier days a campaign against the Turks and more recently the need to rid the Empire of foreigners, notably the Swedes, the French and the Spanish. On the other hand joining with the Swedes and French to turn the combined armies on the emperor and drive him out to Spain was what Kinsky and Trčka had been aiming at since 1631. That much Piccolomini might have heard in Pilsen, although from separate sources, and it will not have worried him that the two propositions were incompatible, requiring Wallenstein to both join with and to drive out the foreigners, but the rest can only have been his inventions or the fantasies of drunken evenings with the Bohemians. Gallas was sceptical, and it was agreed that he should endeavour to dissuade Wallenstein from any such ideas, which the three officers would in the meanwhile not report further. Piccolomini returned to Pilsen, but a week later he sent a confidential agent to Vienna to reveal this alleged plan to the emperor, as well as to the Spanish envoy Oñate and the papal nuncio.[34]

The emperor believed what he was told, as set out in Lamormaini's report to the head of the Jesuit order: 'On 12 January Friedland's secret intrigues eventually came out into the open. He wanted to ruin the emperor and to destroy the House of Austria, to seize the Austrian lands for himself, and to distribute the property of those loyal to the emperor among the participants in the conspiracy.'[35] It may seem surprising that such a fantastic story was accepted in Vienna, but the climate of suspicion at court was such that Wallenstein's former friends, and even those of an independent turn of mind, could no longer argue for a more balanced view, while his enemies exploited the story with no concern as to whether it was true or not. Particularly significant was the Pilsen oath, signed on 12 January and news of which reached Vienna a few days later, which seemed to fit in with and independently confirm Piccolomini's tale of imminent rebellion. Hence instead of serving as a warning to the court not to make a move against Wallenstein the oath convinced them that they had no alternative but to do so, and quickly. The problem was how.

An answer was provided by Prince Gundakar Liechtenstein, brother of Wallenstein's old associate and rival Karl, and himself a former Imperial councillor. Although no longer in favour at court, Liechtenstein's views still found a hearing, and he had considerably influenced the peace memorandum submitted by Trauttmansdorff and his colleagues in January 1633. In December he turned his thoughts to the subject of Wallenstein, and his opinion reached the emperor shortly before Piccolomini's dire warning.[36] Although when he wrote Liechtenstein knew neither of the supposed rebellion nor of the oath, he nevertheless viewed Wallenstein as disobedient, citing specifically his quartering of the army in the hereditary lands, his failure to pursue Bernhard of Weimar, and his orders to Suys to remain in Upper Austria, all contrary to the emperor's commands. This disobedience posed a threat for the future, he claimed, as it might lead Wallenstein into various forms of treachery and rebellion, including moves against the House of Austria in association with France. Hence Wallenstein should be removed from his command, because 'in politics one should always assume and provide against the worst that may happen'.

Arguing hypothetically, at least ostensibly, Liechtenstein continued that should it appear that the general were involved in treachery, and that he could not be removed safely without killing him, then Ferdinand should proceed as follows:

> Select two or three of your confidential councillors, conscientious and well versed in the law, and arrange for them to be thoroughly but secretly informed as to what the generalissimo has effected against Your Majesty, what indications there are of his further intentions, and what particulars are available as to the danger to Your Majesty's person, esteemed House and lands, and to the true religion. They should then be asked to deliver an opinion as to whether, should there be no other sure way of deposing him, Your Majesty might, without violating justice, deprive him of his life, ... as extreme evil calls for extreme remedy, and for the preservation of the state everything must be done which does not go against God.

Ironically, considering Wallenstein's own efforts, Liechtenstein added that once the general had been replaced it would be essential for the emperor to seek peace at the earliest opportunity, because the situation was becoming ever worse, and hence 'as Your Majesty cannot make peace just as you would like it, you must make it as best you can'.

Emperor Ferdinand, often regarded as easy-going, even lazy, for once acted swiftly and decisively. Whether or not Liechtenstein was the principal influence, he followed the advice in his memorandum – apart from making peace – almost to the letter. To the secret tribunal he appointed Eggenberg, still the first minister, Trauttmansdorff, the coming man, and Bishop Antonius of Vienna, a councillor and a churchman. Two of these had long been regarded as Wallenstein's supporters, while Trauttmansdorff did not number among his more committed enemies, but this was negated by the change in their personal attitudes to him which had by then taken place, and by the impossibility of appearing to side with the general in the atmosphere of crisis prevalent at court. They met on 24 January, and they did not need to deliberate long.[37] As a result of their findings an Imperial *Patent* (decree) was drawn up on the same day, informing the army that Wallenstein had been removed from his post, so that they were therefore released from their duty towards him and should instead take their orders from Gallas until such time as a new commander-in-chief was appointed.[38] Those officers who had signed the Pilsen oath were, with the exception of two unnamed individuals, pardoned for any impropriety. This decree, however, was withheld until such time as the emperor should see fit to publish it. So secret were these proceedings that beside the three members of the tribunal and Ferdinand himself they were known only to Lamormaini. The latter reported to the head of his order the key decision which was reached, namely that the emperor authorised his loyal officers, Gallas, Piccolomini, Colloredo and Aldringer, to arrest the conspirators and to bring them to Vienna for trial, but if necessary 'to eliminate them from the numbers of the mortal'. Despite this secrecy, on the very next day Maximilian's representative Richel was told by Trauttmansdorff himself that action against Wallenstein was imminent, although he would give no more details.[39]

A 'dead or alive' warrant has always been a licence to kill, but issued in a form which allows the originators to salvage their consciences by shuffling off the decision on to those who are to carry it out. The prospective executioners were neither happy with their task nor united among themselves. Colloredo took little direct part, while for almost three weeks after 24 January Gallas was at headquarters in Pilsen, rather perplexed as he saw no sign that Wallenstein was preparing a dramatic *coup d'état*. In fact apart from attending to the normal business of the army, to the limited extent that his health permitted, the general seemed to be doing nothing other than to wait endlessly for Arnim, and moreover when the latter did eventually arrive he, Gallas, was to be invited, indeed required, to take part in the negotiations. Piccolomini, safely out of Pilsen commanding the forces in Upper Austria, contacted Aldringer, stationed near him on the Bavarian border, and a steady stream of coded correspondence but little action followed, while each eyed the other, trying to ensure for themselves the lion's share of any benefits which might follow from this affair.[40]

Here Aldringer was at a disadvantage, because whereas Piccolomini stood high in Wallenstein's favour the general had always distrusted him, although respecting his ability, and the relationship had deteriorated further in recent times. They had not met since October 1632, when Aldringer had been detached to return to Bavaria with Maximilian, where he had tarried too long to re-join Wallenstein before Lützen, while his campaigning with Feria had been against the generalissimo's wishes even if not against his direct orders. Wallenstein was anxious to see him, but Aldringer was equally anxious to avoid such a meeting, and he sent a stream of excuses for his failure to go to Pilsen.

As a result he was not well placed to take part in any attempt to arrest or kill Wallenstein. Piccolomini himself became hesitant, perhaps thinking that he might have overplayed his hand. Although courageous on the battlefield he was nervous of having to take the leading part in trying to seize the generalissimo in his own headquarters, surrounded by an army probably more loyal to him as the source of what little pay it received than to the Imperial court which provided nothing.[41]

The planned move against Wallenstein following the tribunal's decision could not long be fully hidden. Some people started to guess; others correctly interpreted the lack of any apparent action as meaning that something was being undertaken in secret. Oñate knew by early February, Maximilian soon afterwards, while on 2 February an Imperial councillor communicated the decision to Aldringer, which he in turn passed on to Piccolomini.[42] At some point the information reached Gallas in Pilsen, whereupon seeing which way the wind blew he abandoned any reservations he might have had. Nevertheless security was tight enough for no hint to have reached Ilow, Trčka or Wallenstein himself, and hence they did not demur when Gallas suggested a further meeting of officers, at which they should all present details of the totals owed to them by the Imperial treasury for their military outlays. In fact he intended this meeting as an opportunity to gather supporters in Pilsen in order to proceed against Wallenstein, and it enabled him to summon Piccolomini and Aldringer in particular. The latter, however, once again found an excuse to absent himself, and when Piccolomini arrived on 11 February he agreed with Gallas, according to his own account, that the undertaking was too dangerous to be attempted because the garrison had been changed and the sentiment of the army was unknown.[43]

On the following day Gallas left Pilsen with Wallenstein's good wishes, using the excuse that he intended to meet Aldringer and accompany him back to headquarters. On 13 February he despatched confidential orders to those senior officers outside Pilsen whom he regarded as trustworthy. They were, he said, in future to obey no orders from Wallenstein, Ilow or Trčka, but only those from himself, Aldringer and Piccolomini. The latter also left Pilsen soon after, reporting to Gallas that 'it was not possible' before he left to distribute copies of his order to the reliable colonels amongst those there assembled, as he had been ordered to do.[44] While Gallas and Piccolomini then set about securing the loyalty of officers and regiments throughout the hereditary lands, other than those in the Pilsen area, Aldringer went to Vienna to urge the need for open action, as well as to draw attention to his own loyal efforts. He met Oñate first, and then on 18 February he was received by Ferdinand. Imperial orders to army commanders followed on the same day, confirming Gallas's earlier ones, and messengers were despatched to allied princes both within and outside the Empire informing them of the situation, much to Maximilian's pleasure and relief.[45]

Ferdinand then issued a proclamation, also dated 18 February and known as the patent of proscription, publicising Wallenstein's alleged plans and announcing his dismissal.[46] Unlike the decree of 24 January this makes no mention of pardon for those who signed the Pilsen oath, no longer a matter of some officers having 'gone rather far and done more than they legally should have', but now described as 'a most dangerous and far-reaching conspiracy against us and our esteemed House'. Regarding Wallenstein himself the first decree had made no accusations, citing only 'highly important and urgent reasons' for making a change in the command. In contrast the proclamation refers to 'definite information concerning his designs to drive us and our esteemed House out of our hereditary kingdom, lands and people, and to take our crown and sceptre for himself', which is described as 'an unheard-of faithless breach of oath and barbaric tyranny for which there are no parallels in history'. Despite this hyperbole, however, careful reading shows that Wallenstein was accused only of harbouring intentions, not of having actually taken any action. Although by implication he was branded as a traitor there was no formal statement to that effect, nor was he placed under the ban of the Empire, and there was likewise no mention of or authority for anyone to arrest him, let alone kill him. Nor was the document sent to Pilsen.

One other matter was not overlooked. Oñate had been the first, so far as the records show, to mention what many others may safely be assumed to have had in mind. At the end of January he had told Piccolomini's confidential factotum Fabio Diodati that there would soon be money enough in the Imperial coffers, the proceeds of the confiscation of the vast Wallenstein and Trčka estates. On the same day as the proscription was published, while Wallenstein still lived and no attempt had yet been made to arrest him, the emperor gave orders for the immediate despatch of troops to seize his and Trčka's possessions.[47] Evidently he was not expecting them to be brought to trial. It was Ferdinand's favourite financial device, now his standard procedure, to pay his debts by sequestering the assets of anyone who could conveniently be classified as a rebel. The veil of legality covering this near-naked expropriation was thin in Bohemia, thinner still in the Palatinate and Mecklenburg, and was now reduced to a three-man tribunal, sitting in secret, hearing no evidence and publishing no judgement, on the basis of which the emperor issued what amounted to a warrant of execution. Scarcely surprising that no attention had been paid to Wallenstein's offers to resign and to go into honourable retirement for what little time was left to him.

14
Assassination Is the Quickest Way
(Molière)

In Pilsen they had still not detected the rumbles of distant thunder which might have warned of the approaching storm. On 17 and 18 February Wallenstein was transacting normal army business and writing to Questenberg about money. He was also arranging the transfer of recently confiscated Bohemian émigré properties to some of his colonels in settlement of Imperial exchequer debts, suggesting that as yet he had no thoughts of changing sides and aligning himself with the Swedes and their exile confederates.[1]

The colonels and generals had gathered at headquarters, but this time only about thirty of them. Gallas, having proposed the meeting, left on 12 February and did not return. Piccolomini stayed a little longer to distribute Gallas's order to those deemed reliable, but thought better of it and departed in his turn. On 17 February Colonel Giulio Diodati, brother of Fabio and another of Piccolomini's henchmen, quietly left Pilsen with his entire regiment, although he had received no such orders, and an equerry sent after him did not return. On 18 February another colonel was sent to summon Gallas, but he likewise did not return.[2] Some of the officers who came to Pilsen had already received Gallas's secret order, so that they were aware of at least part of what was going on, while others probably guessed or had heard rumours. Camp talk, Diodati's disappearance and Gallas's continued absence now made Ilow, Trčka and Wallenstein himself realise that something dangerous was happening.

Wallenstein's first reaction was to seek to clarify his position with the court. On 18 February he sent Max Waldstein with a letter of accreditation and a verbal message to Eggenberg. Two days later, after his meeting with senior officers referred to below, he sent Colonel Mohr Wald with credentials to speak on his behalf to the emperor, Eggenberg, Gallas,

Piccolomini and Aldringer, as well as for Max to speak to Questenberg. Wald first encountered Piccolomini, by then stationed 30 miles southeast of Pilsen at Horazdowitz (Horažd'ovice) with a force of 3000 cavalry, who informed him of Wallenstein's dismissal and sent him on to Gallas. Before travelling further the colonel reported his mission to the head of the Order of German Knights, of which he was a member. He was to tell the emperor and the officers, he wrote, that Wallenstein 'has never thought, still less by word or deed undertaken, to do anything against His Majesty, but should His Majesty prefer to place someone else in command of the army he will gladly resign, asking only that it should be done properly and not by force, and without guilt attaching to him. I am to assure them that he would rather die than commit any act against His Majesty.' The following day Wald reached Gallas, who promptly arrested him, but although he was unable to deliver the messages his mission was duly reported to Vienna. Max reached the court on 22 February and was received by Eggenberg, who refused either to read the credential from Wallenstein or to hear his message, instead advising Max that he should make efforts to clear himself with the emperor as he could do nothing more for his patron. The reason for his journey was nevertheless well known at court.[3]

In this new and threatening situation Wallenstein and his adherents realised that they also had to think about self-defence, pushing them into the very contacts with the enemy which the court imagined to be long established. In the first of these Ilow was the originator and Franz Albrecht the intermediary, but Wallenstein evidently acquiesced in their efforts. On 18 February Franz Albrecht wrote to Arnim that both he and Wallenstein were still anxiously awaiting his arrival in Pilsen, but problems were starting to be apparent – Diodati's disappearance, the continued absence of Gallas and Aldringer, doubts about Piccolomini – although most of the officers and regiments still remained loyal. Nevertheless, continued Franz Albrecht, Wallenstein requested Arnim to station a strong detachment of cavalry near the Bohemian border in case he should require assistance. He himself was leaving for Regensburg to tell Bernhard of Weimar of the generalissimo's peace efforts, and to seek help from him should open hostilities develop between one part of the Imperialist forces under Gallas and the other under Wallenstein.[4]

On Sunday 19 February Wallenstein, from his bed, addressed the senior officers in Pilsen.[5] According to Wald's later testimony he referred first to the important issue of money, acknowledging that in order to lose no time in bringing their regiments back up to strength over the winter the colonels had advanced cash from their own private means, for which he stood guarantor. Unfortunately funds had not been forthcoming from the court to enable him to redeem this obligation, and they should therefore have a further meeting with Ilow at which this problem and possible remedies could be discussed. He went on to say that 'he had been deeply pained to learn that it was being said of him that he was plotting against His Majesty, and planning to alter his own religion'. He assured them that 'at his advanced age he had no thoughts of changing his religion, nor had it ever been his intention to undertake anything against his emperor. All he had done was to seek peace, and although this was not welcome to some at the Imperial court he intended to continue his efforts, as it was his opinion that His Imperial Majesty would enjoy no good fortune unless peace were made.' He ended by saying that as he feared that some kind of outrage might be attempted against him he was concentrating forces around Prague, but this was not, he emphasised, directed against the emperor, and he hoped that all the officers would stand by him. If not it would have been better had they allowed him to resign at their previous meeting, so that he would not have found himself in this danger.

At the subsequent meeting with Ilow the officers affirmed their support for Wallenstein, although according to a report sent to Maximilian shortly afterwards they avoided replying to Trčka's tentative enquiry as to what the position would be 'should it be a different service'.[6] On the following day, Monday 20 February, they were received again by Wallenstein. He was aware, he said, that their earlier oath had been misunderstood or wilfully misrepresented, so he wished to state explicitly that should he ever – and he had no intention of so doing – make even the slightest move against the emperor then all concerned were released from their obligations to him. Hence a new oath of loyalty to the generalissimo containing this provision was circulated and signed.[7] Wallenstein intended this expressly non-rebellious version to be a reassurance to the court, while Ilow and Trčka hoped that even at this late stage a new piece of paper might shore up the crumbling loyalty of the officer corps. Thereafter the colonels dispersed freely to their regiments, although two who were deemed unreliable, one of them Johan Beck, were held back, officially in order to act as observers at the anticipated peace negotiations with Arnim.

Trčka sent out orders for the assembly of forces at Prague, but Gallas forestalled him, and the city and surrounding area were quickly secured by regiments and officers acting under his command. As they were unaware of this in Pilsen the plan was for Trčka to go to Prague on Tuesday 21 February to make arrangements, and for Wallenstein to follow him with the rest of the headquarters on the following day. At this point they were still expecting to be able to act independently rather than having to rely on help from the enemy, which would have prescribed a move in the opposite direction, towards the Saxon border or Regensburg. Trčka duly set out, but he had only gone a short distance when he met a messenger coming in the opposite direction, and his news sent him post-haste back to Pilsen.[8] The proscription proclamation had not yet reached Prague, but Gallas's order that Wallenstein was no longer to be obeyed and the occupation of the city by loyalist troops told their own story. This sudden revelation of the extent to which their situation had deteriorated came as a bolt from the blue to Wallenstein, Ilow, Trčka and Kinsky. There was no time for debate; immediate action was required as an attack on Pilsen might be imminent. They would have to leave as soon as possible, and with opposing forces in Prague to the north-east and in Horazdowitz to the south-east they had to head west, where there was also a better chance that key places had not yet been secured by the loyalists. Their chosen destination was Eger, 50 miles away, the western-most town in Bohemia and only a couple of miles from Saxony in one direction and from the Upper Palatinate and the route to Swedish-occupied Regensburg in the other.

Wallenstein himself issued some of the orders. Anticipating Ferdinand's confiscation he wrote to his Friedland chancellery that all ready cash was to be moved out at once, an instruction which arrived just in time. He also ordered the Irish Colonel Walter Butler, stationed twenty miles west of Pilsen, to stand by and wait for him on the road to Eger with his regiment of dragoons (mounted infantrymen), while Lieutenant-Colonel John Gordon, a Scot commanding the Eger garrison, was instructed to hold the town for him and to ignore any orders coming from elsewhere. Ilow wrote to Franz Albrecht, appraising him of the situation and asking him to persuade Bernhard of Weimar to move his cavalry up towards Eger, while Kinsky sent a letter to Arnim, telling him that Wallenstein was going to Eger, and urging him to make his long-delayed journey to meet him there.[9]

Meanwhile the immediately available troops were mustered to act as an escort, and patrols were sent out to guard against a surprise attack. According to Maximilian's representative in Pilsen, Trčka and Ilow set to plundering the city in order to take with them whatever could be found, realising that their own possessions would be confiscated and to help finance subsequent military action. Baggage was gathered, transport was assembled, and Wallenstein's household made ready, from high officials of his Friedland court down to the humblest servants, some 40 in all, while senior military functionaries and their staff made the number up to around 200. Before dawn the following morning the general received Colonel Beck, still detained at Pilsen, telling him that 'I had peace in my hand; now I have no further say in the matter, but God is just'. Beck was later allowed to leave, together with Bavarian and Imperial representatives still in Pilsen, and on Wallenstein's orders they were provided with a squad of musketeers to ensure their safety. At ten in the morning on Wednesday 22 February Wallenstein and his remaining adherents, with an escort of around 1300 men, mostly cavalry, set out for Eger.[10]

The journey took three days, travelling slowly because of Wallenstein's condition, which confined him most of the time to a horse litter. His health had continued to deteriorate. In early January he told his Spanish visitor Quiroga that 'he would gladly take the strongest poison in order to be free once and for all of the pains he had to endure, were it not that he had to fear hell and the devil'. The Saxon colonel Schlieff saw Wallenstein on 19 February and later observed that he had looked like a corpse. Beck reported that when Wallenstein summoned him earlier at Pilsen he had only been able to sit for a short time, needing to go off for an hour in a steam bath before he could continue the discussion.[11] The 50 miles to Eger must have seemed endless.

The first stop was at Mies (Stříbro), only fifteen miles from Pilsen, by which time Butler and his 900 men had joined the escort. Butler was in a quandary. He later confirmed to Gallas that he had received his order not to obey Wallenstein, although without specifying when, and while he had not been at the most recent Pilsen meeting he must have had some idea of the situation. On the other hand Gallas's authority was based only on his own order, whereas Wallenstein's was backed by his long-standing position and reputation, so for the moment Butler followed his instructions. Nevertheless his regiment was stationed at the front of the column to make it more difficult to defect, and at the overnight stops Butler was billeted in the castles, away from his men outside. On the second night, at Plan (Planá), he secretly sent his chaplain Patrick Taafe off with a message protesting his loyalty to the emperor and asserting that he was only going to Eger under compulsion, which was successfully delivered to Piccolomini the following day.[12] Wallenstein too sent out an envoy, Colonel Breuner, with accreditations to the emperor, Eggenberg and Trauttmansdorff, to deliver yet another message that he was ready to resign and retire into private life. Breuner only reached Pilsen, where he was arrested by Giulio Diodati, but his mission was reported to Vienna. The emperor wrote back to Gallas (although unknown to him Wallenstein was by then dead) that

Breuner's message made no difference to his intentions, 'which I have previously set out to you and my field marshal Count Piccolomini' and which he was to endeavour 'to effect safely in the one way or the other, and as soon as possible'.[13]

Those two, however, were taking no risks. They had been wary of mounting an attack on Pilsen while Wallenstein was still there, and even though they knew of his flight and his destination on the Wednesday afternoon it was not until Friday 24 February, the day upon which Wallenstein eventually reached Eger, that Piccolomini and his 3000 cavalry arrived in Pilsen. Even then they made no attempt at pursuit, relying on Gordon to close Eger's gates to prevent Wallenstein from occupying the town. Hence they expected him to pass it by, escaping from Bohemia into safer territory where he could join up with the Saxons or Swedes. Gallas was greatly angered to learn later that Wallenstein had been admitted to Eger, which presented the threat that he might hold it as a bridgehead in Bohemia until the enemy advanced to his assistance. There was little that Gallas could do about it other than send out light cavalry to harass any approaching reinforcements, apologetically reporting to the emperor that nothing could be undertaken against Eger without artillery, 'and in the present bad weather it is not possible to move up a single gun'.[14]

On the morning of the last day of the journey to Eger a large part of Wallenstein's original escort, 500 cavalry from the regiment of Duke Heinrich Julius of Saxe-Lauenburg, yet another brother of Franz Albrecht, suddenly rode off in response to an order sent by their colonel. Butler could have done likewise but chose to stay, sitting part of the way with Wallenstein, according to Taafe's account, and receiving flattering offers for the future from him as a reward for his loyalty. Before reaching Eger Wallenstein sent for Major Walter Leslie, another Scot and second-in-command of Gordon's garrison regiment. He too, so he said, was invited to travel and talk with Wallenstein so that the latter could attempt to win him over to his plans, but both of these reports are suspect in view of the two officers' parts in Wallenstein's murder, and their subsequent efforts to maximise their rewards from the emperor.

The same problem applies to all accounts of the remaining days of Wallenstein's life, as apart from peripheral details the only sources for the events in Eger are Butler, Gordon and Leslie, together perhaps with Macdaniel, one of Butler's officers. Leslie's written account appears to be his own, Gordon's was edited and amended by someone, probably Piccolomini, while Butler's depends mainly on a letter written by Taafe nineteen years later. There are also references in the *Itinerarium* published by another of his chaplains, Thomas Carve, but he was not in Germany at the time and did not return until 1635, after Butler's death, so that his description of events is at best third hand. Another account is believed to derive at least in part from Macdaniel, but this is not reliably attributed. The basic facts of what happened can be established from these sources, but their claims as to what the officers discussed beforehand and what Wallenstein and Ilow said to them cannot be regarded as reliable. Srbik's reconstruction of the events themselves has not been bettered, and it forms the basis both of Mann's account and of the following description.[15]

Death, a necessary end
(*Julius Caesar*)

Eger was a prosperous town, walled and with a castle on rising ground set aside from the centre. Its focus was the large lower market square and the well-appointed patrician houses around it. Wallenstein knew it well, as it was the natural starting point for military expeditions from Bohemia into Germany. His forces had set out from here against Christian of Denmark in 1625, and against Gustavus Adolphus in 1632. Now it was to be his refuge, although Gallas had sent Gordon orders to bar it to him. Leslie later claimed that these had not been received, but they were in any case difficult orders to follow in such an uncertain situation. The commandant had to make a choice between instructions from afar on the still questionable authority of Gallas, and the demands of the commander-in-chief present at the gate in person, and with, so it was said, a large part of the army not far behind him. Old habits prevailed, and Gordon not only admitted Wallenstein but moved out of his own lodgings to free the best house on the market square for him, as his rank required, while other accommodation was provided for Ilow and Butler, as well as for Trčka, Kinsky and their wives. The escorting troops, now numbering about 1700, made camp outside the walls, leaving only the 700 men of the garrison actually in the town.

Late on that Friday night a messenger from Pilsen caught up with the travellers at Eger, bringing with him a copy of the emperor's original notification to the army of Wallenstein's dismissal, drawn up on 24 January but only now reaching units in the field. This was the first time that he received any official confirmation of the fact, and he never saw the proscription patent of 18 February. According to Leslie, who was present when he received it although probably not privy to the contents, Wallenstein appeared shocked, losing his self-control and venting his anger in threats against the House of Austria. He may well have done so, and he had cause enough, but it also suited Leslie to claim that he had.

It is not certain how much Butler, Gordon and Leslie knew about Wallenstein's dismissal, but during their first tentative private discussion that night they established that they all had their suspicions. These were confirmed by a harangue they received from Ilow on the following morning. He, knowing the loyalty of the troops in and around the town to be critical, set out to win over their commanders. He assured them that the ingratitude of the House of Austria to its commander-in-chief justified all concerned in renouncing their allegiance and switching their service instead to Wallenstein as an independent prince, a step which they would find to be not only right but also profitable. The three officers demurred, so they later claimed, suggesting that perhaps a little time would bring about a reconciliation of emperor and general. Not so, replied Ilow, and moreover Swedish and Saxon troops were on their way and would soon arrive in Eger. A decision and a new oath of loyalty to Wallenstein were needed without delay. The three duly complied, comforting themselves with the thought that an oath given under duress could not bind them, and they then went off to discuss an entirely different plan of action.

They were in a difficult personal situation. Butler had stayed with the entourage on the march from Pilsen, although he could have left with his men as Heinrich Julius's cavalry had done, while Gordon and Leslie had admitted Wallenstein to Eger against orders. Now Ilow had left them in no doubt that the generalissimo had not only been dismissed but had become a rebel. For them to do nothing would be taken as siding with the defectors, and would invite drastic punishment from the Imperialists, while to slip away from Eger at this stage would be regarded as dereliction of duty, with the same consequences. On the other hand to arrest Wallenstein, Ilow and Trčka would be difficult and dangerous. The Irishmen among Butler's troops might well be unconcerned about wider issues and obedient to their officers, but they were encamped outside the walls. The garrison inside the town and holding its gates and defences were mainly Germans, as were most of their junior officers, and as far as they knew Wallenstein was the emperor's commander-in-chief and Ilow was his field marshal, added to which Trčka was colonel and proprietor of their own regiment, Gordon being only his deputy. They might well resist an attempted arrest by foreign officers, and a failed attempt would probably bring about the immediate execution of the perpetrators.

A clandestine assassination with explanations afterwards looked a safer prospect, but raised equally difficult problems of justification and authority. On Saturday morning Gordon may have received 'the necessary information' which Diodati recorded that he sent to him, probably a copy of the first Imperial order not to obey the generalissimo and his associates. It also seems likely that Butler had been given an intimation of the secret sentence on Wallenstein – arrest if possible, death if not – as he surreptitiously sent a captain from Eger with a further message to the Imperialist commanders that he would seize and if necessary kill the generalissimo, notwithstanding the imminent arrival of enemy forces.[16] Nevertheless to assassinate the commander-in-chief on the strength of a verbal message was a daunting prospect. Piccolomini himself had earlier demanded a written order from Gallas before considering an attempt to seize Wallenstein in Pilsen, but as the order was not forthcoming nor was the attempt. The proclamations, even had the three officers seen them, announced only Wallenstein's dismissal and said nothing about arresting him dead or alive. To kill him, and his adherents as well, without even an attempt at an arrest, would not only be against the terms of the secret sentence but could easily expose those involved to a charge of murder, as convenient scapegoats should Piccolomini, Gallas and even the emperor want to absolve themselves of responsibility for the deed. Ironically Ilow had provided them with the way out. If Swedish or Saxon forces were about to occupy Eger an arrest would be ineffectual, as those arrested would shortly be freed. Hence the only way that the emperor's presumed order could be carried out was to kill them before the enemy arrived. That was still a risky undertaking but on balance the least dangerous course, particularly as dead men tell no tales and the only account available of the circumstances leading up to the assassination would be that of the executioners themselves.

Although Gordon was reportedly more reticent about the deed than the others, once the course of action had been decided all three went about planning and organising the details swiftly and efficiently. Butler's Irish dragoons would do all that was necessary, and three of his officers, Major Geraldine and Captains Devereux and Macdaniel, were secretly briefed as to the situation. The garrison duty officer, a German, was instructed to allow 40 of the Irishmen to enter the town at the appropriate time, but probably he was told no more than that they were required for some routine assignment. Dealing with Wallenstein was the lesser problem, as he was in no condition to defend himself, and Ilow had seen no need to post a strong guard around his house, which was patrolled only by four town watchmen whose main duty was to ensure that there was no noise to disturb the general. Ilow and Trčka were another matter, determined fighting men certain to resist fiercely, and senior officers whose orders and appeals for help the German garrison troops were likely to obey. Hence the first plan, to fall upon them in their billets, was rejected. Somewhere more isolated was needed, away from potential assistance and where the noise of an affray would not rouse the guard and the town. The castle met those requirements, and moreover Gordon had moved his residence there to make way for Wallenstein on the market square. What more natural than that the commandant of the town should demonstrate his hospitality by inviting the distinguished visitors to dinner at his lodgings. They accepted, Kinsky too, and Captain Niemann, Ilow's adjutant, was also invited, although Wallenstein was too ill to attend. At around six on the evening of Saturday 25 February they arrived, accompanied only by a few servants.

The assassination squads were already in place. As the guests settled at the table the castle was secured outside by Macdaniel and his men, while the servants were led off to a separate room, where they were given a meal and quietly locked in. The castle's hall was too large and cold for dinner for seven – the three loyalist officers and their four victims – so a smaller panelled room, warmer and more pleasant, had been chosen. Conveniently, this had two adjoining anterooms in which Geraldine and Devereux waited, each with six soldiers, weapons to hand but with no firearms to avoid noise. Suspecting nothing, the guests hung up their swords and made themselves at home. Wine and conversation flowed. As they ate a soldier brought Leslie a key, the sign that the castle outer gate was locked, and he in turn sent an attendant with a message, apparently to the kitchen. Nothing unusual in these minor matters, and the guests took no notice of them, but in fact Leslie's message was to the officers in the anterooms. It was time to act.

Suddenly the fourteen armed men burst into the room, Geraldine to the fore shouting – so the reports claimed – 'Who is a good servant of the emperor?', to which Butler, Gordon and Leslie responded 'Vivat Ferdinandus', seized their swords and made to attack their guests. Kinsky, seated between the table and the wall, was quickly despatched, but the others, soldiers all, grabbed their own weapons and defended themselves manfully. Candles and lanterns were quickly extinguished, and with so many fighting men in a small dark room killing the three targets was not easily accomplished. The servants heard the tumult and broke out of their room, at least two rushing to their masters' aid and dying for their loyalty. Niemann escaped into a corridor but was overtaken and struck down, while Ilow managed to wound Leslie in the hand before he too fell. Trčka, a large, powerful man protected by a thick leather jerkin of the kind often worn in battle, took advantage of the confusion to break out of the room and escape into the castle courtyard, but at the gate he was halted and killed by the Irish sentries. The plan had achieved its full objectives so far. Leslie hurried to the town gates to admit more Irish dragoons to patrol the streets and to ensure that no disturbances followed. Then he assembled the guard, told them briefly what had happened and that it was at the emperor's command, and ordered them to stay quietly at their posts. Gordon was left in charge of the castle and its dead while Butler prepared for the next step.

With the dangerous Ilow and Trčka dead and the town in loyalist hands there was little justification for killing Wallenstein himself, as he could easily have been arrested. However Kinsky and Niemann had already been murdered with no justification whatsoever, not to mention the two servants, as they were not covered by the proscription or by the emperor's secret sentence, and ruthless men who had gone so far were not prepared to risk leaving the principal alive. Ilow's claim that the Swedes and Saxons were approaching still provided the fig-leaf, particularly as he had allegedly boasted over dinner that Wallenstein would shortly have a larger army than ever before. Time was passing, though, and despite the precautions news had reached the town, probably through one of the surviving servants, so that Kinsky's and Trčka's wives were already aware of their husbands' deaths. It was after ten on a stormy night when Butler, Geraldine, Devereux and their soldiers reached the market square. A dozen men were posted at the back of Wallenstein's lodgings, another dozen at the front, and then Devereux and his six tried and trusted stalwarts entered the house. Butler preferred to wait outside.

As they rushed up the stairs to Wallenstein's first-floor chambers they swept one servant aside with passing blows, and at the top they answered the protests of another by stabbing him to death. Devereux was in the lead, armed with a partisan, the short pike with a fearsomely sharp broad blade used in battle by infantry officers. His men kicked the bedroom door open, and he found himself standing face to face with Wallenstein, who had been roused by the storm and noise and had got himself out of bed, perhaps to look out of the window. What each said, if anything, in the brief moment of hesitation is unknown, although contemporary accounts carried many fanciful versions. The most credible is that Devereux uttered a short phrase of abuse as he worked himself up to strike the blow, shouting, according to Gordon's report: 'You evil, perjured, rebellious old scoundrel.' Wallenstein made at most the one-word reply 'Quarter' and the accompanying gesture of submission, the traditional soldier's plea for mercy on the battlefield. Then Devereux ran him through with a single decisive thrust below the ribs and upwards into the chest, killing him almost instantly. As the soldiers crowded into the room one picked up the body and made to throw it out of the window, but that was too much even for Devereux. Instead it was rolled up in a carpet and dragged down the stairs into the street, and shortly afterwards it was taken in a cart to join the others in the castle.

Aftermath

The Saxons did not come, and nor did the Swedes. Franz Albrecht had reached Regensburg on Tuesday 21 February, where he received a cordial reception but no sympathy for his mission from Bernhard of Weimar. The latter was not prepared to move to help Wallenstein, and he was inclined to regard the whole thing as not merely a deception but a trap. The arrival of further letters from Ilow only served to convince him that his suspicions were correct, and that he was about to be attacked by Wallenstein from one direction in Bohemia, Gallas from another, and in all probability by Maximilian's army from Bavaria too. Instead of sending cavalry to Eger he hastily mobilised his forces and prepared his defences against this imaginary onslaught.[17] Disappointed but still unaware of what had taken place, Franz Albrecht tried to return from this fruitless mission, but he was captured by Butler's dragoons *en route* to Eger three days after Wallenstein's death. Despite his protests that he had safe conduct, as a representative of the elector of Saxony taking part in negotiations authorised by the emperor himself, he was held and sent to Vienna. There he spent some time in comfortable captivity, giving his version of events to the enquiry into Wallenstein's affairs, before re-enlisting as an Imperialist officer and serving until his death in battle in 1642.[18]

For most of this time Arnim was still in Dresden, having arrived back from Berlin on 12 February. Nearly a week passed before his instructions to go to Pilsen were issued, together with somewhat wider latitude than before as to what peace terms he could accept from Wallenstein, but still he did not set out. On the 22nd he wrote to Franz Albrecht that he had been ill, but by Friday 24th, the day that Wallenstein reached Eger, Arnim was still delaying. Two days later he and Elector John George – a notorious drunkard – were able to drink, drink and drink again to the news that the generalissimo had finally broken with the emperor, although in fact he was already dead. The following morning Arnim at last set off for his long-delayed meeting with Wallenstein, but he was fortunate that information about the assassination reached him on 2 March, before he had crossed the Bohemian border and before he received a letter bearing Kinsky's seal which the loyalists had sent, hoping to trap him too. He was appalled by the murder. 'I know of no instance where such a thing has happened in the realm of a Christian emperor. As for peace I see little hope for us to cling to, and for my own part I will never in my life be used again in the matter. I shall stick to my profession.' To John George he summed up his view of the Imperial House: '*Sanguine coepit, sanguine crevit, sanguine finis erit*' (starting in blood, flourishing in blood, it will end in blood).[19] Fifteen months later, when Saxony and the emperor came to terms of sorts in the aftermath of a major Swedish defeat at Nördlingen, Arnim resigned his appointment in protest.

There was little such high-mindedness on the Imperialist side, only an undignified scramble for rewards. Butler had promised a month's salary to the troops in Eger to ensure their cooperation, which Gallas duly authorised, adding 500 Reichstaler per man for the twelve soldiers in the assassination squads, as well as 1000 each for Devereux and Macdaniel, while Geraldine received 2000 on account of his higher rank. Butler and Leslie also immediately applied for allocation to them of better – that is more profitable – regiments, which they received soon afterwards, as did Gordon, while Devereux, Wallenstein's actual killer, was promoted from captain to lieutenant-colonel.[20]

That was not enough for the three organisers of the murder. Gordon immediately sent Leslie to give a verbal account of the events at Eger to Gallas, who sent him on to do the same in Vienna, where he pressed for generous recompense for their loyalty. Butler, determined not to be outdone, sent Geraldine to Gallas and Macdaniel to Vienna to do likewise. Arriving there on 3 March, only a day after the first news of the assassination, Leslie was promptly honoured and promoted by Ferdinand, and after converting to Catholicism the following month he went on to become a count three years later. All three principals were granted substantial properties from Wallenstein's estates, while Devereux, Macdaniel and Geraldine received large bounties paid out in cash or property of equivalent value. Butler was not satisfied, and a letter written on his behalf to Schlick complained that everyone in Vienna 'is giving the honour and thanks solely to Herr Leslie and Colonel Gordon, while he [Butler], who was in charge of the Friedland execution, is forgotten, just as though he had done nothing'.[21] Naturally Gallas, Piccolomini and Aldringer, having carefully taken no personal risks, expected to be rewarded too, as did almost everyone even marginally connected with the affair. Most were indeed handsomely treated, Gallas reportedly becoming the largest landowner in Bohemia in consequence, despite which many complained that their portions were too small compared to others who had done less, with Piccolomini the loudest of them all. So generous were the gifts bestowed upon the various claimants, which had to be principally in the form of property since the emperor had as little cash as ever, that the vast Wallenstein and Trčka estates, as well as smaller confiscations, were mostly given away or traded off against outstanding claims from the officer corps. Even so, some of the beneficiaries were still waiting for actual settlement years later.[22]

They did not all have time to enjoy their blood money. Butler died of plague within the year, Aldringer was killed during a retreat, also in 1634, and Devereux likewise fell victim to the plague in 1639. Gordon and Leslie fared better, as did Gallas and Piccolomini. Gordon lived until 1649, and Gallas until 1647, most of the time as commander-in-chief despite his disastrous military performance, while Piccolomini was his alternate during periods of disfavour and ultimately his successor. The newly noble and rich Leslie remained in the army for the rest of the war, finally reaching the rank of field marshal in 1650.[23] Emperor Ferdinand himself survived Wallenstein by three years, dying in 1637, but not before he had been forced to abandon his Edict of Restitution to secure peace with Saxony, although with a face-saving pretence that it was only being suspended for 40 years. Maximilian of Bavaria and John George of Saxony both lived to a ripe old age, dying in 1651 and 1656 respectively, so that both had the dubious distinction of ruling their domains throughout the whole of the Thirty Years War.

Although the Imperial exchequer ended up with little to show from the confiscations they at least cleared some of the accumulated debts to the colonels and generals. In the process, however, a coach and horses had to be driven through any concept of legality. Even had Wallenstein been properly tried and condemned his property could not lawfully have been seized, as it was the subject of an entail in perpetuity granted some years earlier by Ferdinand himself.[24] This provided that while a duke of Friedland could be executed for treason his duchy and estates were exempt from confiscation even in these circumstances, and would pass in full to his heirs. Such privileges were not unique in the highest circles, and this one was well-known in Vienna, but it was simply ignored. Hence Wallenstein's wife could not inherit, and she was left to depend on her relatives for two years, until after eventually making an appeal for clemency rather than justice she was allowed to recover a couple of small properties. Max Waldstein came off better by playing the political game and distancing himself from his dead benefactor. He too was barred from inheriting, but he managed to retain what Wallenstein had already given him, to remain in Imperial service, and to return sufficiently into favour to be allowed a couple of years later to buy Wallenstein's Prague palace at an advantageous price.[25] This, and many of Wallenstein's properties granted to those involved in his death, remained in the respective families for centuries, until they were themselves expropriated by the communist regime after the Second World War.

But of course Wallenstein had not been properly tried and condemned, and a flood of criticism soon arose not only on the enemy side but in Vienna itself. This worried Ferdinand and his councillors enough for a legal commission to be set up to advise on the possibility of a posthumous trial.[26] Its members reported in April 1634, noting in their preamble that Kinsky's widow had written to the emperor demanding legal action against her husband's killers, no doubt motivated, they said, 'by evil people who want only to vilify Your Imperial Majesty'. They rehearsed the accusations against Wallenstein publicised in the patents of 24 January and 18 February, as a result of which and on the emperor's command the people concerned had been executed, 'as being manifestly and permanently engaged in *lèse-majesté*, rebellion and treason ... and by that very fact they have been shown before the world for what they were'. The lawyers contended that the executions and confiscations which followed were justified by 'natural reason', although conceding that 'it might have an appearance more of an authoritarian than a lawful act when a man is executed without trial or sentence'. The core passage in their opinion is worthy of the Queen of Hearts in *Alice in Wonderland* ('sentence first, verdict afterwards!'). 'Because Friedland was so malicious, wanting not only to deprive Your Imperial Majesty and your esteemed House, without lawful grounds or process, of crown, sceptre, land and people, but also to completely eradicate you all, and to subvert the entire commonwealth; and because he was already at the final stage and in the last act of execution, with the necessary means to hand, had he not been prevented by the special providence of God; so it was completely unnecessary to hold a trial or process of law to charge, try or sentence him.' For good measure they quoted Cicero. They also exonerated the killers, on the grounds that in such circumstances any private citizen was entitled, without higher orders or the declaration of a court, to avert the danger by killing the offenders, and as such they were not to be punished but rewarded as liberators of the fatherland. Nevertheless, the commission continued, there were considerable difficulties in holding any kind of posthumous trial. Friends of the accused and other interested parties would have to be allowed to make representations as in normal legal proceedings, as though the issue were in doubt, which would be in contradiction of what had already been done: 'Hence Your Imperial Majesty's reputation and the honour of those who carried out the executions would suffer considerably.' Moreover the exchequer would face problems over the confiscations which had taken place. Nor could a simple declaration of guilt be issued, despite Wallenstein's 'incontestable notoriety', as although a number of the accusations against him were undoubtedly true, they said, notably the plans for depriving the emperor of his lands and distributing them to others, unfortunately there was no actual proof to hand. Hence they could not be repeated in a declaration, but nor could they be omitted, as they had already been publicised, and their absence would cause widespread doubts and speculation because of the implication that, at least on those points, Wallenstein might have been innocent. Better therefore to rely on the original patents as the final word on the subject.

Meanwhile Ferdinand and his confidants were exploring an alternative route to counter criticism by using the press, which soon published versions of the accounts of the principal officers involved. Gordon's relatively simple text had been amended, probably by Piccolomini, and it is noteworthy that the records clerk in Vienna marked Leslie's considerably longer manuscript as the account 'which he brought with him'.[27] Three-quarters of this is devoted to reporting in detail the incriminating things which Wallenstein and Ilow allegedly said, while the planning and actions of the three officers who were responsible for their assassination are much more briefly outlined. This was what they wanted to hear in Vienna and it suited Leslie to oblige them, both in order to help his case for a large reward and to enable him to skate around some potentially much more difficult questions. Wide circulation of these and other versions of the events at Eger in the flysheet press followed, but in relation to Ferdinand's need to demonstrate Wallenstein's guilt they were in the last analysis only hearsay.

Some more substantial evidence was required, but it was not to be found. Piccolomini had hurried to Eger as soon as he heard of the murders, and as the first of the higher command to arrive he had made arrangements for the custody of the documents in Wallenstein's chancery. Three days after the general's death Gallas wrote to the emperor that Wallenstein had burned six hundred documents in Eger on the day before he died. The source of this report was not stated, but the chancery superintendent, eager enough to cooperate in other respects, knew nothing of it.[28] That Wallenstein should have burned papers when he thought that he was safe and about to join up with the Saxons seems unlikely, even more unlikely that he could have done so personally and secretly, given his state of health, but such a claim offered a convenient explanation for the failure to find incriminating documents in his records. None were in fact found; had they been, they would certainly have been published at once. An alternative had to be produced, leading to the idea that Piccolomini, the source of the key information, should write a detailed, signed account for official publication.

Piccolomini arrived in Vienna around 8 March, and he was taken aback by the attitude to the killings which he encountered. Some people, he complained to Gallas in a letter a week later, seemed to doubt whether Wallenstein's guilt had been established, and they even hinted at a conspiracy against him by the Italians and the Spanish. To clarify the matter fully, and on the emperor's orders, he was writing his own account, and he suggested that Gallas should add what he had personally heard from Wallenstein regarding his planned treachery, a proposal which Gallas did not take up. After his return to Pilsen Piccolomini found similar doubts in the army, and he wrote to Ferdinand and Trauttmansdorff complaining that hostile elements were using suspicions of conspiracy against Wallenstein as an excuse not to obey the Italians.[29]

Having written the draft of his account by mid-March Piccolomini became surprisingly hesitant, and by the end of the month Ferdinand was repeatedly enquiring of Fabio Diodati, Piccolomini's secretary in this matter, whether the signed text had yet arrived in Vienna. In early April Marquis Caretto di Grana, a member of the Imperial war council, pointed out to Diodati on the emperor's behalf that the first draft omitted many relevant items from the earlier reports, including some which were central to incriminating Wallenstein, such as his alleged correspondence with Bernhard of Weimar and contacts with the French aimed at displacing the House of Habsburg from the Imperial throne. A revised draft added some but not all of these points, leaving out the most important, and moreover Piccolomini still did not sign.[30] Some months went by, and eventually the plan to publish his statement had to be abandoned, although much of it found its way without direct attribution into a wider account published on behalf of the court in the autumn.

The most credible explanation for Piccolomini's reticence is that he knew much of the information he had provided to be untrue. He was also worried that the emperor was avoiding an open commitment to those behind the killings, and in particular that the 'dead or alive' order was still being kept secret. No evidence to support the charges against Wallenstein had so far been found, and Piccolomini probably had good cause to fear that if contrary evidence later came to light he might be made a scapegoat, particularly if he had given a hostage to fortune by admitting and publicising his own part in the accusations. A curious postscript is provided by a story, the original source of which is unknown, that on his deathbed Gallas asked for an audience with the then Emperor Ferdinand III, as he had to inform him of something in order to save his own soul. Schlick and Khevenhüller were sent to him but Gallas declined to confide in them, instead having a bundle of papers brought to his room and burned.[31]

Leaving no stone unturned in the effort to find some evidence of Wallenstein's guilt, members of his household and headquarters staff, as well as many of his army commanders, were examined by a tribunal in an attempt to identify accomplices in the alleged treason. Nothing emerged. No senior officer would admit the slightest knowledge of any conspiracy or treasonable contact with the enemy, only the well-known and officially sanctioned negotiations with the Saxons. Seven were eventually brought to trial before military courts in May 1634, but on charges which amounted to little more than going on obeying Wallenstein's orders longer than they should have done.[32] Although all were convicted two were promptly released after princely intercessions on their behalf, while four of those condemned to death had their sentences commuted to life imprisonment, but they were quietly freed within a year. Only one was actually executed, the only senior officer outside Pilsen who had sought to assist Wallenstein after the Imperial action against him became known. Conveniently he was also by far the richest, with properties well worth confiscating, as well as providing a token justification for the whole procedure. Ferdinand was so embarrassed that he ordered the verdicts and sentences to be kept secret.[33]

Requiem

As soon as Piccolomini arrived in Eger after the murders he arranged to send the bodies of the victims to be put on public display in Prague, which he reported to Gallas. The latter responded that nothing was to be done until instructions arrived from the emperor, but the corpses had already left and were held instead at Mies, where the general and his escort had halted overnight only a week before. Ferdinand ordered that Wallenstein's body should be handed over to his relatives to bury quietly where they pleased, but that the others were to be interred where they were. Wallenstein had planned a mausoleum and crypt for himself and his closest relatives in the Carthusian monastery which he had founded at Walditz (Valdice), near Gitschin, but at the time of his death the church was unfinished and the tomb not yet built, so that in the meantime his body was temporarily laid to rest in Mies. The church and crypt were eventually completed in 1636, and in May of that year Wallenstein's brother-in-law Cardinal Harrach, his widow Isabella and Max Waldstein arranged for his body, in its rough wooden coffin, to be moved to Walditz, travelling day and night under military escort. There Wallenstein's remains were immediately and privately buried, alongside those of his first wife and infant son, which had been taken there shortly before from their previous resting places.

In 1734 the Carthusians of Walditz commemorated the centenary of the death of their founder, and ten years later they provided his remains with an impressive pewter coffin. However in 1782 the monastery, like many others, was dissolved as a result of reforms made by Emperor Joseph II. A dispute then arose between two of Wallenstein's direct descendants, both wishing to claim the remains and to re-inter them in their respective parts of the family property. This dragged on for three years, but eventually, on 1 March 1785, the coffins were moved, with great pomp and solemnity and in the presence of various descendants, other nobility and curious onlookers. They were taken to the chapel of Santa Anna, in the grounds of the baroque chateau at Münchengrätz (Mnichovo Hradiště, 40 miles north-east of Prague). Here Wallenstein's coffin was placed in a niche off the rear of the nave, with that of his first wife and his infant son below it. Some years later they were moved again, to a niche on the left side of the nave, which was subsequently furnished with a substantial stone memorial plaque. This is still there to be seen today, as the chateau is now a tourist attraction.[34]

15
But Brutus Says He Was Ambitious
(*Julius Caesar*)

> The aura of myth surrounding this lord is so strongly imbued that I can often scarcely prevent myself from believing the tales which are told in such great detail about him, even when I was actually with him at the very moment which is being described.[1]

Thus wrote no less a person than Field Marshal Count Gottfried Heinrich Pappenheim about Wallenstein early in 1630. His problem is understandable, because while Gustavus Adolphus became a legend in his own lifetime Wallenstein had already long since become more myth than man to many of his contemporaries. Tales accumulated around him. He was, so it was claimed, bulletproof, a common soldiers' superstition about those who always seemed to emerge unwounded from the thick of the fray. The story was that he had turned Catholic after miraculously escaping unhurt from a fall, having dozed off on a high window-ledge while serving as a page in the household of the margrave of Burgau. His first wife Lucretia had been, it was incorrectly mooted, much older than him, so that she had resorted to love potions to keep him faithful. It was rumoured that he could not stand the least noise, and even dogs had to be cleared from the district while he was in residence. His tempers were said to be terrible to behold, but he was supposedly submissive to the dictates of the stars due to an obsession with astrology. He was even blamed by some for the outbreak of fires in Prague and Vienna shortly after his arrival in the respective cities early in 1627.[2]

Such colourful details added to the actual drama of his demise to make him an attractive subject for writers, and within a year or two of his death plays appeared on the stages of Madrid and elsewhere, including Henry Glapthorne's *Tragedy of Albertus Wallenstein* in London.

A considerable literature followed, most famously Schiller's play in 1799, but continuing up to the present day. Twentieth-century works include a major novel by the distinguished German author Alfred Döblin and at least half a dozen others. In German popular consciousness Wallenstein the myth and Wallenstein the literary character have largely superseded Wallenstein the man, while even in serious historiography the boundaries are frequently blurred.

The problem in distinguishing between fact, exaggeration and invention is that the tall stories started to appear early in Wallenstein's public career, no doubt because of the interest which his sudden rise to prominence created. They were then deliberately publicised, magnified and exploited by his enemies in the later years of his life, so that they were well-established common knowledge by the time of his death. Early historians of Ferdinand's reign and of Wallenstein's career were naturally aware of and influenced by them, shaping their accounts to conform to this pre-existing popular image of his character. Subsequent biographers took these early works as their sources, drawing on them and passing them on, sometimes further embroidered, from one generation to another, in a manner well demonstrated in Geiger's study of Wallenstein's astrology. By the time document-based historiography developed in the nineteenth century the traditional view of Wallenstein was so well entrenched that the genuine original sources were used principally to confirm rather than to re-evaluate previous concepts.

A second part of the problem lies in the very profusion of these sources. Wallenstein wrote vast numbers of letters, many of them of course exclusively concerned with military matters or the affairs of his estates, but he also maintained a prolific personal correspondence, as well as frequently adding private postscripts to business letters. Other key figures in Wallenstein's life were also active letter-writers, among them Aldringer, Arnim, Collalto, Harrach, and to a lesser extent many of his senior officers. Large collections of their missives have survived in official or family archives, and many have been published. The total of such extant letters and other relevant documents is reported to run into five-figure numbers, but even so there are considerable gaps, and often only one side of any particular sequence of correspondence – and not necessarily all of that – is still available.[3] Moreover there is reason to believe that a considerable amount of uncomfortable material was deliberately disposed of in the aftermath of Wallenstein's assassination. Hence significant difficulties of interpretation arise.

Firstly there is the standard historiographical problem that what happens to be written down, in a document which happens to be preserved, tends to assume a disproportionate significance in the eyes of later historians. Secondly the volume of Wallenstein's correspondence and his habit of jotting down his thoughts of the moment has often made it possible for researchers to find passages which, if quoted out of context, or without acknowledging that he often expressed differing views at different times, appear to support a particular opinion or line of argument. This is not to say that such interpretations are necessarily wrong, merely to warn that their basis has frequently been partial and selective. It is also prudent to note that even descriptions given by contemporaries who knew Wallenstein well cannot necessarily be taken at face value. Arnim, for example, wrote of the general's 'perverse moods' during the later stages of the 1633 peace negotiations, but at the time he was himself angry and frustrated about their failure, and moreover he was not personally present at a number of the relevant meetings.[4]

At the risk of falling into similar error it seems appropriate to conclude with an attempt to give some overview of Wallenstein's character and personality, particularly as this is relevant to the questions of motivation which have inevitably arisen in discussing the military and political aspects of his life. The traditional view, briefly summarised, is that Wallenstein was highly intelligent and a brilliant organiser, but harsh, arrogant, overbearing and vindictive, as well as superstitious, and above all acquisitive and insatiably ambitious. Some of these points were considered in Chapter 5, where it was argued in respect of astrology that there is some basis for the legend, in that Wallenstein did have an interest, but that the indications are that the degree of that interest was not untypical for the period, so that the traditional view is greatly exaggerated. Much the same probably applies to the rest of the picture.

As a young man Wallenstein was clearly personable enough. Although his circle in the university at Altdorf may have been somewhat disreputable he was evidently 'one of the boys'. He did not obtain his post at Matthias's court solely on his brother-in-law Zierotin's recommendation; he had to present himself in person to influential courtiers, and he must have made a favourable impression. The same applies to the wealthy widow Lucretia, née Landek, who did not have to accept him as a husband. So far as can be judged both that match and his second marriage were successful by the standards of the aristocracy of the time, and indeed Isabella's surviving letters suggest an affection which went well beyond the merely dutiful. Around the time of his answer to Ferdinand's call for help at Gradisca in 1617 Wallenstein established friendly relationships with Harrach and Eggenberg, which lasted until the former's death and until shortly before his own death respectively. Much has been said of his enemies at court, but he also had a loyal circle of friends there, among whom these and Questenberg were the most prominent. With Arnim too he established a long-lasting and fateful friendship, to the extent that the Saxon general needed to defend himself on that account to the Swedes in 1632: 'It is, I hear, held against me that the duke of Friedland has been heard to say that I am as dear to him as his own soul. That was already the case four or five years ago.'[5]

Perhaps the most authentic account of Wallenstein's personality and manner is that given by his first biographer, Count Galleazzo Gualdo Priorato, who served under him as a young man before going on to become a colonel, diplomat and notable historian. Although only a junior officer at the time, his social rank will have ensured that he knew the general personally, and his book contains details which suggest direct observation. Thus he notes that it was Wallenstein's custom to thank individually those who had acquitted themselves well in action, and he describes how he would lay his hand on a man's shoulder while praising him publicly, a practice which Priorato says he never forgot however high he himself rose.[6] And, he continues, 'just as Wallenstein always had an open heart and a ready word for the soldiers, so also he allowed free access to his table to each comrade and officer, and he took pleasure in eating in the company of those who had given generously of their labours and wanted the opportunity to quench their thirsts. He often said that nothing was more able to strengthen ties than the offering of wine, which was the real love potion which altered the inclination of the heart. The company and the conversation which took place at the table were the most natural means by which friends were won and *esprit de corps* was developed.' Priorato indicates Wallenstein's easy familiarity with his officers, while his dry sense of humour is apparent in the ironic postscripts which he sometimes added to his letters. Other sources report him employing personal charm to good effect in dealing with diplomatic contacts, and Wallenstein himself wrote in 1626 that 'today I got drunk with the envoy' sent by the elector of Brandenburg.[7]

It is entirely possible that Wallenstein's manner changed in the later years of his life, the period from which most accounts stem, and that the causes were illness, the burdens of a reluctantly resumed command, and the anxieties and frustrations of the fruitless search for peace. The ill get little enough sympathy in their lifetimes, and from posterity they commonly get even less, so that Wallenstein's constant pain tends to be overlooked in assessing his behaviour and actions, in addition to which symptoms of growing stress and depression are clearly discernible. He had always had a sharp and unbridled tongue, and his more caustic judgements were often reported back to their subjects, giving rise to enduring enmities, while later he allowed himself similar freedom on more political topics such as the Jesuits and the Spanish. Even so, accounts of his manner need to be viewed cautiously. Numerous histories and biographies have reported that in 1626 Wallenstein lost his temper with Aldringer over his letters to the court in Vienna, calling him a *Tintenfresser*, usually literally translated as 'ink-swiller', although 'pen-pusher' is a better colloquial equivalent. Few, however, add that moments later the general apologised handsomely, as Aldringer himself recorded in the letter which is the source of the story.[8]

Wallenstein's supposed arrogance largely reflects the climate of the age, in which arrogance could with justice be said to be a characteristic of the aristocracy. The style in which he lived and travelled later in life, surrounded by a court, liveried servants, and a smartly uniformed escort complete with silver-tipped lances, has often been commented upon. However this was the norm for the ruling prince of a significant territory, and in Wallenstein's case the court also functioned as a travelling military headquarters. His brother-in-law Zierotin, a rich Moravian aristocrat but no prince, also lived magnificently, as did Maximilian, who reportedly brought a retinue of 1200 horsemen with him to attend his sister's wedding. Ferdinand himself is said to have arrived at the electoral meeting in Regensburg with an establishment of 3000, requiring 600 wagons, and to have entered the same city in 1622 with a cavalcade of 2000 cavalry, which helps to put into context the report that Wallenstein, as commander-in-chief, arrived in Memmingen in 1630 with an escort of 600 soldiers.[9]

Other aspects of Wallenstein's conduct likewise need to be seen in their context. There are reports of him using whatever influence he could bring to bear to help him gain his ends, for instance in fending off the property-related lawsuits of his first wife's relatives or in having appeals against the confiscation of Bohemian lands which he wished to buy rejected.[10] Again this was usual. Everyone employed any influence they could, particularly in legal matters, on the usually well-founded assumption that their opponents were doing likewise. Wallenstein's vindictiveness has been illustrated by his allegedly deliberate abandonment of Maximilian's Bavaria to Swedish invasion, but more personally by his treatment of one of his own cousins captured in Silesia while fighting on the Danish side. The unfortunate man was despatched back to Friedland and imprisoned in one of Wallenstein's own castles, whereas he let the other captured Bohemian exiles go free.[11] This may be considered alongside Sigmund Smiřický, who as reported in Chapter 4 imprisoned his own daughter, in principle for life, following an unfortunate love affair. The point is that historical figures have to be judged by the standards of their own times, not anachronistically against present-day ones.

Acquisitive in terms of property Wallenstein certainly was, and in this he was typical of the aristocracy not only in this but in most periods. However it was an acquisitiveness bred of opportunity rather than obsession. After he successfully became a major landowner through his first marriage Wallenstein made no apparent effort to progress further until he recognised the unique possibilities presented by the Bohemian confiscations. Thereafter his further major acquisitions were driven as much by the fact that property offered the only prospect of obtaining settlement of any of the emperor's huge debts to him as by other considerations. Mecklenburg had the additional attraction of making him an independent prince directly under the emperor, rather than only a subject of the king of Bohemia, but had other things been equal it is a reasonable speculation that his first priority would have been to make further additions to Friedland as and when opportunities presented themselves. It is evident that his duchies were Wallenstein's main personal interest, as throughout his campaigns, even at the most critical stages, he still maintained a close watch on and control over what was happening on his estates, receiving reports and despatching instructions in a constant stream of correspondence. As his own creation, Friedland held pride of place, which is confirmed by his efforts to secure it for the long term through the entail mentioned in Chapter 14, and the arrangements he made for its inheritance within the family after the death of his infant son.

Wallenstein applied his organisational talents as effectively to his properties as he did to his army. His concentration of his original purchases in Bohemia into a single territory enabled Friedland to be developed far more effectively as an economic unit than had previously been the case. This was assisted by the fact that as generalissimo Wallenstein controlled the army's vast purchasing requirements, and a symbiotic relationship was quickly developed, both assuring the army a reliable source of supplies and providing Friedland with a secure outlet for its products. This applied not only to basic foodstuffs but also to a wide range of commodities, from boots to gunpowder, for which Wallenstein encouraged the establishment or expansion of manufacturing facilities. The profits flowed in part to the populace, who enjoyed a period of considerable prosperity, and in part to Wallenstein through the resulting rents and taxes, which he in turn recycled into financing his army. Through a combination of good fortune in the course of the war and Wallenstein's deliberate protection Friedland also escaped most of the burdens of campaigning and quartering within its boundaries, so that the citizens had much to be grateful for. Physical evidence of prosperity is to be found in the building works which Wallenstein commissioned in little more than a decade, not only palaces and premises for himself and his administration, but also religious foundations and churches, as well as provision of schools, hospitals and orphanages well ahead of the standards of the time.

As a landlord and ruler in Friedland Wallenstein was at the progressive end of the contemporary range, both economically and in the wider context. He was not, of course, a liberal in any later sense, and nor was he unique in his day, but he certainly did not number among the many harsh, grasping and incompetent rulers in the seventeenth-century Holy Roman Empire. Unfortunately many of those who acquired shares of his property following his murder were exactly that, so that with Friedland quickly dismembered its prosperity did not long survive him. While it lasted, however, Mecklenburg and Sagan benefited too, as Wallenstein immediately applied the same approach during his shorter hold on these territories. Mecklenburg's response to Gustavus Adolphus may be seen as one testimonial to his efforts. Once he had established himself in north Germany the Swedish king issued an appeal to the Protestant citizens of the duchy to rise up against the tyrannical Catholic usurper Wallenstein in favour of their old dukes and himself. No-one did, despite the fact that Wallenstein had by then been dismissed at Regensburg and had no army or other substantial means of coercion at his disposal.[12]

In matters of religion Wallenstein has long been regarded as a model of tolerance in an intolerant era, a position which his enemies attributed at best to insincerity in his own beliefs and at worst to atheism or active hostility to the Catholic religion. Both views are exaggerations. After his conversion as a young man Wallenstein remained a conventional practising Catholic for the rest of his life, and his benefactions to the church were generous although not out of keeping with expectations for one of his station and wealth. Early on he took part in, or at least allowed, attempts to pressurise his Moravian tenants into converting to Catholicism, but later he made little more than token efforts to implement Ferdinand's Bohemian recatholicisation policy in Friedland. In Mecklenburg, where he had no overlord, he made no effort at all, allowing Protestant worship to continue undisturbed and even bringing in a Protestant as his chancellor.[13] In his armies he applied no religious criterion, whether to ordinary soldiers or to his field marshals. It has been said that, like Richelieu, his approach to religion in the political world was pragmatic, but that should not be mistaken for personal indifference.

He did, however, become increasingly hostile to the Jesuits over the years. There are indications that Jesuit influence assisted both his initial conversion and his first marriage, but when he made a religious foundation a few years later it was Carthusian, because, it was said, their demands were less exorbitant. During the Danish war he came to see the Jesuits as opposed to peace, seeking religious advantage from military success, while his own opposition to the Edict of Restitution in turn aroused their hostility to him. Lamormaini, formerly inclined to be one of his supporters in Vienna, turned against him on this account, and by the latter days the Jesuits around Ferdinand were among his bitterest opponents and he was among their most outspoken critics.

As a military organiser Wallenstein had few equals in his own or any other age, but as a general he was unusual for the time, not least because he fought few major battles. Lützen, and to a lesser extent the Dessau bridge, alone qualify for this description, as the Alte Veste was not an open-field battle, while Wolgast and Steinau were too one-sided to rate such a description. In part this is attributable to his opponents. On the Hungarian border in 1626 Mansfeld avoided him, and Bethlen Gabor slipped away in the night rather than do battle. In 1627 the Danish forces in Silesia were captured in a series of fortified places rather than making a stand in the field, while Christian retreated back to Denmark as Wallenstein advanced. In 1632 Arnim's Saxons evacuated Bohemia as soon as he moved against them, and Gustavus preferred to attempt a surprise attack on the Alte Veste fortifications from the north rather than confront Wallenstein's army drawn up for battle outside to the west, while at Naumburg the king again declined the challenge. These particular instances demonstrate Wallenstein's successful application of one of the main principles of good generalship, that of concentrating superior forces before engaging the enemy, but they can also be placed in a wider context in which he too was inclined to avoid battles except when he could achieve such superiority. This can be ascribed in large measure to his oft-expressed conviction that the resources of their opponents were much greater than those of the Imperialists, who in consequence were much less able to afford – and hence to risk – a lost battle, as Breitenfeld only too clearly showed.

Wallenstein was also one of the first of a new breed of commander who set out to fight a new kind of war. Henri, Duke of Rohan, a contemporary soldier and military theorist, observed that whereas in the past generals had played the lion, in future they would play the fox, which the British military expert Liddell Hart rather more fulsomely expressed in calling Wallenstein 'the supreme poker player of military history' and 'a grand strategist playing for higher stakes than local military success'. The old style had been to muster one's forces and set out to confront and force the enemy to battle. The new one was to combine military and political strategy to outmanoeuvre the opponent, defeating him if necessary but above all forcing him to make peace without achieving his original objectives. Wallenstein's duel with Gustavus is a prime example. Throughout 1632 Maximilian was pressing him to take immediate and direct action against the Swedes, firstly by moving south to face them before his new army was fully ready, secondly by attacking them in their almost impregnable Nuremberg fortifications, thirdly by pursuing them despite the weaknesses of his own army when they eventually withdrew from Nuremberg, and finally by returning south in the autumn when they again threatened Bavaria. Wallenstein did the opposite. Rather than responding to the Swedish king's thrusts he applied pressure to his Saxon allies, thereby forcing him to make hasty moves in insufficient strength, and as a result he twice caught him at a serious disadvantage. Put simply, Wallenstein acted in a way which forced Gustavus to react, rather than vice versa. As with the Danish campaign earlier and as in the negotiations in Silesia a year later Wallenstein's objective throughout was not to achieve an impressive battlefield victory, where the advantage gained would probably have been temporary, but to force his opponents back north, deprive them of their allies, and leave them little alternative but to make peace. His strategy was neither generally understood nor appreciated at the court, but a later military tribute came from Prince Eugène of Savoy, Austrian commander-in-chief in the early 1700s and himself possessor of one of the highest military reputations of the age, who described him as 'the great Wallenstein'.

The most durable part of the Wallenstein myth is that he was boundlessly ambitious, an opinion maintained even by those modern historians who otherwise exhibit a more balanced approach to earlier traditions. The view is understandable among contemporaries who observed him rise rapidly from obscurity to apparent pre-eminence, both militarily and socially, particularly those who thought that they had cause to fear the direction in which his ambitions were supposed to lead.

Historiography has retained this initial image, but generally without citing any specific evidence to sustain it, implicitly relying on the reverse logic that because he was so successful he must by definition have been inordinately ambitious. In fact, as has been indicated at relevant stages in this book, each step in Wallenstein's upward progress had an inherent logic independent of personal ambition, while the further aims attributed to him were contemporary speculations or the malicious inventions of his enemies.

Wallenstein was conventionally ambitious for his time and class in aspiring to an advantageous marriage, but he pursued neither of the other routes to self-betterment potentially available to him as a younger man. Many noblemen of quite elevated status made careers in the service of the yet more elevated, including most of those who have been mentioned among Ferdinand's councillors. Prince Christian of Anhalt-Bernburg rose high in the service of the electors of the Palatinate, and Wallenstein himself later numbered counts among the senior officials of his household. Gentlemen of his initial status could and did advance in rank and possessions by this route, but although he set his foot on the lower rungs of the ladder with Matthias there is no indication that he made any effort to progress further. The alternative career of a professional soldier was also open to both noblemen and gentlemen long before the start of the Thirty Years War. Among the former to pursue it were Tilly, Arnim and Franz Albrecht of Saxe-Lauenburg, while Aldringer was only one of a number who achieved high rank despite a more modest background. Again Wallenstein made a start but went no further until pressed by changing political circumstances.

Wallenstein's actions following the spread of the Bohemian revolt to Moravia bear the hallmarks not of ambition but of the man of action responding to a new, challenging and personally threatening situation. Rather than await events in the hope of escaping the worst he chose to show his colours and to take his fate into his own hands, exhibiting publicly for the first time the foresight and competence which were the characteristics of his subsequent career. He employed the same qualities to good effect in his property dealing following the defeat of the revolt, but this nevertheless has to be seen as opportunism rather than simple ambition, as such circumstances could not have been foreseen, still less engineered. Doubtless there was an element of ambition underlying the subsequent elevation of Friedland into a principality, although social aspiration might be a more appropriate term, and the move also had much to do with Ferdinand's need to create a new and personally loyal aristocracy in Bohemia.

Wallenstein's offer to raise his first army is likewise more convincingly explained as a response to the threat to his new possessions and status than as a matter of ambition. He was already among the super-rich and he had no need to become a large-scale military entrepreneur in order to add to his wealth. Indeed it was more a case of hazarding a large proportion of what he had. Nor had he shown any previous sign of wanting to be a general for its own sake, while his subsequent conduct clearly suggests that he found it more of a burden than a benefit in practice. His lands were at serious risk if the war went against the emperor, but no-one else was willing or able to finance an army. Again he chose to act rather than to take his chance on events. His elevation to the status of duke may have been a reward but was also a practical step to avoid the anomalous position of the new commander being outranked socially by a number of his own officers, or by Maximilian, his effective opposite number controlling the Catholic League army.

Despite the fears and claims of his enemies there is no evidence that Wallenstein either wished to or did exercise any significant political influence in his capacity as generalissimo. On the contrary, his lack of such influence is clearly shown by his unavailing opposition during his first command to the Edict of Restitution and the Imperial involvement in the Mantuan war in Italy, and during his second to Feria's Spanish expedition aimed mainly at French interests on Germany's southwestern borders. As for wider political ambitions, Maximilian's fears were as fanciful as the later interpretation of historians of a nationalist turn of mind, optimistically supported at most by a few throwaway lines in Wallenstein's correspondence, that he aimed at establishing a centralised power base for the emperor. The general's 'great idea', maintained one such, was that 'the unity of the Empire should stand above the individual princes', so that had he been successful Germany might have emerged as a nation state centuries earlier than was actually the case.[14] The concept is anachronistic and Wallenstein was an unlikely proponent, as a supporter of the established order and an opponent of revolution, even from above, quite apart from the fact that as duke of Mecklenburg he had himself become one of the self-same individual princes.

His acquisition of Mecklenburg was mainly opportunist, both in that it was available and as it was the only such asset on offer worth even a fraction of the emperor's outstanding debts to his general. Again there was probably an element of social aspiration, but this is likely to have been secondary rather than an example of overweening ambition. Later examples of Wallenstein's supposed ambition, including the ambition for revenge after his Regensburg dismissal, depend essentially on unsupported conspiracy theories. Thus it is claimed that although he had always intended to resume his command he delayed doing so in order to enjoy the discomfiture of his adversaries, and to wait for the military position to become so desperate that he could name his own terms. Actually all the indications are that he genuinely had no wish to return to the army, and that he only did so when the Saxon invasion of Bohemia posed a direct threat to his own principal remaining property, this being the common thread between his military involvements in 1619, 1625 and 1631. Purportedly serious mention of the crown of Bohemia was made only by the Swedes and the French, in propositions instigated by exile intriguers, and according to their own report Wallenstein dismissed the idea as 'gross villainy'. Their other fantasies and Piccolomini's fabrications were too absurd to require further refutation.

One other aspect of Wallenstein's career as a general which has been interpreted as ambition was his effort to secure sole command, extending his control first over the armies intended for service in the Empire – in this context Germany – and then to all Imperialist forces wherever they might be. In the process he acquired the rank of full general previously reserved for the head of state, and the unprecedented title of supreme commander or generalissimo. In 1633 he insisted that were the Imperialist army and those of the Protestant electors to unite it had to be under his control, and to the end he resisted the idea that he might share command of the Imperialist army with the emperor's son. This was not, however, a matter of self-aggrandisement but of military logic. Divided commands inevitably prevent the most effective utilisation of resources, while the complex and wide-ranging conflicts in which the Imperialist forces were involved required a single strategic overview. Part of the explanation for Gustavus's military success was that as both king and general he had exactly such a unified command, which he also sought where possible to impose on his allies, and with their lesser resources the Imperialists could not afford to be worse organised than their opponents. Wallenstein and Gustavus also shared a common characteristic of men of high ability in positions of power, that of believing in themselves and in their capacity to perform their functions better than any alternative candidate. In Wallenstein's case this was certainly true, as with a few brief exceptions the Imperialist military performance during the Thirty Years War was generally poor both before and after his period in command. He was not disposed to share control of the army he had created and financed with the kind of old-school cavaliers who had been responsible for the campaign which resulted in his narrow escape at the siege of Göding in 1623. He was sure that he could do better, but such self-belief is not the same thing as ambition, as the merely ambitious often lack the competence to perform at the highest level.

At this distance in time Wallenstein's true personality could not easily be assessed even were it not obscured by contemporary fables and calumnies, and the accretions of the centuries upon them. Arguably it is not of great importance, as his role and place in history are not dependent upon whether he was personally congenial, and it makes little difference to the facts of his achievements whether they were the result of circumstances or ambition. Nevertheless both legend and historiography are replete with highly coloured images of the supposed Wallenstein, so it is therefore worth bearing in mind some cautionary observations about the quality of the evidence upon which they are based. Richelieu warned in his memoirs, with specific reference to Wallenstein although it has a more general applicability, that good or bad reputations derive principally from the last period of life, and although good and bad are transmitted to later ages, because of its own wickedness the world is more inclined to believe the latter than the former. Schiller, himself a historian, wrote that it was Wallenstein's misfortune that his enemies survived him to write his history, while Richelieu noted that after his death many censured him who would have praised him had he lived.[15]

In one of history's little ironies a cousin wrote to Wallenstein from exile in Amsterdam in 1629, telling the general that he had heard that Tilly had Imperial orders to arrest him, or failing that to have him murdered. While thanking him for his concern Wallenstein replied that Ferdinand was 'a just and grateful master who recompenses faithful service in a fashion different from the one of which you inform me'. Elsewhere he wrote of his own 'true, faithful and selfless service', adding that 'had I served God as I have the emperor I would be the holiest of heaven's saints'. He said the same on another occasion: 'If I paid as much attention to my own soul's salvation as to the emperor's service I would certainly not go to purgatory, still less to hell.' Richelieu concurred, noting that 'the emperor never found another, the value of whose service even began to approach Wallenstein's', so that for the worldly-wise cardinal 'Wallenstein's death remains a monstrous example, whether it be of the ungratefulness of his subordinates or of the cruelty of his master'.[16]

One question unanswered by those who ascribe unlimited ambition to Wallenstein is why he devoted so much effort to achieving a negotiated peace rather than an Imperialist victory. Defeating first the Saxons and then the Swedes in 1633 was potentially possible, and Wallenstein's successors did inflict a crushing defeat on the Swedes at Nördlingen six months after his death, although they did not anticipate how temporary would be the effect of their victory. Had Wallenstein achieved such successes in 1633 his standing would have soared to its highest level, and the prospective personal rewards would have been commensurately great, exceeding even what he had already gained. Instead he chose the thankless and ultimately unsuccessful role of peacemaker. 'Ambition', as Shakespeare's Mark Antony said of Caesar, 'should be made of sterner stuff'. The search for peace, however, was never far from Wallenstein's strategy, and he summarised his view of the continuing conflict to Arnim in December 1631: 'As the evidence of this past fourteen years of continuous war has more than sufficed to show, when most of the country lies in ashes they will have to make peace.'[17] That is exactly what happened – seventeen years later.

References

Chapter 1
1. Aretin, Urkunden, 63 f.
2. Hallwich (Ende), II, 529, 533, 186 f.
3. Gaedecke, 293 f.
4. Bonney, 20; Diwald, 298; Parker, 96, 265; Roberts, 167; Wedgwood, 170, 171, 346, 349, 354, 359.

Chapter 2
1. Dvorský, 33, 41; Caspar, XVII, 131 f., 144; XVIII, 219; Hallwich (Briefe), III, 350 f., Khevenhüller (Conterfet), part 2, 219.
2. Mann, 11.
3. Dvorský, 23.
4. Polišenský and Kollmann, 27.
5. Stieve, 212 f.; Förster (Landesfürst), 352 f., 355; Dvorský, 32 f., 35, 37.
6. Murr, 300 ff.; Baader, 14 ff., 24 ff.
7. Matiegka, 34; Polišenský and Kollmann, 19; Krause, 10.
8. Priorato, 9; Khevenhüller (Conterfet), part 2, 219.
9. Mann, 70; Polišenský and Kollmann, 21.
10. Schebek (Wallensteiniana), 252 ff.; Strauss and Strauss-Kloebe, 190, note 1.
11. Polišenský and Kollmann, 25; Schebek (Wallensteinfrage), 532.
12. Palacký, 87.
13. Diwald, 177.
14. Palacký, 86, 88.
15. Mann, 85.
16. Palacký, 86.
17. Chlumecky (Zierotin), 398.
18. Mann, 103.
19. Bilek, 112.
20. Khevenhüller (Conterfet), part 2, 219.
21. Polišenský and Kollmann, 35 f.
22. Polišenský and Kollmann, 26, 36.
23. Mann, 114; Diwald, 67.
24. Duhr, 83; Geiger, 73 ff., 78.
25. Mann, 115.
26. Diwald, 71; Förster (Landesfürst), 327.
27. Polišenský and Kollmann, 40 f.; Strauss and Strauss-Kloebe, 191, note 1.
28. Hurter (Ferdinand), VII, 174.
29. Stieve, 235.
30. Polišenský and Kollmann, 40.

Chapter 3

1. Mann, 133.
2. Mann, 134.
3. Schebek (Wallensteiniana), 258.
4. Hallwich (Fünf Bücher), I, 21.
5. Gindely (Dreißigjähriger Krieg), II, 42.
6. Hallwich (Fünf Bücher), I, 26 ff.; Stieve, 247 ff.; Theatrum, I, 114.
7. Gindely (Dreißigjähriger Krieg), II, 49.
8. Polišenský and Kollmann, 58, 62; Strauss and Strauss-Kloebe, 192, notes 2, 4.
9. Hallwich (Fünf Bücher), I, 37; Stieve, 263; Polišenský and Kollmann, 55.
10. Diwald, 90.
11. Polišenský and Kollmann, 62; Diwald, 147.
12. Dvorský, 123.
13. Hallwich (Fünf Bücher), I, 49.
14. Hallwich (Fünf Bücher), I, 47.
15. Hallwich (Fünf Bücher), I, 53 f.
16. Krause, 9 f., 18 f.
17. Hallwich (Fünf Bücher), I, 58.

Chapter 4

1. Hallwich (Fünf Bücher), I, 74.
2. Hallwich (Fünf Bücher), I, 24; Stieve, 245.
3. Mortimer (Eyewitness), 31, 150.
4. Ernstberger, 86 ff.; Gindely (Gegenreformation), 327 ff.; Newald, 103 ff.
5. Ernstberger, 126.
6. Gindely (Gegenreformation), 327 f.; Parker, 89; Wedgwood, 168.
7. Gindely (Gegenreformation), 342.
8. Ernstberger, 120.
9. Ernstberger, 122.
10. Wedgwood, 167.
11. Bilek, 235 f., 238; Mann, 180 ff.
12. Bilek, 3 ff.; Gindely (Dreißigjähriger Krieg), II, 325 ff.
13. Theatrum, I, 353 f.
14. Mann, 180; Bilek, 218.
15. Bilek, 244 ff.
16. Mann, 183 f.; Gindely (Waldstein), I, 415 ff.
17. Bilek, 21, 22 f.
18. Bilek, 112, 22.
19. Nemethy, 95 ff.
20. Maps of Friedland: Mann, 257; Mann and Bliggenstorfer, 34.
21. Gindely (Waldstein), I, 34, 36.
22. Bilek; Mann, 207 f.
23. Mann, 207.
24. Bilek, 305.
25. Wedgwood, 170; Diwald, 184.

Chapter 5

1. Schiller (Wallenstein), 324.
2. Mann, 94, 95; Diwald, 55.
3. Caspar, XVII, 131f., 144.
4. Text in: Frisch, I, 386 ff.; Helbig, 60 ff.; Strauss and Strauss-Kloebe, 185 ff.; Struve, 26 ff.
5. Strauss and Strauss-Kloebe, 191, note 2.
6. Strauss and Strauss-Kloebe, 188.
7. Polišenský and Kollmann, 30; Diwald, 55; Watson, 53.
8. Strauss and Strauss-Kloebe, 190, note 1; 191, notes 1 and 2; 192, notes 2 and 4.
9. Frisch, VIII.I, 347.
10. Mann, 94; Frisch, VIII.I, 346; Strauss and Strauss-Kloebe, 187.
11. Struve, 25 f.
12. Text in: Frisch, VIII.I, 348 ff.; Strauss and Strauss-Kloebe, 194 ff.; Struve, 33 ff.
13. Struve, 21 f.; Caspar, I, 211.
14. Strauss and Strauss-Kloebe, 214.
15. Strauss and Strauss-Kloebe, 200.
16. Diwald, 55 f.; Mann, 298.
17. Strauss and Strauss-Kloebe, 211, note 1; 212, notes 1, 2, 4; 213, notes 1–3.
18. Struve, 11 f., 17; Geiger, 97.
19. Mann, 564 f.
20. Geiger, 418 f., 165; Förster (Briefe), I, 338.
21. Geiger, 192, 250 f., 293, 305; Bergel (Seni), 54 f.
22. Mortimer (Eyewitness), 75, 97; Aretin, Urkunden, 52; Mann, 562, 591.
23. Mortimer (Eyewitness), 75 f.
24. South Wales Evening Post, 11 July 2007; Mann, 93; Diwald, 55.
25. Struve, 21; Strauss, 200.
26. Mann, 93 ff.; Khevenhüller (Conterfet), part 2, 219; Gindely (Waldstein), II, 5f.
27. Geiger, 39, 40, 165 f., 177, 192 f., 418 ff.
28. Geiger, 420.
29. Goodrick, 135.

Chapter 6

1. Janko, 243 ff.; Mann, 213; Tadra (Bethlen), 445, 446, 451, 452, 455, 456 f., 457 f.; Tadra (Briefe), 300.
2. Förster (Prozeß), Urkunden, 7 ff., 24 ff.
3. Gindely (Waldstein), I, 281 ff.; Tadra (Briefe), 362.
4. Mann, 230.
5. Diwald, 214.
6. Tadra (Bethlen), 443 ff.
7. Hallwich (Fünf Bücher), I, 86, 176 f.; Menčik, 3.
8. Hallwich (Fünf Bücher), I, 171.
9. Mann, 303 ff.
10. Hallwich (Fünf Bücher), I, 238.
11. Tadra (Briefe), 337.
12. Hallwich (Fünf Bücher), I, 243; Hallwich (Berufung), 128.

References 257

13. Gindely (Waldstein), I, 50.
14. Hallwich (Fünf Bücher), I, 183, 173 f.
15. Menčik, 17 f., 20; Hallwich (Berufung), 122 ff.
16. Loewe, 86.
17. Khevenhüller (Annales), X, 802.
18. Polišenský and Kollmann, 101.
19. Prökl, I, 144.
20. Diwald, 344; Hallwich (Fünf Bücher), III, 15.
21. Tadra (Briefe), 356.
22. Chlumecky (Regesten), 8 f., 11.
23. Tadra (Briefe), 300, 301; Chlumecky (Regesten), 16, 17.

Chapter 7

1. Tadra (Briefe), 336, 357.
2. Polišenský and Kollmann, 107.
3. Polišenský and Kollmann, 110.
4. Mortimer (Eyewitness), 141.
5. Mann, 324; Guthrie, 121 f.; Diwald, 350.
6. Diwald, 350.
7. Polišenský and Kollmann, 112.
8. Mann, 324; Theatrum, I, 923; Guthrie, 121 f.
9. Hallwich (Fünf Bücher), III, 43; II, 357.
10. Polišenský and Kollmann, 114 f.
11. Diwald, 354, 359; Mann, 327.
12. Diwald, 357; Polišenský and Kollmann, 118, 120; Tadra (Briefe), 406.
13. Hallwich (Fünf Bücher), I, 483.
14. Parker, 78.
15. Tadra (Briefe), 417, 425; Polišenský and Kollmann, 118 ff.; Mann, 331.
16. Tadra (Briefe), 443 f.
17. Mann, 332.
18. Hallwich (Fünf Bücher), I, 358.
19. Mann, 338 f.; Tadra (Briefe), 316 f., 324, 329.
20. Tadra (Briefe), 300, 324 f., 326 f., 331 f., 337; Gindely (Waldstein), I, 106 ff.
21. Tadra (Briefe), 354, 391.
22. Tadra (Briefe), 338.
23. Schebek (Wallensteinfrage), 52 ff.; Mann, 441 ff.
24. Chlumecky (Regesten), 70; Bartel, 34 ff.; Gindely (Waldstein), I, 372.
25. Tadra (Briefe), 464, 465, 473; Ritter (Untersuchungen), 30, 31.
26. Chlumecky (Regesten), 43; Tadra (Briefe), 482, 485; Gindely (Waldstein), I, 226 f.; Mann, 391.
27. Chlumecky (Regesten), 46.
28. Diwald, 386.
29. Chlumecky (Regesten), 47 f.
30. Mann, 393 ff.; Polišenský and Kollmann, 131 ff.
31. Polišenský and Kollmann, 150 f.
32. Hallwich (Fünf Bücher), III, 331.
33. Diwald, 396 ff.; Mann, 449 f.; Polišenský and Kollmann, 153, 168, 174.

34. Polišenský and Kollmann, 144 f.
35. Schebek (Wallensteinfrage), 64 ff.
36. Diwald, 414 ff.; Mann, 460 ff.
37. Mann, 464, 468.
38. Hallwich (Fünf Bücher), III, 368.
39. Hallwich (Fünf Bücher), III, 434 ff.
40. Chlumecky (Regesten), 109.
41. Tadra (Briefe), 352 f., 466 f.; Hallwich (Fünf Bücher), II, 211, 320; III, 60; Förster (Briefe), I, 320.

Chapter 8

1. Mann, 427 ff.
2. Förster (Prozeß), Urkunden, 93.
3. Diwald, 424; Kampmann, 49.
4. Kampmann, 88.
5. Mann, 421.
6. Villermont, 355; Mann, 511.
7. Förster (Briefe), I, 258, 168.
8. Kampmann, 80, 90 f., 92 f.
9. Lorenz, 93 f.
10. Khevenhüller (Annales), XI, 62 ff.; Kampmann, 94.
11. Hurter (Ferdinand), IV, 342 ff.
12. Diwald, 450.
13. Bireley, 53 f.
14. Theatrum, II, 10 ff.
15. Parker, 98; Wedgwood, 245.
16. Loch, 38, 40, 99.
17. Chlumecky (Regesten), 158, 180, 192, 209, 218; Gindely (Waldstein), II, 182, 192.
18. Wedgwood, 242 f.
19. Chlumecky (Regesten), 157.
20. Hallwich (Fünf Bücher), II, 428 f.; Chlumecky (Regesten), 179 f., 167.
21. Gindely (Waldstein), II, 210; Chlumecky (Regesten), 180, 192 f., 211, 219.
22. Förster (Briefe), II, 37 f.
23. Mortimer (Eyewitness), 45 ff., 164 ff.
24. Mann, 532.
25. Gindely (Waldstein), II, 211.

Chapter 9

1. Mann, 567.
2. Polišenský and Kollmann, 214.
3. Khevenhüller (Annales), XI, 62.
4. Wedgwood, 228.
5. Gindley (Waldstein), II, 265.
6. Tadra (Bethlen), 447; Hallwich (Fünf Bücher), II, 578.
7. Theatrum, II, 163 ff.

References 259

8. Gindely (Waldstein), II, 259; Albrecht (Politik), 442, 444; Mann, 597 f.
9. Gindely (Waldstein), II, 270 f., 276 ff.
10. Gindely (Waldstein), II, 281 ff., 292; Hurter (Geschichte Wallensteins), 376.
11. Theatrum, II, 209 ff.; Diwald, 448; Polišenský and Kollmann, 216.
12. Straka, 182 f.; Chlumecky (Regesten), 242.
13. Khevenhüller (Annales), XI, 1134.
14. Diwald, 439; Polišenský and Kollmann, 215.
15. Ernstberger, 405 f.
16. Ernstberger, 416, 420.
17. Polišenský and Kollmann, 205 f., 216 f.; Diwald, 449.
18. Roberts, 109.
19. Dudik (Enthebung), 18, 72, 85; Hallwich (Briefe), I, 346, 374; Polišenský and Kollmann, 222 f.
20. Diwald, 448; Polišenský and Kollmann, 223.
21. Hallwich (Briefe), I, 147.
22. Mann, 634.
23. Mann, 647.
24. Hallwich (Briefe), I, 538; Irmer (Verhandlungen), I, 119; Förster (Briefe), II, 177.
25. Gaedecke, 309 ff.
26. Diwald, 467.
27. Gaedecke, 107, 108.
28. Dudik (Enthebung), 172 ff.
29. Förster (Briefe), II, 187 f.
30. Dudik (Enthebung), 190.

Chapter 10

1. Albrecht (Auswärtige Politik), 342.
2. Hallwich (Arnim), 170.
3. Hallwich (Briefe), II, 619; Diwald, 489.
4. Mann, 672.
5. Förster (Briefe), II, 197.
6. Dudik (Enthebung), 466.
7. Aretin, Urkunden, 40 f.
8. Förster (Prozeß), Urkunden, 100 f.
9. Zwiedineck-Südenhorst, 198 ff.
10. Dudik (Enthebung), 333 f.
11. Guthrie, 167.
12. Guthrie, 166 ff.
13. Dudik (Enthebung), 407 ff.
14. Guthrie, 166 f.
15. Mann, 680 ff.
16. Khevenhüller (Annales), XII, 24.

Chapter 11

1. Guthrie, 188 f.; Roberts, 170; Ritter (Gegenreformation), III, 536; Hallwich (Briefe), II, 573.

2. Roberts, 138.
3. Mahr (Wallenstein vor Nürnberg), 11 f., plan inside back cover.
4. Mahr (Wallenstein vor Nürnberg), 26 f.
5. Mahr (Wallensteins Lager), 28 f.
6. Mann, 710 f.
7. Hallwich (Briefe), III, 109 f.; II, 689 f.
8. Theatrum, II, 736.
9. The course of the battle: Mahr (Wallensteins Lager), 64 ff.; Guthrie, 189 ff.
10. Sveriges Krig, plan 17, inside back cover.
11. Mahr (Wallensteins Lager), 114, 120; Förster (Briefe), II, 237.
12. Mahr (Wallensteins Lager), 98; Droysen, 70; Monro, 278.
13. Guthrie, 191; Mahr (Wallensteins Lager), 80.
14. Monro, 279; Fronmüller, 81.
15. Monro, 282; Mahr (Wallensteins Lager), 88 f.; Förster (Briefe), II, 238.
16. Förster (Briefe), II, 240 f.
17. Hallwich (Briefe), III, 100, 111; Förster (Briefe), II, 245; Roberts, 174.
18. Hallwich (Briefe), III, 111; Förster (Briefe), II, 245 f.
19. Förster (Briefe), II, 246.
20. Hallwich (Briefe), III, 246 f.
21. Hallwich (Briefe), III, 374 f.
22. Halllwich (Briefe), III, 245 f.
23. Hallwich (Briefe), III, 470 ff.
24. Hallwich (Briefe), III, 485 f., 496, 495.
25. Deuticke, 46.
26. Hallwich (Briefe), III, 480 ff.
27. Hallwich (Briefe), III, 499 ff.
28. Deuticke, 61; Hallwich (Briefe), III, 484, 500; Seidler (Lützen), 28.
29. Deuticke, 47.
30. Deuticke, 59 ff.; Seidler (Lützen), 29.
31. Deuticke, 63; Hallwich (Briefe), III, 500.
32. Deuticke, 58 f.; Seidler (Lützen), 31 ff.
33. Hallwich (Briefe), III, 501; Deuticke, 68; Seidler (Lützen), 39 f.
34. Guthrie, 204, 207.
35. Deuticke, 69; Seidler (Lützen), 41.
36. The course of the battle: Deuticke, 64 ff.; Förster (Briefe), II, 302 ff.; Guthrie, 208 ff.; Seidler (Lützen), 44 ff.
37. Guthrie, 204; Hallwich (Briefe), III, 501; Förster (Briefe), II, 302.
38. Guthrie, 212.
39. Mortimer (Eyewitness), 40.
40. Fritsch, 134.
41. Fritsch, 134 f.

Chapter 12

1. Hallwich (Briefe), III, 754 ff.
2. Irmer (Verhandlungen), II, 98.
3. Mann, 777.
4. Hallwich (Briefe), III, 553, 583.

References 261

5. Seidler (Blutgericht), 16; Förster (Briefe), II, 311.
6. Parker, 131; Wedgwood, 347.
7. Monro, 290; Irmer (Verhandlungen), II, 47.
8. Monro, 310.
9. Irmer (Verhandlungen), II, 20, 45, 54 f.; Hallwich (Briefe), IV, 196 ff., 361 f.; Hallwich (Ende), I, 424, 585.
10. Hildebrand, 23 ff.
11. Hildebrand, 27 ff.
12. Irmer (Verhandlungen), II, 136, ff., 240; Feuquières, I, 155; II, 1 ff., 32.
13. See Chapter 8.
14. Hallwich (Ende), I, 320.
15. Irmer (Verhandlungen), II, 220.
16. Hallwich (Ende), I, 396, 398, 401.
17. Hallwich (Ende), I, 397.
18. Hallwich (Ende), I, 389, 421 f., 457 ff.
19. Srbik, 43; Pekař, I, 362; Förster (Briefe), III, 50 f.
20. Suvanto (Anhänger), 270; Elster, 19; Hallwich (Briefe), IV, 414 ff.
21. Hildebrand, 46.
22. Irmer (Verhandlungen), II, 310 ff.
23. Gaedecke, 192 f.
24. Hallwich (Ende), I, 569 f., 585.
25. Irmer (Verhandlungen), III, 424 f.
26. Gaedecke, 196 ff.; Förster (Briefe), III, 75; Hildebrand, 58 f.
27. Hallwich (Ende), I, 589.
28. Hallwich (Ende), II, 358 f.
29. Hallwich (Ende), II, 80.
30. Hallwich (Briefe), IV, 267 ff., 397 f.
31. Hallwich (Ende), I, 539 f., 586.
32. Irmer (Verhandlungen), III, 35 ff.
33. Irmer (Verhandlungen), III, 448.
34. Suvanto (Politik).

Chapter 13

1. Hallwich (Ende), II, 67 f., 87.
2. Förster (Briefe), III, 92 ff.
3. Aretin, Urkunden, 46 f.; Hallwich (Ende), II, 140 f.
4. Irmer (Verhandlungen), III, 67 ff.; Hallwich (Briefe), IV, 463 f.
5. Mann, 837 f.
6. Hallwich (Ende), II, 155 f., 389 ff.; Förster (Briefe), II, 114 ff.
7. Förster (Briefe), III, 121 ff., 127 f.
8. Hallwich (Ende), II, 403, 406 f.
9. Srbik, 379 f.
10. Mann, 335 f., 430.
11. Hallwich (Ende), II, 155 f., 160 f., 164 f.; Förster (Briefe), III, 135 f.
12. Förster (Briefe), III, 129 ff., 138 ff., 142 f.
13. Irmer (Verhandlungen), III, 95 f.
14. Mann, 844 ff.

15. Mann, 851 f.
16. Ranke, 524 ff.
17. Mann, 991 ff.; Rudhart, 26; Diwald, 15.
18. Jedin, 342 ff.; Irmer (Verhandlungen), III, 426 ff., 441 ff.; Förster (Briefe), III, Anhang, 43 ff.; Dudik (Waldt), 359 f.
19. Hallwich (Ende), II, 186 f.
20. Irmer (Verhandlungen), III, 129 f.
21. Rudhart, 24.
22. Gaedecke, 214 f.
23. Förster (Briefe), III, 448 ff.; Feuquières, II, 215; I, 153.
24. Hallwich (Ende), II, 183 f., 208 f.
25. Feuquières, I, 152 ff.; II, 212.
26. Gaedecke, 329; Irmer (Verhandlungen), III, 154, 246.
27. Gaedecke, 217 ff.; Hallwich (Ende), II, 184 f.
28. Gaedecke, 242, 258, 259, 261, 271, 272.
29. Gaedecke, 252 ff., 263 f.
30. Irmer (Verhandlungen), III, 139 f., 169, 243.
31. Irmer (Verhandlungen), III, 117 f., 138; Srbik, 83.
32. Jedin, 338 ff.
33. Srbik, 82 f.
34. Aretin, Urkunden, 76; Jedin, 341.
35. Srbik, 81, 381.
36. Mitis, 103 ff.
37. Mann, 894.
38. Förster (Briefe), III, 177 ff.
39. Srbik, 381; Irmer (Verhandlungen), III, 170.
40. Mann, 897 ff.
41. Mann, 900, 902.
42. Hallwich (Briefe), IV, 566.
43. Jedin, 348 f.
44. Jedin, 349; Förster (Briefe), III, 192; Irmer (Verhandlungen), III, 257.
45. Aretin, Urkunden, 82 f.
46. Helbig, 32 ff.
47. Irmer (Verhandlungen), III, 215; Förster (Briefe), III, 205 ff.

Chapter 14

1. Hallwich (Ende), II, 223 ff., 226.
2. Mann, 916.
3. Hallwich (Ende), II, 225; Dudik (Waldt), 345 ff.; Srbik, 127.
4. Gaedecke, 280 f.
5. Dudik (Waldt), 337 f.
6. Aretin, Urkunden, 85 f.
7. Dudik (Waldt), 338 f.
8. Irmer (Verhandlungen), III, 362.
9. Hallwich (Ende), II, 521 f.; Srbik, 388; Irmer (Verhandlungen), III, 269 f., 271 f.
10. Prökl, I, 235; Aretin, Urkunden, 88; Förster (Briefe), III, 228, 230.

References 263

11. Rudhart, 27; Irmer (Verhandlungen), III, 466; Förster (Briefe), III, 226 f.
12. Förster (Briefe), III, 317; Mailath, III, 370 f.
13. Hallwich (Ende), III, 240 f.; Srbik, 168.
14. Förster (Briefe), III, 302 ff.
15. Srbik, 148 f., 170 ff., 384 ff., 388 ff.; Mann, 933 ff., 1081; Mailath 368 ff.
16. Irmer (Verhandlungen), III, 305; Förster (Briefe), III, 273, 305.
17. Förster (Briefe), III, 211 f.; Hallwich (Ende), II, 482.
18. Irmer (Verhandlungen), III, 401 ff.
19. Gaedecke, 274 ff., 293 f.; Irmer (Verhandlungen), III, 267, 305 f., 323 f.; Irmer (Arnim), 277.
20. Förster (Briefe), III, 351; Hallwich (Ende), II, 526 f.
21. Förster (Briefe), III, 350, 333; Hallwich (Ende), II, 537 f.
22. Kampmann, 183; Mann, 970 ff.
23. Bücheler, 61 ff., 39 ff.; Schebek (Wallensteinfrage), 396; Murr, 396 f.; Neue Deutsche Biographie, XIV, 331 f.
24. Förster (Prozeß), Urkunden, 88 ff.
25. Mann, 947 f., 971 f.
26. Hallwich (Ende), II, 527 ff.
27. Srbik, 140, 142.
28. Srbik, 140; Förster (Briefe), III, 351; Mann, 948 f.
29. Jedin, 332, 334.
30. Jedin, 333 f.
31. Mann, 981.
32. Dudik, 315; Mann, 964.
33. Förster (Briefe), III, Anhang, 29.
34. Bergel (Reliquien).

Chapter 15

1. Aretin, Urkunden, 38.
2. Murr, 304; Priorato, 9; Diwald, 383 f.
3. Diwald, 11.
4. Gaedecke, 217.
5. Irmer (Verhandlungen), I, 178.
6. Priorato, 29 ff.
7. Mann, 416; Tadra (Briefe), 365.
8. Hallwich (Gestalten), 144, 164.
9. Krause, 65; Wäschke, 57.
10. Polišenský and Kollmann, 36, 40; Gindely (Gegenreformation), 44 ff.
11. Hallwich (Fünf Bücher), II, 133.
12. Diwald, 454 f.
13. Mann, 105, 484, 487.
14. Diwald, 552.
15. Petitot, 105; Schiller (Dreißigjähriger Kreig), 470.
16. Förster (Briefe), II, 66 ff.; Tadra (Briefe), 457, 366;.Petitot, 100.
17. Förster (Briefe), II, 178.

Bibliography

English – Biographies

Mann, G., *Wallenstein: His Life Narrated by Golo Mann*, trans. C. Kessler (London, 1976). (References in the text are to page numbers in the original German publication listed below, as Mann's own references, notes and bibliography are not printed in this English edition.)
Mitchell, J., *The Life of Wallenstein, Duke of Friedland* (London, 1837).
Watson, F., *Wallenstein: Soldier under Saturn* (Bath, 1969; first published 1938).

English – Other Material

Bireley, R., *Religion and Politics in the Age of the Counter-Reformation* (Chapel Hill, NC, 1981).
Bonney, R., *The Thirty Years War 1618–1648* (Oxford, 2002).
Goodrick, A., *The Relation of Sydnam Poyntz 1624–1636* (London, 1908).
Guthrie, W., *Battles of the Thirty Years War: From White Mountain to Nördlingen, 1618–1635* (Westport, CT, 2002).
Liddell Hart, B., *Great Captains Unveiled* (London, 1927). (Contains one chapter on Wallenstein.)
Monro, R., *Monro, His Expedition with the Worthy Scots Regiment Called Mac-Keys*, ed. W. Brockington (Westport, CT, 1999; first published 1637).
Mortimer, G., *Eyewitness Accounts of the Thirty Years War 1618–48* (Basingstoke, 2002). (Mortimer, Eyewitness.)
Mortimer, G., 'War by Contract, Credit and Contribution: The Thirty Years War', *Early Modern Military History, 1450–1815*, ed. G. Mortimer (Basingstoke, 2004), 101–17. (Mortimer, Contributions.)
Parker, G., *The Thirty Years War* (London, 1984).
Roberts, M., *Gustavus Adolphus*, 2nd edn (London, 1992; first published 1973).
Toyne, S., *Albrecht von Wallenstein: A monograph* (Oxford, 1911). (An essay rather than a biography.)
Van Creveld, M., *Supplying War: Logistics from Wallenstein to Paton* (Cambridge, 1977). (Actually contains very little on Wallenstein.)
Wedgwood, C., *The Thirty Years War* (London, 1938).

Sources in Other Languages, Principally German

Albrecht, D., *Die auswärtige Politik Maximilians von Bayern 1618–1635* (Göttingen, 1962). (Albrecht, Auswärtige Politik.)
Albrecht, D., *Die Politik Maximilians I. von Bayern und seiner Verbündeten, 1618–1651*, 2, 5 (Munich, 1964). (Albrecht, Politik.)
Aretin, K., *Wallenstein: Beiträge zur sicheren Kenntniss seines Characters, etc.* (Munich, 1845). (There is another edition of this work, Regensburg 1846, with different page numbering and contents.)

Baader, J., *Wallenstein als Student an der Universität Altdorf* (Nuremberg, 1860).
Bartel, W., *Zur Kritik des Berichtes über die Brucker Conferenz, 25. November 1626* (Marburg, 1890).
Bergel, J., 'Die Schicksale der Reliquien Wallensteins etc.', *Mitteilungen des Vereins für Geschichte der Deutschen in Böhmen*, 72 (1934), 1-19. (Bergel, Reliquien.)
Bergel, J., 'Wallenstein und Seni', *Stifter-Jahrbuch*, 4 (1955), 40–56. (Bergel, Seni.)
Bilek, T., *Beiträge zur Geschichte Waldsteins* (Prague, 1886).
Bücheler, H., *Von Pappenheim zu Piccolomini: sechs Gestalten aus Wallensteins Lager* (Sigmaringen, 1994).
Caspar, M., ed., *Johannes Kepler: gesammelte Werke*, 18 vols (Munich, 1937–59).
Chlumecky, P., *Die Regesten, oder die chronologischen Verzeichnisse der Urkunden in den Archiven etc.* (Brünn, 1856). (Chlumecky, Regesten.)
Chlumecky, P., *Carl von Zierotin und seine Zeit, 1564–1615* (Brünn, 1862). (Chlumecky, Zierotin.)
Deuticke, K., *Die Schlacht bei Lützen* (Giessen, 1917).
Diwald, H., *Wallenstein*, 3rd edn (Esslingen, 1984; first published 1969).
Droysen, G., *Schriftstücke von Gustav Adolf zumeist an evangelische Fürsten Deutschlands* (Halle, 1877).
Dudik, B., *Waldstein von seiner Enthebung etc.* (Vienna, 1858). (Dudik, Enthebung.)
Dudik, B., 'Des kaiserlichen Obristen Mohr von Waldt Hochverraths-Process', *Archiv für Kunde österreichischer Geschichts-Quellen*, 25 (1860), 315–400. (Dudik, Waldt.)
Duhr, B., 'Wallenstein in seinem Verhältnis zu den Jesuiten', *Historisches Jahrbuch*, 13 (1892), 80–99.
Dvorský, F., 'Albrecht z Valdštejna až na konec roku 1621', *Rozpravy České Akademie Cisaře Františka Josefa*, 1, 3 (1892), 367-584. (Although this text is in Czech the documents referred to are printed in German. Pages have dual numbering.)
Elster, O., *Piccolomini-Studien* (Leipzig, 1911).
Ernstberger, A., 'Hans de Witte: Finanzmann Wallensteins', *Vierteljahrsschrift für Sozial- und Wirtsschaftsgeschichte*, Beiheft 38 (1954).
Feuquières, M., *Lettres et négociations du Marquis de Feuquières etc.*, 3 vols (Amsterdam, 1753).
Förster, F., *Albrechts von Wallenstein, des Herzogs von Friedland und Mecklenburg, ungedruckte eigenhändige vertrauliche Briefe etc.*, 3 vols (Berlin, 1828). (Förster, Briefe.)
Förster, F., *Wallenstein als Feldherr und Landesfürst in seinem öffentlichen und Privat-Leben* (Potsdam, 1834). (Förster, Landesfürst.)
Förster, F., *Wallensteins Prozeß vor den Schranken des Weltgerichts etc.* (Leipzig, 1844). (Förster, Prozeß.)
Frisch, C., ed., *Joannis Kepleri Astronomi Opera Omnia*, 8 vols (Frankfurt/Main, 1858–71).
Fritsch, A., 'Tagbuch des Augustin von Fritsch etc.', *Beyträge zur vaterländischen Historie, Geographie, Staatistik, und Landwirthschaft*, ed. L. Westenrieder (Munich, 1788–1806), IV, 105–91.
Fronmüller, G., *Geschichte Altenberg's und der alten Veste etc.* (Fürth, 1860).
Gaedecke, A., *Wallensteins Verhandlungen mit den Schweden und Sachsen, 1631–1634* (Frankfurt/Main, 1885).

Geiger, A., *Wallensteins Astrologie: eine kritische Überprüfung der Überlieferung nach dem gegenwärtigen Quellenbestand* (Graz, 1983).
Gindely, A., *Geschichte des Dreißigjährigen Krieges*, 3 vols (Prague, 1869–80). (Gindely, Dreißigjähriger Krieg.)
Gindely, A., *Waldstein während seines ersten Generalats etc.*, 1625–1630, 2 vols (Prague, 1887). (Gindely, Waldstein.)
Gindely, A., *Geschichte der Gegenreformationen in Böhmen* (Leipzig, 1894). (Gindely, Gegenreformation.)
Hallwich, H., 'Wallenstein und Arnim im Frühjahr 1632', *Mitteilungen des Vereins für Geschichte der Deutschen in Böhmen*, 17 (1878/9), 145–86. (Hallwich, Arnim.)
Hallwich, H., *Wallensteins Ende: ungedruckte Briefe und Akten*, 2 vols (Leipzig, 1879). (Hallwich, Ende.)
Hallwich, H., 'Wallensteins erste Berufung zum Generalat', *Zeitschrift für Allgemeine Geschichte*, 2 (1884), 108–34. (Hallwich, Berufung.)
Hallwich, H., *Gestalten aus Wallenstein's Lager* (Leipzig, 1885). (Hallwich, Gestalten.)
Hallwich, H., *Fünf Bücher Geschichte Wallensteins*, 3 vols (Leipzig, 1910). (Hallwich, Fünf Bücher.)
Hallwich, H., *Briefe und Akten zur Geschichte Wallensteins 1630–1634*, 4 vols (Vienna, 1912). (Hallwich, Briefe.)
Helbig, K., *Der Kaiser Ferdinand und der Herzog von Friedland während des Winters 1633–34* (Dresden, 1852).
Hildebrand, E., *Wallenstein und seine Verbindungen mit den Schweden* (Frankfurt/ Main, 1885).
Hurter, F., *Geschichte Kaiser Ferdinand II*, 11 vols (Vienna, 1850–64). (Hurter, Ferdinand.)
Hurter, F., *Zur Geschichte Wallensteins* (Schaffhausen, 1855). (Hurter, Geschichte Wallensteins.)
Irmer, G., *Die Verhandlungen Schwedens und seiner Verbündeten mit Wallenstein und dem Kaiser*, 3 vols (Leipzig, 1889–91). (Irmer, Verhandlungen.)
Irmer, G., *Hans Georg von Arnim etc* (Leipzig, 1894). (Irmer, Arnim.)
Janko, W., *Wallenstein: ein Charakterbild in Sinne neuerer Geschichtsforschung* (Vienna, 1867).
Jedin, H., 'Die Relation Ottavio Piccolominis über Wallensteins Schuld und Ende', *Zeitschrift des Vereins für Geschichte Schlesiens*, 65 (1931), 328–57.
Kampmann, C., *Reichsrebellion und kaiserliche Acht: politische Strafjustiz im dreißigjährigen Krieg und das Verfahren gegen Wallenstein 1634* (Münster, 1992).
Khevenhüller, F., *Annales Ferdinandeii*, 14 vols (Leipzig, 1721–26; vols I–IV first published 1640–41). (Khevenhüller, Annales.)
Khevenhüller, F., *Conterfet Kupfferstich*. (First published 1640 in volume I of the *Annales*, with un-numbered pages. Re-published in Leipzig, 1722, as volume XIV, parts 1 and 2, of the *Annales*. The section on Wallenstein is on pp. 219–24 of part 2.) (Khevenhüller, Conterfet.)
Krause, G., *Tagebuch Christians des Jüngeren, Fürst zu Anhalt* (Leipzig, 1858).
Loch, V., 'Fürstbischof Johann Georg II. als Präsident der Kaiserlichen Commission etc.', *Bericht über Bestand und Wirken des Historischen Vereins für Oberfranken zu Bamberg*, 39 (1876), 33–105.

Loewe, V., *Die Organisation und Verwaltung der Wallensteinischen Heere* (Freiburg, 1895).
Lorenz, O., 'Briefe Wallensteins, meistentheils über Mecklenburg etc.', *Jahrbücher des Vereins für mecklenburgische Geschichte*, 40 (1875), 89–130.
Mahr, H., *Wallensteins Lager: die Schlacht an der Alten Veste* (Nuremberg, 1980). (Mahr, Wallensteins Lager.)
Mahr, H., *Wallenstein vor Nürnberg 1632: sein Lager bei Zirndorf und die Schlacht an der Alten Veste, dargestellt durch den Plan der Gebrüder Trexel 1634* (Neustadt, 1982). (Mahr, Wallenstein vor Nürnberg.)
Mailath, J., *Geschichte des österreichischen Kaiserstaates*, III (Gotha, 1842).
Mann, G., *Wallenstein: sein Leben erzählt von Golo Mann* (Frankfurt/Main, 1971).
Mann, G. and R. Bliggenstorfer, *Wallenstein: Bilder zu seinem Leben* (Frankfurt/Main, 1973).
Matiegka, J. and J. Malý, *Les caractères physiques d'Albert de Wallenstein, duc de Frýdlant* (Prague, 1934). (Czech with French summary.)
Menčik, F., 'Die Hofrathssitzungen im Jahre 1625 etc.', *Sitzungsberichte der königl.-böhmischen Gesellschaft der Wissenschaften, Classe für Philosophie, Geschichte u. Philologie*, 9 (1899).
Mieck, I., 'Wallenstein 1634: Mord oder Hinrichtung?', *Das Attentat in der Geschichte*, ed. A. Demandt (Cologne, 1996), 143–63.
Mitis, O., 'Gundakar von Liechtensteins Anteil an der kaiserlichen Zentralverwaltung 1605–1654', *Beiträge zur neueren Geschichte Österreichs*, 4 (1909), 36–118.
Murr, C., *Beyträge zur Geschichte des dreyßigjährigen Krieges, etc.* (Nuremberg, 1790).
Nemethy, F., *Das Schloß Friedland etc.* (Prague, 1818).
Neue Deutsche Biographie (Berlin, 1985).
Newald, J., 'Die lange Münze in Oesterreich', *Numismatische Zeitschrift*, 13 (1881), 88–132.
Palacký, F., 'Jugendgeschichte Albrechts von Waldstein, Herzogs von Friedland', *Jahrbücher des Böhmischen Museums*, 2 (1831), 78–89.
Pekař, J., *Wallenstein 1630–1634: die Tragödie einer Verschwörung*, 2 vols (Berlin, 1937; first published in Czech 1933–34).
Petitot, M., *Collection des mémoires relatifs a l'histoire de France, XXVIII* (Paris, 1823).
Polišenský, J. and J. Kollmann, *Wallenstein: Feldherr des Dreißigjährigen Krieges*, trans. H. Langer (Cologne, 1997; first published in Czech, 1995).
Priorato, G., *Lebensgeschichte Albrechts von Waldstein, Herzogs zu Friedland* (Nuremberg, 1769; first published in Italian, 1643).
Prökl, V., *Eger und das Egerland*, 2 vols (Falkenau, 1877).
Ranke, L., *Geschichte Wallensteins* (Leipzig, 1869).
Ritter, M., *Deutsche Geschichte im Zeitalter der Gegenreformation und des Dreißigjährigen Krieges*, 3 vols (Stuttgart, 1889–1908). (Ritter, Gegenreformation.)
Ritter, M., 'Untersuchungen zur Geschichte Wallensteins, 1625–1629', *Deutsche Zeitschrift für Geschichtswissenschaft*, 4 (1890), 14–53. (Ritter, Untersuchungen.)
Rudhart, G., *Einige Worte über Wallensteins Schuld* (Munich, 1850).
Schebek, E., 'Wallensteiniana', *Mitteilungen des Vereins für Geschichte der Deutschen in Böhmen*, 13 (1875), 250–385. (Schebek, Wallensteiniana.)

Schebek, E., *Die Lösung der Wallensteinfrage* (Berlin, 1881). (Schebek, Wallensteinfrage.)
Schiller, F., *The Robbers* and *Wallenstein*, trans. F. Lamport (Harmondsworth, 1979). (Schiller, Wallenstein.)
Schiller, F., *Geschichte des Dreißigjährigen Kriegs* (Zurich, 1985; first published 1791–93). (Schiller, Dreißigjähriger Krieg.)
Seidler, J., *Das Prager Blutgericht 1633* (Memmingen, 1951). (Seidler, Blutgericht.)
Seidler, J., *Untersuchungen über die Schlacht bei Lützen 1632* (Memmingen, 1954). (Seidler, Lützen.)
Srbik, H., *Wallensteins Ende* (Vienna, 1920).
Stieve, F., *Abhandlungen, Vorträge und Reden* (Leipzig, 1900).
Straka, C., 'Albrecht z Valdštejna a jeho doba', *Rozpravy České Akademie Cisaře Františka Josefa*, 44 (1911). (Document referred to is printed in Latin.)
Strauss, H. and S. Strauss-Kloebe, *Die Astrologie des Johannes Kepler* (Munich, 1926).
Struve, O., *Das Horoskop Wallenstein's von Joh. Kepler*, ed. W. Becker (Berlin, 1923; first published 1860).
Suvanto, P., *Wallenstein und seine Anhänger am Wiener Hof zur Zeit des zweiten Generalats 1631–1634* (Helsinki, 1963). (Suvanto, Anhänger.)
Suvanto, P., *Die deutsche Politik Oxenstiernas und Wallenstein* (Helsinki, 1979). (Suvanto, Politik.)
Sveriges Krig 1611–1632, VI, ed. Generalstaben (Stockholm, 1939).
Tadra, F., 'Beiträge zur Geschichte des Feldzuges Bethlen Gabors gegen Kaiser Ferdinand II.', *Archiv für österreichische Geschichte*, 55 (1877), 401–64. (Tadra, Bethlen.)
Tadra, F., 'Briefe Albrechts von Waldstein an Karl von Harrach, 1625–1627', *Fontes Rerum Austriacarum*, 41, 2 (1879). (Tadra, Briefe.)
Theatrum Europaeum, I, *Vom Jahr Christi 1617–1629* (Frankfurt/Main, 1643).
Theatrum Europaeum, II, *Von Anno Christi 1629 biß auff das Jahr 1633* (Frankfurt/Main, 1646).
Villermont, A., *Tilly oder der Dreißigjährige Krieg* (Schaffhausen, 1860).
Wäschke, H., 'Eindrücke vom Kurfürstentag zu Regensburg 1630', *Deutsche Geschichtsblätter*, XVI (1915), 57–76, 103–32, 147–52.
Zwiedineck-Südenhorst, H., *Hans Ulrich von Eggenberg etc.* (Vienna, 1880).

Index

This index is in five sections. Wallenstein himself is indexed chronologically in the first and more generally in the second. The third comprises named individuals, the fourth covers other subjects, and the fifth gives the modern names of places in former Habsburg territories. In the 'people' section titles are shown only for those above the rank of count. Wallenstein's relatives appear with the spelling 'Waldstein', while Emperor Ferdinand II is not indexed (other than in connection with his sons), as he is referred to throughout the book.

Wallenstein – chronology

Birth (1583), 6
School at Goldberg (1597), 8, 13
Academy at Altdorf (1599), 8 f., 13, 53, 242
First military experience (1604), 9 f.
Conversion to Catholicism (before 1607), 11 f., 54, 246 f.
Gentleman of the chamber to Archduke Matthias (1607), 13 f., 15, 17, 54
Zierotin's testimonial (1607), 14, 16, 54, 242
Role in the conflict between Matthias and Rudolf II (1608), 15
First marriage (1609), 11, 15 f., 18, 242, 245, 247, 249
Appointed a Moravian colonel (1610, 1615, 1618), 11, 17 f., 24, 25
Military experience at Gradisca (1617), 18 f., 21, 25, 30 f., 55, 242
Response to the Bohemian revolt (1618), 25
Raises an Imperial regiment and is appointed colonel (1619), 25, 27, 30
Tries to take his Moravian regiment over to the Imperialists (1619), 26, 31
Seizes cash from the Olmütz treasury (1619), 26 f., 31, 35
Property in Moravia confiscated (1619), 27
Military service against the Bohemian rebels (1619–20), 30
Commission for a second regiment (1619), 30
Assigned to special duties (late 1620), 29, 31
Appointed to lead a force against Jägerndorf (1621), 33
Appointed military commandant of Prague (1622), 34, 38
Restores his financial position (by 1622), 36 f.
Member of the Bohemian minting consortium (1622), 38, 42, 45, 79
Property dealings (1622–24), 41 ff., 245 f.
Size of lands purchased in Bohemia (1622–24), 46
Second marriage (1623), 53, 55 f., 60, 68 f., 242
Becomes a count palatine (1623), 69
Becomes a prince of the Empire (1623), 69
Appointed third-in-command of an Imperial army (1623), 71, 76
Promoted to major-general (1623), 72
Besieged at Göding (1623), 69, 71, 76, 79, 80, 92, 252
Proposes raising troops for the emperor (1624), 73, 76 ff.

Appointed as general and becomes a duke (1625), 78
Musters his army in Eger and advances into Germany (1625), 79
Differences with Tilly (1626), 83, 88
Battle for the Dessau bridge (1626), 84 ff., 88–90, 93, 104, 144, 247
Command extended to the Habsburg lands (1626), 89
Campaign against Mansfeld and Bethlen (1626), 90 ff.
Bruck an der Leitha conference (1626), 93 f., 100, 124, 144, 203
Campaign against Denmark (1627), 95 ff.
Attempts to establish a navy in the Baltic (c.1627), 99, 109
Kiel Canal project (1627), 99
Only son born (late 1627), 60, 110
Contact with Gustavus Adolphus (1627–28), 100, 136 f.
Siege of Stralsund (1628), 101 ff., 114, 116, 120, 144, 154
Battle of Wolgast (1628), 103 f., 111, 124, 247
Generalissimo of all Imperial forces (1628), 48, 61, 70, 106
Offered a chance of the Danish throne (1628), 108, 185
Acquisition of the duchy of Sagan (1628), 108
Acquisition of the duchy of Mecklenburg (1628), 106 ff.
Opposition to the Italian war over Mantua (1628), 115 f., 121 f., 188 f., 250
Peace of Lübeck ends the Danish war (1629), 103 f., 135
Opposition to the Edict of Restitution (1629), 113, 121 f., 124, 247, 250
Limits of power as generalissimo (1629),117 ff.
Financial crisis with army funding (1630), 130 f., 137 f.
Dismissal at Regensburg Electoral Meeting (1630), 125 ff., 133, 139, 150, 183, 244, 246, 251

Approaches from the emperor to resume command (1631), 132, 135, 138, 144, 145
Mecklenburg lost as Swedes advance (mid-1631), 134
Contacts Denmark and Saxony on Imperial behalf (1631), 135, 197
Alleged contacts with exiles and the Swedes (1631), 214
Friedland raided by Bohemian exiles (late 1631), 134
Leaves Prague ahead of the Saxon invasion (1631), 135
Temporary reappointment as general (December 1631), 138, 144
Rebuilds the Imperial army (early 1632), 142 ff.
Reappointment agreed at Göllersdorf (April 1632), 144 f.
Receives the duchy of Glogau to offset his losses (1632), 145
Does not aid Bavaria against the Swedish advance (April 1632), 150
Expels the Saxons from Bohemia and Silesia (June 1632), 151
Besieges Gustavus in Nuremberg (July 1632), 2, 153 ff., 164, 167 f., 248
Establishes his camp at Zirndorf (July 1632), 154 ff.
Battle at the Alte Veste (September 1632), 157 ff., 168, 247
Confronts Gustavus at Naumburg (November 1632), 166 f., 247
Sends Pappenheim to take Halle (November 1632), 169
Skirmish at Rippach (November 1632), 169–71
Battle of Lützen (November 1632), 2, 152, 170 ff., 178–82, 186, 196, 200, 217, 247
Prague 'blood tribunal' (early 1633), 180 f.
Contact with exiles and the Swedes (May 1633), 183 ff., 197
Approaches from exiles and the French (mid-1633), 184

Alleged aspirations to the Bohemian crown (1633–34), 3, 183–5, 214, 219, 251
Truces and peace negotiations in Silesia (1633), 186 ff.
Opposition to Spanish intervention under Feria (1633), 188 f., 190
Moves towards replacing him (August 1633), 189
Alleged readiness to defect to the Swedes (1633), 190 f.
Attempts to involve him in a German 'third party' (1633), 191, 195 f.
Attack on Schweidnitz (June 1633), 188
Battle of Steinau and the recovery of Silesia (October 1633), 193, 196, 199, 201, 212, 247
Swedish capture of Regensburg (November 1633), 199 f., 205, 210
Makes his winter headquarters at Pilsen (December 1633), 200
Dispute over winter quarters (December 1633), 201 f., 215
Dispute over the emperor's orders to Suys (1633), 204 f., 215
Declining Spanish support for him (late 1633), 206
Secret decision to dismiss him (December 1633), 205
Refuses troops to escort the Cardinal Infant (January 1634), 206 f.
Increasing influence of Ilow and Trčka (1633–34), 207, 210
First Pilsen oath (January 1634), 207 ff., 213, 215, 217, 219, 223
Renews contacts with the Saxons (January 1634), 211 f.
Kinsky renews contacts with the French (January 1634), 211, 214
Piccolomini claims that Wallenstein plans a *coup d'état* (January 1634), 3, 213–15, 237, 251
Liechtenstein's advice to the emperor (January 1634), 215 f.
Condemned by a secret tribunal (24 January 1634), 3, 216, 218, 220

First patent of dismissal (24 January 1634), 216 f., 235 ff.
Emperor's 'dead or alive' order (January 1634), 3, 217, 229, 238
Gallas takes command of the army (February 1634), 218
Patent of Proscription (18 February 1634), 219, 224, 227, 231, 235 f.
Confiscation of his property (February 1634), 219
Second Pilsen oath (20 February 1634), 222 f.
Flight from Pilsen to Eger (22–24 February 1634), 224 ff.
Murder in Eger (25 February 1634), 3, 59, 61, 227 ff.
Attempts to incriminate him after his death, 3, 235 ff.
The fate of his remains, 238 f.

Wallenstein – general

Ambition, 1, 4, 11 f., 16 f., 19, 21, 77, 99, 109 f., 184 f., 248 ff.
Astrology, 4, 52 ff., 129 f., 240–2
Enemies, 66, 76, 78, 81, 86, 91–4, 100, 103, 122–4, 126, 205 f., 213
Illnesses, 10, 18, 29 f., 56, 59 f., 89, 92, 95, 130, 133, 174, 179, 194, 207, 210, 243
Friedland, lands and duchy of, 18, 42, 45, 47, 56, 69, 78, 106, 109, 117, 134, 137, 179, 224, 244–6, 249
Glogau, duchy of, 145, 214
'Grand manner' in public, 110, 244
Jesuits, attitude to, 187, 190, 244, 247
Languages, 9
Mecklenburg, duchy of, 60, 106 ff., 115, 117, 125, 134 f., 137, 139, 145, 179, 214, 219, 245 f., 250
Name, derivation and spelling of, 6 f.
Officers, choice of, including Protestants, 80 f., 92, 96, 144
Peacemaking efforts, 82, 89, 100, 103 f., 116, 178 f., 182

Physical appearance, 9
Resignation threats and offers, 89, 92, 94, 200, 203 f., 208, 212 f., 220, 222, 225 f.
Sagan, duchy of, 60 f., 66, 108, 117, 134, 179, 214, 246
Spain, attitude of and to, 99, 115 f., 124, 127 f., 188–90, 192, 206, 214, 244, 250
Turkish campaign, attitude to, 99 f., 115, 214

People

Albrecht II, Archduke of Austria, 14
Aldringer (von Aldringen), Johann, 80, 84, 86, 115, 144, 149, 162 f., 166, 168, 182, 189, 199–201, 205, 207, 209, 217 f., 222, 234, 241, 244, 249
Anhalt (*see under* Christian)
Antonius Wolfrath, Bishop of Vienna, 144, 178, 216
Arnim, Hans Georg, 96–8, 100 f., 103, 108, 117, 135, 137, 141 f., 146, 151, 153, 165, 168, 176, 179 f., 185–97

Baden-Durlach (*see under* Georg)
Balbinus, Father Bohuslaus, 17
Banér, Johan, 158
Bassevi, Jakob, 38, 40
Bavaria (*see under* Maximilian)
Beck, Johann, 223, 225
Bernhard, Duke of Saxe-Weimar, 163, 166, 173, 175, 180, 182, 190 f., 199 f., 202, 205 f., 208, 211, 214 f., 222, 224, 232, 237
Bethlen Gabor, Prince of Transylvania, 18, 28, 30, 33, 69, 71–3, 75, 78, 82 f., 86, 89–91, 93, 95, 107, 114, 147, 247
Brahe, Nils, 173
Brandenburg (*see under* George William)
Breuner, Johann Philipp, 225 f.
Brunswick (*see under* Christian)
Bubna, Johann, 183, 185, 211

Bucquoy, Charles Bonaventure de Longueval, 24, 26, 28–30, 33
Burgau, Margrave of (Ferdinand, Archduke of Tyrol), 9, 13, 240
Burgsdorff, 186
Butler, Walter, 224–34

Caesar, Julius, 52, 142, 227, 253
Cardinal Infant (Ferdinand, Archbishop of Toledo), 206–8
Caretto di Grana, Marquis of, 237
Carve, Thomas, 227
Charles I, King of England, 72, 75
Christian I, Prince of Anhalt-Bernburg, 29, 32, 249
Christian II (the Younger), Prince of Anhalt-Bernburg, 34
Christian IV, King of Denmark, 1, 61, 74 f., 79, 82 ff., 106 f., 109, 111 f., 116, 121, 124, 135, 139, 227, 247
Christian, Duke of Brunswick (the 'mad Halberstädter'), 71, 82 f., 91, 107
Cicero, 142, 235
Collalto, Rombaldo, 91, 113–16, 129, 144, 241
Colloredo, Rudolf, 80, 170 f., 214, 217
Cologne, Elector and Archbishop of, 62, 125, 142

Dampierre, Henri Duval, 24
Denmark, King of (*see under* Christian IV)
Devereux, Walter, 229–34
Dietrichstein, Franz, Cardinal Bishop of Olmütz, 24, 26, 33 f., 38, 206
Diodati, Fabio, 219, 237
Diodati, Guilio, 221 f., 225, 229
Diwald, Hellmut, 52, 56, 60, 63, 85, 129
Döblin, Alfred, 241

Eggenberg, Prince Hans Ulrich, 31, 50, 68, 93 f., 132, 135, 138, 144 f., 178, 201, 203, 213, 216, 221, 225, 242
Elizabeth I, Queen of England, 54

England, King of (*see under* Charles I, James I)
Eugène, Price of Savoy, 248

Ferdinand II, Emperor, sons of (*see under* Ferdinand, Leopold Wilhelm)
Ferdinand, King of Hungary (later Emperor Ferdinand III), 61, 125, 128, 203, 213, 251
Feria, Duke of, 189 f., 199, 201, 206, 217, 250
Feuquières, Marquis of, 184 f., 211
France, King of (*see under* Henry IV, Louis XIII)
Franz Albrecht, Duke of Saxe-Lauenburg, 186–8, 190, 192–4, 197, 210–12, 214, 222, 224, 226, 232, 249
Franz Julius, Duke of Saxe-Lauenburg, 190
Frederick V, Elector Palatine ('Winter King' of Bohemia), 27 f., 29, 31–3, 39, 70–4, 107, 109, 125 f., 140, 142, 148
Fritsch, Augustin, 37, 176
Fuchs, Hans Philipp, 83, 86

Gallas, Matthias, 115, 144, 146, 165, 168, 187, 189, 193, 195 f., 201, 207, 209, 214–18, 221–7, 229, 232–4, 237 f.
Geiger, Angelika, 241
Georg, Duke of Brunswick-Lüneberg, 167–70, 180, 182
Georg Friedrich, Margrave of Baden-Durlach, 70, 98
George William, Elector of Brandenburg, 73, 88 f., 96 f., 126 f., 139 f., 187, 190 f., 193–5, 212, 243
Geraldine, 229–31, 233
Glapthorne, Henry, 240
Gordon, John, 224, 226–31, 234, 236
Gustavus II Adolphus, King of Sweden, 2, 4, 61, 74 f., 81, 95 f., 98, 100 f., 109, 111, 113, 117 f., 124, 131, 139 ff., 146 ff., 177 f., 181 f., 185 f., 227, 240, 246–8, 251

Guthrie, William, 85, 150, 153, 173

Halberstädter, the 'mad' (*see under* Christian)
Hardegg, 212
Harrach, Ernst, Cardinal Archbishop of Prague, 93, 139
Harrach, Isabella (married Wallenstein), 59, 68 f., 80, 95, 110, 234 f., 239, 242
Harrach, Karl, 31, 68 f., 72, 76 f., 89, 92–4, 136, 203, 241 f.
Harrach, Katharina (married Maximilian Waldstein), 34, 68
Harrach, Maximiliana (married Trčka), 136
Hatzfeld, Melchior, 169
Heinrich Julius, Duke of Saxe-Lauenburg, 66, 226, 228
Henri, Duke of Rohan, 248
Henry IV, King of France, 19
Holk, Heinrich, 97, 101, 144, 152, 165 f., 169 f., 173 f., 180 f., 188, 191, 207
Horn, Gustav, 148–50, 182, 191, 200, 214
Hungary, King of (*see under* Ferdinand)

Ilow, Christian, 144, 207–11, 214, 218, 221–4, 227–32, 236
Isabella, Spanish Infanta, 206

Jägerndorf, Margrave of, 33
James I, King of England, 28, 72, 74
Johann Ernst, Duke of Weimar, 82, 89 f.
John George I, Elector of Saxony, 27–9, 31, 73, 107, 113, 126, 134, 137, 139, 146 f., 151, 161, 165, 181, 187 f., 190 f., 192–5, 211 f., 232–4
Joseph II, Holy Roman Emperor, 239
Joseph, Father, 125, 128, 184

Kepler, Johannes, 52 ff.
Khevenhüller, Franz Christoph, 65 f., 124, 129, 152, 238
Khlesl, Melchior, Cardinal, 24

Index

Kinsky, Wilhelm, 184, 197, 209–11, 214, 224, 227, 230 f., 233, 235
Kollmann, Josef, 56, 129

Lamormaini, Father Wilhelm, 113, 124, 128, 182, 205, 215, 217, 247
Landek, Lucretia Nekeš (married Wallenstein), 11, 15 f., 18, 21, 44, 56, 60, 68, 239 f., 242, 244
Leopold, Archduke of Austria (brother of Ferdinand II), 66
Leopold Wilhelm, younger son of Ferdinand II, 114, 135
Leslie, Walter, 226–8, 230 f., 233 f., 236
Liddel Hart, Basil, 248
Liechtenstein, Prince Gundakar, 215 f.
Liechtenstein, Prince Karl, 24, 26, 32, 34, 38, 40 f., 44–7, 50
Louis XIII, King of France, 140, 184, 213 f.
Lüneberg (*see under* Georg)
Luther, Martin, 13

Macdaniel, 226 f., 229 f., 233
Magni, Father Valeriano, 93 f.
Mainz, Elector and Archbishop of, 125
Mann, Golo, 5, 52, 57, 60, 63, 65, 85, 179, 227
Mansfeld, Peter Ernst, 24, 28, 30, 33, 71, 74–6, 83–91, 93, 95, 97, 107, 146, 247
Marradas, Balthasar, 10, 80, 92
Martinitz, Jaroslav, 23, 50
Matthias, Holy Roman Emperor, 12–15, 17 f., 20, 22 f., 25, 27, 189, 192, 194, 242, 249
Maurice of Nassau, 75
Maximilian I, Duke of Bavaria (from 1623 Elector), 29, 32 f., 62, 73, 75, 78, 93 f., 100, 107, 110 f., 123–9, 137, 140–2, 145, 148–51, 156, 164, 166
Maximilian, Archduke (brother of Matthias and Rudolf), 18, 21, 24
Mecklenburg, Dukes of, 97, 106–9, 134

Michna, Paul, 38, 40
Monro, Robert, 161–3, 182

Nevers, Karl, Duke of Gonzaga-Nevers, 114 f.
Niemann, Heinrich, 230 f.
Nuncio, Papal (Carlo Caraffa, Bishop of Aversa), 128, 215

Olivares, Gaspar de Guzmán, Duke of Dan Lúcar, 206
Oñate, Iñigo Vélez de Guevara, 34, 206, 215, 218 f.
Oxenstierna, Axel, 157, 161, 163, 178, 181–3, 190–2, 196 f., 199

Palatine (*see under* Frederick)
Pappenheim, Gottfried Heinrich, 147, 151, 164–6, 169–71, 173–6, 180, 240
Philip IV, King of Spain, 19 f., 61, 116, 142
Piccolomini, Octavio, 64, 174, 181, 189, 196, 201, 213 f., 215, 217–19, 221 f., 225 f., 229, 234, 236–8, 251
Poland, King of (to 1632 Sigismund III; then Wladislav IV), 61, 75, 178
Polišenský, Josef, 56, 129
Pomerania, Duke of (Bogislav XV), 101 f.
Pope, the (from 1623 Urban VIII, Maffeo Barberini), 63, 125, 142
Poyntz, Sydnam, 37, 66, 175
Priorato, Galeazzo Gualdo, 66, 243

Questenberg, Caspar (Abbot of Strachow), 129
Questenberg, Gerhard (Imperial councillor), 129 f., 132, 178, 189, 201 f., 204, 207, 221 f., 243
Questenberg, Hermann, 189
Quiroga, Father Diego de, 206 f., 225

Rákóczi, Georg I (György), Prince of Transylvania, 147
Rašin, Jaroslaw Sezyma, 136 f., 184, 197

Richel, Bartholomäus, 205, 212 f., 217
Richelieu, Armand Jean du Plessis, Cardinal Duke of, 74 f., 125, 140, 142, 184, 213, 247, 252
Rohan (*see under* Henri)
Rudolf II, Holy Roman Emperor, 12–15, 17, 20, 61, 64

Savoy, Duke of (to 1630 Karl Emmanuel I), 24, 27
Saxe-Lauenburg (*see under* Franz Albrecht, Franz Julius, Heinrich Julius)
Saxe-Weimar (*see under* Bernhard)
Saxony (*see under* John George)
Schiller, Friedrich, 52, 64, 208 f., 241, 252
Schlick, Heinrich, 87, 97 f., 189, 206, 212, 233, 238
Senno, Giovanni Battista, 61 f., 66
Shakespeare, William, 52, 65, 253
Slavata, Heinrich (Wallenstein's guardian), 7
Slavata, Heinrich (Wilhelm's brother), 23, 43
Slavata, Wilhelm, 7, 23, 43, 50, 136, 206
Smiřický, Albrecht Jan, 43 f.
Smiřický, Heinrich Georg, 43–5
Smiřický, Margareta Salomena, 43, 45
Smiřický, Sigmund, 43, 245
Spinola, Ambrosio, Marquis of Los Balbases, 29, 70, 79
Srbik, Heinrich, 227
Stralendorf, Peter Heinrich, 178
Suvanto, Pekka, 197
Suys, Ernst Roland, 204 f., 215
Sweden, King of (*see under* Gustavus)

Taafe, Patrick, 225 f.
Taxis, Gerhard, 53, 56 f., 66
Thurn, Heinrich Matthias, 10, 23 f., 26, 28–30, 32, 71, 96, 136 f., 181, 183 f., 186–8, 190 f., 193, 196 f., 212

Tilly, Johann Tserclaes, 10, 29, 32, 70 f., 73, 75, 79, 82 f., 89 f., 93, 95, 97 f., 102–4, 108, 112, 123 f., 128, 132–4
Transylvania (*see under* Bethlen, Rákóczi)
Trauttmansdorff, Maximilian, 178, 182, 189, 192–4, 200, 202–4, 208, 211, 216 f., 225, 237
Trčka, Adam Erdmann, 136 f., 184, 187, 191, 196 f., 207, 209–11, 214, 218 f., 221, 223 f., 227 f., 230 f., 234
Trier, Elector and Archbishop of, 142
Turkish Sultan (Osman II in 1622; Murad IV in 1626), 32, 90

Wald, Mohr, 221 f.
Waldstein, Adam (Imperial councillor), 41
Waldstein, Albrecht Carl (Wallenstein's son), 60, 110
Waldstein, Isabella (Wallenstein's wife; *see under* Harrach)
Waldstein, Katharina (Wallenstein's sister), 14, 17
Waldstein, Lucretia (Wallenstein's wife, *see under* Landek)
Waldstein, Maria (Wallenstein's sister), 17
Waldstein, Maria Elizabeth (Wallenstein's daughter), 64, 110
Waldstein, Markyta (Wallenstein's mother), 7, 41, 44
Waldstein, Maximilian (Wallenstein's cousin), 34, 68, 110, 132, 213, 221 f., 235, 239
Waldstein, Vilim (Wilhelm), (Wallenstein's father), 7
Watson, Francis, 52, 56
Weimar (*see under* Johann Ernst)
Weingartner, Johannes, 205 f.
Wellington, Duke of, 84, 178
Werdenberg, Verda, 115
Witte, Hans de, 38 f., 46, 79, 92, 130 f., 133, 146

Zierotin, Karl, 14–16, 24, 38, 54, 242, 244

Other subjects

Augsburg, peace of (1555), 111–13

Ban of the Empire, 32, 70, 106, 219
Bärwalde, treaty of (1631), 140, 148
Battles, descriptions and numbers, 84 f.
Bohemia, election and deposition of king, 15, 17, 19 f., 22, 27
Bohemian revolt, executions (1621), 32
Bohemian Brethren, 7
Bohemian Confession, 7
Bohemian exiles, 32, 71, 96 f., 134–7, 179, 181, 182 ff., 193, 197 f., 221, 245, 251 f.
Braunau, dispute over church at (1618), 23
Breisach, siege of (1633), 189
Breitenfeld, battle of (1631), 132, 134–7, 141, 146 f., 177, 247
Breslau, proposed negotiations (1633), 183, 188–90, 194

Calvinism and Calvinists, 7 f., 27, 112 f., 183, 194
Capuchins, 93, 125, 206
Carthusians, 18, 239, 247
Casale, siege of (1628), 114, 116
Catholic League, 19, 29, 33 f., 72 f., 78, 94, 98, 100, 112, 123, 125, 127, 133, 140 f., 147, 250
Cleves-Jülich, dispute over (1610), 19
Confiscations of property by the emperor, 41 f., 107 f.
Contributions and war financing, 5, 33 f., 77 f., 80, 94, 101, 117, 124, 130, 133, 142, 145, 151, 165, 178
Croats, 170 f.

Donauwörth disturbances (1606–07), 19

Edict of Restitution (1629), 111 ff., 116, 121, 124 f., 141, 182, 194, 206, 234, 247, 250
Electoral title, transfer to Maximilian (1623), 73, 107, 125, 140

Emperor, election of (1612, 1619), 15, 27

Habsburg succession (1618), 20
Halle, capture of (1632), 168–71, 180
Hanseatic League, 99, 102, 113
Heilbronn League, 181 f., 212
Hessisch-Oldendorf, battle of (1633), 182
Honigfelde, battle of (1629), 117
Huguenots, 95, 114
Hussites, 7, 23

Imperial war council, and presidents of, 31, 72, 81, 91 f., 113, 146, 189, 204, 206, 212, 237
Ingolstadt, siege of (1632), 148–50, 154

Jesuits, 3, 13, 15, 17, 20, 124, 186 f., 190, 205, 215, 244, 247

Kipper- und Wipperzeit, 38 f.

La Rochelle, siege of (1628), 114
Leipzig Manifesto (1631), 139
Letter of Majesty (1609), 15, 20, 22
Lower Saxon Circle, 74 f., 106
Lusatia, transfer to Saxony (1620), 29, 31, 107
Lutter, battle of (1626), 90, 93, 97, 104

Magdeburg, siege of (1631), 102, 133, 141, 152, 154
Mantua, war over (1628–31), 114 ff., 121, 124, 126, 140, 188 f., 250
Munich, capture of (1632), 2, 131, 151, 157

Netherlands, truce in (1609–21), 12, 19, 72
Netherlands, war in, 12, 19, 21, 29, 72, 114, 116, 126, 128, 147, 166, 177, 188, 206
Neuhäusel, skirmish at (1621), 33
Nördlingen, battle of (1634), 233, 253

Palatinate, occupation and confiscation of, 29, 32, 70, 72, 74, 107, 125, 139 f., 142, 148, 219
Poland, role in the war, 75, 95, 97, 99, 111, 114, 117, 124, 139
Pomerania, designs on, 136, 212
Prague, Defenestration of (1618), 7, 23, 43
Protestant Union, 19, 29, 70

Rain, battle of (1632), 148 f., 161
Romans, election as King of, 125 f., 128, 214

Spanish party (so-called), 31

Theatrum Europeaum, 85, 157

Uzkok war (1615–17), 18 f.

Werben, Swedish camp at (1631), 133, 154
White Mountain, battle of (1620), 29–31, 34, 37, 41, 43, 70
Witch trials, 62

Zábláti, battle of (1619), 28, 30

Modern place names

(CZ = Czech Republic; PL = Poland; SK = Slovakia)

Braunau	Broumov, CZ	Marienburg	Malbork, PL
Breslau	Wroclaw, PL	Mies	Stříbro, CZ
Brünn	Brno, CZ	Münchengrätz	Mnichovo
Crossen	Krosno Odrzańskie, PL	Neuhäusel	Hradiště, CZ
Eger	Cheb, CZ	Olmütz	Nové Zámky, SK
Friedland	Frýdlant, CZ	Pilsen	Olomouc, CZ
Gitschin	Jičin, CZ	Plan	Plzeň, CZ
Glogau	Glogów, PL	Pressburg	Planá, CZ
Göding	Hodonín, CZ	Reichenberg	Bratislava, SK
Goldberg	Zlotoryja, PL	Sagan	Liberec, CZ
Hermanitz	Heřmanice, CZ	Schweidnitz	Żagań, PL
Honigfelde	Trzciana, PL	Steinau	Świdnica, PL
Horazdowitz	Horažd'ovice, CZ	Stettin	Ścinawa, PL
Karlsbad	Karlovy Vary, CZ	Teschen	Szczecin, PL
Königgrätz	Hradec Králové, CZ		Cieszyn, PL; Český Těšín, CZ
Koschumberg	Košumberk, CZ	Walditz	Valdice, CZ
Lieben	Libeň, CZ	Zablat	Záblatí, CZ
Liegnitz	Legnica, PL	Znaim	Znojmo, CZ